centrum im. willy brandta
willy brandt zentrum

Uniwersytet Wrocławski

German and European Studies of the Willy Brandt Center at the Wroclaw University

Edited by

Prof. Dr. Ireneusz Paweł Karolewski (managing editor)
Prof. Dr. Jochen Roose
Prof. Dr. Krzysztof Ruchniewicz
Prof. Dr. Marek Zybura

Volume 5

Robert Grzeszczak [ed.]

Challenges of Good Governance in the European Union

Nomos

The following book constitutes a part of the research conducted within the framework of the project funded by the grant no. 013/11/B/HS5/03443 „Challenges of good governance in the EU- transfer from governing to governance-what is the most effective way to realise the public mission in the modern multilevel governing system", financed by the National Science Centre of Poland.

The Deutsche Nationalbibliothek lists this publication in the Deutsche Nationalbibliografie; detailed bibliographic data are available on the Internet at http://dnb.d-nb.de

ISBN 978-3-8487-3180-0 (Print)
978-3-8452-7545-1 (ePDF)

British Library Cataloguing-in-Publication Data
A catalogue record for this book is available from the British Library.

ISBN 978-3-8487-3180-0 (Print)
978-3-8452-7545-1 (ePDF)

Library of Congress Cataloging-in-Publication Data
Grzeszczak, Robert
Challenges of Good Governance in the European Union
Robert Grzeszczak (ed.)
369 p.
Includes bibliographic references.

ISBN 978-3-8487-3180-0 (Print)
978-3-8452-7545-1 (ePDF)

1. Edition 2016

Inhalt

The Challenge of Good Governance: An introduction 9
Robert Grzeszczak

Part One: Change of the paradigms: From government to good governance?

Chapter 1: Approaches to (good) governance in the European Union 25
Ireneusz P. Karolewski

Chapter 2: Good Governance and Public Administration 49
Jerzy Supernat

Chapter 3: Good Governance and Human Rights. The Right to Good Administration 63
Michalina Szpyrka

Chapter 4: Think tanks as good governance brokers 79
Monika Sus

Chapter 5: Good governance in the judicial system – enhancing the effectiveness of the judicial protection 91
Jagna Mucha

Part Two: Public participation and government effectiveness

Chapter 1: The development of the concept of EU citizenship through the incremental acceptance of citizens' rights 109
Magdalena Gniadzik

Chapter 2: Tackling discrimination in the European Union 123
Magdalena Gniadzik

Chapter 3: The high level of security 139
Anna Kańciak

Chapter 4: Development of information society services 155
Anna Kańciak

Chapter 5: The good governance rule and balancing the interests of employers and employees in the EU 173
Piotr Kwasiborski

Chapter 6: Good Governance thorough Better Regulation. Looking for the impact analysis approach to the proportionality principle 197
Jędrzej Maśnicki

Chapter 7: The access to e-justice and its benefits for citizens and business environment 229
Jagna Mucha

Part Three: The practice of good governance at the EU and national level

Chapter 1: Initiatives supporting the internal and external security of the EU and its member states 243

Anna Kańciak

Chapter 2: Into the light of good governance – what is the role of transparency in health law? 259

Atina Krajewska

Chapter 3: The impact of the informatisation of the judiciary on the efficiency and effectiveness of public duties – case study. 283

Kamil Mroczka

Chapter 4: The impact of the principles of good governance on the EU Investment Law 299

Jagna Mucha

Chapter 5: Good governance at the local level. The EGTC as a tool for cross-border cooperation 311

Elżbieta Opiłowska

Chapter 6: Mutual recognition of official documents as an example of an initiative that brings the European Union closer to its citizens 331

Ewelina Tomczak / Michalina Szpyrka

Chapter 7: Good governance at the metropolitan level. Examples of institutional practice in selected Polish metropolitan areas 343

Aldona Wiktorska-Święcka

About the Authors 367

The Challenge of Good Governance: An introduction

Robert Grzeszczak

The period of reforms in the EU continues. The times of transition are often more exciting than those of routine and continuity, but they are typically also disorderly and confusing. Old paradigms fade, but new ones only emerge slowly, and their multiplicity leads to protracted phases of co-existence, competition and conflict (Krisch, 2012: 203).

The European Union of the 21st century is confronted with problems that were unknown at the beginning of its functioning. The onset of the second decade of the 21st century sees the reaching of a critical mass concerning the integration process. We can observe a political and substantive crisis of the European Union (hereinafter referred to as the EU), which results from the lack of clearly-defined integration goals and indecision as to the current and future shape of the European Union. Whether the EU internal market of 28 Member States will continue to exist is highly doubtful. Will its original goal remain limited to a federal organisation albeit with an unusual political system or will the EU assume a totally new, postmodern shape that cannot yet be defined? These questions become pressing in the face of a decade-long economic and political crisis affecting the economy of the internal market, sectoral policies of the EU, and the economies of individual Member States.

Therefore, there have been calls for a considerable (far-reaching) change as to how the European Union (as well as its Member States) is governed, which has been reflected in the concept of good governance. The idea has been discussed among international scholars for over two decades, but it is now becoming increasingly applicable in the practice of the European integration process. The elements of good governance can be identified in the actions taken by the European as well as national authorities, for instance in the initiatives aimed at combatting discrimination and social exclusion, bringing Europe closer to its citizens, improving the legislative environment (*Better Regulation scheme*), improving the functioning of justice systems in order to promote the internal and external security of the EU, establishing the principles of a modern approach towards the financing of public authorities, reducing the risk of the disintegration of the internal market, as well as promoting the principles of democratic governance based on the good governance concept, also in third countries, especially the ones located on the borders of the internal market of the EU. However, the governance in the EU is faced with a fundamental problem: decisions are taken on an ad hoc basis, which is related to the fact that the purpose of the integration process has not been clearly defined. Hence, the economic governance has also been reformed only on an ad hoc basis so far. It remains to be seen whether the reforms implemented are effective. The crisis may become a catalyst for the acceleration of the integration project in Europe.

The concept of good governance has been well known among legal scholars as well as within European law and European Studies since the late 1990s. (Rosenau, Czempiel, 1992; Walker, de Búrca, 2007). It is also known across the Member States of the EU and among numerous international bodies and organisations such as the World Trade Organisation. The World Bank was the first to incorporate it into its documents and aid schemes (World Bank, 1991: 1). The concept of good governance implies that significant redistribution of political power, combined with enhancing the presence of non-governmental organisations, epistemic communities, "networked structures" and public-private partnerships, plays a role in improving the efficiency of the state and international organisations (such as the EU).

The White Paper of the European Commission on good governance defines governance as "rules, processes and behaviours that affect the way in which powers are exercised at European level, particularly as regards openness, participation, accountability, effectiveness and coherence." (*A white paper of the European governance*, 2001: 428). Over a dozen years later, the European Commission extended the scope of these rules and values. It indicated that good governance should be based on values such as lawfulness, integrity, impartiality, inclusion, openness, recipient-oriented attitude, reactivity, communication, efficiency, sustainability, vision, reflection, innovation and accountability (EC 2015: 18-19).

As an "*umbrella term*" the notion of good governance is, and probably will remain, ambiguous for a number of reasons. First of all, the objectives of the concept of good governance are diverse, depending on the legal and regulatory environment and the types of entities being part of the governance structure. Environment is defined here as the efficiency of national as well as international legal systems, the legal, economic, cultural and even geographical environment, as well as action levels: central (national) or local, transnational or international (de Búrca, Weiler, 2012: 207; Held, 1995: 17). Good governance is, in the first place, a set of good practices followed by state actors in cooperation with, inter alia, non-state, social and expert organisations. It refers to, for example, the efficient functioning of administration, particularly with respect to the ability to absorb funds effectively and to address collective issues.

The development of the concept of good governance is related to a number of factors typical of the previous century: in the first place, the growing bureaucracy of the state apparatus, formation of other regulatory and executive entities, in particular agencies, as well as the transfer of competencies to institutions independent from the governments of the Member States (Curtin, 2009: 136). Additionally, the processes of the implementation of European Union policies have started to be accompanied by the direct vertical and horizontal cooperation of the institutions of the Member States, which has led to the creation of various kinds of networks. This implies the growth in the importance of territorial units, which, after all, are naturally most interested in the implementation of the idea of good governance.

Good governance standards include, in particular, respect for the principles of democracy and the rule of law, a well-functioning administration, transparency of activities and efficiency, responsiveness and responsibility, ownership and accountability, legitimacy and democracy, and respect for human rights (Curtin, Wessel 2013: 45-47; Farrall, Rubenstein 2009: 191-213; Farall, 2014: 389-408). Legitimacy for good governance can be achieved not only through efficient actions, but also through the participation of stakeholders and deliberative decision-making structures. In the context of good governance, the question also arises as to so-called "good enough governance", which refers to the minimum standards of good governance (Grindle, 2004: 525-548). As the fulfilment of the criteria for good governance is always a question of degree, there is always the issue of the threshold between bad and good governance.

Consequently, good governance leads to a significant improvement in the quality of governance, i.e. the manner and effects of governance. Therefore, the underlying issue is not who governs, but how the governing is being done, which is at the very heart of the thesis of the present research project on "the transition from government to governance."

In other words, there is a tendency to shift away from emphasising the fundamental role of the government in favour of focusing on how governance is being done. This does not mean that democratic legitimacy is becoming less relevant. Good governance entails, however, a departure from solely parliamentary or electoral legitimacy and, at the same time, brings the participation and deliberations of the entities engaged in a given governance structure to the fore. What is meant here is the mode of governance, i.e. the way of exercising authority. In a broad sense, the fundamental function of the (state) authority is integration. It entails curbing natural centrifugal tendencies and ensuring the key role of the central authority in governing a state or an international or transnational structure, e.g. the European Union. Another function relies in the distribution of resources and goods administered by public authorities. The protective function provides external and internal security, whereas the structure-forming function refers to the provision of social mechanisms ensuring that the representatives of all social groups have access to governance (Deryng, 1936: 16).

In a narrow sense, the functions of authority are related to the activities carried out in specific areas, such as law-making (legislative function), appointing or modifying state authorities (creative function), decision-making with respect to government finances, implementation of the budget (budgetary function), as well as influencing the economy, culture, education and science (Grzeszczak, 2011: 22-23; Aiginger, Cramme, Ederer, Liddle, Thillaye, 2012: 1-12).

Governance involves exercising state authority, which entails, inter alia, the process of decision-making and running the state apparatus, ensuring that decisions are abided by. Consequently, governance entails, in principle, the actions related to the exercise of power: law-making, issuing administrative decisions and delivering judgments, and it is equipped with a structured means of enforcement as a necessary component of power. In the strict sense of the term, governance is the task of the government and its departments. In its broader meaning, governance involves also the activities taken by the parliament and the head of state, with a distinction being sometimes made between the power to make decisions and the power to influence them. The latter case encompasses organised pressure groups and processes of lobbying in its broadest sense (Walker, de Búrca, 2007: 517).

Good governance means efficient governance. It involves correlating the actions taken with the costs incurred and the efforts made (workload, time effort etc.) and relating these to projected and achieved effects. Efficient governance regards the ability of the authorities to carry out public policies in a fair and cost-effective manner. In particular, this entails provision of basic social services, improvement of living standards, elimination of poverty, ensuring development and equal opportunities, supporting human resources development, provision of social protection, implementation of employment policies, as well as ensuring environmental protection and sustainable development. Good governance means also a democratic governance- it is understood as openness and transparency of the functioning of public authorities, as well as the possibility to engage citizens in administrative tasks (Supernat, 2009: 644–649). Democratisation is related to the establishment of auditing procedures, accountability of public authorities and administration for the actions taken, as well as delimitation. It is naturally, democratisation is also related to management processes and it involves the obligation to respect human rights, including the rights of minorities, which is a normative element.

Good governance involves ensuring political stability and efficient foreign policy, including provision of internal and external security. However, as political systems need to be able to respond to social changes, crises and emerging challenges, stability is not an end in itself. In this context, the concept of "resilience of governance" emerges, understood as the ability to respond to crises and to tackle them through appropriate and creative governance (Duit at al., 2010: 363-368).

Additionally, good governance means the elimination of an excessive administrative burden facilitates economic development, enhances the regulatory environment, and eliminates over-regulation (inflation of standards and rules). This is linked to the proposal for developing smart administration, which, "guided by the principles of logic, the criteria of rationality and the requirements of fairness. It is able to enrich the values underpinning it without any additional organisational, financial and human efforts." Another proposal refers to the provision of an efficient tax system and public debt policy. This would lead to liberalisation of trade, attraction of foreign investment as well as enhancing the privatisation of state-owned enterprises.

This book is divided into three parts. In the first part "Change of the paradigms: From government to good governance?" the first chapter of Ireneusz P. Karolewski provides an overview of the concept of good governance in the European Union. The EU has discovered the concept of good governance through development policies of the World Bank, UNDP and the OECD. Since 1990s it has used the term in various contexts, both regarding the institutional architecture of the EU and the ENP. However, there are still serious issues with the very concept, as the EU does not make clear how the democratic component of good governance should look and nor does it coherently act in tune with coherent democracy concepts. In addition, the good governance is challenged increasingly by the complexity of the EU, as the EU is expected to provide fewer and fewer solutions to the collective problems of the Europeans. The inability of the EU to deliver goods and solutions to problems in accordance with the heterogeneous European citizenry has been visible in the context of the recent crisis such as the sovereign debt crisis and the refugee crisis. The EU's capability to perform has been under serious pressure and is very likely to remain so.

The next chapter by Jerzy Supernat focuses on good governance and public administration. He argues that good governance in the administrative domain doubles standards for public administration. Public administration from a good governance perspective should be a truly composite concept: administrative-public, which means that it should embrace both bureaucratic-technical values (efficacy) and political values (mostly democracy and the rule of law). Such composite public administration may be termed good administrative-public governance. The idea of good administrative-public governance requires the strengthening of two relevant capacities: administrative capacity (through institutionalization of European administrative multi-level space) and public capacity (by guaranteeing the accountability of public administration).

In the following chapter Michalina Szpyrka presents an analysis of human rights and good governance. Good governance is strictly linked to human rights as both these concept place the individual at the heart of their concerns. Although it is still impossible to precisely determine the relation between good governance and human rights, there are certain links between these two areas. At European Union level, the concept of links between good governance and human rights is best reflected in the implementation of the right to good administration. The execution of this right – both in a narrow and a broad sense – contributes to enhancing the image of public administration and bringing it closer to the citizen.

Monika Sus examines the policy advice in the transition process. She argues that think-tanks as brokers of good governance are an important factor in the process of transition towards a good governed state. By playing different roles in the policy system, they can contribute to greater transparency, inclusion and effectiveness of the policy making process. At the same time, their sole existence is not enough for the enhancement of the policy system and it has to be followed by the willingness of different stakeholders of the decision making process to cooperate with the think tanks, use their advice and provide them access to the policy process.

Issues concerning good governance in the judicial system are the subject of analysis by Jagna Mucha. She claims that in line with the concept of good governance, government does not have exclusive jurisdiction over governance. Good governance implies the existence of other actors involved in governing, such as judges who ensure the legality of the government's actions. Efficient, accessible judicial institutions control public administration by limiting its discretion and guarantee that the rights of the applicant of the administrative proceedings are ensured. In this sense, effective judicial system shall guard the principle of good governance, which is particularly challenging at the EU level.

The second part of the book focuses on selected issues of public participation and government effectiveness. In the first chapter Magdalena Gniadzik pays attention to the development of the concept of EU citizenship through incremental acceptance of citizens' rights. EU citizenship was intended as a means of strengthening the position of citizens of EU member states within the framework of EU law. However, the current jurisprudence of the Court of Justice concerning the right to free movement may be interpreted as heading towards the return to a situation where this right to free movement is granted only for those who are wealthy and well-integrated with the host state. Furthermore, in extreme situations EU citizen could be deprived of the right to social protection, among other rights, because of the lack of sufficient link to any of the member states. These tendencies may result in a negation of the very substance of the EU citizenship's status.

The same author continues her analysis in the next chapter devoted to anti-discrimination framework and employment. She argues.that the European Union, despite undoubtedly important achievements in its fight against discrimination in work and employment, has some structural problems, which hinder or even preclude an effective realisation of the adopted anti-discrimination objectives. The main role plays diversified level of social development and cultural as well as historical experience of particular member states, which often results in fundamental differences in their approach to issues surrounding equal treatment in EU member states. The consequence is the impossibility of reaching a consensus and adopting common and binding legal regulations. The necessity of reaching a consensus also delays amendments to the existing regulations which could be a response to the rapidly advancing social change. It seems, however, that the most destructive element is the lack of engagement in the implementation of already existing legislation or strategies. This casts a significant doubt over the effectiveness of the EU's anti-discrimination policy, and is therefore the largest threat for the idea of good governance in the context of the European Union's anti-discrimination law and policy.

The next contributor, Anna Kańciak, analyses the relationship between good governance and security policy. The realisation of good governance in the scope of the high level of security is compared with problems resulting from interpretation of art. 67 TFEU. The exclusive competences of Member States (art. 4. 2 TEU) in the area of national security, which includes decisions on actions to provide it, will influence the effectiveness of security at the European level. The evaluation, whether the EU "is making efforts" in order to ensure the high level of security must take into account the scope, the effectiveness, and the appropriateness of the initiatives taken at the EU level to support security.

Anna Kańciak is also the author of the next chapter entitled "Development of information society services". It examines the close relation between the digitisation of the citizen's life and the level of development and functionality of information and communication systems. However, the problem appears at the stage of developing legal grounds and common standards of using new technological opportunities and the realisation of appointed action.

The good governance rule and balancing interests of employers and employees in the EU is examined by Piotr Kwasiborski. In his view the concept of good governance should be followed also in the area of employment law-making process through the operation of the so called social dialogue. The overriding aim of the social dialogue is to balance the employers' and employees' interest. Such balance is said to be nurtured at the EU level mainly through the operation of the EESC, a body supposed to guarantee the appreciation of interests of both the employers and employees during the EU legislation process. Practically the influence of EESC is however very limited and therefore a challenge of good governance in this area is to assure that EU decision-makers have greater respect to the EESC's recommendations.

An overview of good governance through the concept of better regulation is presented by Jędrzej Maśnicki, who shows the direct link between good governance, better regulation, and the principle of proportionality. The good governance principles encapsulated in the EC's better regulation agenda should be broadly recognized, not only by the EC's internal staff, but also by other institutions. The well-performed decision-making process is crucial for the provision of good governance through the examination of legislative competences of EU institutions. It should be enhanced by a more strict approach to the proportionality principle examined by the CJEU during the review of the EU measures. In examining the validity of EU acts the CJEU should take into consideration the quality of information, which lays behind the decision-making process. The form most plausible to deliver it is an impact assessment described in detail by the better regulation instruments.

With regard to the access to e-justice, Jagna Mucha demonstrates its benefits for citizens and business environment. She claims that the right to the effective access to justice constitutes one of the fundamental pillars of a democratic legal order. However, it turned out to be a challenge to facilitate comprehensive, equal access to justice across the whole EU. Therefore, the European Union has introduced a tool to ensure an easier management of the cross-border cases, namely the European e-Justice Portal. Although it is an important source of information about the functioning to the judiciary in the European Union and all its member states, the experience gathered so far allows us to submit its functionality to some critical review.

The third part of the book contains case studies of the practice of good governance at the EU and national level. The first case study of Anna Kańciak deals with the initiatives supporting the internal and external security of the EU and its Member States. The strategic guidelines in AFSJ and the common foreign policy and security (CFSP) constitutes the signs of good governments of the EU at the international level. The European Union obliged to ensure the high level of security (art. 67. 3 TFEU), bringing the added value added through strategic guidelines (art. 68 TFEU), coordinates the actions at the European level. Thereby it is undeniable that the criterion of the participation is met by the EU. With respect to decisions of Art. 4. TEU, the EU makes efforts to formulate guidelines for the EU security policy.

The next chapter by Atina Krajewska aims to address the issue of transparency of global health law in the context of its constitutionalisation. First the author explains the importance of global health law for the EU and its Member States. Subsequently, she analyses the development of global health law, which is marked by extraordinary proliferation of actors and a wide range of norms, accompanied by perhaps a comparatively modest process of juridification. The institutional and normative plurality and lack of transparency hinders the creation and sustainment of coherent responses to global health challenges. The chapter aims to determine whether global health law can be seen as a societal fragment and an autonomous system of global society. It analyses different reasons underlying the lack of transparency, including the scarcity of classical international law instruments and the proliferation of soft law.

Kamil Mroczka analyses the impact of government informatization on the efficiency and effectiveness of public duties - case studies. He claims that high degree of standardisation and computerisation of the judiciary and the use of "Rechtspfleger", especially in the branches with a high numbers of cases (land registry, business registry, family law, enforcement cases, and payment orders), enable courts to keep the costs low and allow the revenue (derived from court fees) to be distributed to other parts of the court system (for example, criminal proceedings).

The impact of the principles of good governance on the European Investment Law is explored by Jagna Mucha, who claims that the materialisation of the concept of good governance is considered to be of utmost importance for the amount of the investments made in the EU. Not surprisingly, investors locate their capital in these countries, since there is a stable, legal framework regulating the working of the transparent public administration. Therefore, the concept of good governance has a significant influence on the directions of the EU investment policy and on the EU law. With varying degrees of success the EU institutions aim at guaranteeing legal certainty and transparency as regards the conditions under which investors shall operate and resolve their disputes.

Good governance at the local level is examined by Elżbieta Opiłowska. She claims that European Grouping for Territorial Cooperation instrument can be an effective tool to facilitate cross-border cooperation by fulfilling the principles of good governance. It may provide an operative instrument towards harmonisation and unification of cross-border cooperation in the EU. However, there are still some challenges and shortcomings to be faced by local authorities. Differences in national and regional competences may complicate the construction process of the grouping and slow down the functioning of projects in areas handled by different levels across EU.

Next, Ewelina Tomczak and Michalina Szpyrka, deal with the question of mutual recognition of official documents as an example of an initiative that brings the European Union closer to its citizens.

In the last chapter of the book, Aldona Wiktorska-Święcicka analyses the operation of good governance at the metropolitan level. The aim of the case study is to provide an in-depth reflection on institutional practice in Poland in the context of the implementation of *good governance* standards in selected metropolitan areas. In the chapter the author examines the basic issues concerning metropolitan areas as well as their governance with regard to *good governance* standards. She discusses the question of innovation associated with the paradigm in question as well as directions and challenges connected with *metropolitan governance* in Poland, including its institutional dimension.

The book aims at presenting the concept of good governance, the recommended initiatives and forms of implementation as well as at answering the question of how the crisis influences the performance of integration tasks and the condition of the Member States. The situation in Poland serves as the prime point of reference for the presentation of relevant national policies.

The first objective of the book is to verify the hypothesis that 21st century is the time of transition from government to governance, which is connected with the proposal to introduce the good governance system in the EU and in the Member States. Therefore, the issues which have been examined by the project team involve theoretical considerations regarding political and legal initiatives related to the good governance programs. The research project concentrated on the period between 2009-2016, covering the time between the enforcement of the Lisbon Treaty and the time when legislative acts implementing its provisions will come into force or the relevant new institutional solutions will be implemented.

The second objective of the book is to precisely and systematically analyze issues which constitute the concept of good governance in the EU. Thirdly, in the book the hypothesis is posed that an element of good governance is the ability to fulfil the social needs of EU citizens. In order to evaluate this hypothesis, the particular issues will be analyzed. Efficiency in fulfilling the social needs of the EU citizens is an essence of this concept.

The objective of the book is to determine optimal measures for wielding power, to formulate a coherent concept of good governance and the methods of its realization in practice. This should be particularly important and useful when the good governance concept is defined non-uniformly and when it is designated for very distinct goals.

The realization of the principle of good governance includes a number of detailed EU initiatives, of which the research project refers to the latest ones. The book concerns one of the most significant problems, namely the functioning of the public sector in theory and in practice. The objectives were formulated in reaction to the discussion, initiated a decade ago, concerning the role of the state in 21st century, the future of EU integration and challenges of globalisation (Majone, Cambridge 2009: 43). Currently, good governance is associated with the improvement of management methods in the European Union in all aspects of the realisation of domestic and EU policies. As such it goes beyond the issues of state capacity and the effectiveness of management. The importance of issues related to social participation in the work of administration and verification of public authorities' decisions is growing. Indirectly all the issues mentioned above refer to social legitimisation of public actions in the European Union.

References

A white paper of the European governance, COM(2001) 428.

Aiginger K. and Cramme O. and Ederer S. and Liddle R. and Thillaye R. (2012), 'Reconciling the short and the long run: governance reforms to solve the crisis and beyond', WWWforEurope Policy Brief, Issue 1.

Curtin D. (2009), 'Executive Power of the European Union Law: Practices, and the Living Constitution', Oxford: Oxford University Press.

Curtin D. and Wessel R. A. (eds.) (2013), 'Good governance and the European Union: reflections on concepts, institutions and substance', Oxford: Oxford University Press.

de Búrca, G. and Weiler, J. H. H. (2012), 'The worlds of European constitutionalism', Cambridge: Cambridge University Press.

Deryng A. (1936), 'Zagadnienie podziału funkcji władzy państwowej, Stała Delegacja Zrzeszeń i Instytucyj Prawniczych R.P.', Warszawa.

Duit A. at al. (2010), 'Governance, complexity, resilience', Global Environmental Change 20.

European Commission (2015), 'Quality of Public Administration: A Toolbox for Practitioners', Luxembourg: Publications Office of the EU.

Farall J. (2014), 'Rule of Accountability or Rule of Law? Regulating the UN Security Council's accountability deficits', *Journal of Conflict Security Law,* 19(3): 389-408.

Farrall J. and Rubenstein K. (eds.) (2009), 'Sanctions Accountability and Governance in a Globalised World', Cambridge: Cambridge University Press.

Grindle M. S. (2004), 'Good Enough Governance: Poverty Reduction and Reform in Developing Countries', *Governance: An International Journal of Policy, Administration, and Institutions*, 17 (4): 525- 548.

Grzeszczak R. (2015), 'The concept and practice of good governance in the European Union', *International Journal of Social, Education, Economics and Management Engineering* 9(2): 449- 453.

Grzeszczak R. (2011), 'Władza wykonawcza w systemie Unii Europejskiej', Warsaw: University Press.

Held D. (1995), 'Democracy and the Global Order: From the Modern State to Cosmopolitan Governance', Cambridge: Cambridge University Press.

Krisch N. (2012), 'The case for pluralism in postnational law', in: J.H.H. Weiler, G. de Búrca (eds.), *The Worlds of European Constitutionalism*, Cambridge University Press.

Majone G. (2009), 'Europe as the Would-be World Power', Cambridge University Press.

Rosenau J. and Czempiel E.O. (1992), 'Governance Without Government: Order and Change in World Politics', Cambridge: Cambridge University Press.

Supernat J. (2009), 'Transparentność w funkcjonowaniu instytucji Unii Europejskiej', in: P. J. Suwaj, D. R. Kijowski (eds.), 'Patologie w administracji publicznej', Warsaw: Wolters Kluwer business.

Walker N. and de Búrca G. (2007), 'Reconceiving Law and New Governance', *Columbia Journal of European Law*, 13(3): 519- 537.

World Bank (1991), 'Managing Development - The Governance Dimension', Washington D.C.

Part One:
Change of the paradigms:
From government to good governance?

Chapter 1: Approaches to (good) governance in the European Union

Ireneusz P. Karolewski

Key words: Multi-level Governance, Democratic Deficit, Good Governance, European Neighbourhood Policy

Introduction

The term "good governance" has often been equated with "governance", as the governance discourse became popular in social and legal sciences in the beginning of 1990s. At that time, the notion of "governance without government" entered both International Relations and International Public Policy (e.g. Rosenau and Czempiel, 1992; Reinicke, 1998). Inspired by the breakdown of communism and the revival of the free market as well as perpetuated by the neoliberal economics of the minimal state the concept ascribed a greater role to non-state actors, networks, private-public partnerships and civil society actors with regard to the solution of public problems and the provision of public goods. The growing popularity of "governance" and "good governance" resulted from a conviction that non-hierarchical forms of governance with voluntary coordination, rather than the traditional "command and control" politics could be far more effective and efficient than state-centred decisions.

The notion of "governance without government" was followed by a series of related concepts such as "governance with government" and politics "in the shadow of hierarchy" (Mayntz and Scharpf, 1995), as the initial hype about the irrelevance of the state was replaced by more realistic approaches. These approaches highlighted the importance of state participation in public policy formulation and implementation but still focused on non-hierarchical decision-making processes.

Against this backdrop, the EU has become the epitome of "governance with government", as scholars tend to view it as a nested political system with a plethora of various actors including national governments, supranational institutions, transnational interest groups, expert networks and advocacy coalitions. All these actors interact in a highly complex multilevel system in which the power is exercised through coordination and consensus-seeking, rather than a vertical type of decision-making (Risse-Kappen, 1996). Some scholars go even so far as to argue that the power in the multilevel governance of the EU shifted from the centre (governments of the EU member states) to the periphery and has brought about a new type of actor, the so-called "interface managers"—actors controlling the information flow between different levels of decision making (Beck and Grande, 2007). Regardless of whether it is the case or not, there seems to be a consensus in the European Studies that the governance system of the EU is based on the dispersion of authority, rather than its centralization (e.g. Hooghe and Marks, 1996).

In addition to the non-hierarchical nature of governance, the notion of "good governance" introduced a further legitimacy dimension into the discourse. Against this backdrop, governance is not only about solving societal problems but also about the democratic legitimacy of the decision-making involved. While "governance" is mainly concerned with administrative reforms, sound financial management, predictability, fighting corruption as well as the opening of the state to non-state actors, "good governance" focuses on human rights, political participation and democracy. In other words, good governance is more ambitious, since it both aims at the increase of the administrative performance of the state (via reforms and inclusions of non-state actors) and the inclusion of democratic criteria into public decision-making. Within the EU it is closely connected to both the notion of the EU's democratic deficit and the EU's external Europeanisation policies, that is the EU's attempts to liberalise and democratise its neighbouring countries, for instance with the European Neighbourhood Policy.

Good Governance: Evolution of a concept

The concepts of "governance" and "good governance" have been discussed in the context of the EU for some time now. Both arrived in the EU discourse via Development Studies and became popularised through the World Bank Reports of 1989, 1992 and 1994. The World Bank has introduced the term "good governance" analogous to sound development management (World Bank, 1992), mainly in crisis-ridden countries of Africa and Latin America. It included capacity-building in the public sector, more accountability with regard to the management of public finances, a better legal environment and more transparency. This understanding was quite different from the idea that successful socio-economic development can be based on a minimum state, which was epitomized by the so-called Washington consensus (e.g. Williamson, 1990) focusing on free market. The notion of the minimal states was increasingly put into question, as it became apparent that replacing the state by the market can also generate negative outcomes, for instance by depriving the poorest parts of the society, in particular in Africa, of the most basic public goods. Already in 1989 the World Bank Report (1989: 60) concluded that the hitherto approach to development policy based on the reduction of state activity was conducive to an acute failure in "the exercise of political power to manage a nation's affairs", rather than improving governance (see also Börzel/ Pamuk/Stahn, 2008).

The World Bank Report of 1994 (World Bank, 1994) put new aspects onto its governance agenda where the state remained central but suggested more decentralization and civil society participation. It focused on three elements of governance that were deemed essential: "(i) the form of political regime; (ii) the process by which authority is exercised in the management of a country's economic and social resources for development; and (iii) the capacity of governments to design, formulate, and implement policies and discharge functions" (World Bank 1994).

A further advancement of the concept of good governance was carried by the United Nations Development Programme (UNDP, 1997), which similarly to the World Bank, focused on sound economic, political and administrative authority in order to manage a country's affairs. In contrast to the state-centred approach of the World Bank, the UNDP amended its definition by extending governance to "comprise the mechanisms, processes and institutions through which citizens and groups articulate their interests, exercise their political rights, meet their obligations and mediate their differences" (UNDP, 1997: 2). In 2002, the UNDP went even further and introduced the term "democratic governance", which explicitly highlighted the political dimension.

In turn, the EU adopted the concept of good governance from the World Bank, UNDP and the OECD with the latter joining the discourse it in the beginning of the 1990s. Even though the OECD shared the governance conceptualisation of the World Bank (OECD/DAC 1995), it dispersed the term more widely, mostly through its working group on "Participatory Development and Good Governance". In addition, the OECD put more emphasis on participation, human rights and democratisation, as it acknowledged that the governance failures are likely to result also from political factors than just administrative mismanagement (see also Börzel/ Pamuk/Stahn, 2008).

For many years, there was not much interest by the EU in good governance, as the only development policy that the EU has formulated, was the preferential trade treatment of the former colonies of some EU member states. This approach (since 1975 and through the 1980s) was economic by default and largely ignored issues such as human rights, participation and rule of law, which is noticeable with the series of the Lomé agreements the EU signed with the APC (African, Caribbean, and Pacific) countries. However, with the end of the Cold War, the EU has adopted the conceptual shift regarding governance too. This is quite visible through comparison of the individual Lomé agreements. The Lomé IV Convention of 1989 ignored human rights and democracy, whereas its updated version of 1995, the Lomé IV Bis declares these aspects essential for the agreement. In this agreement, the EU has reacted to the advancement of the discourse on good governance and embraced the introduction of political principles in its approach to governance. The Lomé Agreements have been replaced in 2000 by the Cotonou Agreement, which open the EU's concept of good governance to non-state actors. The state still remains central but the new approach includes non-state actors into the political dialogue and declares them subjects of development aid (European Commission, 1998; Börzel/Pamuk/Stahn, 2008; Santiso 2001).

Governance in the EU: How good is it really?

The EU and previously the EC have introduced its internal reforms through a series of negotiations of the EU Treaty. For decades, democracy within the EU was not an issue and human rights were not even mentioned in the original Rome Treaties that gave birth the the European integration process in 1957. For a long time, the EU has been a project of political elites and the EU's legitimacy was based on the so-called "permissive consensus" (Lindberg and Scheingold, 1970), that is, the acceptance by the EU societies that political elites can manage the process more effectively and without the democratic participation of the societies. Consequently, the EU legitimacy was entirely based on its ability to perform, for instance its capability to establish a single European market, beneficial to all citizens. In this sense, the EU aimed at governance performance based on a narrow understanding of administrative capacity and efficient decision-making. However, the failures of the EU to secure the support of the citizens became visible with the Maastricht Treaty and the subsequent treaties of Amsterdam and Nice. In some EU counties the newly negotiated treaties were subject to referendums, of which some failed. The failed referendums in Denmark (1992) on the Maastricht Treaty and Ireland (2001) on the Nice Treaty showed certain limitations of the EU legitimacy and brought about discussions on its democratic legitimacy. These discussions had already started in the course of 1990s but with the series of failed referenda they ceased to be a merely academic topic and acquired political relevance (e.g. Höreth, 1998; Scharpf, 2003; Grimm, 2015).

That is why in 2000 the European Commission declared the reform of European governance one of its major strategic objectives. As a response to a growing demand for more democracy and transparency, the Commission published a White Paper in 2001 which applied the concept of good governance to the institutional dynamics of the EU. The White Paper focused mainly on improving democratic legitimacy and highlighted the necessity of strengthening the participatory dimension of the EU. In the opinion of the Commission, the concept of European governance shall be comprised of five key principles of good governance: openness, participation, accountability, effectiveness and coherence. All these principles should be integrated with a framework bringing together member states, European institutions and civil society (European Commission 2001).

As Tanja Börzel, Yasemin Pamuk and Andreas Stahn (2008: 21) point out, the good governance concept applied to internal dimension of the EU is much more democracy-oriented than its external application, as it calls for more involvement of regional and local actors and civil society. In particular, the latter seems to play a crucial role in the White Paper, as it supposed to give "[…voice to the concerns of citizens and delivering services that meet people's needs' (Armstrong, 2002). This opening towards civil society actors has been crucial given the growing uneasiness with the EU's complex political system.

The EU's political system has been often equated with the "multilevel governance", an unconventional system of governance with a multitude of actors and complex interactions, which are of non-hierarchical nature. Gary Marks was one of the first scholars to use the term "multilevel governance" (MLG) to describe the EU's transnational policy networks in which local, regional, national and supranational governments collaborate in order to find collective solutions binding for all (Marks, 1993: 402–3). In addition, the MLG perspective stresses that in the EU various actors operating at different territorial levels are increasingly interlocked and interdependent in their decision-making. In this sense, the EU can be viewed as a case of "governance with government", where the government engages as a partner of other actors, public and private ones, rather than a tradition top-down "command and control" state. What makes the EU particularly complex is the numerous governments, a plethora of experts groups and advocacy coalitions as well as a multitude of nongovernmental organizations, organized both nationally and transnationally, who are all involved in collective decision-making. Within this myriad of actors, various decision-making procedures and informal politics, the EU has probably excelled more than any other state organization known to date. Still, there are other labels for the EU political system including multi-tiered governance, polycentric governance or "fragmegration", the latter depicting the seemingly contradictory processes of integration and fragmentation, which in fact both take place in the EU simultaneously (Bache and Flinders, 2004: 5).

The MLG approach assumes that decision-making competencies are shared by political actors at different levels. Actors such as supranational institutions (the European Commission, the European Court, and the European Parliament) exert power in policy-making, which is independent from the governments and executives of the member states. Member states remain influential, however, only as one actor type among others (Hooghe and Marks, 1996). Furthermore, the levels of decisions, also referred to as arenas, are intertwined, meaning that sub-national actors can influence the policy-making by circumventing their own nation states. The sub-national actors can operate in both national and supranational arenas, creating transnational associations and coalitions, since states no longer provide the only interface between supranational and sub-national arenas. Consequently, multilevel policy-making occurs when actors from different levels make interdependent decisions with regard to collective tasks and are in need to coordinate their policies to fulfil those tasks. Even though majority decision-making is possible in the EU, multi-level coordination is achieved by negotiating policy outcomes.

Hooghe and Marks (2004: 6) systematized the scholarly literature on multilevel governance and came to an insight that:

> "A common element across these literatures is that the dispersion of governance across multiple jurisdictions is both more efficient than and normative-

> ly superior to the central state monopoly. Most important is the claim that governance must operate at multiple scales in order to capture variations in the territorial reach of policy externalities. Because externalities arising from the provision of public goods vary immensely—from planet-wide in the case of global warming to local in the case of most city services—so should the scale of governance."

Against this background, we can argue that MLG actually reflects the very idea of good governance, as it responds to transnational challenges and provides public goods for a variety of European actors. Moreover, it is inclusive, since it involves many actors, experts and networks, both public and private. Some scholars even point to democratic legitimacy through MLG, as it not only supposed to solve collective problems within the EU but also allows for the participation of groups who are affected by a given EU regulation. The idea of the normative superiority of multilevel governance is striking, in particular when compared with literature on the democratic deficit of the EU, which highlights a serious lack of transparency in the decision-making system of the EU and a resulting problem of the (un)accountability of the decision-makers.

That is why there are doubts about how good the good governance in the EU really is, both regarding the governance output and its democratic legitimacy. For instance, the capability of the EU to provide collective goods through a multilevel decision-making system can be asymmetrical depending on the type of negotiation, the type of coupling between the actors and the policy field involved. Depending on the type of interaction between the actors (bilateral or multilateral), negotiations in the multilevel system are burdened with a different degree of conflict. In multilateral negotiations, many different interests have to be considered; hence the probability that distributive issues will arise is higher. In addition, the conflict potential in the multilevel system depends on the type of policy. Regulatory policies reduce the autonomy of member states by setting binding rules, which generates conflicts over the vertical division of competencies between member states and the EU, while distributive or redistributive policies, which channel resources of one group of states to another, are burdened by the contradictory interests of actors. Since negotiations in the multilevel system of the EU include cross-cutting interest conflicts, agreement is only possible when actors show willingness to cooperate (Benz, 2003).

The multilevel system of the EU encompasses four levels of negotiation (Grande, 2000). Firstly, it is the inter-community level of negotiation, at which supranational actors such as the Commission, or transnationally organized interest groups negotiate or coordinate their policies. Secondly, it is the inter-national level of negotiation, at which officials of the member states, national experts or nationally organized interest groups interact at the supranational level (in various councils and committees of the EU such as COREPER or COSAC). Thirdly, it is the intra-national level of negotiation, at which national actors (public and private) interact in the national arenas in order to convey their European policies or positions. An additional, fourth level of negotiation consists of supranational actors' lobbying in the national arenas to gain support for their policies (for example, the representatives of the European Commission in the member states, which is the so-called reverse lobbying).

Furthermore, there is a new type of political actor who interacts at the interface of many different levels and arenas and thus controls the flow of information, which is a relevant power resource. These "interface managers" represent their institutions in committees, councils and negotiation rounds on different levels (Beck and Grande, 2007). Formal power, good public relations and public legitimacy are in the multi-level system less important. The real power resource is the information about the preferences of other actors, the capacity to form coalitions and to successfully communicate across the boundaries of different arenas. In this perspective, power is shifted from the centre of the political system to its peripheries, where there is even less transparency and actors possessing power are not necessarily elected.

This brings us to pathologies of MLG in the EU. Irrespective of its problem-solving capacity, the MLG also develops pathologies of political responsibility. It is lacking transparency for an outside observer, in this case most of the EU citizens. Citizens cannot easily learn who influences given political decisions in the EU, particularly under circumstances of power shifts from known political actors such as governments to the peripheries of the political system. This lack of transparency leads to a dilution of political responsibility. This is why political actors have strong incentives to apply new legitimacy strategies such as "blame avoidance", "scapegoating" and "credit claiming", which allow the governments to escape the political control of the national public opinion. The actors can shift responsibility onto other political actors; they can claim unjustified credit for the negotiation success or use the EU as a diversion from their own mistakes. By the same token, they can utilize their national electoral obligations as an argument in the negotiations within the multi-level system, thus playing two-level games. Ulrich Beck and Edgar Grande point to a "paradox of weakness" in the multi-level system. They argue that in the complex multi-level decision-making process, governments cannot use any hierarchical steering methods, thus appearing weaker. However, they have the capability of avoiding some of the constraints that infringe their power at the national level. In particular, states can escape the pervasive influence of public opinion or even the national interest groups. In this perspective, national governments become stronger due to the multi-level system (Beck and Grande, 2007). This puts the issue of inclusiveness, democracy and accountability into a different light.

EU good governance and potential performance deficiencies

While many scholars praise the MLG as a case of good governance, others highlight its deficiencies, regarding in particular its performance, that is, the ability to solve collective problems. One of such points of critique is the heterogeneity and complexity of MLG, which heavily influences the decision performance of the EU, since the expanding EU causes not only the decision-making structures to grow more complex, but also places a burden on the “social choice” in the EU, which is the ability to construct a common will in the EU (cf. Arrow 1951). It means that given the growing heterogeneity of societal groups, their interests and identities, the formation of public good from actors' preferences that ought to be the essence of decisions made in every democratic political system becomes more difficult (cf. Dahl and Tufte, 1971). With more societal heterogeneity, there is a growing chance that more political actors (be they voters or collective actors such as parties or state bureaucracies) will not be able to rediscover their preferences in the decisions made at the European level. In this sense, the EU might not even be able to determine in whose name it is making decisions and how far the problems at hand are serious and to whom.

Consequently, growing cultural, normative and economic differences increase the distance between the decisions of the EU and the individual preferences. This entails potentially an increasing number of conflicts, their increased intensity, and according to tendency a less popular acceptance of the EU. Tsebelis and Yataganas (2002) conclude with regard to the changes in the EU’s decision-making system (included in the Nice Treaty in 1999 as well as its modified version in the Constitution in 2004) that the difficulty of reaching a consensus increases as a result of the extension of veto powers within the Council. They expect the role of unelected actors such as judges and bureaucrats in the EU to become more significant, since it will be more difficult to change the legislative status quo, while the implementation and interpretation of legislation will offer courts and bureaucracy more discretion and hence scope of action. This development shifts not only power to unelected actors, but also makes the gap between the preferences of citizens and the European policies larger.

Regarding the output dimension of the EU legitimacy, the growing complexity of the EU generates an increased number of veto players – political actors who have an effective influence on the decision-making system. George Tsebelis (2006) suggests convincingly that with the increasing number of political actors (and the plurality of political actors is the key feature of MLG), who either determine agenda-setting or possess power to veto collective decisions, the difficulty of decision-making grows considerably. More actors' influence in the decision-making process indicates problems of reaching a consensus or the delay of the decision-making procedure, also including a higher probability of decisional blockades. Schneider, Drüner and Dobbins (2006) point to a similar danger of legislative gridlock, and stress also the greater negotiation complexity, growing preference divergence and a stronger status quo orientation with every EU enlargement. Relatively homogenous preferences of the new members (after the EU Eastern Enlargement) are expected in environmental, social and consumer policies. However, in other policy fields, such as agricultural policy, fishery and trade policy, the heterogeneous preferences of the new members will fit into the existing status quo orientation of old members, thus rendering the entire system more rigid and resistant to change. This conclusion is also confirmed by the spatial analysis by Zimmer, Schneider and Dobbis (2004), who suggest that enlargement is likely to increase the significance of conflict in the EU.

The increased conflict potential of the EU after its enlargements means that it will be more difficult to assure an output-legitimacy of the EU. Even though the major output of the EU consists in its regulatory activity, the EU draws its main attractiveness for the majority of countries from its distributive and redistributive activity, in particular with regard to the poorer EU members of South and Eastern Europe who, not least thanks to the EU resources, already experience or still hope for accelerated economic growth and modernization. The enlarged EU has already begun to face more distributional conflicts than before. Yet less distributional power clearly decreases the attractiveness of EU membership, thereby diminishing the output-legitimacy of the organization. Against this background, the good governance is challenged increasingly by the complexity of the EU, as the EU expected to provide less and less solutions to collective problems of the Europeans. Of course, some of the described challenges are worst case scenarios and are unlikely to occur. Still, the inability of the EU to deliver goods and solutions of problems in accordance with the heterogeneous European citizenry has been visible in the context of the recent crises including the sovereign debt crisis and the refugee crisis. The EU's capability to perform has been under serious pressure and is very likely to remain so.

Good governance and democratic legitimacy

As mentioned above, the concept of good governance combines performance (provision of public goods and solutions to collective problems) and democratic legitimacy (democratic participation, democratic accountability). However, some scholars have argued that democratisation of the EU brings more dangers than benefits to the organization. I would like to focus here on arguments formulated by Andrew Moravcsik, as they are the most pronounced regarding the issue and reflect also other similar positions in the EU discourse.

Andrew Moravcsik claims that that democratisation of the EU might be dangerous because it would be accompanied by greater politicisation, which in turn is likely to undermine the legitimacy of the EU (Moravcsik, 2006: 222, 237). Moravcsik's argument is partly reasonable regarding the possible impact of further politicisation on the EU's legitimacy. Nevertheless, few would agree that the recent politicisation of the European Union has been caused by outstanding opportunities for citizens to influence the political process at the European level. In contrast, the politicisation of the European Union can be traced back to other reasons such as increasing distribution conflicts, since many EU policies now produce winners and losers or the growing importance of majority rule for European decision-making. This has been quite visible in the context of the EU's refugee crisis 2015-16. Moreover, Moravcsik (2006: 236) dismisses widespread complaints about the so-called "democratic deficit" of the European Union. Thus, so Moravcsik's argument goes, the diagnosis of a democratic deficit at the European level is a misconception, since the EU is measured by inappropriate normative benchmarks. Compared to the empirical standards, valid in the EU member states, the European Union does not need to be afraid of any judgement regarding its democratic content. However, there are several problems with this point of view. Focusing on the practice of governance in the national democracies within the EU, Moravcsik entirely overlooks that many of them suffer from democratic shortfalls themselves. This observation is made by scholars who seek to provide a conceptual framework for studying the democratic quality of democracies (e. g. Beetham 1994; Diamond and Morlino 2004) as well as by empirical evidence from several studies on the erosion of political support that most contemporary democracies are facing (e. g. Norris, 1999; Pharr and Putnam, 2000; Cain et al., 2003; Dalton, 2004). Moreover, the EU member states are losing some of their democratic quality precisely because EU policymaking erodes democratic procedures within the nation-states without sufficient compensation at the European level (Kohler-Koch et al., 2004: 200). Furthermore, Moravcsik claims that the European Union does not really suffer from a "democratic deficit," at least compared to its member states. This argument is mainly justified by the fact that in contemporary democracies many important decisions are insulated from both party competition and public opinion. Accordingly, also the institutional architecture of the EU would not significantly differ from the main features of its member states (Moravcsik, 2006: 232, 239; see also Moravcsik, 2002, 2004). In fact, there are good reasons for why some institutions such as constitutional courts, administrative bureaucracies, police, armies and central banks should be protected from unsteady majorities and fickle voters. The main reason is that democracies are also political systems which have to produce certain public goods. Without providing basic results neither democracies nor any other type of political order will survive. The delegation of certain responsibilities to insulated institutions and their experts therefore aims to guarantee both effective and efficient outputs. However, this argument is problematic when applied for the purpose of justifying the democratic character of the European Union, as it conflates democracy and the rule of law. In the words of Marc Plattner (2004: 107): "There is always a tension, almost a kind of schizophrenia, within liberal democracy, as it simultaneously tries to affirm and to limit popular vote". In this sense, the European Union does not suffer from a weak constitutional pillar but from an imbalance between the constitutional and the popular one caused by "the continuing expansion of the constitutional pillar to the detriment of the popular one" (Mény, 2002: 4). Yet, Moravcsik (2006:

237) promotes a "Europe of results" by recommending "to depoliticize European constitutional evolution through an incremental, piecemeal strategy of implementing effective policies and modest institutional reforms". These quotations highlight that Moravcsik advocates the so-called output-paradigm that many representatives of empirical democratic theory share. This paradigm does not try to justify the idea of democracy intrinsically but rather by emphasizing its positive consequences for the people (Lord, 2004: 7). Accordingly, a great number of scholars strive to "release" the notion of "democracy" and "democratic" from the irksome burden of its participatory component, which only endangers the further success of the democratic idea in a changing world (Buchstein and Jörke, 2003: 474). In this sense, good governance becomes reduced to governance, as the very idea of democracy refers to the people's right to collective self-determination by guaranteeing the citizens' right to influence the decisions they are affected by. Moreover, the overemphasis on the output-dimension, detrimental to the input-dimension of democracy, creates a blurred distinction between democratic political systems and other regime types. In other words, other forms of government, such as a benign technocracy or a benevolent dictatorship, might also produce satisfying results which are in close accordance with the preferences of the majority of the population (Lord, 2004: 13). Perhaps these polities are even more successful than democracies, since they do not need to deal with the unpredictable effects of citizen participation. However, these forms of government have nothing to do with democracy, precisely because they are in contrast to the people's right to collective self-determination. These polities rest on heteronomy inasmuch as the people have no voice in the determination of the community's fate. Against this background, good governance in the EU is closely related the notion (and practice) of democratic deficit. In particular, it should focus more strongly on the participatory aspects, rather than the constitutional elements, which are in the EU strong due to its treaty-based character.

Exporting Good Governance?

In addition to the internal aspects of good governance within the EU, the EU uses the concept with regard to its external policies, for instance the European Neighborhood Policy (ENP). The EU has five main policies towards third countries in Europe: the (former) EU-Enlargement policy (relating mainly to Central and Eastern Europe); the Stability and Association policy (regarding South Eastern Europe); the EU–Russia policy and the EU–Central Asia policy, the last one being clearly not related to Europe, but is considered a part of the so-called "EU-Ostpolitik"; and the European Neighbourhood Policy that embraces the remainder of the former Soviet countries including Ukraine, Belarus, Moldova, Georgia, Azerbaijan and Armenia. It is not always evident whether the grouping follows coherent geographical criteria or the rather more specific interests of foreign and international policies of the EU and its member states.

The ENP was launched in 2003 to offer the EU's Eastern neighbours an alternative to membership. The countries of the former Soviet Union and the Southern Mediterranean were viewed to be the main neighbouring regions of the enlarged European Union, with which the EU wanted to develop strategic relations. In 2004, the European Commission published the ENP Strategy Paper (European Commission 2004) which became one of the most essential documents of the ENP. The Paper highlights that good governance is a principle of cooperation with the ENP countries, even though it does not contain any clear-cut definition of the term.

In December 2006, the European Commission published a paper on the Strengthening of the ENP (European Commission 2006), which depicts good governance in the context of the fight against corruption. The paper states "that the EU has a vital interest in seeing greater economic development and stability and better governance in its neighbourhood" (European Commission 2006: 7). Despite the emphasis on the governance performance in the neighbouring countries, the Commission also stresses the participatory aspects of good governance, as it demands the "appropriate participation by civil society representatives as stakeholders in the reform process, whether in the preparation of legislation, the monitoring of its implementation or in developing national or regional initiatives related to the ENP" (European Commission 2006: 8).

In a sense, the EU's external policy of good governance relates to some extent to different aspects of the enactment of European norms. As the European norms, procedures and regulations become adopted in non-European countries, we can point to a transfer of the European "institutional identity", as good governance became one of the key aspects of the EU's self-image. This is in tune with the concept of Europeanisation offered by Radaelli (2003: 30) who argues that Europeanisation consists of processes of (a) construction (b) diffusion and (c) institutionalisation, of formal and informal rules, procedures, policy paradigms, styles, "ways of doing things", and shared beliefs and governance norms which are first defined and consolidated in the making of EU decisions.

The EU has used a variety of instruments of transferring its institutional identity in third countries. All EU external policy instruments can be divided into two types, including positive and negative ones. Positive instruments involve providing certain benefits to the targeted states such as prospective membership, closer cooperation, financial incentives, grant aid, technical assistance or the establishment of political dialogue, whereas negative instruments are usually associated with sanctions or pressure on the state elites, for example, by supporting oppositional civil society groups if they fail to comply with the requirements of the normative actors. Both types of policy instruments can be conducive to identity transfer to third countries. Even transgovernmental functional cooperation in individual policy sectors can function as a transmission belt for identity transfer. For instance, technical cooperation offers the EU the possibility of promoting democratisation indirectly, through the "back door" of joint problem-solving. Since even technical cooperation is anchored in the EU's *acquis communautaire* and has a goal of transferring European legal and administrative standards to the ENP countries, these rules and standards often contain elements of democratic governance that were developed for advanced liberal democracies of the EU.

In the theoretical discourse, we can identify three major arguments about the causal workings of norms regarding their transfer to other countries. Firstly, "identity giving" actors can apply incentives and rewards to change the behaviour of other actors in tune with the governance norms of identity-givers. Here, the learning processes of "identity receiving" actors can ensue, as soon as they show behavioural adaptation regarding the transferred norms. This perspective is rooted in instrumental rationality, and therefore it questions the autonomous role of governance norms vis-à-vis the creation of identities. Here, the so-called conditionality policies are deemed to be the right tools for the transfer of governance norms, provided they are applied in an effective manner. Effective conditionality policies mainly work through learning processes on the part of the identity recipients. In this sense, the norm-orientated behavioural conditioning of actors occurs as long as the learning process is progressing or remains at least stable. In particular, conditioning works when the targeted governments expect the promised rewards to be greater than the costs of norm compliance. However, instrumental rationality also implies that the identity recipients can be aware of conditioning processes and resist them by pretending that identity transfer took place. This can be observed, for instance, in cases where countries adopt EU norms but do not implement them. In this context, identity generation outside the EU is dependent on the two-sided credibility of the EU (Karolewski, 2011). On the one hand, the subjects of the EU identity politics have to be certain that they will receive the promised rewards after meeting the EU's demands. On the other hand, they also have to believe that they will receive the reward only if they fully meet the requirements. Secondly, it is believed that interactions and communication between the identity producing actors and the identity-adopting actors can lead to the internalisation of norms and identities by the latter, rather than their manipulative pseudo-adaptation. This argument is in tune with the (neo)-functionalist perspective pointing out that the long exposure to the norms of the EU can draw other countries into the EU's identity orbit. A means to ascertain a durable exposure to EU norms and ongoing interactions between the EU and the objects of identity transfer is the establishment of common institutions, which convey the EU norms of governance on the one hand and integrate other actors on the other hand. However, not only is the durability of exposure to the EU's norms crucial but also the consistency of the EU's normative arguments. If the EU communicates inconsistently regarding the norms or normative self-images, for instance, by using diverging normative standards for different countries, it undermines its identity transfer (Karolewski, 2011). One of such positive self-images is the EU as a normative power. Here, the EU stresses its progressive stance, for instance in rejecting the death sentence or in promoting and implementing environmental policies. By so doing it asserts its leading role and depicts, for instance, the US as a laggard. In other words, the EU promotes its positive image as the forerunner in the fight against climate change, thus claiming its moral supremacy. Consequently, the EU uses the vanguard–laggard dichotomy in order to describe its own identity in contrast to other countries, in particular the US. In this context, the consistency of the EU's normative self-images is central, as they convey the EU supremacy. Cracks in the normative consistency of norms and normative self-images of the EU render the exposure to the EU norms less effective and might even question the very appropriateness of a given norm.

Thirdly, we can discern the Habermas-inspired argument of normative persuasion, which is supposed to be based on the unselfish exchange of arguments with the goal of finding consensus, rather than negotiating on the basis of individual interests. Whereas instrumental rationality and the interactionist perspectives imply a one-directional framework of identity-giver and identity-recipient, the persuasion mechanism includes both parties in the identity-making endeavour. According to Checkel (2007, 227), "when normative suasion takes place, agents actively and reflectively internalize new understandings of appropriateness". As a consequence, this perspective suggests inclusive socialisation, where all actors act according to the logic of appropriateness of shared norms. This can take place, for instance, through the political dialogue which the EU practiced within the ENP.

The EU already applied this mixture of conditionality and socialisation in the pre-accession process in 2004 regarding Central and Eastern Europe. However, the conditionality strategies of the EU were accompanied by strong normative arguments of reuniting Europe, of the "return to Europe" of the Central and Eastern European countries, while this type of commitment has been lacking concerning the contemporary ENP. The EU has applied socialisation towards the post-Soviet countries mainly through networking, in which the adoption of EU norms is not a legal obligation but a political commitment. This stems from the flexibility of the approach, according to which the EU's *acquis communautaire* can, but does not have to, serve as a model for stimulating third countries to adopt European regulations, rules and norms. Notwithstanding the lower degree of obligation and precision, monitoring is assured at the political level. ENP countries' progress in fulfilling their action plan commitments is assessed every 18 months by the European Commission in "progress reports". This unilateral assessment is complemented by a consensual monitoring structure in the joint Association Councils. Therefore, even in this case the EU uses both socialisation and conditionality strategies. While conditionality was important in terms of making the political elites in the Central Eastern European states comply with EU requirements, it is also clear that the society and the political elites of these countries shared a strong desire and consensus on the need to "return to Europe" and to "break with the communist-past". The EU and the Western states also played this common identity card by emphasising, "we are all Europe and belong together" and used it to reinforce and legitimise the requested reforms. Regarding the ENP countries, both conditionality and socialisation strategies are weaker, since the EU does not offer any EU membership to these countries. In this sense, identity transfer is not backed up by a real identity offer. Therefore, the conditionality requirements cannot be supported easily by decisive identity transfer. Such identity transfer is associated with ambivalent feelings in large parts of these societies as Ukraine, Moldova and Belarus. Unlike the Central and East European countries those three lack the notion of breaking with the past and returning to Europe, and also have close links to Russia. This was quite visible in Ukraine during the 2014-2015 crisis where large parts of the society were willing to oust the then president Janukovych for his anti-EU course but Russia still enjoyed popular support in Crimea and the Donbas. Most EU scholars suggest meanwhile that the EU's ability to transfer norms of good governance to countries with divided societies and ambivalent political elites is quite limited (Karolewski, 2011), even though the EU made good governance one of the key aspects of its institutional identity.

Conclusions

In this chapter I have argued that the notion of governance and also good governance are central to the understanding to how the EU defines itself. The EU has become an epitome of "governance with government", a nested political system with a plethora of various actors including governments of the member states, transnational interest groups, supranational institutions, expert networks and advocacy coalitions. All these actors interact in a highly complex multilevel system in which the power is exercised through coordination and consensus-seeking, rather than a vertical "command and control" model of decision-making. The good governance concept introduces an additional legitimacy dimension into the discourse. In this context, governance is not only about solving societal problems but also about democratic legitimacy and deeper normative content. While "governance" is mainly concerned with administrative reforms, sound financial management, predictability, fighting corruption as well as the opening of the state to non-state actors, good governance focuses on human rights, political participation and democracy.

While the EU has used the concept of good governance widely with regard to both its internal politics and external politics, there are numerous issues with both the theory and practice of good governance in the EU. First, there is the question of the EU's democratic deficit. The EU has not dealt with this in any serious way so far. The White Paper on Governance mentions for instance participation and accountability, no serious democratic reforms have been introduced into the institutional system of the EU. The Lisbon Treaty introduced some changes such as the enhanced role of the national parliaments or the European Citizens' Initiative but all these new measures have not mitigated the EU's democratic deficit in any meaningful way. I have argued that the standards of good governance within the EU should be measured against the background of the citizens' expectations, rather than by murky standards of democracy. Oftentimes, both in theory and practice, the EU uses performance-oriented standards of democracy by conflating the rule of law and democracy. The delegation of certain responsibilities to insulated institutions and their experts to guarantee both effective and efficient outputs should not be conflated with democracy. It becomes even more problematic, when such arguments are applied to justify the seemingly democratic character of the European Union. A scholarly sound debate on the EU's legitimacy requires a disclosure of the conception of democracy one uses. Every democracy, be it national or European, needs normative benchmarks, which cannot be derived from its actual workings. Otherwise, we fall into the trap of circular reasoning by stating that democracy should be what it is, a fundamental fallacy. There are conceptual consequences for using the wrong-footed notion of democracy in the context of the EU, particularly when it is based on the benchmarks of the nation-state. Even though democracy is a complex concept encompassing many components, the self-determination of the citizens is still the cornerstone of its normative justification. Otherwise, we might need to start justifying democracy even in nation-states solely in accordance with their capability to produce economic growth or welfare. This is particularly relevant in the context of the EU capability to produce public goods or solve problems. As I have suggested, the system of multi-level governance in the EU is subject to growing complexity and heterogeneity, not least due to various enlargements. There are several pathologies of the MLG including lack of transparency and dilution of political responsibility. A negative consequence of the growing complexity and heterogeneity of the EU's MLG will undoubtedly be the deepening dilution of political responsibility. Citizens will be even less capable of ascribing political outcomes and thus responsibility for mistakes or undesirable political solutions to specific political actors. This is a dangerous tendency, since the legitimacy of the entire EU might be at stake here. Citizens unable to control political decision-makers are more likely to question the legitimacy of the EU political system, thus withdrawing their "diffuse support" (David Easton).

Against this background, the good governance is challenged increasingly by the complexity of the EU, as the EU is expected to provide fewer and fewer solutions to the collective problems of the Europeans. The inability of the EU to deliver goods and solutions to problems in accordance with the heterogeneous European citizenry has been visible in the context of the recent crisis such as the sovereign debt crisis and the refugee crisis. The EU's capability to perform has been under serious pressure and is very likely to remain so.

The export of the EU's good governance has not been very successful. From the Southern Dimension of the ENP only Tunisia made democratic progress. With the annexation of the Crimea and the war in Donbas caused serious limitation of the EU's impact on its neighbours. Even after the signing of the Association Agreement with Ukraine in 2014, serious problems of democratic governance in Ukraine remained. It is certainly connected with an external identity dilemma of the EU. First, the EU refuses to offer a perspective of formal membership to countries in its neighbourhood such as Belarus, Ukraine or Moldova, undermining its credibility as a benevolent "identity hegemon". Second, the EU does not always live up to its positive self-images, which questions the EU's credibility as an "identity hegemon". Cracks in image consistency promote therefore an instrumental approach to the EU by third countries, which poses a challenge to the EU's external identity politics, which good governance is part of.

In sum, the EU has discovered the concept of good governance through development policies of the World Bank, UNDP and the OECD. Since 1990s it has used the term in various contexts, both regarding the institutional architecture of the EU and the ENP. However, there are still serious issues with the very concept, as the EU does make clear how the democratic component of good governance should look and nor does it coherently act in tune with coherent democracy concepts.

References

Armstrong K. A. (2002), 'Rediscovering Civil Society: The European Union and the White Paper on Governance', *European Law Journal* 8(1), 102-132.

Arrow K. J. (1951), 'Social Choice and Individual Values', New Haven: Yale University Press.

Bache I., Flinders M. (2004), 'Themes and Issues in Multilevel Governance', in: I. Bache, M. Flinders, *Multi-level Governance*, Oxford University Press, 1-14.

Beck U., Grande E. (2007), 'Cosmopolitan Europe', Cambridge: Polity Press.

Beetham D. (1994), 'Defining and Measuring Democracy', London: Sage.

Benz A. (2003), 'Mehrebenenverflechtung in der Europäischen Union', in: M. Jachtenfuchs, B. Kohler-Koch (eds.), *Europäische Integration*, 2nd ed., Opladen, 317-351.

Börzel T., Pamuk Y., Stahn A. (2008), 'Good Governance in the European Union, Berlin Working Paper on European Integration No. 7', FU Berlin, http://www.fuberlin.de/europa (accessed: 2.3.2016).

Buchstein H., Jörke D. (2003), 'Das Unbehagen an der Demokratietheorie', *Leviathan* 31, 470-495.

Cain B. E., Dalton R. J., Scarrow S. E. (eds.) (2003), 'Democracy Transformed? Expanding Political Opportunities in Advanced Industrial Democracies', Oxford: Oxford University Press.

Checkel J. (2007), 'Social Mechanisms and Regional Cooperation: Are Europe and the EU Really All That Different?', in A. Achary, A. I. Johnston (eds), *Crafting Cooperation: Regional International Institutions in Comparative Perspective,* Cambridge, Cambridge University Press, 221-243.

Dahl R. A, Tufte E. R. (1973), 'Size and Democracy', Redwood City: Stanford University Press.

Dalton R. J. (2004), 'Democratic Challenges, Democratic Choices. The Erosion of Political Support in Advanced Industrial Democracies', Oxford: Oxford University Press.

Diamond L., L. Morlino (2004), 'The Quality of Democracy. An Overview', *Journal of Democracy* 15, 20-31.

European Commission (1998), *Commission Communication to the Council: Democratisation, the Rule of Law, Respect for Human Rights and Good Governance: the Challenges of the Partnership between the European Union and the ACP States*, Brussels.

European Commission (2001), *Communication from the Commission of 25 July 2001 "European governance - A white paper"* (COM(2001) 428 final - Official Journal C 287 of 12.10.2001).

European Commission (2004), *Communication from the Commission. European Neighbourhood Policy, Strategy Paper*, Brussels.

European Commission (2006), *Communication from the Commission to the Council and the European Parliament on Strengthening the European Neighbourhood Policy*, Brussels.

Grande E. (2000), 'Multi-level Governance: Institutionelle Besonderheiten und Funktionsbedingungen des europäischen Mehrebenensystems', in: E. Grande, M. Jachtenfuchs (eds.), *Wie Problemlösungsfähigkeit ist die EU?*, Baden-Baden: Nomos, 11-30.

Grimm D. (2015), 'The Democratic Costs of Constitutionalism: The European Case', *European Law Journal* 21(4), 460-473.

Hooghe, Liebset and Marks, Gary (1996), 'European Integration from the 1980s: State-Centric versus Multi-Level Governance', *Journal of Common Market Studies* 34: 341-378.

Höreth M. (1998), 'The Trilemma of Legitimacy. Multilevel Governance in the EU and the Problem of Democracy. ZEI Discussion Papers: 1998, C 11".

Karolewski I. P. (2011), 'European Identity Making and Identity Transfer', *Europe-Asia Studies*, 63:6, 935-955.

Kohler–Koch B., Conzelmann T., Knodt M. (2004), 'Europäische Integration – Europäisches Regieren', Wiesbaden: VS Verlag.

Lindberg L., Scheingold S. (1970), 'Europe's Would-be Polity', Englewood Cliffs: Prentice-Hall.

Lord Ch. (2004), 'A Democratic Audit of the European Union', Houndmills: Palgrave.

Marks G., Hooghe L. (2004), 'Contrasting Visions of Multi-level Governance', in: I. Bache, M. Flinders, *Multi-level Governance*, Oxford University Press, 15-30.

Marks G. (1993), 'Structural Policy and Multilevel Governance in the EC', in A. Cafruny, G. Rosenthal (eds), *The State of the European Community,* Vol. 2*: The Maastricht Debates and Beyond*, Boulder: Lynne Riener, 391–410.

Mayntz R., Scharpf F. W. (eds) (1995), 'Gesellschaftliche Selbstregulierung und politische Steuerung', Frankfurt a.M: Campus.

Mény Y. (2002), 'De la démocratie en Europe: Old Concepts and New Challenges', *Journal of Common Market Studies,* 41:1-13.

Moravcsik A. (2002), 'In Defense of the Democratic Deficit: Reassessing Legitimacy in the European Union', *Journal of Common Market Studies*, 40: 603-624.

Moravcsik A. (2004), 'Is there a 'Democratic Deficit' in World Politics? A Framework for Analysis', *Government and Opposition*, 39: 603-624.

Moravcsik A. (2006), 'What Can We Learn from the Collapse of the European Constitutional Project?', *Politische Vierteljahresschrift*, 47: 219-241.

Norris P. (ed.) (1999), 'Critical Citizens. Global Support for Democratic Government', Oxford: Oxford University Press.

OECD/DAC (1995), 'Orientations on Participatory Development and Good Governance, Paris'.

Pharr S. J., Putnam R. (eds.) (2000), 'Disaffected Democracies. What's Troubling the Trilateral Countries?', Princeton: Princeton University Press.

Plattner M. F. (2004), 'A Skeptical Afterword', *Journal of Democracy,* 15: 106-110.

Radaelli C. M. (2003), 'The Europeanization of public policy', in K. Featherstone, C. M. Radaelli (eds.), *The Politics of Europeanization*, Oxford: Oxford University Press, 27–56.

Reinicke W. H. (1998), 'Global Public Policy. Governing without Government? Washington, D.C.', Brookings Institution Press.

Risse-Kappen T. (1996), 'Exploring the Nature of the Beast: International Relations Theory and Comparative Policy Analysis Meet the European Union', *Journal of Common Market Studies* 34(1): 53-80.

Rosenau, J. N., Czempiel E. O. (eds.) (1992), 'Governance without Government: Order and Change in World Politics', Cambridge University Press.

Santiso C. (2001), 'International Co-operation for Democracy and Good Governance: Moving toward a Second Generation?', *European Journal of Development Research,* 13(1): 154-180.

Scharp F. W. (2003), 'Problem-Solving Effectiveness and Democratic Accountability in the EU', MPIfG Working Paper 03/1.

Scharpf F. W. (1988), 'The Joint-Decision Trap: Lessons from German Federalism and European Integration', *Public Administration,* 66: 239-278.

Schneider G., Dobbins M., Drüner D. (2006), 'Legislation in an Ever-Widening European Union: Gridlock, Chaos and Rentseeking?', Mimeo, University of Konstanz.

Tsebelis G., Yataganas X. (2002), 'Veto Players and Decision Making in the EU after Nice', *Journal of Common Market Studies,* 40: 283-307.

Tsebelis G. (2006), 'The European Convention and the Rome and Brussels IGCs: A Veto Players Analysis', in: T. König, S. Hug (eds), *Policy-making Processes and the European Constitution: A Comparative Study of Member States and Accession Countries*, London, 9-22.

Williamson J. (1990), 'What Washington Means by Policy Reform', in: J. Williamson (ed.), *Latin American Adjustment: How Much Has Happened?*, Washington, Institute for International Economics.

World Bank (1989), 'Sub-Sahara Africa. From Crisis to Sustainable Growth. A Long-term Perspective Study', Washington, DC.

World Bank (1992), 'Governance and Development', Washington, DC.

World Bank (1994), 'Governance. The World Bank's Experience', Washington DC.

Zimmer Ch., Schneider G., Dobbins M. (2005), 'The Contested Council: The Conflict Dimensions of an Intergovernmental Institution', *Political Studies,* 53: 403-422.

Chapter 2: Good Governance and Public Administration

Jerzy Supernat

Key words: governance, good governance, administration, public administration

The terms 'good governance' and 'public administration' have both gained – the former quite recently, the latter much, much earlier – prominence in academic literature and practice. In spite of their wide application, neither term is easy to grasp due to their complexity and evolution resulting in their diversification into many usages (Rhodes, 2000). Regarding the term 'good governance' it's sufficient to mention its intensive usage not only by the European Union (EU) – both in internal and external relations[1], but also in developmental policies (international development cooperation) by other international organizations, such as the World Bank, the Organization of Economic Cooperation and Development (OECD), the

1 The EU's understanding of good governance is reflected *inter alia* in the Cotonou Partnership Agreement signed in Cotonou on 23 of June 2000, which replaced the Lomé Convention and provides the basis for the ACP-EU partnership until 2020. Article 9 restates the separation of human rights, democratic principles and the rule of law from good governance: 'In the context of a political and institutional environment that upholds human rights, democratic principles and the rule of law, good governance is the transparent and accountable management of human, natural, economic and financial resources for the purposes of equitable and sustainable development. It entails clear decision-making procedures at the level of public authorities, transparent and accountable institutions, the primacy of law in the management and distribution of resources and capacity building for elaborating and implementing measures aiming in particular at preventing and combating corruption. Good governance, which underpins the ACP-EU Partnership, shall underpin the domestic and international policies of the Parties and constitute a fundamental element of this Agreement', the Partnership Agreement between the members of the African, Caribbean and Pacific Group of States of the one part, and the European Community and its Member States of the other part, Official Journal of the European Union L 287, 4 November 2010. The Cotonou Agreement, thus, spells out the promotion of good governance in a broader political sense.

United Nations[2], and by individual states – EU member states[3] and other (non-member) states. This usage is far from unified as the above-mentioned entities view the line between 'governance' and 'good governance' differently. In documents issued by these entities governance and good governance appear *inter alia* as a form of political system, the process by which authority is exercised in the management of a country's economic and social resources for development, the capacity of governments to design, formulate, and implement policies and discharge functions[4].

The above brings us to a different understanding of 'good governance' – either as a narrower, more administrative concept, or as a wider more political concept[5]. *Nota bene* both approaches are in line with the dual na-

---

2 The term 'democratic governance' was also launched by these entities in order to draw more attention to the political dimension of good governance and not focus good governance exclusively on economic processes and administrative efficiency.

3 E.g. the British and Irish Ombudsman Association (BIOA) underlines that governance arrangement in any complaint-handling scheme should promote and support the following six principles: independence, openness and transparency (*inter alia* clear delegation arrangements, including levels of authority), accountability, integrity, clarity of purpose (i.e. ensuring that stakeholders know why the scheme exists and what it does, and what to expect from it) and effectiveness, *Guide to principles of good governance*, BIOA, October 2009.

4 Sometimes good governance tends to be equated with governance, which on one hand is disputable, but on the other acceptable as each concept has normative and political implications (good governance deeper than governance which allows to see it as legitimate governance): they refer to institutionalised modes of coordination that aim at provision of public goods rather than serving individual needs (Scharpf, 1999). The transformation of governance into good governance was explained by the European Commission as follows: 'As the concepts of human rights, democratisation and democracy, the rule of law, civil society, decentralised power sharing, and sound public administration gain importance and relevance as a society develops into a more sophisticated political system, governance evolves into good governance', Communication from the Commission to the Council, the European Parliament and the European Economic and Social Committee – Governance and development, COM/2003/0615 (4).

5 E.g. good governance as understood by the European Commission in 2001 is a strong political concept: 'Five principles underpin good governance (…) in this White Paper: *openness, participation, accountability, effectiveness and coherence*. Each principle is important for establishing more democratic governance. They underpin democracy and the rule of law (…) The application of these five principles reinforces those of proportionality and subsidiarity', *European Governance: A White Paper*, COM (2001) 428. More on the concept of good governance in this document see the insightful text of Curtin D. and Dekker I. (2005). And of course, the EU's enlargement policy has implicitly endorsed the promotion of good governance

ture of public administration. Public administration is a political institution as it is *public*, and is, and should be, an effective institution as it is also *administrative*. The usage of the word 'public' in 'public administration' brings us many specific connotations, including: the rule of law, the constitution, political power, democracy, input-oriented legitimacy, society-orientation, respect for human dignity and rights, accountability, transparency, participation, consensus, politics, policy, change, values, mission, steering, etc. On the other hand, the word 'administration' in the term 'public administration' typically produces rather different connotations, including: efficacy, effectiveness, efficiency, economy, output-oriented legitimacy, state-orientation, order, bureaucracy, bureaucratic power, management, planning, organization, motivation, coordination, control, division of work, hierarchy, centralization, unity of direction, policy implementation, predictability, stability, permanence etc. This means providing a clear distinction between 'public' and 'administrative' in 'public administration' which is of critical importance for functions and activities of fundamental categories of administrators: political-administrators for whom work is a vocation, administrators (managers) for whom work is a career, and administrators (office staff) for whom work is a paid job[6]. In any event, there is no doubt that public administration, as an institution, due to its composite nature, should be good, sound and proper in both legal and non-legal terms[7]. The outcome of this is that good administration in EU administrative law is both a general principle, comprising legal and non-legal rules, and a fundamental right, which is a public subjective right of a fundamental nature – a notion with a double status (an umbrella no-

---

principles and elements both in a narrow as well as in a wider sense. As a result good governance principles are relevant both for the EU (for the public administration of the EU) and for the member states (for public administrations of the member states).

6 The insightful well documented description and analysis of this issue in British public administration was given by G.K. Fry (1995). Broader comparative approach to the field (employing evolution in the field from personal servants through state servants, public servants, the civil service as protected service to the civil service as professional service) was offered by H.A.G.M. Bekke, F.M van der Meer (2000).

7 Here one can recall that R. Dworkin (1977: 28 and 31) approaches law as more than written rules only as he includes into law general principles as well, which legitimizes different non-legal principles of good governance and good administration.

tion[8], an indeterminate notion, an open-ended notion, etc.)[9]. These dimensions of good administration may be significantly strengthened by the codification of EU administrative procedures (Schwarze, 2012: 301-304). The first step towards codifications of EU administrative procedures can be seen in the European Parliament resolution of 15 January, 2013. The resolution includes recommendations to the Commission on a Law of Administrative Procedure of the European Union[10], resulting in the Commission's Proposal for a Regulation of the European Parliament and of the Council on the Administrative Procedure of the European Union's institutions, bodies, offices and agencies (see footnote 11).

Regarding the term 'public administration' A. Dunsire (1973) in his account of the development of the term 'administration' – from the seventeenth century to the early twentieth century – identified fifteen meanings that have been given to the term throughout its history. The meanings of 'administration' listed by him clearly show the difficulty we face in our field: we use the same term for different things. Let's take a look at the first two completely opposing meanings of 'administration' on his list: '>>help<< or >>service<< pure and simple (with no notion of >>direction<<)' and '>>direction<< or >>government<< pure and simple (...), with connotations of >>service<< or >>help<< entirely suppressed or remote' (Dunsire, 1973: 2). All of the meanings and usages of the term 'administration' analyzed by A. Dunsire are relevant for a text like this (understanding that no 'single' usage is necessarily correct should stop us from entering into endless heated debates on what administration is). However, meaning number nine is of special importance to the text: 'work of directing, or establishing the principles of, the execution or implementation of the laws, or of public policy, as contrasted with both the determi-

8 Here one can analyze good administration as the umbrella notion including umbrella principle and umbrella right: a general principle of good administration being the umbrella principle, and a right to good administration being the umbrella right.

9 H.C.H. Hofmann, G.C. Rowe and A. H. Türk explain good administration as 'a framework concept drawing together a range of rights, rules, and principles guiding administrative procedures with the aim of: ensuring procedural justice, public administration adherence to the rule of law, and sound outcomes from administrative procedures'. They justly stress that the principles of good administration have developed in close connection with the precept of procedural justice and the principle of the rule of law (Hofmann et al., 2011:190).

10 2012/2024(INL).

nation of those laws or that policy, and the detailed or routine stages of such execution or implementation' (Dunsire, 1973: 16-17). Its importance flows first and foremost from the fact that it defines *public* administration, and secondly from the fact that it stresses the differences between administration and the work of the Parliament or legislature (bearing in mind that administration also deals with legislation) on one hand, while on the other, between administration (political and administrative/bureaucratic administration) and routine or mechanical clerical work, i.e. technical administration. The distinction between political administration and technical administration is visible in article 298.1 of the Treaty on the Functioning of the European Union (TFUE) which reads: 'In carrying out their missions, the institutions, bodies, offices and agencies of the Union shall have the support of an open, efficient and independent European administration'. Setting aside the possibility that the term 'European administration' denotes administrations of the member states of the European Union[11], article 298.1 TFUE allows us to identify three levels in the Union administration: political administration (European Council and Council), administrative/bureaucratic administration (European Commission[12], bod-

11 Such a possibility excludes the Proposal for a Regulation of the European Parliament and of the Council on the Administrative Procedure of the European Union's institutions, bodies, offices and agencies 'having regard to the Treaty on the Functioning of the European Union, and in particular Article 298 thereof' which defines in article 4 'Union's administration' as 'the administration of the Union's institutions, bodies, offices and agencies' and states in article 2.3 that 'This Regulation shall not apply to the administration of the Member States', text of the Proposal available at: http://www.emeeting.europarl.europa.eu/committees/agenda/201601/JURI/JURI%282016%290128_1/sitt-1457625, accessed10 February 2016.

12 However, it cannot be denied that the European Commission is to some extent a political institution as mutual permeating political and executive elements is typical for administration. The elegant orthodox paradigm of public administration in the form of politics-administration dichotomy was from the very beginning in contradiction with bureaucracy's real world and with what could be empirically observed; namely, that, in practice, administration is not a technical and value-neutral activity separable from politics, that administrations routinely engage in politics, that administration is politics (politics is generically defined as the authoritative allocation of values (Easton, 1965: 21)). The above was convincingly proved by the Noble prize winner H.A. Simon (1947) and D. Waldo (1948). Especially D. Waldo submitted powerful arguments that administration is a strong form of politics and therefore each endeavor to separate administration from politics is doomed to failure. As a consequence it may be stated, as did J.M. Gaus (1950: 168), that: 'A theory of public administration means in our time a theory of politics also'. At

ies, offices and agencies), and technical administration (European administration). The existence of these three levels in the Union administration, coupled with the vertical complexity of administrations of the member states indicates that administration in the EU is multi-level administration[13].

The multi-level character of the EU administrative system, which is sometimes described as a European Administrative Space (EAS), has been intensively discussed (e.g. Piattoni, 2010; Olsen, 2002). The debate on the EU administrative system carries with it two concepts: a multi-level administrative system and a multi-level governance. The multi-level administrative system has often been referenced and discussed in recent public administration based literature (Egeberg, 2006), it is also complemented by and overlapped with political-science based literature (Hooghe, Marks, 2001) that tries to conceptualize the European administrative system as a multi-level governance. Both concepts bring to bear a complementary understanding of the EU multi-level administrative system. Multi-level, in this administrative context, means that a new platform emerges that interlinks the national institutional structures with other corners of the EU system. It consists of separate institutions on the supranational level (the Commission, the Council and EU offices and agencies) and separate institutions on the national level, although the supranational level does not always integrate well into the national level or into the existing national systems of governmental accountability: political, parliamentary, legal, administrative, financial et cetera. The first are able to act relatively independently from Member State governments and institutions, while at the same time the institutional interconnectedness exists between supranational and national institutions across levels of government. This interconnectedness between two levels may breed in the decisional processes suboptimal decisions that are accepted by all participants at the lower level[14]. In other

the same time, the conclusion that there is no politics-administration dichotomy cannot lead to the conclusion that politics and administration is more or less the same thing. Prominent public administration scholars H.G. Frederickson and K.B. Smith (2003: 40) state clearly that it would be wrongheaded to approach the subject of public administration on such assumption.

13 Possible conceptualizations and logics regarding multilevel administration are discussed by A. Benz (2015) and E. Grande, M. McCowan (2015).

14 Such decisional pathology (a specific common denominator) of decisional processes involving two levels is known in literature as the joint decision trap (Heritier, 2015).

words, the multi-level character of the EU administrative system means that the emerging platform includes the paradoxical mix of institutional independence and institutional interconnectedness across different levels of government. Understanding the dynamics of this mix of administrative independence and administrative interdependence is critical for a proper understanding of the multi-level character of the EU administrative system (Bauer, Trondal, 2015: 17). Also, as the EU multi-level system of administration/governance is a complex and dynamic system of negotiations between European and national, public and private etc. entities, negotiation skills should be placed high among administration and governance skills and arts.

The EU administrative system, especially when viewed as a multi-level administrative system, is characterized – as referred to above – as a European Administrative Space. Observation of developmental trends taking place in this space allows us to identify a shift to a higher level in the process of its formation. This, in turn, allows us to distinguish two progressive phases of scientific study regarding EAS: European Administrative Space I (EAS I) and European Administrative Space II (EAS II) (Trondal, Guy Peters 2015: 81-82). This indicates a clear development towards a European Administrative Space[15] not only as a hypothesis, but also as an accomplished fact. The development towards a European Administrative Space is *inter alia* due to the transformative power of the EU and its institutions. Analyzing the outcomes of this transformative power for the Polish executive branch and public administration, R. Grzeszczak observes the emergence of a European administrative merger between them: 'EU

15 According to OECD definition: a European Administrative Space denotes that public administration operates and is managed on the basis of common European principles, rules and regulations uniformly enforced in the relevant territory (OECD/Sigma, 1999: 15). The idea of a unique European administrative convergence stressing that convergence is European stands in contrast to two other possible ideas: namely of a global administrative convergence (suggested by the New Public Management) and national (domestic, local) administrative robustness. According to the last idea, Europe and the world are likely to continue, at least for some time, with a variety of administrative models (public administrations being collections of partly autonomous institutions with identities, traditions and dynamics of their own). As for conditions and factors of an administrative convergence, either European or global, it may be fuelled both by the attractiveness of one model (convergence as/by attractiveness), and by imposition of one model (convergence as/by imposition).

law affects all areas of Polish public administration, including the law it applies. The organizational structure of administrative bodies as well as the scope of their powers and the ways in which these powers are exercised with regard to foreigners and foreign entities has been affected too. This process is so advanced that one could even argue that there has been an administrative merger of its own kind. Not only do the public servants of the member states cooperate, advise and help one another before international decisions are made by the EU, but they are also directly involved in the actual decision-making at the EU level' (Grzeszczak, 2015: 30). EAS I features the convergence of administrative policies and systems studied mostly by comparative public administration (Knill, 2001). More recent waves of study on EAS II frame the EAS as featuring an emergent common administrative order through the development of new institutional constellations and configurations including institutional independence, integration and cooptation (Trondal, Guy Peters, 2015: 82-88). Independence, integration and cooptation can be seen as necessary conditions for the creation and function of European Administrative Space. This space cannot exist without institutionalizing some degree of independent administrative capacity at the European level (without European institutions that are able to function relatively independently from national governments and national institutions). Good examples of the institutionalization of independent administrative capacity at the European level can be seen in European agencies (regulatory or decentralized agencies). However, the analysis of their rule-making powers shows the limitations of their independence and a certain discrepancy between their status as regulatory agencies and their real regulatory power (Chiti, 2013). The rise of European Administrative Space may also require a certain level of integrity in regard to independent administrative capacity. This embraces two kinds of integration: the inter-institutional integration of administrative structures at the EU level, and the intra-institutional integration of each institution, which brings about internal administrative hierarchies: of which, the administrative integration of the Commission is an example. Finally, cooptation means that independent and integrated European administrative capacity is able to co-opt some administrative national sub-centers, including domestic offices and agencies. This integration and cooptation may exceed EU administrative structures as EU institutions may co-opt other international organizations – thus integrating global administrative space.

The institutional development in the EU and the strengthening of the institutional (organizational, structural) capacity of EU public administration

(EU administrative capacity, administrative ability, administrative capability) is of critical importance for implementing Union law and policies. *Nota bene* it is of critical importance not only for EU public administration but also for administrations in its Member States as article 197 TFUE section 1 reads: 'Effective implementation of Union law by the Member States, which is essential for the proper functioning of the Union, shall be regarded as a matter of common interest', and next, the first sentence in section 2 points to the administrative capacities of the Member States: 'The Union may support the efforts of the Member States to improve their administrative capacity to implement Union law'. Traditionally, the EU gave only modest attention to administrative issues. Only after the Commission crisis, which reached a climax when the Santer Commission resigned in 1999 after allegations of fraud, mismanagement, and nepotism, was administrative reform moved to the top of the Commission agenda. Traditionally, the EU administration was, and still is, a mostly political administration: the Commission's administrative capacities in terms of staff and budget are modest in relation to its tasks. The implementation of the Union law and policies usually takes place through national administration and by shared administration (shared management)[16]. In addition to the strengthening of Union (and Member States) administrative capacities, good governance requires institutional safeguards (mostly the institution of the rule of law) in order to limit governmental authority and prevent it from acting arbitrarily. The establishment of an effective legal framework should ensure the predictability and accountability of administrative actors. This framework could also be used to prevent specific actors from arbitrarily circumventing or changing the *rules of the game* at the expense of

---

16 The other method found the following characteristics in the article 59.1 of the Regulation (EU, EURATOM) No 966/2012 of the European Parliament and of the Council of 25 October 2012 on the financial rules applicable to the general budget of the Union and repealing Council Regulation (EC, Euratom) No 1605/2002: 'Where the Commission implements the budget under shared management, implementation tasks shall be delegated to Member States. The Commission and the Member States shall respect the principles of sound financial management, transparency and non-discrimination and shall ensure the visibility of Union action when they manage Union funds. To this end, the Commission and the Member States shall fulfil their respective control and audit obligations and assume the resulting responsibilities laid down in this Regulation. Complementary provisions shall be laid down in sector-specific rules', Official Journal of the European Union L 298/1.

other actors or society as such. This calls for the parallel process of strengthening both public administration, and good governance (democratic institutions) or the strengthening of public administration bound by the rule of law with at least a minimum level of democracy; including free and fair elections, the separation of power on a horizontal and vertical level, and the limiting and control of power through a functioning judiciary. In summary, good public administration requires good and democratic governance.

The recent example of the complex approach to public administration and good governance sketched above can also be found in the Charter for Multilevel Governance in Europe drawn up by the Committee of the Regions of the European Union at the 106th plenary session on 2nd and 3rd of April 2014. The objective of this Charter is to connect regions and cities across Europe, whilst also promoting multi-actorship with societal actors. The Committee both states and affirms that they stand for a multilevel governance in Europe "based on coordinated action by the European Union, the Member States and regional and local authorities according to the principles of subsidiarity, proportionality and partnership, taking the form of operational and institutional cooperation in the drawing up and implementation of the European Union's policies". Multilevel governance as understood by the Committee includes both fundamental values and democratic principles (those listed above, plus openness, transparency, citizen participation, partnership, fundamental rights protection, etc.), and rather administrative and technical standards including strengthening institutional capacity building, creating networks, and cooperating closely by thinking beyond traditional administrative borders, procedures and hurdles (a European mind-set)[17]. The Committee believes that a commitment to

17 H. Cleveland was the first to use the word governance as an alternative to the phrase public administration prophetically wrote: 'The organizations that get things done will no longer be hierarchical pyramids with most of the real control at the top. They will be systems – interlaced webs of tension in which control is loose, power diffused, and centers of decision plural. Decision-making will become an increasingly intricate process of multilateral brokerage both inside and outside the organization which thinks it has the responsibility for making, or at least announcing, the decision. Because organizations will be horizontal, the way they are governed is likely to be more collegial, consensual, and consultative. The bigger the problems to be tackled, the more real power is diffused and the larger the number of persons who can exercise it – if they work at it' (Cleveland 1972:13).

the fundamental values, principles and processes underpinning multilevel governance will bring new modes of dialogue and partnership across public authorities in the European Union. Promoting dialogue and partnership between interested institutions (with increasing the involvement of regional and local authorities) was stressed as an element of good governance (*dobre rządzenie*) in Poland's regional policy declared in the document Nationwide Strategy of Regional Development 2010-2020: Regions, Cities and Rural Areas issued by the Council of Ministers on the 13th of July 2010.

In conclusion, current public administration in the EU requires building administrative capacity, the core of which is institutional (organizational, structural) capacity, which also includes personal capacity. In other words, administrative capacity may be equalized with the institutionalization of administrative space or, to be more specific, institutionalization of European administrative multilevel space. This institutionalization concerns organizations and structures, but also people, a specific example being the people who work for the Commission and European offices and agencies. Being public, public administration has always had a strong public arm. The concept of good governance with all its democratic principles stresses the importance of this arm in relation to the other bureaucratic arm. Therefore, public administration as seen from a good governance perspective (from this perspective it may be termed: the administrative core of good governance and the administrative governance) must embrace varying sets of complementary qualities: it must be effective but also legal and democratic (there must be a corollary between facts and legal norms), it must be a leader but also a servant, it must command specialist expertise but also be representative of the public that it serves, it must be independent but also accountable, it must be efficient and economic but also responsive, it must be internally focused and externally oriented, it must posses classified information but also be open and transparent and so on and so forth. In other words, good governance in the domain of public administration doubles standards for public administration. Public administration from a good governance perspective should be a truly composite concept: administrative-public. Though the term 'administrative-public public administration' is substantially justified, it still sounds a bit awkward; hence, the composite concept of good public administration may be expressed better by the term 'good administrative-public governance'.

Conclusions and recommendations

Good governance in the administrative domain doubles standards for public administration. Public administration from a good governance perspective should be a truly composite concept: administrative-public, which means that it should embrace both bureaucratic-technical values (efficacy) and political values (mostly democracy and the rule of law). Such composite public administration may be termed good administrative-public governance. The idea of good administrative-public governance requires the strengthening of two relevant capacities: administrative capacity (through institutionalization of European administrative multi-level space) and public capacity (by guaranteeing the accountability of public administration).

References:

Bauer M.W., Trondal J. (2015), 'The Administrative System of the European Union', in: M.W. Bauer, J. Trondal (eds.), *The Palgrave Handbook of the European Administrative System*, New York: Palgrave Macmillan: 1-28.

Benz A. (2015), 'European Public Administration as a Multilevel Administration: A Conceptual Framework', in: M.W. Bauer, J. Trondal (eds.) *The Palgrave Handbook of the European Administrative System*, New York: Palgrave Macmillan: 31-47.

Cleveland, H. (1972), 'The Future Executive: A Guide for Tomorrow's Managers', New York: Harper & Row.

Chiti E. (2013), 'European Agencies' Rulemaking: Powers, Procedures and Assessment', *European Law Journal*, 19(1): 93-110.

Curtin D., Dekker I. (2005), 'Good Governance: The Concept and its Application by the European Union', in: Curtin D. and Wessel R.A., *Good Governance and the European Union. Reflections on Concepts, Institutions and Substance*, Antwerp: Intersentia: 3-20.

Dunsire A. (1973), 'Administration. The Word and the Science', London: Martin Robertson.

Dworkin R. (1977), 'Taking Rights Seriously', Cambridge: Harvard University Press.

Easton D. (1965), 'A Systems Analysis of Political Life', New York: Wiley.

Egeberg M. (ed.) (2006), 'Multilevel Union Administration', London: Palgrave Macmillan.

Frederickson H.G., Smith K.B. (2003), 'The Public Administration Theory Primer', Oxford: Westview Press.

Gaus J.M. (1950), 'Trends in the Theory of Public Administration', *Public Administration Review*, 10(3):161-168.

Grande E., McCowan M. (2015), 'The Two Logics of Multilevel Administration in the EU', in: M.W. Bauer, J. Trondal (eds.), *The Palgrave Handbook of the European Administrative System*, New York: Palgrave Macmillan: 48-65.

Grzeszczak R. (2015), 'The European transformation of the legislative, executive and judicial power in Poland', in: I.P. Karolewski, M. Sus (eds.), *The Transformative Power of Europe. The Case of Poland*, Baden-Baden: Nomos: 21-35.

Heritier A. (2015), 'Fritz W. Scharpf, The Joint Decision Trap: Lessons from German Federalism and European Integration', in: S.J. Balla, M. Lodge, E.C. Page (eds.), *The Oxford Handbook of Classics in Public Policy and Administration*, Oxford: Oxford University Press.

Hofmann H.C.H., Rowe G.C., Türk A.H. (2011), 'Administrative Law and Policy of the EU', Oxford: Oxford University Press.

Hooghe L., Marks, G., (2001), 'Multi-Level Governance and European Integration', New York: Rowman&Littlefield Publishers.

Knill C. (2001), 'The Europeanisation of National Administrations', Cambridge: Cambridge University Press.

Olsen J.P., (2002), 'Towards a European Administrative Space?', ARENA Working Papers WP 02/26.

Piattoni, S. (2010), 'The Theory of Multi-Level Governance', Oxford: Oxford University Press.

Rhodes, R.A.W. (2000), 'Governance and Public Administration', in: J. Pierre (ed.), *Debating Governance. Authority, Steering, and Democracy*, Oxford: Oxford University Press: 54-90.

Schwarze, J. (2012), 'European Administrative Law in the Light of the Treaty of Lisbon', *European Public Law*, 18(2): 285-304.

Scharpf F.W. (1999), 'Governing in Europe. Effective and Democratic?', Oxford: Oxford University Press.

Simon H.A. (1947), 'Administrative Behavior. A Study of Decision-Making Processes in Administrative Organization', New York: Macmillan.

Trondal J., Guy Peters B. (2015), 'A Conceptual Account of the European Administrative Space' in: M.W. Bauer, J. Trondal (eds.), *The Palgrave Handbook of the European Administrative System*, New York: Palgrave Macmillan: 79-92.

Waldo D. (1948), 'The Administrative State. A Study of the Political Theory of American Public Administration', New York: Ronald Press.

Chapter 3: Good Governance and Human Rights. The Right to Good Administration

Michalina Szpyrka

Key words: good governance, human rights, right to good administration

Introduction

The concept of good governance is organically linked to human rights, which, without good governance, cannot be respected and protected in a sustainable manner. The Committee on Economic, Social and Cultural Rights considered that "Good governance is essential to the realisation of all human rights, including the elimination of poverty and ensuring a satisfactory livelihood for all."[1] It is therefore beyond doubt that human rights and good governance are mutually reinforcing and can be achieved on a number of different levels, as further elaborated later in this chapter.

The concept of good governance can be reflected in different activities of the state and its agencies as well as other subjects of international law. In the light of the objective pursued by this book, which is to present new challenges for good governance in the European Union, the main part of this chapter outlines the realisation of the concept of good governance in the EU through the right to good administration laid down by Article 41 of the Charter of Fundamental Rights of the European Union (hereafter referred to as the "Charter"). The chapter details a concept of links between human rights and good governance developed by the United Nations High Commissioner for Human Rights. The next part provides an assessment of the realisation of the concept of good governance and human rights in the European Union in the context of the right to good administration. Conse-

1 Substantive Issues Arising in the Implementation of the International Covenant on Economic, Social and Cultural Rights: General Comment 12, The right to adequate food (Art. 11), Economic and Social Council United Nations, 12 May 1999, E/C. 12/1999/5, available at: http://www.ohchr.org/EN/Issues/Development/GoodGovernance/Pages/GoodGovernanceIndex.aspx (accessed: 30.1.2016).

quently, the scope and objective of the right to good administration in the EU as well as the rights of individuals that stem from it have been presented.

The considerations are an attempt to address whether the implementation of the right to good administration fosters the implementation of the concept of good governance in the European Union, thereby contributing to effective protection of human rights. To answer this question it is necessary to show what has been achieved. Due to the limitations of the present paper, let me focus on the actualisation of the right to good administration in Poland: systematising the rules of conduct for public officials, implementation of e-administration and the pl.ID scheme.

The concept of links between good governance and human rights

As mentioned above, the concept of good governance is organically linked to human rights as it places individuals at the heart of its concerns and ensures the broad participation of society in the activities of public administration. Yet, the relationship between good governance and human rights is complicated, inter alia due to the different origin and application of these two notions. The concept of good governance is a result of transitions and an extension of the function of public administration following the development of civil society. It obliges public administration to involve citizens in handling their own affairs. Conversely, human rights apply to everyone. They are universal, inalienable, inviolable and inherent. They cannot be conferred by the state or entities subject to international law as they are inherent to the human being. Therefore, the scope and coverage of these two terms are different. However, as will be explained in the course of this paper, good governance and human rights are mutually reinforcing as the concept of good governance relies not only in protecting individuals from the authorities, but also in taking care of their problems. This qualitative difference results from the observation of human rights (Kisielewicz, 2009: 15).

A seminar held in 2004 by the Office of the United Nations High Commissioner for Human Rights (OHCHR) and UNDP led to the conclusion that the interaction between good governance and human rights should be facilitated:[2]

> "Human rights principles provide a set of values to guide the work of Governments and other political and social actors... Moreover, human rights principles inform the content of good governance efforts: they may inform the development of legislative frameworks, policies, programmes, budgetary allocations and other measures. On the other hand, without good governance, human rights cannot be respected and protected in a sustainable manner. The implementation of human rights relies on a conducive and enabling environment. This includes appropriate legal frameworks and institutions as well as political, managerial and administrative processes responsible for responding to the rights and needs of the population."[3]

Furthermore, "governance is central for effective policy formulation and implementation, including for the integrated delivery of essential services, such as education, water, sanitation and health."[4]

Human Rights Council Resolution 7/11 recognises that "transparent, responsible, accountable and participatory government, responsive to the needs and aspirations of the people, including women and members of vulnerable and marginalised groups, is the foundation on which good governance rests and that such a foundation is an indispensable condition for the full realisation of human rights, including the right to development."[5] Human Rights Council Resolution 19/20 additionally emphasises that multiple good governance principles such as accountability, transparency, integrity, non-discrimination, equality, participation and efficiency are also the principles of human rights. Most importantly, in the light of the mutually reinforcing relationship between good governance and human rights, good governance should be implemented through a broad interpretation of the existing principles and human rights.[6]

---

2 E/CN.4/2005/97, available at: http://ap.ohchr.org/documents/alldocs.aspx?doc_id=10340 (accessed: 20.1.2016).

3 Good Governance Practices for the Protection of Human Rights (United Nations publication, Sales No. E.07.XIV.10), p. 3. see also E/CN.4/2005/97, para. 8.

4 Global Thematic Consultation on Governance and the Post-2015 Development Framework: Consultation report, 2013, sect. 4.1.1.

5 Resolution 7/11, *The role of good governance in the promotion and protection of human rights,* Human Rights Council, 27 March 2008, available at http://ap.ohchr.org/documents/E/HRC/resolutions/A_HRC_RES_7_11.pdf (accessed 31.1.2016).

6 Resolution 19/20, *The role of good governance in the promotion and protection of human rights*, Human Rights Council, 19 March 2012, available at: http://ap.ohchr.org/documents/dpage_e.aspx?si=A/HRC/19/L.26 (accessed: 31.1.2016).

Also the OHCHR addressed the mutually reinforcing relationship between good governance and human rights. It developed a concept of links between good governance and human rights in four areas, namely: *democratic institutions, delivery of State services, rule of law and anti-corruption measures*. This indicates how a variety of actors are engaged in the realisation of human rights through good governance.

The area of *democratic institutions* identified by the OHCHR focuses on good governance reforms which allow the public to participate in policymaking through either formal or informal consultations. Another goal of the reforms is to establish mechanisms for the inclusion of multiple social groups in decision-making processes, particularly at the local level, to make sure that the representatives of all social groups, and not only some of them, are engaged in local politics. Finally, the reforms carried out in this area may contribute to encouraging civil society and local communities to be open about the issues they find important.

As regards *the delivery of State services*, good governance reforms are intended to advance human rights. This is possible due to the improvement of the state's capacity to fulfil its obligations concerning the provision of public goods and services, which are essential for defending multiple human rights, such as the rights to education, health and food safety. Reform initiatives in this realm are intended to establish mechanisms ensuring wide access to these services and paths for the participation of the public in decision-making processes (see more: Kjoer and Kinnerup, 2002: 1-18).

The area of *the rule of law* focuses on legislative measures and reforms to the existing institutions, ranging from penal systems to courts and national parliaments, so that they implement the existing legislation more effectively, thereby contributing to the better protection of human rights. In the realm of *the rule of law*, good governance reforms may involve reforms of individual legislative acts, awareness-raising activities, education on the national and international legal frameworks in force, as well as reforms of the existing institutions.

Although the links between corruption, *anti-corruption measures* and human rights have not yet been fully explored and described, it is undeniable that anti-corruption measures constitute part of the good governance framework. In this regard, good governance is implemented through anti-corruption measures based on principles of transparency, accountability and social participation. Reform initiatives undertaken in this area may involve establishing institutions such as anti-corruption commissions as well as mechanisms for exchanging information, monitoring government's use of public funds and implementing anti-corruption policies[7] (see more: Buckley, 2002: 173-201).

The right to good administration

The above concept of links between good governance and human rights developed by the OHCHR is reflected in the right to good administration laid down in Article 41 of the Charter. The right to good administration represents an embodiment of good governance in the European Union. It should be noted that good governance implemented through good public administration is a fundamental condition for the development of democracy. The possibility to distribute social resources and public services, the guarantees for equality for everyone before the law thanks to adequate regulation, as well as curbing corruption and the misuse of power are the foundations for well-functioning society that advances human rights.

In the European Union, the right to good administration is defined as a bundle of rights of an individual who is a party to administrative proceedings conducted before public administration bodies in the case-law of the Court of Justice of the European Union (CJEU). This has been possible as the CJEU monitors the activities of EU bodies, including those which perform administrative functions, such as the European Commission and EU agencies. These bodies carry out administrative proceedings involving various entities (antitrust entities, state aid entities, anti-dumping entities), as a result of which they make rulings that, in a material sense, are also administrative acts (Szydło, 2004: 93). The CJEU has not only created the right to good administration understood as a set of rules for the functioning of public administration, which has the power to settle the affairs of individuals, but it also propagates this right (Niewiadomski, 2003:16).

After a long period of elaborating the right to good administration in the case-law of the CJEU, the right was laid down in Article 41 of the Charter and was included in the catalogue of fundamental rights (Addink et al., 2010:116).

---

7 *Good governance Practices for the protection of human rights*, Office of United Nations High Commissioner for Human Rights, United Nations, New-York and Geneva, 2007, available at: http://www.ohchr.org/Documents/Publications/GoodGovernance.pdf (accessed 31.1.2016).

It should be noted that, in the strict sense, the right to good administration is of a procedural nature (Szydło, 2004: 93). This implies that everyone may legitimately request public administration bodies to take action in a specific manner. However, this does not mean that public administration bodies may be requested to give a specific decision or to grant specific benefits (Kańska, 2004: 301). A correlation of the components of the EU right to good administration, which cannot be discussed in detail here due to the nature of this paper (Dutheil de la Rochere,2008: 157- 172), is that the obligations are imposed on the Union institution and not the member states directly. Also the European Code of Good Administrative Behaviour approved by the European Parliament on 6 September 2001 is an intra-EU document which gives substance to the right to good administration. The document, which serves as a recommendation for EU institutions, is a set of principles intended to be a benchmark for national administrations. These principles, laid down in Articles 4-20 of the Code, "apply to all relations of the Institutions and their administrations with the public, unless they are governed by specific provisions." Therefore, the Code applies not only to individual public administration matters which result in the enactment of an administrative measure, but all the relations of public administration with the society, which should resemble the relations of a client and a service provider (Lipowicz, 2005: 11). Legal scholars claim that the European Code of Good Administrative Behaviour contributes to the codification of the principles of administrative proceedings at the Union level (Sole, 2011: 139). In this context, it is also pertinent to mention that in 2008 in Poland there was an attempt to codify the provisions of administrative law. The Polish Commissioner for Human Rights drew up a draft of a bill under the title *General Provisions of Administrative Law* primarily designed to enhance the implementation of the citizens' right to good administration. The draft was prepared on the basis of detailed examination of the implementation of the right to good administration by local and regional authorities performed by the Office of the Commissioner for Human Rights. Unfortunately, it has never been implemented.[8]

The right to good administration understood in the same way as in the Charter, the case-law of the CJEU and the European Code of Good Administrative Behaviour was also incorporated in the case-law of the Polish

8 „Prawo do dobrej administracji", RPO-MAT.60, Warszawa 2008, available at: https://www.rpo.gov.pl/pliki/12124042030.pdf (accessed: 30.1.2016).

courts. The Polish Constitutional Court referred to it several times and, although it noted that the right to good administration was not laid down in the Constitution of the Republic of Poland,[9] the components of this right should be taken into account in law-making.[10] Following the example of the Constitutional Court, Polish administrative courts also started to make reference to the principle of good administration in their case-law, with the result that, even if no reference has ever been made to the right to good administration in the Polish Constitution, its individual components are observed in the Polish legal system (Wyrzykowski et al., 2012: 31).

Examples of the implementation of the right to good administration

In the light of the above considerations, the question arises whether examples of the implementation of the right to good administration are to be found at member state level. If the answer is affirmative, it is also important to determine whether it is implemented only in a narrow sense or also in a broad sense. The analysis of the actions taken in this regard at the national level, which include standardising the rules as well as initiatives aimed at bringing public administration closer to the citizens and facilitating access to the services provided by the public administration using the latest technologies, suggests that public administration strives to come closer to the citizens and to meet their expectations. Streamlining public administration, opening the authorities to the needs of citizens and ensuring adequate standards of handling administrative affairs testifies to the application of the provisions of the European Code of Good Administrative Behaviour and an active implementation of the right to good administration, both in a narrow and in a broad sense. The following section presents several examples of how the right to good administration is implemented in Poland.

An example which should certainly be given here is the creation and incorporation in the Polish legal system of labour regulations applying to public officials, which were laid down in the Civil Servants' Code of Conduct established by the regulation of the President of the Council of Minis-

9 In its judgment SK 54/05 Polish Constitutional Court linked the right to good administration and the principles of democratic rule of law and the rule of law.

10 For example the judgment: K52/02 and P 37/09.

ters.[11] The Code was devised as a result of the implementation of the Council of Europe Committee of Ministers Recommendation No. R/ 2000/10 dated 11 May 2000 to Member States on codes of conduct for public officials and entered into force at the request of the Head of the Civil Service after consulting the Council for Civil Service (Opaliński, 2011: 181). This document is not only a set of public officials' standards of conduct which were earlier laid down in multiple legal acts, such as the Constitution of the Republic of Poland, provisions of the Civil Servants Act, the Civil Code, the Administrative Procedure Code and various acts of domestic law. It standardises the most fundamental principles of public officials' conduct based on the requirements of conscientiousness, impartiality, a kind and friendly attitude towards the applicant, and, at the same time, is an expression of general rules of conduct that allow public servants to keep the dignity of the office they represent.

The code defines administration as public service provided to all citizens on the basis of the provisions of applicable laws, thereby referring to the European model of good administration (Opaliński, 2011: 182). According to the Code, the main objective of exercising public authority is to implement the principle of the democratic rule of law and, at the same time, protect the legitimate interests of citizens. Therefore, the role of public officials is to perform their tasks on the basis of the rule of law and the ability to favour the interest of the public over their own interest. This applies also to the personal life of public officials, who should equate the consent to enter public service with the consent to have their right to privacy limited.[12]

The Code also requires officials to demonstrate fairness defined as taking a conscientious and comprehensive approach to examining each case. Under this requirement, officials should be guided by creativity in solving problems and should take account not only of the provisions of administrative law but also their own sense of justice. In practice, this means that difficult decisions should be taken by striking a fair balance between the public interest and the legitimate interest of the party to the proceedings, particularly in conflict situations (Opaliński, 2011: 183).

Another requirement imposed by the Code is for public officials to constantly improve their professional skills. This requirement is linked to the

11 Zarządzenie nr 114 Prezesa Rady Ministrów z dnia 11 października 2002 r. w sprawie ustanowienia Kodeksu Etyki Służby Cywilnej (M.P. No. 46/ 683).

12 § 2 pkt 9 The Code.

aim of acquiring the widest possible expertise on the existing legislation in the field covered by a given office. Civil servants may improve their professional skills by, among others, acquiring the certificate of an "e-official" developed in order to assess the basic digital literacy skills of civil servants. The certificate was endorsed by the ECDL Foundation in Dublin, which is indicative of its high standard.[13]

The provisions of the Code are based on stressing the need for vertical and horizontal cooperation between public officials as well as drawing on the expertise of others in areas not limited to administrative law. Adopting such an approach, along with a kind and friendly attitude towards all the applicants and a general concern for high-quality interpersonal relations, as suggested by the Code, should serve to handle affairs in a comprehensive and complex way.[14]

The Code also imposes the duty of impartiality, which is understood as elimination of corruption mechanisms as well as any suspicions about the links that may potentially be established between the public and private interests. In this sense, impartiality also means an obligation to refrain from accepting any benefits for the actions taken that are directly linked to the function performed by the official. It also prohibits entering into employment relationships that may conflict with the carrying out of professional duties. The Code also lays down the standard criteria of impartiality, such as the equal treatment of the parties, which is related to, on the one hand, prohibition of discrimination and, on the other hand, prohibition to favour any interest groups and demonstrate any personal relationship with the parties involved in public service activity. According to the Code, public officials' impartiality is subject to social control, which is reflected in the right to information on proceedings that are under way.[15]

The statement made in the Code concerning the prohibition to accept any benefits from the parties has not been formulated properly as it may be concluded that it does not cover the cases where benefits are accepted from non-parties that, in this way, attempt to gain the favour of a civil servant or express their gratitude for the outcome of proceedings that are already closed. The Code only lays down limitations concerning the possi-

13 More information on the web: https://www.ecdl.pl/e-urzednik (accessed: 10.1.2016).

14 § 3 The Code.

15 § 4 The Code.

bility to enter into employment relationships with the party to the proceedings conducted by a given office (Opaliński, 2011: 186).

The importance of public officials' impartiality was additionally emphasised by the introduction of the obligation to demonstrate fairness and professionalism, which is expressed in the principle of the political neutrality of public officials resulting from the requirement of non-politicisation of civil servants.[16] Non-politicised service is a demonstration of the professional way in which civil servants carry out their duties and of the fact that they are free from any influence by political parties that seek to obtain a favourable decision. Hence, the principle of neutrality encompasses the obligation to refrain from being a member of, and forming, political parties as well as a ban on participation in initiatives that pursue political objectives. Civil servants are obliged to follow the strategy of the state, which is directly linked to the obligation to settle administrative affairs in an impartial and objective way, irrespectively of one's own political opinion.[17]

As the standards for impartiality can be considered as unfortunate, including regulations concerning accepting benefits only from entities that are parties to proceedings, no sanctions for non-compliance with the Code and no indication of the authority responsible for supervising the application of the Code, the Code was revoked by the order of the President of the Council of Ministers concerning the guidelines for compliance with public service principles and concerning the code of conduct of civil servants.[18] The order introduces reformed rules of conduct of civil servants, whilst maintaining all the basic standards adopted in Civil Servants' Code of Conduct, eliminating the shortcomings of the previous regulations as well as ensuring continuity in the implementation of the right to good administration by public officials. It should be noted that the rules of conduct of civil servants are directly related to the protection of human rights during the performing of public administration duties, which reinforces the assumption that there is an organic link between human rights and the

---

16 Art. 1 of the Act of 21 November 2008 on civil service (Dz. U. 2008 r., No. 227/1505).

17 § 4 The Code.

18 Zarządzenia nr 70 Prezesa Rady Ministrów w sprawie wytycznych w zakresie przestrzegania zasad służby cywilnej oraz w sprawie zasad etyki korpusu służby cywilnej z dnia 6 października 2011 r. (M.P. No. 93/953).

good governance concept realised through the right to good administration.

The development of modern technologies as well as wide access to the Internet and telecommunications networks have made it necessary to revise the traditional attitude towards the way the citizen communicates with the state (the office). It has become essential to implement modern solutions aimed at facilitating the access to public administration through the use of available technology (Kasprzyk, 2011: 346). The basic assumption of e-administration is the use of ICT by public administration bodies to improve their accessibility and to streamline the process of providing public services. Facilitating the access to public administration is expected to encourage citizens to participate in democratic processes and to raise their confidence in the state.[19]

Transforming public administration into e-administration is linked to the necessity of changing internal administrative processes as well the overall administration structure. In order to make this possible, it is essential to set up a unit within a given office which will be responsible for accepting recommendations sent to the office by electronic means and ensuring communication between the customer and the office ("front office"). Another basic requirement is to create a unit responsible for the execution of orders ("back office"), with rules of functioning that will be transparent to the customer. The orders accepted by back-office employees should be executed in an automated way and in accordance with the procedures in force. Such a structure requires smooth electronic communication and data exchange between different institutions. To this aim, it is necessary to provide a secured Internet connection.[20]

In Poland, the implementation of e-administration started with the project "Strategy for development of information society in Poland until 2013."[21] This document sets out provisions concerning the main developments of public administration as regards improving the access to, and efficiency of, public services through the use of available information technology. The basic idea of the project is to gradually eliminate paper-based

19 More information on the web: http://www.eadministracja.pl/informacje-o-elektronicznej-administracji (accessed: 31.1.2016).

20 More information on the web: http://www.eadministracja.pl/informacje-o-elektronicznej-administracji (accessed: 30.1.2016).

21 More information on the web: https://mac.gov.pl/files/wp-content/uploads/2011/12/Strategia-v. 3.03.pdf (accessed: 31.1.2016).

document workflow and to replace it with documents in electronic form as well as to enable citizens to access the offices via the Internet. The rules laid down in the project were further elaborated in the "Integrated State Informatisation Scheme" adopted on 8 January 2014.[22] The main objective of the new scheme is to boost the efficiency of e-services provided to citizens and, at the same time, develop the existing as well as creating new electronic systems.

One of the results of the implementation of e-administration in Poland is the launch and constant development of the www.epuap.gov.pl electronic platform (Electronic Public Administration Services Platform), which has significantly improved the access to public services. ePUAP was modernised and expanded and is currently available as ePUAP2. The catalogue of services that can be provided via the platform was divided into 20 transparent modules, which facilitates navigation. The platform is a communication system enabling public bodies to provide their services via a single point of access over the Internet. Continuous development of ePUAP is expected to boost the interoperability of public administration and reduce the cost of document exchange between citizens and public officials as well as between public officials. Obviously, the platform itself is not perfect yet as it does not allow citizens to handle all administrative affairs over the Internet. For example, they may submit applications for identity cards; however, as regards the application for replacement of a driving licence, they need to visit the office. By typing in, respectively, the postcode or place of residence, citizens can learn where the competent office is located. However, this service is still not mature enough as a list of all state institutions in a given town is displayed and the user needs to check whether a given institution is competent to handle a particular affair or not, which is a major drawback. It also has to be noted that not all the e-administration services are "linked" to the platform, one of these being the submission of the tax return. Despite the fact that the catalogue of services provided via the platform includes a module covering taxes, levies and duties and, under this module, there is a tab dedicated to submitting personal and corporate tax returns, the user is not redirected to a webpage enabling the submitting of the tax return over the Internet. In my opinion, this needs

22 Uchwała Rady Ministrów nr 1/2014 z dnia 8 stycznia 2014 r. w sprawie przyjęcia programu rozwoju „Program Zintegrowanej Informatyzacji Państwa", available at: https://mac.gov.pl/files/pzip_-_uchwala_rm.pdf (accessed: 31.1.2016).

to be enhanced, especially as submitting tax returns over the Internet is becoming increasingly popular.

Despite certain shortcomings, the implementation of e-administration in Poland is heading in the right direction. Replacing, to a significant extent, paper-based document workflow with a paperless environment, putting innovative technological solutions into practice as well as widening the scope of e-administration public services significantly improves its functioning. The individuals that make use of these services, including persons with disability and the elderly, are able to handle multiple administrative affairs at any time and from any location, which is timesaving and enhances the professionalism of public administration services. This, in turn, is an example of the implementation of the right to good administration.

One of the most important recent initiatives concerning the modernisation of public administration services undertaken by the Polish government is the pl.ID scheme[23] implemented by the Ministry of Interior. Initially, the objective of the project was to create a new identity document with an embedded computer chip with electronic signature. However, this idea has been dropped and a particular focus has been put on the modernisation of information infrastructure and PIN (Personal Identification Number) database as well as harmonisation and integration of all state registers. The key assumptions are improvement of the quality of population registration, providing technical assistance to implement the system of electronic identity (e-ID), creating a database of state registers and improving the circulation of information in public administration by making it possible to find all the information on an applicant by entering the PIN.

The pl.ID scheme provides for the establishment of an information infrastructure system, encompassing population registration, identity cards and civil status registration. The system will include up-to-date personal data as well as data related to the legal and administrative status of a citizen, which will make it a reliable source of information. The system will be properly secured to protect all the personal data.

The scheme provides also for an application that will ensure that the System of State Registers (SSR), which is under preparation, delivers its full potential. The ŹRÓDŁO ("SOURCE") application will be made available, free of charge, to all the entities that will use the SSR in future. The project designers argue that the ŹRÓDŁO application is being created

23 More informations on the web: http://plid.obywatel.gov.pl/ (accessed: 31.1.2016).

based on suggestions from public officials, which means it will respond to their expectations. The main ideas of the application are: 1. online access to data, 2. access only to data necessary to handle a given affair, 3. smart forms that will be filled in automatically on the basis of the data in the system, 4. automatic data verification, 5. smart search engines, 6. predictive text and additional descriptions of the blocks to be completed, 7. graphics facilitating data analysis (e.g. R.I.P next to the PIN of a deceased person), 8. reports and summaries necessary for statistics, 9. clear marking of individual action buttons indicating the order in which the tasks are to be performed, 10. responsiveness of the application – automatic adjustment to the size of the screen. All these features are expected to facilitate the work of public officials using the application, hereby contributing to administrative affairs being handled in a comprehensive and quick way.

At the time of writing, it is impossible to envisage the effects of the implementation of the pl.ID scheme. It should, however, be pointed out that the planned modernisation of the existing ICT technology, the activities aimed at the integration of state registers, and providing public officers with an advanced tool is an initiative that, beyond doubt, brings the state closer to the citizen and facilitates the access to public administration, which is no longer understood as an office "flooded with documents", where it is necessary to get through a long and complicated procedure in order to handle an affair, but a citizen-friendly, modern and well-managed institution.

Conclusion

The concept of good governance is organically linked to human rights as it places individuals at the heart of its concerns and ensures broad participation of the society in the activities of public administration. Although the mutual relationship between good governance and human rights cannot be fully defined due to different origins and application of these two terms, it is possible to determine the links between them in the areas of *democratic institutions, the delivery of State services, the rule of law and anti-corruption measures.* In the European Union, the concept of links between good governance and human rights is best advocated through the right to good administration laid down in Article 41 of the Charter of Fundamental Rights. In the strict sense, this right reflects the right to a fair trial in administrative proceedings, and in the broad sense, it needs to be executed each time public authorities contact and are contacted by citizens. Although the right to good administration is directed mainly at EU institutions, good administration initiatives are undertaken also on the member state level. The examples of such initiatives in Poland are the standardisation of Civil Servants' Code of Conduct, implementation of the e-administration system as well as the pl.ID scheme, which make public administration more open, accessible and citizen-friendly. Elimination of obstacles and opening the offices to the needs of citizens results in the fact that, in this area, human rights are put in practice, which demonstrates that the realisation of the concept of good governance enhances the protection of human rights.

References

Addink H., Anthony G., Buyes A., Flinterman C. (2010), 'Human Rights &Good Governance', Utrecht: 116.

Buckley M (2002), 'Anti- Corruption Initiatives and Human Rights : the Potentials', in. H.O. Sano, *Human Rights and Good Governance. Building Bridges,* Hague: Kluwer Law International: 173-201.

Dutheil de la Rochere J. (2008), 'The EU Charter of Fundamental Rights, Not Binding but Influential: the Example of Good Administration', in: A. Arnull, P. Eeckhout, T. Tridimas (eds), *Continuity and Change in EU Law: Essay in Honour Sir Francis Jacobs,* Oxford: Oxford University Press: 157-172.

Kańska K. (2004), 'Towards Administrative Human Rights in EU. Impact of the Charter of Fundamental Rights', *European Law Journal,* 10(3): 296-326.

Kasprzyk B. (2011), 'Aspekty funkcjonowania e-administracji dla jakości życia obywatela', www.ur.edu.pl/file/15858/027.pdf (accessed: 31.1.2016).

Kisielewicz J. (2009), 'Istota i zagadnienia good governance', *Administracja: teoria, dydaktyka, praktyka,* 2(15): 7-32.

Kjoer M., Kinnerup K. (2002), 'Good Governance- How Does It Relate to Human Rights?', in. H.O. Sano, *Human Rights and Good Governance. Building Bridges,* Hague: Kluwer Law International: 1- 18.

Lipowicz I. (2005), 'Prawo obywatela do dobrej administracji', https://www.nik.gov.pl /plik/ id,1555.pdf (accessed: 30.1.2016).

Niewiadomski Z. (2003), 'Czy prawo do dobrej administracji jest pojęciem normatywnym?' in: Z. Niewiadomski , Z. Cieślak., *Prawo do dobrej administracji. Materiały ze zjazdu Katedr Prawa i Postępowania Administracyjnego Warszawa- Dębe 23- 25 września 2002 r.,* Warszawa: 16.

Opaliński M. (2011), 'Europejskie standardy dobrej administracji', *Zeszyty Naukowe Wyższej Szkoły Bankowej we Wrocławiu,* no. 26/2011, p. 181.

'Prawo do dobrej administracji', RPO-MAT.60, Warszawa (2008),: https://www.rpo.gov.pl/pliki/12124042030.pdf (accessed:31.1.2016).

Sole J. P. (2011), 'EU Law, Global Law and Right to Good Administration', in: E. Chiti, B. G. Mattarella (eds), *Global Administrative Law and EU Administrative Law: Relationships, Legal Issues and Comparision*, Berlin: Springer: 139.

Szydło M. (2004), 'Prawo do dobrej administracji jako prawo podstawowe w unijnym porządku prawnym', *Studia Europejskie*, 1: 87-107.

Wyrzykowski M., Ziółkowski M. (2012), 'Konstytucyjne zasady prawa i ich znaczenie dla interpretacji zasad ogólnych prawa i postępowania administracyjnego', in: R. Hauser, Z. Niewiadomski, A. Wróbel (eds), *System Prawa Administracyjnego*, Warszawa: C. H. Beck: 31.

Chapter 4: Think tanks as good governance brokers

Monika Sus

Key words: think tanks, good governance benchmarks, decision-making process, participation

By looking at different aspects of good governance, the volume aims to analyse the conditions which support the transition from government to governance assuming that good governance leads to a significant improvement in the quality of governance both the manner and effects of the process. In line with the underlying hypothesis of the book, this chapter introduces a concept of *good governance brokers* which are to be defined as actors and mechanisms that facilitate the process of transition towards a good governed state.

Following the definition of good governance adopted for the sake of this volume which outlines it as a set of good practices followed by state actors in cooperation with, inter alia, non-state-, social and expert organisations and taking into account other definitions of the concept (European Commission 2001; Goga, 2009; Curtin D. and Wessel R. A., 2013), there is one aspect which all definitions have in common. It is the involvement of different actors and the major role of the private and civic sector in the decision-making process. Political spaces in which diverse players, such as informal groups, organizations and individuals seek to influence public policies are a precondition for the transition process from government to governance. Against this backdrop, the aim of the chapter is to shed light into the linkage between policy advice and good governance. I argue that building capacity for making sound, well-thought-out, evidence-based policy is an essential aspect of the good governance agenda and explain that by focusing on a particular actor of policy advice – think tanks. By looking at the roles which think tanks play in policy process, I will show why think tanks can be understood as good governance brokers.

The primary proposition for the article is that a system of power in a good governed state needs actors intermediately between different normative and institutional worlds, as political parties no longer have a monopoly of discourse on the state and politics. Acting at the interface between science, politics and societies, think tanks are the link between the different communities and foster communication between them. From the conceptual point of view, think tanks can be examined through different theoretical lenses. The commonly used approach to examine think tank influence by assessing the motivations of the experts who work for them draws on theories of policy networks and on the concept of epistemic communities (Stone, 1996). Another way of examining think tanks implies looking at them through the lens of the elite theory and treating them as a mouthpiece for the promotion of elite interests in the policy planning process (Domhoff, 2002).

The chapter proceeds as follows. It starts with theoretical remarks about the definition of a think tank and the recent trends within the market place of ideas. It then turns to the roles which think tanks play in the political process. As Richard Haas, Director of the Policy Planning U.S. Department of State from 2001 and 2003, put it "today's think tanks offer five principal benefits - they generate "new thinking" among U.S. decision-makers, provide experts to serve in the administration and Congress, give policy-makers a venue in which to build shared understanding on policy options, educate U.S. citizens about the world, and provide third-party mediation for parties in conflict" (2002). Taking his statement in consideration, the five most common functions of think tanks in the political life will be introduced and analysed. In conclusion I present a linkage between roles of think tanks and the transition process towards good governance and explicitly refer to their brokerage function.

With regard to data and sources, the chapter draws on secondary literature on the general role of think tanks and policy advice in the decision-making process and public life. Furthermore, it is based on my own research of the Polish and German marketplace of ideas that I have been carrying out since 2007. Since that time I have published a book and several articles and book chapters of the topic[1], for which I have conducted num-

1 Sus M. (2008) 'Foreign Policy think tanks on the example of Poland and Germany' in: J. Elvert, S. Schirmann (eds.) *Changing Times: Germany in the 20th-century Europe*, Peter Lang: Brussels-Bern, 321-339; Sus M. (2011) *Doradztwo w polityce zagranicznej Polski i Niemiec. Inspiracje dla Polski na przykładzie wybranych ośrodków eksperckich*, Wroclaw University Press: Wrocław; Sus M. (2012) 'Think tanki w polskiej polityce zagranicznej. Współczesne wyzwania' in: A. Bąkowski, J. Szlachetko (eds) *Think tanki jako fenomen światowy*, Gdanski University Press: Gdańsk, 116-141; Sus M. (2016) 'Still lagging behind? Foreign Policy Think Tanks in Poland - the origins and contemporary challenges' in: D. Abelson, S. Brooks, X.

ber of interviews with think tank experts and with policy-makers both in Poland and in Germany.

Think tanks - origins and definition

The concept of a think tank emerged in the USA during the Second World War and denoted a solitary place, frequently a bunker (tank), where experts and military strategists discussed tactics of guided actions (think). After the war the term think tank was used to refer to non-governmental and politically independent analytical institutions, acting as non-profit organizations, whose experts discussed the problems of the modern world at conferences and meetings with politicians and drew up written analyses. Over time, the concept of a think tank has been expanded. In Anglo-Saxon and German political science literature from the mid-80s there is an ongoing discussion about the modern sense of the term. Today, many political scientists apply it not only to describe non-governmental institutions but also those whose operating costs are financed with public assets. In addition, many research centres, known as think tanks, are not politically independent. A case in point is offered by German political foundations – the Konrad Adenauer Foundation associated with the CDU, the Friedrich Ebert Foundation associated with the SDP or by the American Heritage Foundation and the American Enterprise Institute for Public Policy Research, presenting a conservative ideology and associated with the Republican Party. They are partisan think tanks. In my view, two definitions of this concept commonly found in the literature of political science are particularly worth quoting. The prototype definition of this concept, still valid in the U.S., defines think tanks as non-profit, non-governmental organizations that conduct research oriented on politics, make analyses, recommendations and advice on internal affairs (Day 2000: 103). A broader definition was created in 2003 by Martin Thunert who is one of the leading German experts in this field. According to him, the think tank can be described as "funded by private or state institutes, whose primary task is to conduct scientific, interdisciplinary research and comment on important political topics" (2003: 31). A much broader understanding of the think

---

Hua (eds) *Think Tanks, Foreign Policy and Geo-Politics: Pathways to Influence*, Routledge: London (forthcoming).

tanks is offered by the UNDP which defines them as "organisations engaged on a regular basis in research and advocacy on any matter related to public policy. They are the bridge between knowledge and power in modern democracies" (UNDP 2003:6). In opposition to the growing scholarly interests with regard to policy advice in US and in countries of Western Europe, this topic still occupies only a small group of researchers in Poland. For this reason it is difficult to indicate a generally accepted definition of the term think tank. Jacek Czaputowicz defines it as analytical or expert centres which are "a bridge between science and the world of politics" and whose mission is "to provide knowledge, enabling the proper decision-making by selecting the information and revealing it to the decision makers at the right time" (2010: 217-18). Tadeusz Kaczmarek uses a similarly broad definition, specifying think tanks as independent research institutions, whose purpose is to shape the process of politics (2011: 19), while Michał Mierzwa of the Bureau of Research Chancellery of the Sejm defines think tanks as "organizations conducting research, analyses and advising on domestic or international issues, in terms of public politics" (2011: 2). On the basis of the above-mentioned definitions, I propose to define the term think tanks as independent, in the organizational sense, centres performing analytical and project-based activity, whose task is to support politicians, administration and the public opinion with knowledge, ideas and scenarios of solutions as well as shaping the debate between the public and the decision makers. This definition is broad enough to include various types of think tanks.

Drawing on the existing literature there are five types of think tanks to be distinguished:

- Independent civil society think tanks established as non-profit organisations (such as Civil Development Forum, pol. Forum Rozwoju Obywatelskiego FOR);
- Policy research institutes located in or affiliated with a university (Centre for Political Analysis of the University of Warsaw, pol. Osrodek Analiz Politologicznych OAP);
- Governmentally created or state sponsored think tanks (such as Polish Institute of International Affairs, pol. Polski Instytut Spraw Miedzynarodowych PISM);
- Corporate created or business affiliated think tank (such as EY's Think Tank for Business Performance & Innovation);

- Political party think tank (such as Civic Institute, pol. Instytut Obywatelski IO).

In the 1970's the proliferation in think tanks started and continues up to the present-day. In 2015 there were 6846 think tanks worldwide (McGann 2016:30). The main reasons for the growth of think tanks are globalisation and technological revolution that lead to an increased demand for timely and concise information and analysis. Moreover, the end of national governments' monopoly on information, increasing complexity and technical nature of policy problems as well as crisis of confidence elected officials in several countries worldwide stimulate the development of the market place of ideas. Despite the fact that the growing number of think tanks is a global phenomenon, there are essential differences between their distributions among countries[2]. "The missing link of Polish politics" – this is how Wawrzyniec Smoczyński, a Polish journalist defined think tanks in his article of 2009 (2009: 38). However, in the recent ranking published by the American Pennsylvania University "Global Go-To Think Tanks," Poland is classified in 4th position in terms of the number of think tanks in Central and Eastern Europe (CEE) (McGann 2016: 32). The author indicates that there are 42 such institutions in Poland, 122 of them in Russia, 54 in Romania and 47 in the Ukraine. Poland is far behind the Western countries – in Great Britain there are 288 think tanks, in Germany 195, while in France 180. The United States remain a Mecca of think tanks with 1835 of expert institutions, followed by China which ranks second with 429 think tanks (ibid.: 30).

Think tank roles in policy process

The intention of the examination of the different roles policy research institutes play is not to look for the impact of any particular think tank, but rather to assess the structural impact of this kind of actor. The central function that think tanks fulfil is to support decision-makers in understanding and making informed choices about various political issues both domestic and international. However, there is also a wide range of other critical roles think tanks play in political life at different stages of the poli-

2 See more about the reasons for the uneven development of think tanks among countries: Stone 2004: 5-9.

cy cycle, from its beginning with definition of the problem to the evaluation of political decisions and their impacts. On the next pages various roles of think tanks are presented while keeping in mind the overall aim of this chapter, which is to show why and to what extent these organisations can be understood as good governance brokers.

Informed voice in policy debates

One of the most central roles performed by think tanks is to carry out basic research on policy problems and policy solutions. In this regard think tanks are similar to universities but their approach to research is predominantly policy oriented both by dealing with issues that pose a current challenge for a country and by presenting the research outcomes in a way that is accessible for policy makers and for the non-specialist broader audience. Moreover, think tanks not only identify the emerging problems but also transform them into policy issues by showing their relevance for political life. At the same time, they bring social science research into the public domain and play a crucial role in the spreading of knowledge and relevant information (e.g. via media) about current policy problems in society. The public information function reveals the educational character of some think tanks. By organising conferences and seminars, they aim to improve public awareness about policy problems and contribute to a better informed society. The knowledge and expertise housed in think tanks has become an important element of public debate in many liberal democracies.

Solutions for political problems

Another important role of think tanks is to provide advice on issues that are immediate policy concerns for policy-makers and to assist in formulation of policies. Against the backdrop of the growing complexity and interconnectivity of several policy areas due to globalisation and rapidly changing world, this function of think tanks has become crucial in recent years. They support policy makers by translating complex, multidimensional issues into problems which are possible to handle and by pointing out available solutions and their political implications. Furthermore, proposing different options for pressing political decisions can only work if the research institutes meet the time-sensitive demands of the practitioners and if they can present their ideas in a way which is useful for policymakers. Crucial for fulfilling this function, is the knowledge among experts about the specifics of the policy cycle and about the most effective mechanisms for approaching decision makers. To perform this function, think tanks usually organize short briefings, seminars or reach out for written forms such as short expertise and policy briefs.

In addition to that think tanks, unlike policy makers, have the ability to address long-term issues and overarching themes which might not be of urgent relevance for the current political life but which could develop in this direction. By having the long-term perspective and engaging in foresight analyses, think tanks provide an added value to the short-term oriented policy world.

Watchdogs over government

Think tanks are present at different stages of a policy cycle, including the last stage – the evaluation of implemented policy choices. By assessing decisions made by politicians, think tanks are able to identify flaws in policies and to contribute to the greater effectives of the decision making process. In this way they can also control policy makers and fulfil legitimizing function on behalf of the society. Thus, think tanks increase the accountability of ruling parties and can potentially act as counter power to the government.

Forum for ideas exchange

Serving as a forum for the exchange of ideas among key stakeholders of the decision making process from various both public and private institutions with different political orientations as well as between them and the public opinion is another task that think tanks often accomplish. Through different formats, such as conferences, seminars and roundtables, think tanks seek to stimulate debate about relevant political issues and facilitate information sharing among various participants of political life. These kinds of think tanks activities contribute to the broadening of perspectives and enhanced dialogue among actors from different communities who normally have limited opportunities to meet and discuss problems with each other. Moreover, in the case of especially conflicted issues, think tanks can play a mediating function between the government and the public opinion by elaborating on different policy options without taking sides.

Providing a supply of personnel for the policy world

The originally American phenomenon of *revolving doors* implies movement between legislators and regulators (parliaments and governments) and the think tank world (Haas, 2002: 7-8). Usually, it takes place after elections when the winning party takes charge of the administration and numbers of staff members of the previous one move on to research organisations. Despite the criticisms of the mechanism which impute a too close involvement of the think tanks into the daily political life by offering positions to former decision makers, there are also advantages of the process. Politicians and members of the administration who had gained some experience by working in a think tank are more aware about the added value experts can offer them once they are back into the world of the politics. At the same time, think tank experts who worked in the administration better understand the nature of the policy-making process which is one of the basic conditions for effective advising. While well-developed in the United States, it remains very limited in Poland. There are two main reasons for that. The first is the professionalisation of the civil service in Poland which makes it difficult and often also not financially rewarding for officials from MFA to change their job and become a think tanker. Quitting a position in the administration means resigning from the status of a civil servant and makes the return very difficult, if not impossible. Revolving doors can happen within high ranked positions which are political and depend of the government being in power. There are a few examples of high officials who change their career from a think tank to the administration. One of the leading illustrations is a first-rate Polish expert on Russia – Katarzyna Pełczynńska-Nałęcz who was a director of the OSW and moved to the MFA to become Polish ambassador in Moscow in 2014. Another example is Paweł Szałamacha, the founder of the Sobieski Institute who recently became minister of finance.

Conclusions

It is close to impossible to single out and to measure think tanks influence on the policy process due to the involvement of other actors as interest groups, social movements and academic communities and the ambiguity of decision making[3]. However, the difficulty of quantifying their impact does not hide their aspirations to influence policy framing. Think tanks are unquestionably one of the essential stakeholders in liberal democratic states and according to Haas *"of the many influences on U.S. foreign policy formulation, the role of think tanks is among the most important and least appreciated"* (2002).

Taking the general importance of think tanks in the political life as a given, lets turn to the main question of this chapter – the brokerage role of think tanks in the transition process towards good governed state. In general terms policy oriented research institutes act as bridge between the policy world and other epistemic communities such as academia or civil society, which seem to be one of the prerequisites for a good governed state. In order to present further aspects of the brokerage role, we have to establish benchmarks of good governance. A point of reference is offered by White Paper on European Governance published by the European Commission which pointed out five essential criteria for ensuring good governance: openness of the functioning of the institutions, wide participation and inclusive approach throughout the policy chain, accountability of legislative and executive, effectiveness of the policies and coherence of policies and actions (2001: 10). Even though the principles were defined with regard to the policy process in the European Union, they seem to be universal for the overall approach of good governance. By playing a set of different roles from prominent discussion partner, via knowledge provider to mobilization force of civil society, think tanks (along with other actors) contribute several of the above-mentioned criteria. They boost the transition towards good governance by enhancing the participation of diverse stakeholders in the political life, by providing transparency and greater accountability of the governing elites as well as by supporting the inclusive

3 Despite this fact, researchers have been making efforts to estimate think tank's influence by indicators such as media citation, requests for commentary, citations by other experts and academics, requests for meetings with decision-makers, the amount of money they receive for their research from various donors etc. However, the ultimate claim about the factual impact on policy makers remains ambiguous.

character of the policy process. In the consequence of the greater inclusion of policy advising, the dynamics of the decision making process has changed and the different stages of the policy cycle has been extended to actors outside the government. It is especially visible with regard to the agenda setting and to the identification of options – in these phases of the decision making process think tanks can play an important role by identifying problems and by increasing numbers of alternative solutions. Since one of the core roles of think tanks is to assess the government´s policy, they can be also involved in the last stage of the policy cycle – the evaluations of chosen decisions.

There is an important final remark to be made. The existence of think tanks in modern societies does not necessary have to mean that they contribute to the transition process towards good governance in an essential way by changing the manner the policy is debated and decided. The demand from the politicians for being advised and their openness for cooperation with policy oriented research communities is a supreme prerequisite for the brokerage function of think tanks. Even though policy making is driven by interest not by ideas, think tanks can make an effective contribution to the process of transition towards good governance if there is awareness about their functioning both among decision makers and society.

References

Czaputowicz J. (2010), ´Rola ośrodków eksperckich w procesach decyzyjnych polityki zagranicznej Polski´, in: S. Bielen (eds) *Polityka zagraniczna Polski po wstąpieniu do NATO i do Unii Europejskiej. Problemy tożsamości i adaptacji*, Warszawa: Difin, 216-228.

Day J.A. (2000), ´Think Tank in Western Europe´, in: *Think Tank & Civil Societies. Catalyst for Ideas and Action*, J.G. McGann, K.R. Weaver (eds), New Jersey: Transaction Publishers.

Domhoff, William G. (2002), 'Who Rules America: Power & Politics', 7th Edition. New York: McGraw Hill.

Haas R.N. (2002), ´Think Tank and U.S. Foreign Policy: A Policy-maker's Perspective ´, *U.S. Foreign Policy Agenda. An Electronic Journal of the U.S. Department of State*, vol. 3.

Goga L. G. (2009), ´Good Governance in the EU´, *Acta Universitatis Danubius : Juridica*, vol.5(1): 173-181.

Kaczmarek T. (2011), 'Kto kieruje globalizacją? Think tanki, czyli kuźnie idei', Warszawa: Difin.

McGann J.G. (2016), ´Global "Go-To Think Tanks"´, Report 2015: Philadelphia.

McGann J. G. and Johnson E. C. (2005), 'Comparative Think Tanks, Politics and Public Policy,, Cheltenham: Edward Egar Publishing.

Mierzwa M. (2011), 'Think Tanki, *Biuro Analiz Sejmowych*, 12, available at: http://orka.sejm.gov.pl/WydBAS.nsf/0/AEE487CF31D5A165C12578B00047620D/$file/Infos_104.pdf (accessed 1.03.2016).

Smoczynski, W. (2009), 'Myślą i rządzą', *Polityka*, 40: 38-40.

Stone, D. (1996), 'Capturing the political imagination. Think Tanks and the Policy Process', New York: Frank Cass.

Stone, D. and Denham A. (2004), 'Think tanks traditions. Policy research and the politics of ideas', Manchester and New York: Manchester University Press.

Sus, M. (2008), 'Foreign Policy think tanks on the example of Poland and Germany', in: J. Elvert and S. Schirmann (eds) *Changing Times: Germany in the 20th-century Europe*, Brussels-Bern: Peter Lang 321-339.

Sus, M. (2011), 'Doradztwo w polityce zagranicznej Polski i Niemiec. Inspiracje dla Polski na przykładzie wybranych ośrodków eksperckich', Wrocław: Wroclaw University Press.

Sus, M. (2012), 'Think tanki w polskiej polityce zagranicznej. Współczesne wyzwania ', in: A. Bąkowski, J. Szlachetko (eds), *Think tanki jako fenomen światowy*, Gdańsk: Gdansk University Press, 116-141.

Sus, M. (2016), 'Still lagging behind? Foreign Policy Think Tanks in Poland - the origins and contemporary challenges' in: D. Abelson, S. Brooks, X. Hua (eds) Think Tanks, *Foreign Policy and Geo-Politics: Pathways to Influence*, London: Routledge. *(forthcoming)*

Thunert M. (2003), 'Think Tank in Deutschland – Berater der Politik', *Aus der Politik und Zeitgeschichte*, 51: 30-41.

Chapter 5: Good governance in the judicial system – enhancing the effectiveness of the judicial protection

Jagna Mucha

Key words: right to effective judicial protection, accountability of judicial system, materialisation of good governance concept, Court of Justice of the European Union

Introductory remarks

The concept of good governance was introduced in 1990's by the World Bank and it designates general principles relating to the way in which state authorities are to operate. More specifically, the said concept gives insight into the manner of exercising authority in a given state in order to improve the standard of living of citizens and to provide an investor-friendly environment. Having a wide range of applications, the concept of good governance can be implemented worldwide and therefore it operates successfully both at the national and international level. In particular, the concept is widely applied in the law of the European Union, playing part in a number of normative solutions, as will be discussed in the following.

Good governance requires the existence of balance between the three, separated powers: the executive, the legislative and the judiciary. The said concept refers mainly (but not only) to the first of them, since undoubtedly it is the executive power which is authorised and responsible for governing the state. However, in line with the said concept, government does not have exclusive jurisdiction over governance, which implies the existence of other actors involved in governing, such as judges who ensure the legality of the government's actions. Strong judicial systems in which the law is duly enforced are vital to good governance (Sachiko, Durwood, 2005: 15). Hence, the interpretation of law included in the court judgements and its proper enforcement make a huge contribution to the quality of governance. An efficient, accessible judicial system controls public administration by limiting its discretion and it guarantees that the rights of the applicant of the administrative proceedings are ensured. A well-functioning, independent, impartial judiciary adjudicating in line with the rule of law prevents public administration from abusing its stronger position in relation to individuals and legal entities. In case of any conflict arising out of the administrative proceeding, the individuals are assured that there is a competent, third party, unbiased and impartial court of law which will resolve the dispute.

The concept of good governance may also be said to have influence on the functioning of the judicial institutions, since they are entrusted with the function of the public authorities. Such application of the said concept emerges from the fundamental right to have the case dealt within a reasonable time by independent and impartial court of law. As a consequence, in a case in which the court does not adjudicate within a reasonable time, the party whose right to the effective legal protection was infringed may bring action for the damages caused by lengthy proceedings. In what follows, the chapter discusses the relationship between the concept of good governance and the judicial system. Overall, it elaborates on how the EU legal framework is influenced by the said concept. To be more specific, it first briefly presents the principles of good governance and their application to the judicial system at the EU level. It discusses on how the principles of accountability, predictability, legal framework, transparency and access to information, as well as the principle of participation, are reflected in the EU legal system. Secondly, it presents the normative consequences of the application of the concept in the EU primary and secondary law. Finally, it presents the interpretation of the relevant provisions delivered by the Court of Justice of the European Union (hereinafter referred as "the Court") with special consideration of the right to effective judicial protection and the consequences of the breach of this right caused by lengthy proceedings.

Interplay between good governance principles and the system of justice

The quality of governance depends on the implementation of the good governance principles in the decision-making process. These principles are referred to all actors involved in this process. In the broad sense, apart from the governmental structures, governance also comprises other entities functioning under the rule of law, such as - *inter alia* - legislators and courts (Cioclea, Pascal, 2010). In view of the above, the principles of good governance find their application not only to public administration, but they also relate to the judicial system.

In line with the approach introduced by the World Bank, there are three dimensions of governance, namely: (i) accountability of public authorities, (ii) predictability and legal framework for development, as well as (iii) information and transparency (World Bank, 1991). Sometime later there appeared the fourth dimension of good governance, referred to as participation. It needs to be stated at this point that those principles constitute the foundation of a very broad concept, discussed here, and thus are open to multifarious interpretations (Strand, Retzl, 2014: 2). The aim here is to demonstrate the way these principles are applied to the EU law in the context of the judicial system.

(i) Accountability of public authorities

It may be deduced from the definition of good governance, as introduced by the World Bank, that the principle of accountability refers to those public authorities which shall bear the financial and economic responsibility for their actions. This element of the concept of good governance is reflected against the background of the EU law by the principle of the liability of a member state for the loss and damage to individuals resulting from the breach of the member state's obligation under EU law and from the principle of the liability of the European Union for any damage caused by its institutions or by its servants in the performance of its duties.

According to the first principle, an individual whose rights were infringed may sue a given member state and claim damages to compensate for the loss suffered in connection with the breach of the EU law. Thus, public authorities are accountable for their actions which are to the detriment of individuals. Such a principle was firstly introduced by the Court in relation to damages resulting from the failure of a member state to implement a directive to its domestic, legal order (Cases C-6/90 and C-9/90, *Francovich and Bonifaci,* ECLI:EU:C:1991:428), to a wrong or incomplete transposition (*Dillenkofer*, ECLI:EU:C:1996:375). Therefore, at first the principle of liability was limited only to the authorities responsible for the implementation of the EU law. In the later jurisprudence the Court extended the principle of the liability of member states to the breaches of the EU law caused by the domestic court adjudicating in the last instance (Case C-224/01, *Köbler,* ECLI:EU:C:2003:513). Consequently, the parties whose rights were infringed by the court of a member state adjudicating in a case involving EU law could bring an action for the damages caused by such court. However, not only domestic institutions and courts are liable for the infringements of the EU law. According to Article 340 paragraph 2 of the Treaty on the Functioning of the European Union (hereinafter referred to as the "TFUE")[1], in the case of there being any damages caused by the EU institutions or EU servants in the performance of their duties, the damaged entity may request redress from the Union.[2]

(ii) Predictability and legal framework

The dimension referring to predictability and legal framework are said to be interlinked; that is they are mutually supportive and reinforcing. Predictability refers to the functioning of legal framework, which means that it assumes the existence of laws and their fair and consistent application by public authorities (Srivastava, 2009).

As presumed by the concept of good governance, rights and obligations are enforced though legal mechanisms in an impartial manner. In view of the above, the legal framework implies that the scope of governmental actions shall be regulated by specific, clear rules and regulations. In line with those rules the representatives of public administration shall issue lawful decisions. Due to the clear provisions individuals and entrepreneurs may learn about the requirements which they have to fulfil in order to successfully to have their case resolved and in order to assess the duration of the proceeding. Proper application of those rules shall be controlled by impartial, unbiased public authorities. It needs to be stated here, that only an effective judicial system operating along the lines fitting in with the concept of good governance may ensure the proper working of administrative institutions in the sense discussed here. In order words, the value of the relevant legal provisions depends on the mode of their enforcement which is the foremost task of the public courts.

The existence of a stable legal framework is the way to ensure predictability, which refers both to the governmental and judicial decision-

1 Consolidated version of the Treaty on the Functioning of the European Union, Official Journal of the European Union no. C-326/47, dated 26 October 2012.

2 Discussion on the interpretation of this provision by the Court is provided in the point 4 of this chapter.

making. Without precise provisions applied by state organs, the outcome of the administrative decisions would be difficult to foresee. The absence of predictability would discourage specific entities from conducting business, since they could not assess the business risk and calculate the transaction costs in an unpredictable and unstable environment. On the other hand, predictability refers also to the adjudication and it concerns the manner of interpretation and enforcement of legal rules. It assures that the cases with similar statement of the facts will be adjudicated equally.

As regards the EU context predictability refers to the application of the EU law by the state organs and its coherent enforcement by the national courts in each member state. It is enhanced by the principle of consistent interpretation of the national law and the system of preliminary questions referred by national courts to the Court. In line with the first of these, national courts and all the authorities applying law, including public administration authorities shall interpret the national laws in conformity with the EU law (Sawyer, 2007). Such a principle was at first formulated by the Court in relation to interpretation of national law in accordance with the EU directives (Case C-14/83 *von Colson,* ECLI:EU:C:1984:153). In line with this principle, national courts shall interpret the national law implementing the directives in line with the subject and purpose of those directives. The Court emphasised that such harmonious interpretation aims at ensuring the effectiveness of the EU law and ensuring wide legal protection of individuals. In the later case law the Court extended the obligation of interpretation of the national law to all the acts of the EU law. According to the Court, national law shall be interpreted in line with the EU law as far as possible (Case C-106/89 *Marleasing,* ECLI:EU:C:1990:395).

Another instrument which enhances predictability in the EU is the mechanism of preliminary rulings provided in Article 267 of the TFUE. According to this provision, national courts may or shall request the Court to give a preliminary ruling concerning the interpretation of the EU law in order to adjudicate the pending case properly. Such mechanism is vital in order to ensure coherent interpretation and application of the law in the entire European Union.

(iii) Transparency and access to information

In order to bring about the concept of good governance, the principles of accountability, predictability and legal framework must be supplemented by access to the public information and by the transparency of the decision-making process. A transparent way of governing and administrating allows citizens to scrutinise and evaluate the way public power is exercised and to participate in public affairs. It involves the right of citizens to request documents and the obligation of public authorities to provide those documents. It is a way to enhance the citizens' involvement and understanding of the process of governance and to increase the efficiency of the operating of the relevant institutions at the same time. Application of those rules allows the state to reach the level of modern and open administration.

Exploiting the principle of transparency and access to documents has a positive influence on the institutional capacity of the judiciary and it increases its legitimacy and authority among government and citizens. One may claim that open access to the information on court proceedings increases the level of the societal trust to the system of justice. It helps to break the stereotypes of the justice system, *inter alia* regarding the lengthy duration of proceedings and indolence among judges. Further, in the transparent system of justice which is monitored by society, judicial institutions are truly motivated to assure the highest degree of professional care and conduct. What is more, transparency also contributes to judicial independence, since judges are aware of the fact that the public investigates their performance. For the same reason it also protects judicial institutions from corruption and arbitrariness. From what was said above there emerges a clear link between the principle of transparency and accountability.

Transparency and access to documents play a vital role in the system of multilevel governance in the European Union. Those principles apply to a wide range of relations between the European Union and the Member States and the EU institutions or organs and the EU citizens. Both principles have fundamental meaning. In the relevant literature of the subject it is emphasised that access to public documents strengthens the democratic credentials of EU documents, whereas transparency enhances legitimacy and the confidence of the EU citizens in the EU institutions (Augustyn, Monda, 2011). According to the Court, transparency "enables citizens to participate more closely in the decision-making process, to guarantee that the administration enjoys greater legitimacy and is more effective and more accountable to the citizen in a democratic system and to contribute to strengthening the principles of democracy and respect for fundamental rights" (Case C-41/00 P, *Interporc,* ECLI:EU:C:2003:125).

Due to the prominent role of those principles in the EU law, it is discussed in the relevant literature of the subject as to whether the principles of transparency and access to documents shall be recognised as the general principles of EU law (Karageorgou, 2013). It is worth mentioning that although the Court referred to those principles in its case law (Joint cases C-39/05 P and C-52/P *Turco,* ECLI:EU:C:2008:374) it did not formally recognise them as autonomous, self-standing general principles.

(iv) Participation

The last principle of the concept of good governance is related to the participation of the different interest groups in the governing process. The groups are formed by the individuals and professionals who are gathered in trade unions, nongovernmental organisations or other associations. The aim of the groups is to represent the interests of those entities and to take these into consideration while implementing and exercising public policies (Ferri, 2015).

In the EU the principle of participatory society has a substantial meaning. In the legal framework of the European Union it is emphasised that an open, transparent and regular dialogue between the EU institutions, representative associations and civil society plays a significant role in the functioning of the Union. Furthermore, it is emphasised that broad consultations with the parties concerned are vital to ensure that the European Union is coherent and transparent.

In the relevant literature of the subject it is pointed out that the principle of participation may concern involvement of society not only in the legislative and executive but also in judicial system (Beters, 2015: 313). As far as the latter is concerned, participation may include the contribution of citizens to the decisions of lay judges. The participation of the social factor has also a vital role in the functioning of the judicial system, since it guarantees that the citizens have a practical influence on this sphere of the public life, Through their participation in the system of justice the citizens actively participate in the process of governing of the state and at the same time they take part in making decisions about the future of other citizens. However, it must be noticed that the issue of the social participation in the system of justice may be viewed as a controversial one. So far as it is not questioned that the social activity is needed, there is no consent as regards the scope and for of this activities.

Moreover, the issue of participation may be discussed in relation to the court and administrative proceedings regarding public matters in which various groups of interest may take part. Such proceedings concern mainly environmental matters, such as, for example, preparation of certain plans and programmes related to environment. Against the EU law background, non-governmental institutions and other civil society organisations may intervene in the cases pending before the Court, provided that they can establish an interest in the result of the case submitted to the Court (Uruena, 2012: 247).

Normative provisions related to the concept of good governance included in the EU law

The EU legal framework is clearly influenced by the concept of good governance, which is noticeable both in primary and secondary EU law. Notably, this influence is twofold. On the one hand, there are provisions in which the concept is referred directly. On the other hand, there are other relevant provisions which do not refer to said concept directly, but they refer to the specific elements of the concept.

Relating to the first situation, the EU legislator refers to the concept indicating the necessity of the promotion of good governance. Such reference is provided in the TFUE and in the Treaty on the European Union (hereinafter referred to as "the TEU")[3]. Article 15 of the TFUE states that the EU institutions and its other organs shall conduct their work as openly as possible in order to promote good governance and to ensure the participation of civil society. Similarly, Article 21 (2) h of the TEU indicates that in order to promote an international system based on the good global governance, the European Union shall define and pursue common policies and actions, as well as it shall work for a high degree of cooperation in all the fields of international relations. Interestingly, there is no explicit reference to the concept of good governance in the Charter of Fundamental Rights of the European Union (hereinafter referred to as "the Charter").[4]

---

3 Consolidated version of the Treaty on European Union, Official Journal the European Union no. C-326/13, dated 26 October 2012.

4 Charter of Fundamental Rights of the European Union, Official Journal of the European Communities no. C-364/1, dated 18 December 2000.

As regards the second approach, where the issues related to the concept of good governance are treated indirectly, there are many references to the specific elements of good governance, both in primary and secondary EU law. Some provisions in point here refer directly to the principle of transparency. The most important one is Article 1, paragraph 2 of the TUE which foresees that in the EU decisions are taken as openly as possible and as closely as possible to the citizen.[5] As far as the principle of accountability is concerned, there is a landmark rule included in the Article 340 of the TFUE, according to which the EU shall remedy any damage caused by its institutions or by its servants in the performance of their duties.[6] It also provides that the servants bear personal liability towards the EU.[7] Further, Article 11 of the TUE refers to the accountability of government to the national parliaments and citizens.[8] In turn, the principle of participation is included in Article 11 paragraphs 1-2 of the TUE under which the EU institutions shall give the citizens the opportunity to acquaint them with their views and to publicly exchange these in all areas of EU actions, as well as to maintain an open, transparent and regular dialogue with the representative associations of civil society.

Additionally, some significant regulations regarding the elements of good governance are involved in the Charter. Article 41 of the Charter deserves particular prominence in this context, since it sets forth the right to good administration. In line with this provision, every person has a right to have their affairs handled impartially, fairly and within a reasonable time by the EU institutions and bodies. This right comprises the right to be heard, the right of access to files and the obligation of the administration to give reasons for its decision. Article 42 of the Charter is also worth mentioning since it grants the EU citizens and the entrepreneurs with a registered base in the EU the right of access to the documents of EU institutions. Last but not least, for the purpose of clarity of further discussion about the application of good governance principles, one should also point out Article 47 of the Charter which provides a right to a fair and public hearing within a reasonable time conducted by a an independent and impartial tribunal.

5 Above mentioned wording is literally repeated in the Article 10 paragraph 3 of the TUE.
6 Art. 340 paragraph 2 of the TFUE.
7 Art. 340 paragraph 4 of the TFUE.
8 Art. 10 paragraph 2 of the TUE.

Implementation of the principles of good governance is also noticeable in secondary EU law. By way of example, regulations regarding public access to documents of EU institutions[9] and the access to information, public participation in decision-making and access to justice in environmental matters shall be mentioned here.[10] There are also legal regulations providing for public participation in the drawing up of certain plans and programmes related to the environment.[11]

Application of the principles of good governance by the Court and the General Court

The fundamental role of the judiciary is to guard the principles of good governance (von Davitz, 2010: 13). Thus, in day to day work, judicial institutions are confronted with cases concerning the application of good governance principles. At the EU level, it is the task of the Court and the General Court to interpret relevant provisions of EU law regarding good governance and to adjudicate on the application of its principles.[12] In view

9 Regulation (EC) no. 1049/2001 of the European Parliament and the Council of 30 May 2001 regarding public access to European Parliament, Council and Commission documents, Official Journal of the European Communities dated 31 May 2001, no. L 145/34.

10 Regulation (EC) no. 1367/2006 of the European Parliament and the Council of 6 September 2006 on the application of the provisions of the Aarhus convention on access to information, public participation in decision-making and access to justice in environmental matters to community institutions and bodies, Official Journal of the European Communities dated 25 September 2006, no. L 264/13.

11 Directive 2003/35/EC of the European Parliament and of the Council of 26 May 2003 providing for public participation in respect of the drawing up of certain plans and programmes relating to the environment and amending with regard to public participation and access to justice Council Directives 85/337/EEC and 96/61/EC, Official Journal of the European Communities dated 25 June 2003, no. L 156/17.

12 For reference to the principle of transparency see: case C-41/00 P *Interporc Im- und Export GmbH op. cit,,* case C-552/07 *Commune de Sausheim v. Pierre Azelvandre*, dated 17 February 2009, ECR 2009 I-00987; For more on the principle of access to documents see: C-350/12P *Council of the European Union v. Sophie in't Veld,* dated 3 July 2014 (not yet published); C-404/10 P *European Commission v. Éditions Odile Jacob SAS,* dated 28 June 2012; C-135/11 P *IFAW Internationaler Tierschutz-Fonds gGmbH v. European Commission* dated 21 June 2012; For more on the principle of accountability see: case T-54/99 *max.mobil Telekommunikation*

of the fact that the issue related to the effective functioning of the justice system and the potential claims related to lengthy proceedings is a burning issue these days, in the context of our discussion the Court most often referred to the principle of accountability, which will be presented in the following.

The General Court referred to the principle of accountability of European institutions by reference to Article 41 of the Charter concerning the right to sound administration. In the *max.mobile v. Commission* (Case T-54/99 *max.mobil Telekommunikation Service GmbH v. Commission*, ECLI:EU:T:2002:20) regarding the interpretation of competition law, the General Court emphasised that the Commission is obliged to undertake a diligent and impartial examination of the submitted complaints within a reasonable time. The General Court stated that fulfilment of this obligation shall be further amenable to the judicial review, in line with the principle involved in Article 47 of the Charter. According to the General Court, "(...) it is in the interests both of the sound administration of justice and of the proper application of the competition rules that natural or legal persons who request the Commission to find an infringement of those rules should be able, if their request is rejected either wholly or in part, to institute proceedings in order to protect their legitimate interests. "

The issue regarding the obligation of the public authorities to act within a reasonable time and their liability for lengthy proceedings was also raised many times in the EU case law in relation to the judicial proceedings. The main question considered by the Court was to determine a way of assessing the appropriate remedy for lengthy proceedings and the court competent for adjudicating on the damages. It is worth mentioning, however, that the approach of the Court is incoherent and that it has changed considerably over the years.

The first landmark judgment in this respect was issued by the Court in the *Baustahlgewebe* case (Case C-185/95 P, *Baustahlgewebe*, ECLI:EU:C:1998:608). In the said case the applicant brought an action to the Court of the First Instance (presently the General Court) for annulment of the decision in which the Commission imposed a fine upon the undertaking or alternatively for the reduction of the said fine. Because of the fact that the duration of the proceedings before the Court of the First In-

Service GmbH v. Commission, dated 30 January 2002, ECR 2002 II-00313; case C-185/95 P, *Baustahlgewebe GmbH v. Commission of the European Communities*, dated 17 December 1998, ECR 1998 I-08417.

stance was excessive, the applicant appealed to the Court claiming that his right to a hearing within the reasonable time laid down in Article 6 of the European Convention for Protection of Human Rights and Fundamental Freedoms[13] (hereinafter referred as "the ECHR") was infringed. Therefore, it requested the Court to set aside the judgment of the Court of the First Instance or – alternatively - to reduce the amount of the imposed fine. Considering the request of the applicant, the Court referred to the duration of the proceeding, which lasted 5 and a half years. It gave some general guidelines regarding the duration of the proceedings, stating that "(…) reasonableness of such period must be appraised in the light of the circumstances specific to each case and, in particular, the importance of the case for the person concerned, its complexity and the conduct of the applicant and of the competent authorities" (Case C-185/95 P, *Baustahlgewebe*, ECLI:EU:C:1998:608). In the case in question the Court held that the proceedings did not satisfy the requirement concerning completion within a reasonable time. According to the Court, such excessive duration of the proceedings shall be qualified as a procedural irregularity. Thus, "(…) for the reason of economy of procedure and in order to ensure an immediate and effective remedy (…)" the Court set aside a part of the contested judgment in so far as it sets the amount of the imposed fine and reduced it (Case C-185/95 P, *Baustahlgewebe*, ECLI:EU:C:1998:608).

However, such an approach according to which, due to the lengthy proceedings, the Court itself is competent to set aside contested judgements and reduce the fines imposed by the Commission, did not hold in the subsequent judgments of the Court. In the latest case law, discussed below, the Court concluded that excessive duration of the administrative and judicial proceedings constitutes a ground for lodging damage claims to the General Court. According to those judgments, lengthy proceedings can be considered as procedural irregularity, but they do not constitute a ground for setting aside a judgement.

In the *Der Grüne Punkt* case (Case C-385/07 P, *Der Grüne Punkt – Duales System Deutschland,* ECLI:EU:C:2009:456), the company abusing its dominant position argued that lengthy proceedings before the General Court caused an infringement of its right to have the case dealt with within the reasonable time. Therefore, it claimed that the Commission's decision

13 Council of Europe, European Convention for the Protection of Human Rights and Fundamental Freedoms, as amended by Protocols Nos. 11 and 14, 4 November 1950.

shall be annulled and the award of the General Court shall be set aside. It argued that the fundamental right to effective legal protection set in Article 47 of the Charter and in Article 6 of the ECHR was breached, since the proceedings before the General Court were excessively long. According to the Court, duration of the proceedings is not the only factor which shall be taken into the consideration while assessing whether the case was adjudicated within a reasonable time. It interpreted the general wording of "reasonable time" according to which "(...) the reasonableness of the period for delivering judgment is to be appraised in the light of the circumstances specific to each case, such as the complexity of the case and the conduct of the parties. [...]." Further it elaborated that "the complexity of the case or the dilatory conduct of the applicant may be deemed to justify a duration which is prima facie too long" (Case C-385/07 P, *Der Grüne Punkt*, ECLI:EU:C:2009:456). Against this background, the Court admitted that the duration of the proceedings was lengthy and it cannot be justified by any of the above mentioned circumstances. However, according to the Court, such procedural irregularity did not affect the outcome of the dispute and therefore setting aside of the General Court's award would not remedy the infringement of the right to the effective legal protection. Nevertheless, the Court referred to the principle of accountability in relation to the concept of good governance stating that the damage caused by lengthy proceedings shall be remedied. According to the Court, the failure to adjudicate within a reasonable time shall be brought as a separate action for damages under second paragraph of Article 340 of the TFUE[14] in connection with Article 268 of the TFUE.[15]

The position of the Court presented in the *Der Grüne Punkt* case (C-385/07 P, *Der Grüne Punkt*, ECLI:EU:C:2009:456) concerning the action for damages caused by infringement of the right to effective legal protection was further developed in the subsequent judicial practice of the Court, *inter alia*. in the judgments: *Kendrion* (Case C-50/12 P, *Kendrion*, ECLI:EU:C:2013:771), the *Groupe Gascogne* (Case C- 58/12 P, *Groupe*

14 In line with this paragraph "In the case of non-contractual liability, the Union shall, in accordance with the general principles common to the laws of the Member States, make good any damage caused by its institutions or by its servants in the performance of their duties.".

15 In line with the Article 268 of the TFUE "The Court of Justice of the European Union shall have jurisdiction in disputes relating to compensation for damage provided for in the second and third paragraphs of Article 340.".

Gascogne, ECLI:EU:C:2013:770) and *Gascogne Sack Deutschland* (Case C-40/12 P, *Gascogne Sack Deutschland,* ECLI:EU:C:2013:768). In these cases the Court stated directly that it stays within the jurisdiction of the General Court (and not the Court) to adjudicate on the damages caused by the breach of Article 47 of the Charter. More precisely, it stated that "(...) it is therefore for the General Court (...) to determine such claims for damages, sitting in a different composition from that which heard the dispute giving rise to the procedure whose duration is criticised (...)." It is worth mentioning that such an approach was expressed by the Advocate General previously in the opinion to the *Der Grüne Punkt* case[16], in which he stated that the General Court shall have jurisdiction to adjudicate on the above mentioned damages. Conversely, such an approach was criticised in the doctrine as it could raise doubts as to the impartiality of the General Court which acts as a judge in its own case (Beumer, 2013, Caro 2013).

Conclusions

It emerges from the discussion presented above that the interplay between good governance and an effective system of justice may be analysed from two different perspectives. In line with the first of them, the role of the judiciary is to safeguard the good governance principles by enforcing the law in line with which the government shall perform. In this sense, it is emphasised here that an effective system of justice ensures the legality of government's actions and controls the public administration in exercising its power. Such a judicial system limits administrative discretion and prevents public authorities from abusing their position towards entities. In other words, effective judicial system safeguards good governance. The examples serving as illustration of the normative consequences of the good governance in the EU law provide a clear background for the discussion in point. As presented, the relevant legal provisions of primary and secondary EU law refer to the concept both in a direct and indirect way. In spite of being highly abstract and vague they clearly constitute a conceptual framework for the key right of various entities and thus they are increasingly referred to in judicial proceedings.

---

16 Opinion of the Advocate General - Yves Bot - to the case C-385/07 P, *Der Grüne Punkt Punkt – Duales System Deutschland GmbH v. Commission of the European Communities*, dated 31 March 2009, para.316-323.

Secondly, the discussion revolved around the issue related to the implementation of the said concept to judicial practice. It emerges from the discussion in point that the judicial institutions shall not only guard good governance but also that they shall apply the principles of good governance while adjudicating. The analysis of the case law allows the conclusion that the application of the various elements of good governance concept to the administration of justice is increasingly important. It emerges from the developing case law discussed here that in the context of effective judicial protection the Court often revolves around the principle of accountability which plays a significant role in relation to increasing amount of claims on damages caused by lengthy judicial proceedings.

References

Augustyn M., Monda C. (2011), 'Transparency and access to documents in the EU: Ten years on from the adoption of regulation 1049/2001', http://www.eipa.eu/files/repository/eipascope/20110912103927_EipascopeSpecialIssue_Art2.pdf (accessed: 31.1.2016).

Beters B. (2015), 'Towards the Europeanisation of participation? Reflecting on the functions and beneficiaries of participation in EU environmental law', [in:] C. Fraenkel-Haeberle, S. Kropp, F. Palermo, K.P. Sommermann, *Citizen participation in multi-level democracies*, Leiden: Brill Nijhoff.

Beumer E. (2013),'The Recent Landmark Cases on the Reasonable Time Requirement: Is the Court Caught Between Scylla and Charybids?', *European Law Blog*, http://europeanlawblog.eu/?p=2093 (accessed: 4.2.2016).

Caro de Sousa P. (2013), 'Case Comment: Gascogne (C-40/12 and C-58/12) and Kendrion (C-50/12)', Decmber 6, 2013, http://eutopialaw.com/2013/12/06/case-comment-gascogne-c-4012-and-c-5812-and-kendrion-c%E2%80%915012/ (accessed: 4.2.2016).

Cioclea A.E., Pascal M. (2010),'New approaches on good governance in the European Union',http://ssrn.com/abstract=1651862

Ferri D. (2015), 'Participation in EU Governance: A "Multi-Level" Perspective and a "Multifold" Approach', [in:] C. Fraenkel-Haeberle, S. Kropp, F. Palermo, K.P. Sommermann, *Citizen Participation in Multi-level Democracies*, Leiden: Brill Nijhoff.

Karageorgou V. (2013), 'Transparency principle as an evolving principle of EU law: regulative contours and implications http://www.right2info.org/resources/publications/eu-karageorgou-vasiliki-transparency-principle-as-an-evolving-principle-of-eu-law (accessed: 31.1.2016).

Sachiko M., Durwood Z. (2005), 'Rule of law, good governance and sustainable development', http://www.inece.org/conference/7/vol1/05_Sachiko_Zaelke.pdf (accessed: 2.2.2016).

Sawyer K. (2007), 'The principle of 'interprétation conforme': How far can nor should national courts go when interpreting national legislation consistently with European Community Law', *Statute Law Review,* 28: 165-181.

Strand J.R., Retzl K.K. (2014), „Good governance within the World Bank: Assessing recent reforms", Presentation at the 2014 Annual Meeting of the International Studies Association, Toronto, http://papers.ssrn.com/sol3/papers.cfm?abstract_id=2409126 (accessed: 4.2.2016).

Srivastava M. (2009), 'Good governance- Concept, Meaning and Features: A detailed study', http://ssrn.com/abstract=1528449 (accessed: 31.1.2016).

Uruena R. (2012), 'No citizens here: Global Subjects and Participation in the International Law', Leiden: Martinus Nijhoff Publishers.

von Davitz T. (2010), 'Good governance in the hands of the judiciary: Lessons from the European example', *Potchefstroom Electronic Law Journal* ,13(1): 2-16.

World Bank (1991), 'Managing Development: The Governance Dimension, A Discussion Paper', August 29, 1991, Washington, D.C, http://www-wds.worldbank.org/external/default/WDSContentServer/WDSP/IB/2006/03/07/000090341_20060307104630/Rendered/PDF/34899.pdf (accessed: 4.2.2016).

Part Two:
Public participation and government effectiveness

Chapter 1: The development of the concept of EU citizenship through the incremental acceptance of citizens' rights

Magdalena Gniadzik

Key words: citizenship of the European Union, equal treatment, right to reside, real link test, civil and political rights

Introduction

EU citizenship was introduced by the Treaty of Maastricht and was intended as a means of strengthening the position of citizens of EU member states within the framework of EU legislation. EU citizenship creates a direct legal bond between an individual and the European Union. However, it also has a second dimension as it influences the relations between a citizen of one member state and other member states, as well as impacts the citizen's relations with their country of origin. It is also often emphasised that EU citizenship is a process in progress rather than a ready and shaped institution of law (Poptecheva, 2014: 86; Kostakopulou, 2014: 449). A characteristic feature of EU citizenship is the fact that it is defined by the rights resulting from the status of an EU citizen.

Political rights of EU citizens

Democratic legitimisation is conditioned by the possibility for citizens to exert influence on the process of decision-making. As far as the relation between the EU and an individual citizen is concerned, the most important rights are the passive election right (the right to vote) and the active election right (the right to stand for election) to the European Parliament. These rights, however, had been granted to citizens of EU member states long before the introduction of EU citizenship, by the adoption of the Act on Direct Elections to the European Parliament of 1976.[1] Members of the European Parliament are elected in a universal, direct, free, proportional and secret ballot. Currently, all EU citizens who live in the territories of any EU member states enjoy their voting rights. Elections to the European Parliament, however, do not fulfil the criterion of material equality as the voting powers differ across EU member states. The division of seats in the Parliament was defined through political decisions and was meant to prevent marginalisation of the states with lower population densities. It is therefore correct to claim that the division reflects the fact that the equality among the states has outweighed the equality of the Union's citizens (Cielen, 2008: 73-74). Beyond doubt, the lack of joint lists of candidates to the European Parliament results in treating MEP's more as representatives of states rather than representatives of voters.

The Treaty of Maastricht introduced voting rights for EU citizens in local elections, including EU citizens living outside their country of origin. These rights are described in detail in the provisions of Directive 94/80/EC, which includes the relevant anti-discriminatory regulations.[2] The voting right for local elections is limited to the elections of the first (basic) tier of municipal authorities in a given country. The municipalities concerned have been defined for particular member states and are listed in the annexe to the directive. As an exception to the principle of non-discrimination, the directive also permits the possibility of reserving the positions of managers of executive authorities, their deputies or members of an executive body of a basic-level local authority for the citizens of the country where the election is being held. Moreover, member states may take away from citizens of other member states who have been elected members of executive authorities in local elections the right to designate delegates who can vote in a parliamentary assembly or to elect the members of that assembly. It must be underlined that the right to vote in local elections does not automatically mean the right to vote in other forms of exercise of direct democracy, such as local referendums or ballots on legislative initiatives. Importantly, one of the postulated possibilities as re-

1 Act concerning the election of the representatives of the Assembly by direct universal suffrage OJ L 278, 08.10.1976, p. 5–11.

2 Council Directive 94/80/EC of 19 December 1994 laying down detailed arrangements for the exercise of the right to vote and to stand as a candidate in municipal elections by citizens of the Union residing in a Member State of which they are not nationals, OJ L 368, 31.12.1994, p. 38–47.

gards bringing the EU closer to its citizens and increasing the citizens' impact on the decision-making process is the proposed introduction of EU-wide referendums (Atickan, 2013: 126-142).

In future, an important role for the shaping of EU citizens' roles in the Union's decision-making process may be played by the European Citizens' Initiative introduced by the Treaty of Lisbon. According to Article 11 TEU, "not less than one million citizens who are nationals of a significant number of Member States may take the initiative of inviting the European Commission, within the framework of its powers, to submit any appropriate proposal on matters where citizens consider that a legal act of the Union is required for the purpose of implementing the Treaties". The initiative was described as not only symbolic but also tangible and significant in terms of increasing the EU's democratisation. It was also presented as a change comparable to the introduction of the first direct elections to the European Parliament, although it was also underlined at the same time that the change would not be capable of solving all of the EU's problems associated with democratic legitimisation (Bordino, 2015: 40 and 42, and a different perspective in Dougan, 2012: 289). Still, the main shortcoming of the institution is the lack of obligation (for the EU's institutions) to adopt the acts of law required by the citizens. Experts also indicate possible difficulties in collecting one million signatures and the limitation of the proposed activities to the scope of authority of the Commission, which results in the possible rejection of a proportion of socially significant initiatives that go beyond EU law and its application (Dougan 2012: 289). The practice so far has not proven this new legal institution successful. The required number of signatures has so far been collected only for three initiatives. Moreover, in each of these initiatives the Commission decided not to draft proposals of the postulated acts of law.[3]

Another right that must be mentioned here is the right to consular protection granted by Article 23 TFEU. As EU citizens travel to third countries more frequently, their effective protection constitutes a growing challenge for consulates. The right to consular protection, despite its limitations, is therefore an appropriate means of ensuring effective protection for EU citizens who are not represented abroad in emergencies. Further-

3 http://ec.europa.eu/citizens-initiative/public/initiatives/successful; (accessed 02.03.2016).

more, it is also a tool to strengthen the European identity and promote the institution of EU citizenship itself (Poptecheva, 2014: 253).

EU citizenship as a link with the scope of application of EU law

A revolutionary change in the meaning of EU citizenship may have been initially suggested by ruling in *Zambrano* (Case C-34/09, *Zambrano*, ECLI:EU:C:2011:124), where Article 20 for the first time became a stand-alone and independent (from Article 21 TFEU) source of rights for the citizen. The court ruled in its judgment that "(...) article 20 TFEU precludes national measures which have the effect of depriving citizens of the Union of the genuine enjoyment of the substance of the rights conferred by virtue of their status as citizens of the Union." As a result of the judgment legal scholars presented the relevant concepts and postulates aimed at amending the previous approach by recognising the fact that systematic and grave violations of fundamental rights by a member state deprive EU citizenship of its substance and importance. Therefore, in each similar situation an individual should have the right to refer to Article 20 TFEU in the so-called Reversed Solange doctrine (von Bogdandy, 2012: 489-520), or by turning EU citizenship into an independent link with EU law (Kochenov, 2012: 369-396). However, in its following judgments (such as: Case C-434/09, *Mc Carthy*, ECLI:EU:C:2011:277; Case C-256/11, *Dereci*, ECLI:EU:C:2011:734; Case C-40/11, *Iida*, ECLI:EU:C:2012:691; Case C-86/12 *Alokpa*, ECLI:EU:C:2013:645) the Court of Justice went in the opposite direction and narrowed down the concept of the substance of EU citizenship law to the right of not being forced to leave the European Union's territory.

According to the Court, "(...) the mere fact that it might appear desirable to a national of a Member State, for economic reasons or in order to keep his family together in the territory of the Union, for the members of his family who do not have the nationality of a Member State to be able to reside with him in the territory of the Union, is not sufficient in itself to support the view that the Union citizen will be forced to leave Union territory if such a right is not granted." The Court excluded the right to family life from the scope of substantial rights of EU citizens, thereby also excluding the possibility of an extension of the application of legal protection of EU citizens and protection by the EU's fundamental rights beyond the scope of application of EU law. The Zambrano judgment, therefore, only created a new link with EU legislation, just as judgment in *Rottman* (Case C-135/08, *Rottman*, ECLI:EU:C:2010:104). In the judgment, it is not only the threat of losing EU citizenship, but also the threat of being forced to leave the EU's territory, that constitutes a sufficient reason to apply EU law.

Consequently, the problem of assigning the links between factual situations and the scope of EU law and its application remains a current issue. It is only after such a link has been found that an individual is covered by the scope of rights resulting from EU citizenship. This state of affairs leads to a fairly case-based practice of formulation of such links, and to an uncertainty as to the possibilities of qualifying even very similar cases in the same way. In her opinion regarding the Zambrano case, Advocate General Sharpston asked what character and length of stay in a different member state lets one assume that there indeed is a link with EU law. Such questions and doubts were answered later by judgment in *O and B.* (Case C-456/12, *O and B.*, ECLI:EU:C:2014:135) where the Court ruled that if during an EU citizen's effective stay in a host country based on Article 7 (1 and 2) of directive 2004/38[4] (for stays longer than three months) his or her family life developed or solidified, then it is necessary for the citizen to be able to lead his or her family life after his or her return to the country of origin – and therefore the derived right of stay must be given to the citizen's family member (who is a citizen of a third country). If such derived right was non-existent, EU citizens could be discouraged from exercising their right to freedom of movement granted by Article 21(1) TFEU.

The right of EU citizens to freedom of movement: the changing models of integration

The most important right granted to EU citizens by the Treaties is the right to freedom of movement and the associated prohibition of discrimination

4 Directive 2004/38/EC of the European Parliament and of the Council of 29 April 2004 on the right of citizens of the Union and their family members to move and reside freely within the territory of the Member States amending Regulation (EEC) No 1612/68 and repealing Directives 64/221/EEC, 68/360/EEC, 72/194/EEC, 73/148/EEC, 75/34/EEC, 75/35/EEC, 90/364/EEC, 90/365/EEC and 93/96/EEC, OJ L 158, 30.4.2004, p. 77–123.

on the grounds of national citizenship. The key role in extending the rights of migrating EU citizens and their families has been played by the relevant judgments of the Court of Justice. The point of departure was the claim (frequently cited) from judgment in *Grzelczyk* (Case C-184/99, *Grzelczyk*, ECLI:EU:C:2001:458) that the status of an EU citizen ought to be the fundamental status of citizens of member states, thus enabling citizens in identical situations to exercise the right to equal treatment, regardless of their countries of origin. However, it must be emphasised that the Court's approach to the importance of EU citizenship and the resulting rights has been changing over time.

Most importantly, as regards the right to freedom of movement of economically inactive EU citizens and members of their families, two models of integration have been impacting the Court's approach. According to the first model, the so-called residence model (Thym, 2015: 34-36) or the so-called perfect assimilation (Verschueren, 2007: 333) the responsible state (particularly in terms of social protection) should be most of all the state on whose territory the individual is residing. Additionally, in this model the scope of the right to equal treatment increases with the duration of the individual's stay. It does not assess the degree of integration of the individual with the society of the host country. In turn, the integration model (Thym, 2015: 36-39) investigates the concrete circumstances such as the person's link with the labour market, family bonds or other personal relations with the host country. Within the second model, the acquisition of the right to equal treatment is conditioned by the ability to prove a certain level of integration with the host country. The first model is, beyond doubt, far easier to apply for a country's judiciary and administration. The second model makes it possible to investigate individual cases and personal situations as well as defining the circumstances that will be taken into account and the minimal conditions that will need to be satisfied in order for the individual to be assessed as integrated to a sufficient extent.

Initially, the Court of Justice referred to both models in an attempt to extend the scope of the right to equal treatment of the EU's migrating citizens. However, it was later shown that the qualitative model prevailed. The key role in the process was played by the concept of the test of the so-called real link between the citizen who exercised his or her right to freedom of movement and the host country or the country of origin. The concept was developed by the Court in the following rulings: *D'Hoop* (Case C-224/98, *D'Hoop*, ECLI:EU:C:2002:432), *Grzelczyk*, *Collins* (Case C-138/02, *Collins*, ECLI:EU:C:2013:860), *Trojani* (Case C-456/02, *Troja-*

ni, ECLI:EU:C:2004:488), or *Bidar* (Case C-209/03, *Bidar*, ECLI:EU:C: 2005:169). According to the concept, member states may limit access to different benefits for citizens of other member states and provide access to benefits only to the citizens who are sufficiently integrated with the society of the host country, and only in situations where there is the real link between the citizen and the host country.

On the one hand, this construct granted integrated migrants (and EU citizens at the same time) the right to equal treatment, also as regards their access to social benefits. On the other hand, however, it enabled host states to limit the number of beneficiaries so as to avoid a unrational burden on their social protection systems caused by the migrating EU citizens. The real link test was therefore also a tool to counteract the phenomenon of the so-called "benefit tourism" (social tourism), i.e. situations where individuals move to a country only to take advantage of the country's more generous social protection system (compared against the social protection system in their country of origin, see also Verschueren, 2007: 333). The real link test also defined the fundamental difference between the status of migrating employees and economically inactive EU citizens, as the former were entitled to equal treatment thanks to their economic activity, regardless of the level of their integration (more on this issue in O'Brien, 2009: 1109-1115).

At that time the Court of Justice attached a lot of importance to the evaluation of the level of integration based on an evaluation of the entirety of individual circumstances – i.e. the importance of individualised assessment. The Court emphasised that member states must not limit themselves to one criterion only, e.g. length of residence, as this single criterion would not necessarily reflect the strength of the individual's link with the society.

A change was introduced by Directive 2004/38 which is, in a way, derived from both the residential and the integration-based models. The directive introduced a system of a gradual extension of rights, depending on the length of stay in the host country. The final outcome of the process of change was to construct a right of permanent stay, to be granted after five years of legal residence in the host country. The identification of the level of integration with the length of residence may, however, be regarded as a contradiction of the real link concept. The directive departed from the requirement of individual assessment of the real link, as it is not in every case that the length of residence is the circumstance that will indicate the level of integration of the individual with the host society. The Court, however, approved the system in its ruling in *Förster* (Case C-158/07, *Förster*, ECLI:EU:C:2008:630), thus contradicting its own previous judgments.

The impact of concerns resulting from the so-called social tourism on the legal status of EU citizens

Importantly, as a result of the financial crisis there have been significant concerns about the looming threat of social tourism within the EU, i.e. the threat of citizens migrating to the countries with comparatively high social benefits. This has led to attempts at limiting the scope of rights granted to mobile EU citizens – particularly those who are economically inactive. It seems, however, that the scale of the phenomenon has been overestimated to a significant extent.

According to the data presented by the European Commission in its communication entitled "Free movement of EU citizens and their families: Five actions to make a difference"[5], at the end of 2012 14.1 million EU citizens lived in a different member state than the one of their origin (2.8% of the total population of the EU). The percentage of third country citizens residing in the EU at the same time amounted to 4.0%. Employment rate among the EU's mobile citizens amounted to 67.7% and was higher than in the years 2005-2012. It was also higher compared with the employment rate of 64.6% among citizens living in their countries of origin. Of the unemployed mobile citizens, 79% lived in a household with an employed person, whereas 64% used to work in their countries of origin.

According to the Commission's communication, mobile EU citizens did not avail themselves of social benefits to a larger extent than did the citizens of host countries. In the investigated 13 countries, they constituted less than 1% of the beneficiaries (citizens of any EU member state) of non-contribution-based social benefits in 6 countries; in 5 countries the range was between 1 and 5%, and the range was between 5 and 15% only in 2 countries. In most member states, mobile citizens also paid (statistically speaking) more taxes and contributions than they received from the social protection systems in their host countries (in other words, they were

5 Communication from the Commission to the European Parliament, the Council and the European Economic and Social Committee - Free movement of EU citizens and their families: Five actions to make a difference, COM (2013) 837.

net payers). The Commission also did not notice any connection between the generosity of social protection systems and the exercise of the right to freedom of movement by EU citizens.

The concerns regarding social tourism, however, have influenced the most recent rulings by the Court of Justice. The shift is visible, in particular, in the judgments in the following cases: *Brey* (Case C-140/12, *Brey*, ECLI:EU:C:2013:565), *Dano* (Case C-333/13, *Dano*, ECLI:EU:C: 2014:2358), and *Alimanovic* (Case C-67/14, *Alimanovic*, ECLI:EU:C: 2015:597). In these cases, the Court ruled that an EU citizen may demand equal treatment in access to social benefits (equalling that of the citizens of the host country) only if his or her stay in the territory of the host country meets all the criteria set out in Directive 2004/38. This results in the conclusion that each situation where the EU citizen who has not yet acquired the right to permanent stay loses his or her means of maintenance results in the loss of the right to stay and the right to claim equal treatment (see also Verschueren, 2015: 370-379). It seems that the judgments are an effect of a certain paradigm shift as regards the interpretation of the substance of EU citizenship and the right to freedom of movement. This is reflected in shifting away from the premise that lay at the foundation of the previous rulings (i.e. the scope of rights granted to EU citizens increasing with the lengths of residence in the host country, is aimed at contributing to their integration with the society of the host country). Currently, integration is a pre-condition that facilitates the acquisition and maintenance of the right of stay and equal treatment. Therefore, we can even say there is an obligation to strive for integration with the society of the host country. Moreover, integration is no longer perceived solely as the existence of an economic and personal bond with the host country, but also as subordination to the values of the host socicty (Coutts, 2015: 539-537).

If host countries are not obliged to show responsibility and financial solidarity with EU citizens who may be in financial trouble, the question to ask is whether such an obligation should always rest on the country of origin. The answer to this question is provided by the Court's rulings concerning the systems of support for students who study abroad. In the judgment in *Martens* (Case C-359/13, *Martens*, ECLI:EU:C:2015:118) the Court ruled that a member state may verify whether there are any links between the beneficiary and the society of the paying state; however, the verification must not be based only on one criterion such as the place of residence or the length of residence. Among the circumstances to be taken into account by the host country the Court listed citizenship, length of of education, family bonds and professional links, knowledge of foreign languages – among other elements. The Court's position, therefore, seems to be that countries of origin are in principle responsible for the provision of financial assistance to their own citizens – due to the link resulting from citizenship. However, the Court also deems it possible for member states to exclude support for persons who are unable to show evidence of a link with the country of origin – as long as the general provisions of EU law are complied with. It must also be noted that the Court's position is highly similar to the one it initially presented in its judgments concerning host countries. However, the current line of ruling may lead (in extreme situations) to an EU citizen pronounced (in his or her specific situation) as not linked to any of the member states and, consequently, deprived of the right to social protection, among other rights. At the current developmental level of EU legislation, EU citizen status will not protect the person from the consequences of such situations.

The so-called Brexit Deal with the United Kingdom

The concerns regarding the phenomenon of social tourism were also one of the main points of the recent negotiations between the United Kingdom and the remaining member states. The compromise between the parties developed as a result of the negotiations is intended to deter British citizens from voting in favour of Brexit in the referendum, on June 23, 2016. According to the declaration of heads of states and governments (accompanying document of the conclusions from the meeting of the European Council on February 18-19, 2016[6]) the United Kingdom is not obliged to participate in further European integration efforts, which is also to be expressed in future Treaties. As regards the rights of EU citizens to the freedom of movement, the declaration stipulates the following: member states "have the right to define the fundamental principles of their social security systems and enjoy a broad margin of discretion to define and implement their social and employment policy, including setting the conditions for access to welfare benefits". A Member state might refuse to grant social benefits to persons who do not have sufficient resources to claim a right of

6 http://www.consilium.europa.eu/en/press/press-releases/2016/02/19-euco-conclusions/; (accessed 02.03.2016).

residence in the case of benefits tourism. Furthermore the member state can reject claims for social assistance by EU citizens who are entitled to reside on their territory solely because of their job-search, even if such benefits are also intended to facilitate access to the labour market of the host state. The Commission is obliged to submit proposals for amending regulation No 883/2004 in order to enable member states to index child benefits for children residing in a state other than that where the worker resides to the conditions of the state of the child's residence. Until 1 January 2020 this rule should apply only new claims made by EU workers, but from that date states can extend indexation to already existing claims to child benefits.

Regulation No 492/2011 is as to be amended as to provide so called alert and safeguard mechanism that will respond to situations of serious inflow of EU workers. A Member State could notify the Commission and the Council that such a situation exists on a scale that affects essential aspects of its social security system, , or which leads to difficulties which are serious and liable to persist in its employment market or are putting an excessive pressure on the proper functioning of its public services. The Council (after a proposal from the Commission) could then authorise the state concerned to restrict access to non-contributory in-work benefits for newly arriving EU workers for a total period of up to four years from the commencement of employment. However access to such benefits should gradually increase in order to take account of the growing connection of the worker concerned with the labour market of the host Member State. The limitation might apply to EU workers only during a period of 7 years.

Importantly, the agreement is to become binding if Britons decide to stay in the EU in the upcoming referendum. The agreement does not impact the legal situation of migrant EU citizens in a direct manner. It is merely a commitment to introduce changes to the acts of derived law in some unspecified future. The real impact of the agreement on mobile EU citizens will depend on the details of the changes to be proposed by the Commission. If the changes permit an overly extensive limitation of the principle of equal treatment, without the necessity to prove a real threat to the social system of the member state, it is highly likely that such changes will be deemed as a violation of the Treaties by the Court of Justice.

On the other hand, the Court in its rulings has always tried to take into account the concerns of the member states that need to cope with large-scale migration. The necessity to combat the phenomenon of social tourism has always been a premise justifying the limitations of the rights of mobile EU citizens. Along with the diminished importance of the proportionality principle and limited rights to social benefits, this facilitated protection of own social systems by particular member states even before the so-called Brexit-deal. From the perspective of the concept of good governance, the compromise marks a move away from the paradigm of bringing the EU closer to its citizens. What also contradicts good governance is the division of EU citizens into the better and the worse, depending on when they chose to exercise their right to freedom of movement. Importantly, the possibility of limiting the access to benefits is not only to be exercised by the United Kingdom, but also by any other member state. If the planned changes are indeed introduced and taken advantage of by further member states, a real threat may ensue for the right to freedom of movement and, consequently, EU citizenship. A return to a situation where the right to settle down in a different country is only for the wealthy and for those who have integrated well with the host country will mean a negation of the very substance of the legal institution of EU citizenship.

References

Atickan E.O. (2013), 'Direct Democracy: Remedying The Democratic Deficit', [in:] Lauresen. F, *The EU and Eurozone crisis*, Farnham.

von Bogdandy A. et allia (2012), 'Reverse Solange – Protecting the essence of fundamental rights against EU Member States', *Common Market Law Review*, 2: 489-520.

Bordino G. (2015), 'A new right for democracy and development in Europe', Brussels.

Poptcheva E-M. (2014), 'Multilevel citizenship. The right to consular protection of EU citizens abroad', Brussels.

Coutts S. (2015), 'Union citizenship as probationary citizenship: Onuekwere, *Common Market Law Review*, 2: 531–545.

Cieleń A. (2008), 'Prawa polityczne obywateli Unii Europejskiej', Warszawa, 229.

Dougan. M, Shuibhne N.N. Sapveanta E. (2012), 'Empowerment and disempowerment of European Citizenship', Oxford.

D. Kochenov, R. Plender (2012), 'EU Citizenship: From an Incipient Form to an Incipient Substance? The Discovery of the Treaty Text', *European Law Review*, 4: 369-396

Kostakopoulou D. (2014), 'When EU Citizens become Foreigners', *European Law Journal*, 4: 447–463.

O'Brien C. (2009), 'Social Blind Spots and Monocular Policy Making: The ECJ's Migrant Worker Model', *Common Market Law Review*, 4: 1107–1141.

Thym D. (2015), 'The elusive limits of solidarity: Residence rights of and social benefits for economically inactive Union citizens', *Common Market Law Review*, 1: 17–50.

Verschueren H. (2015), 'Preventing "benefit tourism" in the EU: A narrow or broad interpretation of the possibilities offered by the ECJ in Dano?', *Common Market Law Review*, 2: 363–390.

Verschueren H.(2007), 'European (Internal) Migration Law as an Instrument for Defining the Boundaries of National Solidarity Systems', *European Journal of Migration and Law*, 3: 307 – 346.

Chapter 2: Tackling discrimination in the European Union

Magdalena Gniadzik

Key words: anti-discrimination policy, European Union, discrimination, equal treatment, disability, parents' rights, same-sex relationships, anti-discrimination directives

The legal foundation of anti-discrimination efforts in the European Union and the associated limitations

In order to make an assessment of the EU's anti-discrimination laws and policies we must first of all recognise their characteristic feature, i.e. the fact that they predominantly focus on employment (Schiek, 2011: 20), which is a reflection of the historic scope of competencies vested in the European Communities and, subsequently, in the EU by the EU's member states. However, we can also say that the basis of European integration has been the fight against special forms of discrimination i.e. discrimination based on citizenship.

According to Article 2 TEU, one of the fundamental goals of the European Union is to combat social exclusion and discrimination as well as to support social justice and protection, equal opportunities for men and women, inter-generational solidarity and the protection of children's rights. According to Article 10 TFEU, when defining and implementing its policies and action the EU strives to combat all forms of discrimination on the grounds of gender, race or ethnic origin, religion or belief, disability, age or sexual orientation. Along these lines, Article 9 TFEU also obliges member states to comply with the requirement to foster high employment rates, ensure appropriate social protection, and combat social exclusion. According to Article 21(1) of the Charter of Fundamental Rights, it is prohibited to discriminate on the grounds of gender, race, skin colour, ethnic or social origin, genetic traits, language, religion or belief, political or other opinions, belonging to a national minority, property, birth, disability, age or sexual orientation.

Article 19 TFEU defines the power standard which facilitates adoption of binding legislation and which is necessary to combat all forms of discrimination based on gender, race or ethnic origin, religion or belief, disability, age or sexual orientation. The article authorises the Council to unanimously adopt such legal measures after permission granted by the European Parliament, i.e. by means of a special legislative procedure. In exceptional cases the European Parliament and the European Council may (within the regular procedure) adopt basic principles regarding UE incentives; this, however, excludes harmonisation of national legislation. A different principle has been defined as regards the legal measures ensuring gender equality in employment, including the equality of remuneration. According to Article 157(3) TFEU, such legislation shall be adopted by means of the ordinary legislative procedure.

It must be emphasised that the requirement of making unanimous decisions in most areas of combating discrimination constitutes a significant constraint on the EU's activities aimed at meeting the objective of non-discrimination. It is frequently the case that reaching an agreement including all member states (representing different traditions and sensitivities as regards equal treatment of different social groups) is very difficult indeed, or even impossible (see also Zawidzka-Łojek, 2015: 45).

A good example here may be the proposed directive on the implementation of the equal treatment principle regardless of the person's religion or belief, disability, age or sexual orientation. The directive was prepared by the EC in 2008[1] (more on the proposed directive in Ellis, 2013: 372-379 and Schiek, 2011: 40) and was aimed at broadening the scope of protection against discrimination on the above-mentioned grounds to include areas other than employment. The proposed directive introduced prohibition of discrimination in the following areas: social protection including social security and health care; social privileges; education, access and delivery of generally available goods and services, including accommodation and transportation. The prohibition was directed at all entities, both private and public, including public institutions. However, in the case of access to goods and services, the prohibition only referred to the scope of professional or business activity of the entities. The proposed directive was to complement Directive 2006/54.[2] Due to the objections of certain

1 Proposal for a Council Directive on implementing the principle of equal treatment between persons irrespective of religion or belief, disability, age or sexual orientation, COM (2008) 426 final.

2 Directive 2006/54/EC of the European Parliament and of the Council of 5 July 2006 on the implementation of the principle of equal opportunities and equal treatment of

member states, the work on the directive was put on hold in 2012 and renewed in December 2014. Still, however, it seems that the adoption of this important and necessary directive is a very long way off.

Implementation of the adopted plans and strategies

A significant problem in the field of combatting discrimination in the EU is also the tardiness in the implementation of already adopted strategies and other legislation which defines action plans in the field. An example here may be the extent of implementation of the Strategy on Disability 2010-2020: A Renewed Commitment for a Barrier-Free World[3] (more on the strategy also in Zawidzka-Łojek, 2015: 228-232). The Strategy has replaced the EU's action plan for the years 2004-2010[4] (more on the previous disability policy in Ventegodt Liisberg, 2011: 73-81); its particular components have been developed based on an analysis of the implementation of the action plan. The Strategy is intended as a framework for the actions taken by member states and its role is to coordinate the EU's actions aimed at improving the situation of disabled persons. The Strategy's general objective is to guarantee disabled citizens full access to their rights, and to ensure their full participation in social and economic life. This issue is a significant social problem as evidenced by the relevant studies: across the EU, an average of 16% of citizens aged 16-64 are affected by disability or long-term health problems, although the proportions in particular member states vary quite significantly. Additionally, 52% of the disabled population in the EU are unemployed (Boeri, 2015: 225-226). The Strategy is also meant to ensure the complete implementation of the UN Convention on the Rights of Disabled Persons (concerning the Convention and its influence on the European Union law and judgements of the Court of

men and women in matters of employment and occupation (recast) OJ L 204, 26.7.2006, p. 23–36.

3 Communication from the Commission to the European Parliament, the Council, the European Economic and Social Committee and the Committee of the Regions - European Disability Strategy 2010-2020: A Renewed Commitment to a Barrier-Free Europe, COM (2010) 636 final.

4 Communication from the Commission to the Council, the European Parliament, the European Economic and Social Committee and the Committee of the Regions - Equal opportunities for people with disabilities: A European Action Plan, COM(2003) 650 final.

Justice see also in: Zawidzka-Łojek, 2015: 223-228) in EU and national legal orders, as well as including the Convention in all EU policies. There are eight principal action areas in the Strategy. These are: accessibility, participation, equality, employment, education and training, social protection, health and external activities.

The point of departure for the Strategy's implementation was the oversight of application and implementation of Directive 2000/78/EC, performed by particular member states. The directive sets out the framework for equal treatment in work and employment[5] and introduces prohibition of discrimination on the ground of disability in the labour market (among other grounds).[6] The next planned step was to adopt the directive implementing the principles of equal treatment of persons regardless of their religion or belief, disability, age or sexual orientation. However, the fact that the directive has not been adopted casts doubt over the likelihood of meeting the objectives set out by the strategy.

In the strategy, a lot of importance was attached to combatting the barriers encountered by persons with disabilities. Therefore, the key term in the strategy is accessibility understood as provision of equal access to disabled person's physical environments, transport, technology and ICT systems as well as other facilities and services. The flagship initiative in the EU in this area is the so-called Act on Accessibility aimed at optimising the market of goods and services accessible for disabled persons and the elderly. The initiative is particularly important because after its adoption manufacturers of goods and service providers will not have to align their products or services with different national legislations. The Commission intended to prepare the relevant directive first in 2012 and then in 2013. Eventually, the proposal was prepared as late as in December 2015.[7]

Work is also still under way on a different act of law necessary to include disabled persons' participation in social life. The act is the directive

---

5 Council Directive 2000/78/EC of 27 November 2000 establishing a general framework for equal treatment in employment and occupation, OJ L 303, 2.12.2000, p. 16–22.

6 Such an analyse was prepared jointly for directives 2000/78 and 2000/43. The Commission in the report form 17.01.2014 stated that, despite of initial difficulties, all 28 member states implemented both directives, COM (2014) 2 final.

7 Proposal for a Directive of the European Parliament and of the on the approximation of the laws, regulations and administrative provisions of the Member States as regards the accessibility requirements for products and services, COM (2015) 615 final.

on the accessibility of the websites of institutions of the public sector, intended to define the technical regulations for publishing content of websites of public institutions in the EU's member states. The planned directive is to pertain only to certain types of websites, e.g. websites containing information on social security services, health care services, tax returns, modes of reporting crimes to the police, issuance of identification documents and other official documentation, or catalogues of public libraries. We must note that according to the Commission's announcements accompanying the EU's digital agenda, websites of public institutions were to be fully accommodated to the needs of persons with disabilities by 2015.

However, we must also indicate some acts of law which are important for persons with disabilities and which have been successfully adopted. For example, an important act is Regulation 181/2011 concerning the rights of passengers in coach and bus transport.[8] According to the regulation, carriers, travel agents and organisers of trips cannot refuse bookings, tickets or boarding of persons on the ground of disability or motor impairment, unless the construction of the vehicle or the infrastructure (such as bus stops or stations) physically prevents such persons from boarding the vehicle or leaving the vehicle. In such situations, however, a disabled passenger may demand that a person of his/her choice assists him/her, whereby such an assistant must be able to support the disabled person. If the passenger is refused such assistance, they may choose to either have the fare reimbursed and be transported free of charge to the point of departure, or to continue their journey or diverted journey with an alternative, reasonably accommodated transport service to the passenger's destination. Moreover, member states are obliged to designate bus and coach terminals with assistance points for disabled persons and persons with reduced mobility. Similar provisions were introduced by Regulation 1300/2014 concerning technical interoperability specifications relating to accessibility of the Union's rail system for persons with disabilities and persons with reduced mobility[9]. Both regulations are aimed at empower-

---

8 Regulation (EU) No 181/2011 of the European Parliament and of the Council of 16 February 2011 concerning the rights of passengers in bus and coach transport and amending Regulation (EC) No 2006/2004, OJ L 55, 28.2.2011, p. 1–12.

9 Commission Regulation (EU) No 1300/2014 of 18 November 2014 on the technical specifications for interoperability relating to accessibility of the Union's rail system for persons with disabilities and persons with reduced mobility, OJ L 356, 12.12.2014, p. 110–178.

ing disabled persons to travel freely. Another initiative also worth mentioning is the European Parking Card i.e. a document authorising its holders to park in the spaces designated for disabled persons and recognised across the EU in all its member states. The Commission has also published information concerning the principles of use of parking spaces by persons with disabilities in all EU member states.

An attempt at assessing the actions aimed at the Strategy's implementation, therefore, does not produce a clear result at this moment. Of course, it must be emphasised that in many areas covered by the Strategy the Union is only a supportive authority that complements and coordinates the activities implemented by particular member states. To a large extent, it is the task of the EU's member states to take actions that can truly improve the situation of disabled persons. The objectives of the directive have been formulated very broadly and generically, which, on the one hand, reflects the scale of the problems encountered by disabled person, but on the other hand – it hinders an assessment of the directive's implementation and effectiveness. Beyond doubt, the activities aimed at improving disabled persons' access to transport services must be evaluated positively. However, the lack of two key pieces of legislation i.e. a European Act on Accessibility and the new anti-discrimination directive is a significant barrier impeding the EU from meeting the Strategy's objectives. It is also a proof of a lack of engagement on the part of EU and member state institutions, despite the initial enthusiasm that accompanied the adoption of the Strategy. Without regaining that enthusiasm, it will not be possible to improve the situation of disabled persons in the European Union. Public consultation and a review of the Strategy announced by the Commission on 22 December 2015 may become a good opportunity to change the situation and involve NGOs to a more significant extent in the process of improving the situation of disabled persons in the EU.

The status of protection standards in light of the changes taking place in European societies

Anti-discrimination law – in order to be an effective tool to increase social participation – must also be up-to-date with the changes taking place in European societies. Even the fairest provisions may prove more harmful than beneficial if they do not reflect the dynamic shifts in social relations. The current status of the protection of parent's rights in the EU may serve as an illustration of the problem (see more on the protection of pregnant women and young mothers in Maliszewska-Nienartowicz, 2013: 31-39 and Zawidzka-Łojek, 2015: 142-148). As has been aptly described in the doctrine, the protection of women during pregnancy and maternity is an exception from the general principle of equality. On the one hand, the protection takes into account the differences between men and women and responds to the specific needs of pregnant women and women looking after young children. On the other hand, the protection may lead to the risk of fossilisation or even the deepening of discrimination rather than to fostering equal opportunities – in particular if the protection is too intensive (Schiek, 2009: 218). Such opinions most typically pertain to the threat of the deterioration of women's situation in the labour market, resulting from the provisions concerning protection of pregnant women and mothers. Ironically however, the protection of women may also fossilise the traditional division of labour between the parents (Zawidzka-Łojek, 2015: 143 with references) and even lead to discrimination against fathers in the process of bringing up children.

Currently, EU legislation contains regulations pertaining to both maternity leave and parental leave. The right of female employees to maternity leave was introduced by Article 8 of Directive 92/85.[10] According to the directive, only female employees are entitled to maternity leave. Parental leave, in turn, are intended for both parents with the employee status introduced by Directive 96/34.[11] The leave has now been extended to four months based on Directive 2010/18.[12] Because both types of leave co-exist and because of the maternity leave in national legislation usually exceeding the period of 14 weeks stipulated by Directive 92/85, we have encountered the possible problem of granting the right to male employees (fathers) in the case of the mother not having the official status of an employee.

10 Council Directive 92/85/EEC of 19 October 1992 on the introduction of measures to encourage improvements in the safety and health at work of pregnant workers and workers who have recently given birth or are breastfeeding, OJ L 348, 28.11.1992, p. 1–7.

11 Council Directive 96/34/EC of 3 June 1996 on the framework agreement on parental leave concluded by UNICE, CEEP and the ETUC, OJ L 145, 19.6.1996, p. 4–9.

12 Council Directive 2010/18/EU of 8 March 2010 implementing the revised Framework Agreement on parental leave concluded by BUSINESSEUROPE, UEAPME, CEEP and ETUC and repealing Directive 96/34/EC, OJ L 68, 18.3.2010, p. 13–20.

The ruling in case *Roca Alvarez* (Case C-104/09, *Roca Alvarez*, ECLI:EU:C:2010:561) presented a broadened scope of the rights of carers in the context of the Spanish regulations according to which mothers with employee status were entitled to feeding breaks at work for the first nine months after birth. Fathers with employee status, in turn, were entitled to feeding breaks only if the mother of the child also had the status of a salaried employee. The Court of Justice ruled that the provisions introduced non-equal treatment based on gender of salaried mothers and salaried fathers. Significantly, the ruling emphasized that the situations of male and female employees who were also parents of young children are comparable due to the necessity of possible reduction of daily working time resulting from the necessity of provision of childcare. The decisive premise for the Court's ruling was the fact that the feeding break was not dependent upon the mother actually breastfeeding the child, and that is why it was ruled that fathers were entitled to the break, too (on condition that the child's mother also had the status of an employee). The break was therefore perceived as the time devoted to childcare and a means of reconciling family and professional life after expiry of maternity leave. This led the Court of Justice to rule that the break was intended to ensure protection of the biological condition of a woman after birth, or the protection of the special relationship between the mother and her child.

However, in its subsequent ruling *Montull* (Case, C-5/12 *Montull*, ECLI:EU:C:2013:571) concerning the corresponding Spanish provisions on the benefits compensating the loss of remuneration due to suspension of employment contracts for the duration of maternity leave, the Court did not rule there was any discrimination based on gender. The right of father-employees to receiving the benefit was dependent upon the acquisition of the right by the mother and its subsequent transfer to the father, while the rights of mother-employees were independent of the status of the child's father. It must also be noted that the Court of Justice based its ruling on its interpretation of Directive 92/85 – despite the fact that the questions of the national court did not pertain to the directive. The Court ruled that the Spanish provisions implemented the right to maternity leave despite the Spanish court's suggestion that the part of the leave (after the statutory 6 weeks) which the employed mother may transfer to the child's father may be treated as a parental leave.

The Court in its response repeated that the right to maternity leave exercised by the employed mother served, firstly, to ensure protection of the woman's biological condition during and after pregnancy, and secondly, to ensure the special relationship between the mother and her child in the post-natal period and to prevent any disturbance of the relationship resulting from accumulated, profession-related tasks. The Court also ruled that the national provisions fostered different treatment on the ground of gender, yet they did not constitute prohibited discrimination according to Article 2(3) of Directive 76/207 (currently: Article 28(1) of Directive 2006/54 concerning the equal treatment of men and women, according to which the directive does not violate the provisions protecting the rights of women, in particular as regards pregnancy and maternity). The Court indicated that the right to maternity leave served to ensure protection of the woman's biological condition during and after pregnancy, as well as ensuring the special relationship between the mother and her child in the post-natal period and preventing any disturbance thereof resulting from accumulated, profession-related tasks.

In its most recent ruling, *Maïstrellis* (Case, C-222/14 *Maïstrellis*, ECLI:EU:C:2015:473) the Court evaluated the provisions of the Greek Civil Service Code. According to these provisions, a judge who is also a father is, in general, entitled to a parental leave, but cannot avail of the leave if his wife is not employed. This pertains to all situations except the one in which the child's mother is deemed incapable of meeting the demands of upbringing due to a serious illness or disability.

The Court also reminded that Directive 96/34 granted both parents their individual right to at least three months of parental leave. The purpose of the leave is to facilitate the reconciliation of the parental and professional obligations of the employed parents, as well as encouraging men to accept an equal part of family duties. According to the Court, the national provisions constituted an example of direct discrimination on grounds of gender, as the fact of being a parent alone was not sufficient (in thc case of men) to avail them of thc leave, while the same fact was sufficient in the case of women with the same status. The Court also shared the opinion of its Advocate-General and stated that taking away the right to parental leave from the father because of his wife's professional status was by no means a measure of improving the health and safety of pregnant women and young mothers or breastfeeding mothers in the workplace. Therefore, as the Court ruled, it was not covered by Article 28(1) of Directive 2006/54 concerning equal treatment of men and women, (according to which the directive does not infringe the provisions protecting the rights of women, in particular as regards pregnancy and maternity).

The above-mentioned rulings indicate, firstly, that the nature of the status of employed fathers depends on the name of the leave and its related rights granted by the national lawmakers. If a member state interprets the national provisions as provisions that support the exercise of the right to maternity leave, then taking away individual rights from men will not constitute discrimination on the grounds of gender. What is surprising, however, is the Court's lack of a unified and consistent understanding of the aims of maternity leave or parental leave. It must be noted at this point that after the initial period of compulsory maternity leave, which indeed is aimed at facilitating the physical and mental regeneration of the mother in the post-natal period, the remaining part of the leave is mostly spent by looking after the child and creating a bond with the child. If national legislation makes it impossible for the employed woman to assign the second part of the leave to the child's father, then there is no justification for limiting the father's right to the second part of the leave as the child's mother herself does not in fact acquire the right to maternity leave. It is also important to pay attention to the protection of the right of the child to be looked after one of the parents in the initial period of its life. In contemporary European societies, more and more parents wish to equally participate in the upbringing and care of their children, so the decision as to which parent looks after the child during the first year if its life should be left to the discretion of the parents. This is particularly significant from the point of view of the demographic issues currently faced by the Union's member states.

The fact that legal provisions do not seem to catch up with the social changes is evidenced even more clearly by the following two cases: *Z* (Case, C-363/12 *Z*, ECLI:EU:C:2014:159) and *C.D.* (Case, C-167/12 *C.D.*, ECLI:EU:C:2014:169). Both cases are pending investigation by the Court of Justice. The Court will make decisions regarding the right to maternity leave in the case of the so-called surrogate mothers. In the first case, the contracting mother was the child's genetic mother. In the second case, the egg came from the surrogate mother, but it was the contracting mother who was granted full and permanent parental care over the child. In these two cases the questions from the relevant national courts focused on the contracting (employed) mother who looks after the child since its birth and her right to paid maternity leave or adoption leave – particularly if the child is being breastfed. Additionally, the national courts asked if granting the contracting mother the right to maternity leave was a case of discrimination on the grounds of gender or on the grounds of disability.

As these cases were not treated jointly in the preparation for court proceedings, two inconsistent opinions of two Advocates-General were prepared. Advocate-General Kokott in her opinion on case *C.D.* (Opinion of 26.09.2013, ECLI:EU:C:2013:6000) indicated that the fact that the structure and content of Directive 92/85 had the monist biological concept of motherhood as its point of departure should not deprive the contracting mothers of all protection. She argued that when the directive was adopted the lawmaker may have not have taken into account the situation where the female pregnant employee and the feeding female employee are actually two different persons. According to Advocate-General Kokott, the situation of a breastfeeding mother looking after the child is most definitely comparable to the situation of a breastfeeding biological mother. Moreover, the application of Directive 92/85 for mothers looking after the child, regardless of whether the mother breast-feeds the child or not, would be aligned with the protective objective of the directive as regards the relationship between the mother and her child. Moreover, the Advocate-General stated that contracting mothers should be subject to protection to an even larger extent than biological mothers as the former need to face the challenge of creating a bond between them and the child, integrating the child with the family and learning the role of the mother. On the other hand, surrogate mothers should also be protected as women who have recently given birth, which means there is a necessity to divide the period of maternity leave between the contracting mother and the surrogate mother.

On the other hand, Advocate-General Nihls Wahl in his opinion (Opinion of 26.09.2013, ECLI:EU:C:2013:604) stipulated that contracting mothers were not covered by the subject scope of Directive 92/85. In his opinion, the protection of health and safety ensured by the maternity leave is intended as a measure only designed for the women who have given birth. However, the objective of protection of the special bond between the mother and the child may be understood solely as a consequence of birth. Otherwise, the scope of protection defined by Article 8 of Directive 92/85 would also need to include mothers who have adopted a child or, in fact, any other parent who undertakes to fully look after his or her newly-born child.

The Court of Justice followed Advocate-General Wahl and his opinion in both cases. The Court underlined the fact that maternity leaves are aimed at protecting the health of the mother in the special situation of vulnerability resulting from pregnancy. Although the leave is also designed to protect the special bond between the mother and her child, this requirement refers only to the period of time immediately following pregnancy and birth. This means that an employed contracting mother is not covered by the provisions of Article 8 of Directive 92/85, even if she is also breastfeeding the child. This means that member states are not obliged to grant such employees the right to maternity leave, but the directive is not an obstacle to a possible introduction of more favourable provisions for such persons. The Court did not see any discrimination on the grounds of gender or disability in either of the cases. The conservative rulings of the Court may be justified by the lack of a common approach of member states to the issue of surrogacy and the great social sensitivity surrounding this issue. It has also been indicated that as the Union has no authority to adopt a common regulation of the problem, the decision is at the discretion of particular member states (Finck, 2015: 297-298). However, sooner or later the issue will require a systemic solution.

Discrimination on the grounds of sexual orientation as a special case

Discrimination on the grounds of sexual orientation as a special case is a topic surrounded by high social sensitivity. Consequently, the European societies and public authorities in particular member states have adopted a varied range of attitudes to one of the most crucial issues for homosexual persons i.e. official recognition of same-sex relationships. Importantly, this area has seen significant changes over the last decade and currently from the Union's 28 member states only 8 have not introduced provisions concerning civil partnerships or same-sex marriages.[13]

The EU has no authority over family law and therefore the decision to introduce (or not) provisions regarding civil partnerships or same-sex marriages is at the sole discretion of particular member states. However, differentiation of the status of homosexual persons impacts their right to the freedom of movement which is exercised by the EU's citizens and members of their families. The circle of persons regarded as family members of a freely moving citizen of the EU and therefore entitled to the right of entry and stay in the territory of the host country is defined by Directive

---

13 These countries are: Bulgaria, Greece, Lithuania, Latvia, Poland, Slovakia, Romania and Italy.

2004/38.[14] Article 2 of the directive stipulates that family members include among others: spouse and the partner with whom the Union citizen has contracted a registered partnership, on the basis of the legislation of a Member State, if the legislation of the host Member State treats registered partnerships as equivalent to marriage and in accordance with the conditions laid down in the relevant legislation of the host Member State.

According to the doctrinal view expressed in Article 2, there only exists an obligation to recognise marriages to the extent to which the host country's citizens would be recognised by their own country. This means that only those member states which have made it possible for same-sex couples to enter into marriage or civil relationships are obliged to recognise the partnerships or marriages entered into in other member states. However, in the member states where there is no form of legal recognition of same-sex relationships, persons in such relationships are treated solely as partners in accordance with the stipulations of Article 3(2b) of the Directive (Guild, 2014: 34-36 and Peers, 2014: 209).

This means that in some member states homosexual couples (both the ones in a partnership or marriage and those who have not been able to enter into a partnership or marriage due to a lack of relevant legal provisions in their countries) will be treated only as partners in the meaning of Article 3 (2) of Directive 2004/38. Consequently, they will be obliged to prove to the authorities of the host country that their relationship is permanent, which will undoubtedly result in a state of uncertainty as to whether they will be recognised as members of one family or not (see also Guth, 2011; 198). Additionally, according to ruling in case *Rahman* (Case, C-83/11 *Rahman*, ECLI:EU:C:2012:519) the status of a partner as defined by Article 3 (2) of Directive 2004/38 does not provide any significant guarantees. The Court of Justice has ruled that host countries are not obliged to accept every application for permission to enter or stay in the host country filed by family members of an EU citizen who are not covered by the notion of family member as defined by Article 2 (2) of the directive. National legislation should merely indicate the criteria enabling such persons to receive

---

14 Directive 2004/38/EC of the European Parliament and of the Council of 29 April 2004 on the right of citizens of the Union and their family members to move and reside freely within the territory of the Member States amending Regulation (EEC) No 1612/68 and repealing Directives 64/221/EEC, 68/360/EEC, 72/194/EEC, 73/148/EEC, 75/34/EEC, 75/35/EEC, 90/364/EEC, 90/365/EEC and 93/96/EEC, OJ L 158, 30.4.2004, p. 77–123.

administrative decisions following their applications for permission to enter and stay in the host country, based on a detailed analysis of their personal circumstances, whereby such decisions should contain a justification if the permission is refused. Each applicant also has the right to appeal against the decision to the relevant court.

This means that Directive 2004/38 does not protect to a sufficient extent the right to respect of family life of single-sex couples – both the couples who entered into a civil partnership and the ones who were unable to do so – and therefore may discourage such persons from exercising their right to move freely within the EU due to their uncertain status. It also seems that the current shape of Directive 2004/38 is also inconsistent with the ruling of the European Court of Human Rights in case Oliari vs. Italy (Judgement of 24.06.2015, in case no. 18766/11 and 36030/11 Oliari vs. Italy, ECLI:CE:ECHR:2015:0721JUD001876611), stipulating that Italy violated Article 8 of the European Convention on Human Rights by not guaranteeing homosexual couples the right to enter into a formal and legally protected relationship. Although it may be argued whether or not the ruling produces an obligation on all states-parties to the Convention to introduce legal regulations enabling homosexual couples to enter into a form of legally recognised relationship, the obligation to recognise that the persons who have entered into a partnership or a marriage turn into family members is the very core of the right to respect for one's family life. According to Article 52 (3) of the Charter of Fundamental Rights, the rights in the Charter, reflecting the rights guaranteed by the European Charter of Human Rights, have the same scope and relevance as the rights stipulated by the Convention. The Court of Justice ruled that the right to family life defined by Article 7 of the Charter of Fundamental Rights reflects the contents of Article 8 of the European Convention on Human Rights – ruling *McB* (Case, C-400/10 *McB*, ECLI:EU:C:2010:582) – thus the Court also confirmed the impact of the interpretation adopted by the European Court of Human Rights regarding Article 8 of the Convention on the range of rights granted by Article 7 of the Charter of Fundamental Rights. The above means that a refusal to grant permission to enter and stay for a person who has entered into a same-sex civil partnership or marriage is a case of discrimination on the grounds of sexual orientation, and a case of violation of Article 7 of the Charter of Fundamental Rights at the same time.

It may therefore be concluded that the task of effective implementation of the principle of equal treatment rests, to a large extent, on the EU's member states. This, however, does not mean that the impact of EU anti-discrimination law and policy on the real lives of citizens of EU member states is insignificant. The European Union undoubtedly has important achievements in its fight against discrimination in work and employment. However, there are also some structural problems to be observed in this area and these problems hinder or even preclude an effective realisation of the adopted anti-discrimination objectives. The most significant problem, and the problem that is impossible to eliminate at the same time, is clearly the diversified level of social development and cultural as well as historical experience of particular member states, which often results in fundamental differences in their approach to issues surrounding equal treatment in EU member states. The consequence is the impossibility of reaching a consensus and adopting common and binding legal regulations. The necessity of reaching a consensus also delays amendments to the existing regulations which could be a response to the rapidly advancing social change. It seems, however, that the most destructive element for the trust of individuals and NGOs to EU institutions and the idea of integration is the problem of the lack of engagement in the implementation of already existing legislation or strategies. This casts a significant doubt over the effectiveness of the EU's anti-discrimination policy, and is therefore the largest threat for the idea of good governance in the context of the European Union's anti-discrimination law and policy.

References

Boeri T., Patacchini E., Peri G. (2015), 'Unexplored Dimensions of Discrimination', Oxford: Oxford University Press.

Ellis E., Watson P. (2012), 'EU Antidiscrimination Law', Oxford: Oxford University Press.

Finck M., Kas B. (2015), 'Surrogacy leave as a matter of EU law: CD and Z', *Common Market Law Review*, 52: 281-298.

Guild, E. Peers S., Tomkin J. (2014), 'The EU Citizenship Directive. A Commentary', Oxford: Oxford University Press.

Guth J. (2011), 'When is a Partner not a Partner? Conceptualisation of 'family' in EU Free Movement Law', *Journal of Social Welfare and Family Law* 2: 193-204.

Maliszewska-Nienartowicz J. (2013), 'Ochrona kobiet w związku z ciążą i macierzyństwem w świetle wybranych orzeczeń Trybunału Sprawiedliwości', *Europejski Przegląd Sądowy*, 3: 31-39.

Peers S., Hervey T., Kenner J., Ward A. (eds.) (2014), 'The EU Charter of Fundamental Rights. A commentary', Oxford: Oxford University Press,.

Schiek D., Chege V. (eds) (2009). 'European Union Non-discrimination Law. Comparative Perspectives on Multidimensional Equality Law', Abington: Routledge-Cavendish.

Schiek D., Lawson A. (2011), 'European Union Non-discrimination Law and Intersectionality', Farnham: Ashgate.

Smolin M. (2013), 'Zasada równości płci. Studium komparatystyczne standardów Rady Europy i Unii Europejskiej', Warszawa: Instytut Wydawniczy EuroPrawo.

Ventegodt Liisberg M. (2011), 'Disability and employment', Cambridge: Intersentia.

Zawidzka-Łojek, A. Szczerba-Zawada A. (eds) (2015) 'Prawo antydyskryminacyjne Unii Europejskiej', Warszawa: Instytut Wydawniczy EuroPrawo.

Chapter 3: The high level of security

Anna Kańciak

Key words: European Union, security, threats, Area of Freedom, Security and Justice, level of security

Introduction

The level of security and the question as to whether it is possible to ensure security in Europe after the events of 2015 have become the main interest of EU institutions and bodies as well as the decision-makers and law enforcement authorities of member states. The growing risk of terrorism resulting from the activities of the so called Islamic State, terrorist attacks in Paris in November 2015, the influx of migrants from Asia and Africa to Europe as well as the crisis in the East following Russia's military intervention in Ukraine have again sparked a debate on the level of security of the European Union as well as the means and measures for ensuring security.

Europol's analyses conducted in 2015, which were presented in an interim threat assessment regarding serious and organised crime in Europe (SOCTA)[1] and a terrorism threat assessment,[2] indicate that these two phenomena remain significant threats to the security of the European Union. The aim of Europol's annual threat assessments is not to capture the current situation but only to present the risk of specific threats. They are a way to bring the issues to the notice of EU decision-makers rather than to serve as a basis for taking the necessary countermeasures. What has become more valuable are the regular weekly reports of Europol and Frontex

---

1 Interim SOCTA 2015: an update on serious and organised crime in the EU, http://www.statewatch.org/news/2015/mar/eu-europol-interim-SOCTA-7271-15.pdf (accessed: 6.1.2016).

2 The EU Terrorism Situation and Trend Report (TE-SAT), European Police Office 2015, https://www.europol.europa.eu/latest_publications/37 (accessed: 6.1.2016).

on the main migratory routes, the numbers of migrants, their origin and the resulting threats.

As illegal migration, organised crime and terrorism are interrelated, addressing each of these phenomena separately would have a negative impact on the development of mechanisms ensuring security in the EU. On the other hand, the urgency, extent and significant consequences of the problem make it impossible to adopt a complex approach. As a result, the EU departs from general assessments and endeavours to take more specific measures by drawing up thematic strategies and action plans. EU initiatives concerning various threats and the problems they trigger are becoming increasingly targeted.

Each of the documents the EU devises and the mechanisms it implements contribute to raising the effectiveness of the EU's action as regards ensuring the safety of its citizens. In the context of the reflection on a high level of security the following questions seem rudimentary: What is the EU's task concerning security? What is its potential for action in this area? How does it deliver on its commitments? The assessment of good governance in terms of the ensuring of security by EU decision-makers should be preceded by an explanation of what security and a high level of security mean.

Good governance is a constituent part of the political system of the European Union. It is the basic instrument for stabilising and stimulating the society and refers to procedures regarding decision-making and developing regulations (Ruszkowski, 2015: 257). The model of European governance was presented by the Commission in 2001 in a White Paper on European governance,[3] which points to the accountability, coherence, efficiency and effectiveness of the powers exercised at European level. Due to Treaty provisions and the exclusive competence of member states in the area of breaches of public security on their territory, not all the indicators of the overall governance model can be applied to the Area of Freedom, Security and Justice (hereafter: the AFSJ) (Case 41/74, *Yvonne van Duyn v Home Office,* ECLI:EU:C:1974:133).

The assessment of the examples and effects of good governance in the EU within the AFSJ should be divided into two stages. During the first stage, reference should be made to theoretical considerations, including the clarification of the basic concepts, legal bases and strategic objectives,

3 European Governance – A White Paper, COM (2001) 428, 25.7.2001.

which will be presented in this chapter. The second stage is the assessment of practical solutions and soft-law instruments.[4]

The framework of this study does not allow for a multidimensional analysis of all the issues related to security, including a number of practices of a legal nature at central, state, local, supranational and international level. This chapter will focus on the first dimension, i.e. the concept of security in the EU, the concept of a "high level of security" and the Treaty bases for ensuring a high level of security in the European Union in the context of good governance.

Security concepts

According to Zenon Trejnis, security is a complex and multidimensional category subject to changes in time and space, which systematically expands with human development to include new challenges and threats as well as new means and methods of eliminating them (Trejnis, 2011: 18). Security is also perceived as a basic human need for peace and confidence, which can only be enjoyed if there is no feeling of insecurity (Czaputowicz, 2012: 22). Definitions of security found in the literature explicitly stress the anthropocentric nature of this phenomenon, describing it as a need individuals, social structures and states have (Turczyński, 2010: 15). In view of a large number of definitions, in this study the most general understanding of security is adopted: the entity's feeling of certainty concerning its existence, survival, possession, functioning and development (Zięba, 2012: 8).

Security policy at national and international level requires a solid legal basis, an institutional system and expertise. Existing publications in the area of international law, political science and international relations referring to European security or security in the European Union in the title do not seek to explain this concept.[5] Furthermore, these terms are often used interchangeably. I support the thesis that diverging definitions of this term

4 More: chapter 4 part III.

5 Example: Wrzosek, M. (2013) *Współczesne zagrożenia w obszarze bezpieczeństwa europejskiego*, Warszawa. Wawrzyk, P. (2012) *Bezpieczeństwo wewnętrzne Unii Europejskiej*, Warszawa. Aleksandrowicz, T. R. (2011) *Bezpieczeństwo w unii Europejskiej*, Warszawa. Mierzejewski, D. J. (2011) *Bezpieczeństwo europejskie w warunkach przemian globalizacyjnych*, Toruń.

result from the fact that representatives of individual fields of science perceive and describe security in the light of knowledge and terminology in their particular field (Cieślarczyk,2009: 9).

On the other hand, the plurality of views and opinions facilitates the understanding of security at the level of the European Union in relation to the interpretation of the relevant Treaty provisions.

In the Treaty on the Functioning of the European Union (hereafter: the TFEU),[6] the notion of security is referred to in Article 2(4) of Title I in the context of the EU's competence to define and implement a common foreign and security policy (hereafter: the CFSP). The next reference to security is made in Article 4(2) TFEU on shared competence. This article refers to an area of freedom, security and justice, which is another field alongside the CFSP (Miąsik, 2012: 105-106).

As one of the three components of the AFSJ, an area of security must be interpreted taking into account the issues covered by provisions, i.e. border control, asylum and migration, judicial cooperation in civil matters and judicial cooperation in criminal matters. At this stage, this leaves no doubt as to the internal dimension of security. The next provision on security is Article 67(3) TFEU, which requires the Union to endeavour to ensure a high level of security. However, the types and dimensions of security are not indicated explicitly. Researchers claim that it covers the security of individuals (Bazzocchii, 2011: 194); however, it must be interpreted in the context of the framework set by Article 67, taking account of Article 72 TFEU, where the concept of internal security is reflected. This article is of vital importance in the context of the reflection on security as it introduces the so-called law and order and internal security clause. Under the clause, the areas of internal security and law and order are the responsibility of member states.

Some claim (Case C-100/01, *Oteiza Olazabala* ECLI:EU:C:2002:712 and the opinion of Advocante General Tizzano to this case, ECLI:EU:C:2002:266) that the terms included in the above clause should be merged into one notion of public order and security. However, combining them with the adjective "public" may lead to confusing the security of the AFSJ with public security addressed in the context of internal market freedoms (e.g. Articles 36, 45, 52, 202 TFEU). This can be justified by the EU ob-

6 Treaty on European Union and the Treaty on the Functioning of the European Union Official Journal OJ C 326, 26.10.2012, p. 47–390.

jectives set in Article 3 TEU, which guarantee the free movement of persons in an area of freedom, security and justice without internal frontiers. Yet, the context, wording and different purposes of individual provisions do not allow the establishing of a direct link between these articles and consider them as the same (Miąsik, 2012: 695).

The Court of Justice took a position on the meaning of the concept of "public order and security" by determining the extent of individual words. In its judgement in the Tsakouridis case, (Case C-145/09, *Panagiotis Tsakouridis*, ECLI:EU:C:2010:708) it found that public security refers to both internal and external security of a member state (Case C-145/09, paragraph 43). Hence, public security, a term broader than internal security, covers both the internal situation of a member state and its external security.[7]

Advocate General Yves Bot addressed this issue in a more comprehensive manner (Opinion of Advocate General Bot, Case C-145/09, ECLI:EU:C:2010:322). In his opinion, he referred to the fact that there is not much case-law of the CJEU concerning security. He stressed that the Court of Justice had never clarified the meaning of the term. Reference was also made to the statement of the CJEU that this notion covers both the internal and external dimensions of security. The Advocate General clarifies that external security refers to the security of a member state in its relations with other countries. Internal security is more difficult to define and poses the question regarding its relation to the notion of public order. A position by the Court on the cases of Oteiza Olazabal (Case C-100/01, *Oteiza Olazabala* ECLI:EU:C:2002:712) and Johnston (Case 222/84, *Marguerite Johnston,* ECLI: EU:C:1986:206) indicates, however, that creating exhaustive definitions for both terms is very difficult and, what is more, artificial (Case C-145/09, paragraph 68).

The dimensions of security become more clear if we refer to the distinction between *purely internal (national) affairs* and the *EU affairs* made with respect to internal market freedoms (Storskrubb, 2014: 208-209). Applying this distinction to the issue under consideration, *purely internal security* would cover situations where it is impossible to use EU protection

7 Appealing to the judicial decision of the Court of Justice of the EU the position of the Court should be referred according to which the public security can to be disturbed not only by the threat to functioning of main institutions and the public service, but also disturbing foreign relationships or the peaceful coexistence of nations. More: Miąsik, D., Półtorak, N., Wróbel, A. *Traktat o funkcjonowaniu...696.*

mechanisms or where the situation of a given state is outside the scope of the Treaties on which the EU is founded, for example if a state resorts to opt-out (Martenczuk, 2008: 522-523). In turn, "EU security" has a cross-border component as it refers to the protection of the interests of more than one member state. While it may seem a novelty to apply the distinction made in the context of internal market freedoms to describe security as internal security, the concept of EU security could be applied and could give rise to a new line of research and analyses of the security of the European Union.

To pursue the deliberations on the concept of security referred to in Title V of the TFEU it is important to determine its scope. In this area, there are EU documents that complement the Treaties and allow the understanding of different components of security. At the same time, as soft-law instruments, they do not have legally binding force. The first of them is the European Security Strategy (ESS)[8] adopted years before the entry into force of the Treaty of Lisbon. It provides for a clarification of the terms used by the EU legislator in the TFEU. The strategy takes a broad approach to security, taking into account sources of conflicts in the world as well as their relevance for the EU's foreign policy. Furthermore, it addresses threats to the EU, both internal and external. This is expressed explicitly in the objective of the ESS, which is to advance the EU's security interest.[9]

The second document is the EU Internal Security Strategy in Action,[10] which addresses the internal dimension of security only. The strategy provides for a European internal security model and covers all the areas of the AFSJ. This counterbalances the opinion of legal scholars, who adopt a broad approach to the Treaty notion of "security" (Article 67 TFEU).

Besides the notions of security referred to in Article 67 TFEU, internal security (Article 72) and public security (Article 36 and others), there is a notion of national security. Article 73 TFEU presents yet another meaning

---

8 European Security Strategy, Brussels, 12 December 2003, http://www.consilium.europa.eu/uedocs/cmsUpload/78367.pdf (accessed: 6.1.2016).

9 Ibidem, 10.

10 Communication from the Commission to the European Parliament and the Council The EU Internal Security Strategy in Action: Five steps towards a more secure Europe, Brussels 22.11.2010, COM(2010) 673 final.

of security which has to be read in the light of Article 4(2) TEU[11] regarding the exclusive competence of member states in the field of maintaining law and order and safeguarding national security.[12]

In the literature, national security is defined as one of "the basic functions of each state, involving addressing threats, both external and internal ones, to the functioning and development of the nation and state" (Miąsik, 2012: 699). It must take into account both external and internal factors comprising, inter alia, the geographical, historical, demographic, economic and sociological context (Łebkowska, 2011: 45-48). Under this approach, external security is taken account of as well, which makes the scope of security wider.

Such a broad interpretation of national security under Article 73 TFEU in the context of the scope of Title V of the TFEU on the AFSJ seems wrong and could lead to the conclusion these provisions are inconsistent or even illogical. Hence, if cooperation in the fields of justice and home affairs was to take into account, to the same extent as foreign policy, it would be pointless to create the AFSJ along with its institutional and legislative framework.

It is difficult to agree with the statement that all the provisions under Title V of the TFEU refer to the security of both an individual and the entire EU, considering all its aspects – both the external and internal, particularly in the context of practical actions of the relevant bodies in the field of justice and home affairs, but also from a theoretical perspective. To claim that the EU legislator wanted to include the elements of the AFSJ as well as foreign and security policy under Title V of the TFEU would undermine the concept of separating these areas, both in primary and derived law. Furthermore, this would blur the differences between the EU home and foreign affairs.

In conclusion, the scope of Articles 72 and 73 TFEU and the fact that they need to remain compatible with the objectives of the part of the Treaty in question, suggest that they both refer to the security of member states, though using different adjectives. Moreover, in order to ensure consistency of the Treaties, internal and national security should be treated as one and the same concept. Hence, the external component should be governed by the rules on the CFSP.

---

11 Consolidated versions of the Treaty on European Union, OJ C 326, 26.10.2012, p. 1–390.

12 Art. 4.2 TEU.

In light of Treaty obligations, the concept of "EU security" or "Union security" is correct and can be considered as justified by many of the Union's activities. It would also not be a mistake to add the adjective internal/external in order to reduce the scope of the term, which is supported by both documents on security and the practical objective of differentiating between its dimensions. The tendency to use the term "EU internal security" can be seen as a consequence of constant referring to the pre-Lisbon division between the external (II) and internal (III) pillar (Wawrzyk, 2012: 67,140). Yet, going back to this division would not fully deliver on the targets set by the EU legislator with respect to the Union's internal security policy (Wolf 2012: 63).

A high level of security

Article 67(3) of the Treaty on the Functioning of the European Union refers to different levels of security. The EU legislator required the Union to ensure a high level of security. This implies that entities can be more or less secure. Ensuring a high level of security is of vital importance for states and their citizens as it is essential for pursuing other goals and priorities, such as survival, territorial integrity, political independence and quality of life (Czaputowicz, 2012: 23).

The fact that there can be different levels of security results from the nature of this term. It is possible to define heterogeneous notions by pointing to their permanent features. In the case of security, its multidimensionality should be taken into account, in the context of different areas of life and entities, the relation with the environment, real and potential threats as well as their type, source, scope and duration (Stefański, 2013: 61). On this basis, a security paradigm is created which is subject to changes, including globalisation processes, as a result of which a transition takes place from the level of force to threats that are not related to the military aspect (Rosicki, 2010: 31). The only permanent components of security are: features of internal security (described on the basis of processes, phenomena and events taking place), dimensions of international security (global, regional, sub-regional and local), features of entities of security[13]

13 Entities of security – every entity acting on purpose (individual or collective), considered from a point of view of his security. With reference to the considered security from the political perspective the basis types of entities of security are states,

(subjective, objective, processual) as well as criteria determining the functioning and development of an entity of security (challenges, threats and opportunities) (Stefański, 2013: 61-62).

The implementation of a certain paradigm is related to identifying a specific level of security and the methods of achieving it. Article 67(3) TFEU provides for four types of methods for achieving a high level of security:

- measures preventing and combating crime, racism and xenophobia;
- measures for coordination and cooperation between police and judicial authorities and other competent authorities;
- mutual recognition of judgments in criminal matters;
- approximation of criminal laws.

This article does not constitute an independent legal basis for secondary legislation or actions taken by member states (Miąsik, 2012: 1021). It is the subsequent chapters of Title V of the TFEU that specify the extent to which the EU may adopt measures to promote a high level of security.

Ensuring a high level of security is one of the main objectives of the AFSJ (Bosse, 2012: 84); however, the TFEU does not clarify what this expression means and how it can be measured. In the Treaty, the EU legislator often uses the concept of a "high level". For instance, it can be found in Article 9 TFEU, according to which the EU shall take into account the requirements linked to the promotion of a high level of employment and education in the context of the protection of social goods. Article 114(3) TFEU takes a high level of protection as a base for health, safety, environmental and consumer protection in the approximation of EU legislation. The concept of a high level is also referred to in Article 148 TFEU in the context of increasing employment. The above mentioned provisions are not related to security in terms of protection of an individual, a state or the EU. Article 114(3) mentioned above also does not concern security understood as public security (Article 36 TFEU, Article 52 TFEU), but only the technical security of products, services and economic activity. Further-

---

organizational units of states and international organizations, as well as non-national structures. According to: National Security Bureau, The Dictionary of National Security Bureau: proposals od new terms from the field of security, https://www.bbn.gov.pl/pl/bezpieczenstwo-narodowe/minislownik-bbn-propozy/6035,MINISLOWNIK-BBN-Propozycje-nowych-terminow-z-dziedziny-bezpieczenstwa.html (accessed: 18.3.2016).

more, Article 114(3) provides for the concept of a high level in relation to ensuring the adequate quality of the EU rules adopted and improving the quality of the legislation developed. This does not mean that, when drawing up legislation, the Commission should act in support of implementing the highest standards in particular areas, which influence the establishment and functioning of the internal market, but rather to prevent a significant reduction of the level of protection and the quality of life. Similarly, ensuring a high level of employment should be understood as an obligation to maintain a low level of unemployment.

More precise information on the meaning of a "high level" is provided by the Commission in soft-law instruments, which specify how the concept of a high level is to be construed for particular areas. One example is the Commission Communication on the application of the Unfair Commercial Practices Directive Achieving a high level of consumer protection Building trust in Internal Market.[14] In the context of unfair commercial practices, the Directive ensures that consumers are not misled and exposed to aggressive marketing practices and that the information provided by EU entrepreneurs is understandable, correct and justified. This allows consumers to make informed and rational choices. Contrary to the provisions of the TFEU, which contain no quantifiers that would lead to the conclusion that a high level of security has been reached, in the Directive the Commission indicated specific aspects to be assessed.

A "high level" has been clarified by the Commission in a Communication on critical information infrastructure protection "Protecting Europe from large scale cyber-attacks and disruptions: enhancing preparedness, security and resilience."[15] There, a "high level of security" is seen as a factor shaping the trust of users of information technology systems. The level of security is influenced by the following factors: diversity, openness, interoperability, usability, transparency, accountability, auditability of different components and competition. Taking action in order to ensure

---

14 Communication from the Commission to the European Parliament, the Council and the European Economic and Social Committee On the application of the Unfair Commercial Practices Directive Achieving a high level of consumer protection Building trust in the Internal Market, COM (2013) 138 final.

15 Communication from the Commission to the European Parliament, the Council, the European Economic and Social Committee and the Committee of the Regions on Critical Information Infrastructure Protection - "Protecting Europe from large scale cyber-attacks and disruptions: enhancing preparedness, security and resilience, COM(2009) 149 final.

that these conditions are met is a measurable process aimed at achieving higher levels of system security.

It is also the term "level" that makes it very difficult to clarify a high level of security and to verify whether it has been reached under the provisions of the Treaties. In the literature, there are diverging interpretations of the meaning of this term in the context of security. Michał Brzeziński distinguishes three levels of security, i.e. security of an international system, a state and an individual / the society (Brzeziński, 2013: 6). This is consistent with the view that there are three levels of security: individual, national and international (Trejnis, 2011: 5). A broader approach provides for a local, sub-regional, supra-regional and global level (Sekściński, 2013: 50). The term "level" appears also with respect to the internal and external aspect of security (Rosicki, 2010: 31). However, the context implies that the diversity of meaning of this term may result from the semantic layer of the notion rather than the willingness to introduce different levels of security.

The above considerations constitute a proof that there are divergent interpretations of this term in the literature. The above views distinguishing between different levels of security with respect to states, citizens and international organisations are related to the personal and material conceptual scope of security. This supports the view that the nature of security is disputed and multidimensional (Miszalskiet al., 2011: 5).

For future reflections, a provisional and general definition of security should be adopted in order to clarify the concept of a "high level". In the literature, it is held that:

- security is the freedom of entities – individuals, social groups, states and organisations – from threats to their fundamental values (Trejnis, 2011: 5); and
- a state opposite to threats, a synonym of the lack of threats, protection from threats as well as confidence resulting from the lack of threats and (or) effective actions aimed at preventing or eliminating them (Zięba, 2012: 7).

The above position indicates that the definition of security is created in a negative way, in close connection with the existence of threats and their nature. The concept of a "high level of security" may be clarified by analogy by basing the definition on the gradation of the level of threats.

Therefore, it is appropriate to refer to standard security measures and alert states as regards operational procedures for the management of crisis situations. The system of security specified in the Commission Decision[16] encompasses standard security measures and three alert states corresponding to the existing threat. The standard security measures and the alert states, from level one to level four, corresponding to increasing threat levels, are identified by the colour codes 'WHITE', 'YELLOW', 'ORANGE' and 'RED'.

Assuming that security is equivalent to the lack of threats, it shall be presumed that the category of a "high level of security" means a low level of threat. In the security system of the Commission, it corresponds to the 'WHITE' code, i.e. when no particular security threat has been identified. In this case, the standard security measures are applicable. They indicate a normal security situation and provide for a minimum acceptable level of security. In other words, they are the basic security measures.[17]

The level of security is a certain state of security measured in objective terms,[18] which, as has been determined, requires certain security measures. Therefore, one should refer to the degrees of risk that a threat will emerge. The gradation and measurability of security levels is related to the influence of factors determining the level of security. In the literature, a distinction is made between external and internal factors (Ciekanowski, 2011: 25). The most important external security factors include:

- relationships with neighbouring countries;
- presence and position in Euro-Atlantic structures;
- legislative and legal situation stabilising European security as new political, economic, military and civilisation challenges emerge.

Internal security factors include mostly political, economic and social aspects, which can be of both a creative and a destructive nature. If the latter is the case, they not only dampen the state's capacity but also increase its vulnerability to external pressures (Grosset, 2010).

Combining the meaning of the notion of security and the concept of a "high level of security", as referred to by the EU legislator in the Treaty,

16 Commission Decision of 15 December 2006 establishing the Commission's standard security measures and alert states and amending its Rules of Procedure as regards operational procedures for management of crisis situations, OJ L 32, 6.2.2007, p. 144–160.

17 Appendix 1 to the Decision 2007/65/EC Security alerts states in the Commission.

18 http://encyklopedia.naukowy.pl/Bezpiecze%C5%84stwo_wewn%C4%99trzne# (accessed: 7.1.2016).

increases the understanding of the European security model proposed by the Commission.[19] This initiative, which was developed in 2010 during the Spanish presidency, consists of common tools and a commitment to:

- recognise the relationship between security, freedom and privacy;
- improve cooperation and solidarity between member states;
- involve all of the EU's institutions;
- address the causes of insecurity (and not just the effects);
- enhance prevention and anticipation;
- involve, as far as they are concerned, all sectors which have a role to play in public protection – political, economic and social;
- recognise a greater interdependence between internal and external security.

The notion of a "level" as per the Treaty may not be analysed in isolation from the remaining words of the concept of a "high level of security" and the scope of Title V of the TFEU. For the implementation of the EU's objective specified in Article 67(3) TFEU, the European security model is based on principles and values of the EU, i.e. respect for human rights and fundamental freedoms, the rule of law, democracy, dialogue, tolerance, transparency and solidarity.

The EU's role as regards ensuring a high level of security relies in developing joint political strategies and legal bases as well as supporting practical collaboration in areas such as police and judicial cooperation, border management and crisis management. The actions taken by the EU in pursuit of the objective of Article 67(3) TFEU consists of reducing the level of threat by adopting a series of measures related to, among other things, combating crime, illegal trade and terrorism, protection of critical infrastructure, enhancing security by better border management, improving cyber-security, better crisis management, improving system interoperability, enhancing external policy, including prevention of conflicts and peace building efforts.

The European security model developed in 2010 was to contribute to the creation of an area of freedom, security and justice. A wide range of activities were to respond to the challenges regarding the protection of rights and freedoms, deepening cooperation and solidarity between mem-

---

19 Draft Internal Security Strategy for the European Union: "Towards a European Security Model", 7120/10.

ber states, addressing the causes of insecurity (and not just the effects), preventing threats and anticipating attacks, involving all sectors (political, economic, social, etc.) and recognising the interdependence between internal and external security in establishing a "global security" approach with third countries.

Summary

Discrepancies in the meaning of a high level of security make it more difficult to judge whether the European Union carries out its work properly in compliance with the Treaty. Before forming an opinion on this subject, several elements should be verified. First of all, the meaning and context of the notion of "security" should be interpreted. The programming nature of Art. 67(3) TFEU supports the adoption of a broad definition, without narrowing security down to the external and internal or EU and national dimension. A general definition of this term, as the most adequate one, allows clarifying the meaning of the concept of a "high level of security", which has not been clarified so far in EU legislation and the literature.

The lack of a definition and the application of the notion of a "high level" in different contexts and in relation to numerous areas justifies the adoption of a negative definition. Defining security by reference to the lack of threats allows the explaining of both what a high level of security means and what factors may have impact on achieving it.

Implementing good governance in the context of a high level of security will face difficulties resulting from the interpretation of Article 67(3) TFEU. The exclusive competence of member states (Article 4(2) TEU) as regards national security and the decisions taken by national authorities in order to ensure it will have a significant impact on the effectiveness of security at EU level. On the other hand, the EU exercises its powers as regards shaping the AFSJ (Article 4(2) TFEU) by taking necessary measures, mainly under Chapter 4 and 5 of Title V of the TFEU.

Evaluation of the effectiveness of the EU actions in light of the developments in 2015 indicates that a satisfactory level of security under the AFSJ has not yet been reached. In keeping with the adopted definition, a high level of insecurity in the EU means that the level of security is low. In light of the Treaty, at the first stage of theoretical considerations it should be considered that the idea of good governance is not being implemented. Yet, it would be a mistake to adopt an unequivocal position and criticise the EU. Evaluation of whether the EU "endeavours" to ensure a high level of security must take into account the scope, effectiveness and appropriateness of the initiatives undertaken to enhance security, as described more fully in Chapter 4, Part III.

References

Aleksandrowicz, T. R. (2011), 'Bezpieczeństwo w Unii Europejskiej', Warszawa: Difin.

Mierzejewski, D. J. (2011), 'Bezpieczeństwo europejskie w warunkach przemian globalizacyjnych', Toruń: Wydawnictwo Adam Marszałek.

Bazzocchi, V. (2011), 'The European Charter of Fundamental Rights and the Area of Freedom, Security and Justice' in: Federico, G. Di (ed), *The EU Charter of Fundamental Rights: From Declaration to Binding Instrument*, Netherlands: Springer: 194.

Bosse, G. (2012), 'From "Villains" to the new Guardians of Security in Europe? Paradigm shift in EU Foreign Policy towards Libya and Belarus' in: Kaunert, Ch. Léonard, S. (eds), *European Security Governance and the European Neighborhood after the Lisbon Treaty,* London: Routledge: 84.

Brzeziński, M. (2013), 'Bezpieczeństwo społeczne z perspektywy bezpieczeństwa wewnętrznego', *Zeszyty Naukowe WSOWL*, 3 (169): 5-18.

Ciekanowski, Z. (2011), 'Wpływ czynników warunkujących poziom bezpieczeństwa państwa', Prace Naukowe Akademii im. Jana Długosza w Częstochowie, Seria: Res Politicae, vol. IV: 25.

Cieślarczyk, M. (2009), 'Teoretyczne i metodologiczne podstawy badania problemów bezpieczeństwa i obronności państwa', Siedlce: Uniwersytet Przyrodniczo-Humanistyczny w Siedlcach: 9.

Czaputowicz, J. (2012), 'Bezpieczeństwo międzynarodowe. Współczesne koncepcje', Warszawa: PWN: 22-23.

Grosset, R. (2010), 'Czynniki kształtujące poziom bezpieczeństwa państwa, Organizacja i zarządzanie strategiczne', *CNBOP-PIB: Kwartalnik,* 3: 9-16.

Łebkowska, J. (2011), 'Bezpieczeństwo – teoretyczny wymiar ponadczasowej wartości', *Przegląd Strategiczny*, 1: 37-50.

Martenczuk, B. (2008), 'Variable geometry and the external relations of the EU: The Experience of Justice and Home Affairs' in: Martenczuk, B. Thiel van, S. (eds.), *Justice, Liberty, Security: New Challenges for EU External Relations,* Brussels: ASP - Academic & Scientific Publishers: 522-523.

Miszalski, W. Trejnis, Z. Popiel, H. Jagusiak, B. (2011), 'Studia Bezpieczeństwa Narodowego w Wojskowej Akademii Technicznej' in: Jagusiak, B. (ed.), *Studia bezpieczeństwa narodowego,* Warszawa: WAT: 5.

Rosicki, R. (2010), 'O pojęciu i istocie bezpieczeństwa', Poznań. http://wnpid.amu.edu.pl/images/dokumenty/bibliografie_pracownikow/Remigiusz_Rosicki/R_Rosicki_O_pojeciu_i_istocie_bezpieczenstwa.pdf (accessed: 6.1.2016)

Ruszkowski, J. (2010), 'Ponadnarodowość w systemie politycznym Unii Europejskiej', Warszawa: Wolters Kluwer: 257.

Sekściński, A. (2013), 'Bezpieczeństwo w ujęciu teoretycznym. Geneza i współczesne rozumienie w naukach politycznych', *e-politykon,* 11: 42- 79.

Stefański, M. (2013), 'Kształtowanie bezpieczeństwa publicznego jako priorytet funkcjonowania państwa; in: Urbanek, A. (ed.), *Wybrane problemy bezpieczeństwa. Dziedziny bezpieczeństwa*, Słupsk: Wydawnictwo Społeczno-Prawne: 61.

Storskrubb, E. (2014), 'Civil justice: the contested nature of the scope of EU' in: Ripoll Servent, A. Trauner, F. (eds.), *Policy change in the Area of Freedom, Security and Justice: How EU institutions matter*, London: Routledge: 208-209.

Trejnis, Z. (2011), 'Nauki o bezpieczeństwie nową dyscypliną w dziedzinie nauk społecznych?' in: Jagusiak, B. (ed.), *Studia bezpieczeństwa narodowego*, Warszawa: WAT: 5,18.

Turczyński, P. (2010), 'Bezpieczeństwo europejskie', Wrocław: ATLA2: 15.

Wawrzyk, P. (2012), 'Bezpieczeństwo Wewnętrzne Unii Europejskiej', Warszawa: Oficyna Wydawnicza Łośgraf: 67,140.

Wolff, S. (2012), 'The new EU's Internal Security Architecture Implementation Challenges' in: Larsen, F. (ed.), *The Lisbon Treaty: Institutional Choices and Implementation,* Farnham: Ashgate: 63.

Wrzosek, M. (2013), 'Współczesne zagrożenia w obszarze bezpieczeństwa europejskiego', Warszawa: Wydawnictwo Menedżerskie PTM.

Zięba, R. (2012), 'O tożsamości nauk o bezpieczeństwie', *Zeszyty Naukowe AON*, 1(86): 7-22.

Websites

http://www.statewatch.org/news/2015/mar/eu-europol-interim-SOCTA-7271-15.pdf (accessed: 6.1.2016).

https://www.europol.europa.eu/latest_publications/37 (accessed: 6.1.2016).

http://encyklopedia.naukowy.pl/Bezpiecze%C5%84stwo_wewn%C4%99trzne# (accessed: 7.1.2016)

http://www.consilium.europa.eu/uedocs/cmsUpload/78367.pdf (accessed: 6.1.2016).

Chapter 4: Development of information society services

Anna Kańciak

Kay words: information society, online services, electronic commerce, digitalisation

Introduction

In order to evaluate the quality, effectiveness, efficiency, cohesion, engagement and openness of EU actions taken to foster the emergence and development of information society services it is necessary to provide at least a general characteristic of the elements in this field, i.e. the development of information and communication technology systems as well as changes in the functioning of the internal market and the EU society. A factor that generates the process of transformation from traditional to electronic forms is the ongoing digitalisation that takes place as technology develops. It has led to the emergence of a digital single market, information society and online services. These three issues, which are interrelated, will be discussed in this chapter in the context of the evaluation of good governance in the European Union.

The effects of information and communication technology (ICT) systems can be seen in a change of the form and functioning of information, which is one of the fundamental resources of society of the 21st century (Mendes et al., 2004: xi). Information is a public good which is of interest to three groups of entities, i.e. governments, the private sector and private persons. Generating, distributing and using information should be a two-way process that allows both accessing it easily and using it in a productive way. This means that citizens are informed about the services available to them and instructed how to use them. Such a system requires a change to the citizen-oriented public sector and the creation of a sociocentric management model. Ensuring the comprehensive and continuous accessibility of public sector services is possible thanks to information and communication technology systems and the dissemination of digital information. The growing use of ICT systems has made them an intrinsic part of citizens' daily life. At the same time, online services have become a key factor for stimulating the development of Europe's economy and society.[1]

The last few decades have seen the process of social adaptation of information technologies to specific areas of the life of Europeans, contributing to the creation of a new, digitalised form of society. Its innovative nature results from a combination of two elements. The first one is information and communication technology systems mentioned above as well as their use in order to communicate and fulfil social roles by every individual at every stage of the socialisation process. Another element, closely related to the first one, is an increase in the number of citizens, directly proportional to the qualitative level of their skills and knowledge concerning the use of digital forms of services. The combination of these two factors results in social events moving in time and space at a fast pace, which is seen as one of many signs of globalisation (Wegner-Kowalska, 2013: 28). Changes related to high-speed data and information transfer are possible due to technical progress and modern technologies. This has contributed to the creation of a new standard of information exchange across international and cultural borders.

According to the European Parliament, the use of information and communication technologies by the public sector constitutes a fundamental basis for the development of a digital society,[2] which is directly related to states' economic and social progress. One element of this process is the creation of an area without internal borders, both in the context of the implementation of the free movement of goods, the freedom to provide services and the freedom of establishment and in the context of eliminating legal and technological barriers in the cyberspace. The growth of e-commerce and better access to online services have allowed for a transition from traditional economy mechanisms to a digital single market. Indispensable elements in the creation of this market are broadband networks and the Internet, which generate changes in social and economic fields (Pietrzak, 2013: 95). Better access to knowledge and services for the pub-

1 Communication from the Commission to the European Parliament, the Council, the European Economic and Social Committee and the Committee of the Regions on Critical Information Infrastructure Protection - "Protecting Europe from large scale cyber-attacks and disruptions: enhancing preparedness, security and resilience", COM(2009)149.

2 European Parliament resolution of 11 December 2012 on completing the Digital Single Market (2012/2030(INI)), OJ C 434/2, 23.12.2015, 25.

lic and private sectors contributes to the creation of an innovative society functioning on the basis of the mechanisms of competition, which in turn boosts e-commerce and the development of online services.

The above confirms a close link between the digitalisation of the citizens' life and the level of sophistication and functionality of ICT systems. Consequently, the development of the infrastructure of information and communication technologies influences social cohesion, economic growth and the competitiveness of the EU itself.

Evaluation of the implementation of good governance principles in the area under consideration will mostly refer to the services based on the ideas of information society and e-commerce.

The idea of information society

The idea of information society became widespread in Europe in 1994 after the publication of the so-called Bangemann Report[3] entitled "Europe and the Global Information Society." It contains recommendations of the High Level Group on Information Society for the European Council. According to Bangemann, information society has the potential to improve the quality of life of Europe's citizens and the effectiveness of social and economic organisation as well as to increase coherence. It is difficult to derive from this sentence an exhaustive definition of information society, but it allows for identification of four interrelated and interdependent features of the European society of the digital age. Improving the quality of life is intrinsically linked to economic organisation. The development of the state's economy increases the economic capacity of the society and, proportionally, the quality of life of EU citizens. This, in turn, enhances the functioning of the society and the processes of its development, organisation, ownership and integration. A higher quality of life combined with the involvement of citizens will, in turn, contribute to better social cohesion. The description of information society provided by Bangemann constitutes a coherent chain of interrelated elements, which, due to information and communication technologies, could function effectively within the framework of the industrial revolution taking place at that time.

3 Bangemann Report, Europe and the Global Information Society (1994), http://www.cyber-rights.org/documents/bangemann.htm (accessed: 3.2.2015).

This approach differs significantly from a long list of definitions referred to in publications on this issue (Nowak, 2009: 1-9). The notion of information society was very quickly incorporated into the works related to the use of information and communication technologies; however, no definition was provided and only tasks were set. The stage of transition from traditional to information society was referred to by the European Commission in 2002.[4] This is reflected in the changes in all the aspects of citizens' life: work, education, management, industry and trade. The success in this area enables a substantive development of Europe, its competitiveness, employment opportunities and far-reaching economic, social and legal consequences.

Eleven years after the publication of the Bangemann report, the Commission did not significantly change its approach to defining information society. In fact, it only paraphrased the description of information society in a document entitled "i2010 – A European Information Society for Growth and Employment."[5] Under this concept, information society promotes growth and jobs in a manner that is in line with sustainable development and prioritises better public services and quality of life.

The next milestone with respect to information society was a document related to the process of computerisation of citizens' life – a Digital Agenda for Europe. In the agenda, the Commission does not use the term "information society", referring to "digital society" instead. To build a digital society, effective interoperability between IT products and services is required.[6] The European Parliament adopted a similar approach, considering information and communication technologies used by the public sector as a fundamental basis for the development of a knowledge-based digital society.[7]

---

4 Communication from the Commission to the Council and the European Parliament, eEurope 2002. Impact and priorities. A communication to the Spring European Council in Stockholm, 23-24 March 2001.

5 Communication from the Commission of 19 May 2010 to the European Parliament, the Council, the European Economic and Social Committee and the Committee of the Regions – *"i2010 – A European Information Society for growth and employment",* COM(2005) 229 final.

6 Communication from the Commission of 19 May 2010 to the European Parliament, the Council, the European Economic and Social Committee and the Committee of the Regions – *Digital Agenda for Europe,* COM(2010) 245 final/2.

7 European Parliament resolution of 11 December 2012 on completing the Digital Single Market (2012/2030(INI)), OJ C 434/2, 23.12.2015, 25.

In view of the large number of tasks and goals related to the development of information society, the fact that the key terms have not been defined and that they are used interchangeably might be considered as a serious shortcoming of the European Commission's actions. However, what should be stressed is the complementary nature of the activities planned and the logical sequence of the results expected, which reflects the influence of information society on the creation of e-administration and the shaping of the information space in Europe.

Information society, with its potential for improving quality, implies changes in the social, economic and legal fields. As a result, it primarily affects the shape of the public sector, but, following the changes taking place, it also influences the model of the private sector. As an integral part of information society, information and communication technologies affect the quality and functionality of, and the extent to which, appliances, applications, databases, services and networks are used. Thus, their role is not only of a creative nature, but it also relates to services. The Digital Agenda for Europe indicates five areas where they are used and defines explicitly the benefits resulting from them, i.e. addressing climate change, health care, empowering patients, promoting cultural diversity and creative content as well as improving transportation efficiency and mobility.

The last, but no less important benefit of the use of ICT in the service of society is e-administration. The importance of digital administration was stressed by a ministerial conference in Malmö in 2009 which led to the unanimous adoption of a declaration on eGovernment. It was recognised that "eGovernment had not only become mainstream in national policies but had also reached beyond national boundaries to become an important enabler to deliver European-wide policy goals across different sectors, from justice to social security, to trading business services and beyond."[8]

The interaction between information society and e-administration is best illustrated by e-administration services. Their scope allows for identification of three groups of recipients and entities that build information society. As targeted and personalised activities, e-administration services primarily serve citizens. They are of importance for the private sector, where entrepreneurs remain a separate group of society that plays an important role. E-administration services also provide an added value to the

8 Ministerial Declaration on eGovernment approved unanimously in Malmö, Sweden, on 18 November 2009, https://ec.europa.eu/digital-agenda/sites/digital-agenda/files/ministerial-declaration-on-egovernment-malmo.pdf (accessed: 21.11.2015).

functioning of public administrative authorities by cost reduction and time saving. As a result, e-administration ought to have the features of smart administration, where the services support streamlined administrative procedures, facilitate information exchange and simplify interaction, thereby empowering users and improving the efficiency, effectiveness and transparency of the entities involved.[9]

Researchers claim that there can be no development of information society without the smooth functioning of e-administration, understood as integrated IT solutions allowing the transforming and improving of internal administration processes and providing e-public services (Ziemba, 2012: 332). This confirms the view that information and communication technologies are the common denominator in the creation and development of e-administration as well as in the emergence of information society.

This also implies that e-administration is a necessary component in the process of the shaping of information society. This view is supported by an overall assessment of the documents drafted in the last two decades on the use of information and communication technologies for the development of society in Europe. As a backbone of information society, ICTs are a necessary instrument or even a stimulus for social, economic and technological progress. They are vulnerable to threats and criminal acts to the same extent as they shape and simplify social and economic life and the entire public sector.

As a rule, the concepts of information society have not changed along with the development of e-administration and the growing use of ICT systems and there have just been modifications to the way information society is described. One example is the Commission's Cybersecurity Strategy of the European Union[10] from 2013, which refers to the notion of a global information society. In 2015, in a communication entitled "A Digital Sin-

9 Communication from the Commission of 19 May 2010 to the European Parliament, the Council, the European Economic and Social Committee and the Committee of the Regions – Digital Agenda for Europe, COM(2010) 245 final/2, 37.

10 Joint Communication from the Commission to the European Parliament, the Council, the European Economic and Social Committee and the Committee of the Regions - Cybersecurity Strategy of the European Union: An Open, Safe and Secure Cyberspace, JOIN(2013) 1 final.

gle Market Strategy for Europe,"[11] the Commission returned to the idea of digital society. In the communication, it explained that digital society consists of "citizens and businesses (that) have the necessary skills and can benefit from interlinked and multi-lingual e-services, from e-government, e-justice, e-health, e-energy or e-transport."[12]

The above is a significant achievement in the work on the idea of information society. After over 20 years of work during which discrepancies in the terms used could be seen, the Commission communicated the meaning of the concept of digital society. By replacing the term "information" with the notion "digital", it stressed the importance of information and communication systems and the impact of the process of digitalisation on the formation of digital society.

To sum up, it should be noted that the process of transformation of information society was influenced by the use of ICT systems, which allowed it to mature and develop at a fast pace. New services offered as part of information society are provided from the very beginning in a digital form, as underlined by the European Commission in 2005 in the "i2010 – A European Information Society for Growth and Employment"[13] initiative.

From the perspective of economic growth, and particularly from the perspective of businesses and consumers, the most important branch of the economy influenced by the Internet is e-commerce. Already in the 1980s the Internet had become a tool to promote countless goods and services all over the world, which allowed consumers to make their purchases irrespective of their location. Entrepreneurs could in turn carry on their business and establish new forms of cooperation. Consequently, transfer rate, the low cost of copying and disseminating information and the global nature of the Internet, based on a system of open communication, have started to influence economic growth and investments (Jaroszek, 2009: 5). This has encouraged the development of e-commerce transactions, and the

11 Communication from the Commission to the European Parliament, the Council, the European Economic and Social Committee and the Committee of the Regions - A Digital Single Market Strategy for Europe, COM/2015/0192 final.

12 Ibidem, 17.

13 Communication from the Commission to the European Parliament, the Council, the European Economic and Social Committee and the Committee of the Regions "i2010 – A European Information Society for growth and employment", COM(2005) 229 final, 4.

production driven by e-commerce has started to create favourable conditions for the development of economic freedoms, allowing for the free movement of goods, services and capital as well as the free movement of elements new to the internal market, i.e. information, technology and communication (Fangfei Wang, 2011: 6). E-commerce allows for a reduction of costs, attracting new investors and eliminating physical limitations as regards offering attractive prices and the development of trade.

In view of the development of a vibrant digital market, the Commission developed the concept of a virtuous cycle of the digital economy[14] and suggested taking on a series of activities related to, among other things, the development of e-commerce, with special reference to facilitation measures for businesses, cross-border online transactions and a single market for telecommunications services.

Information society services

Information society services play an important role for e-commerce and the creation of a single digital market. The services were defined in Directive 2000/31[15], which refers to Article 1(2) Directive 98/34/EC, as amended by Directive 98/48/EC. According to the wording of this article, an information society service is any service normally provided for remuneration, at a distance, by electronic means and at the individual request of a recipient of the service. Such services are usually provided on the basis of an agreement and in an electronic form (Gołaczyński, 2007: 63).

Also the Court of Justice referred to the definition of information society services in a case concerning defamation of a citizen of Cyprus.[16] In its judgment in this case, the CJEU found that the notion of "information society services" referred to in Article 2(b) of Directive 2000/31 covers online information services the remuneration for which is provided not by recipient, but by means of commercial advertisements posted on the web-

14 Communication from the Commission of 19 May 2010 to the European Parliament, the Council, the European Economic and Social Committee and the Committee of the Regions – Digital Agenda for Europe, COM(2010) 245 final/2, 4-5.

15 Directive 2000/31/EC of the European Parliament and of the Council of 8 June 2000 on certain legal aspects of information society services, in particular electronic commerce, in the Internal Market ('Directive on electronic commerce'), OJ L 178, 17.07.2000, p. 0001 – 0016.

16 Case C-291/13, Reports of Cases: not yet published.

site. Examples of information society services include *caching* and *hosting*. Pursuant to Article 13 of E-Commerce Directive, *caching* is the automatic, temporary and intermediate storage of data performed for the purpose of accelerating the renewed access to this information. *Hosting*, which is referred to in Article 14 of the directive, regards the storage of third party data.

Article 21 of the directive, which introduced the so-called review clause, turned out to be relevant for the development of information society services (Gęsicka, 2014: 182). It requires the Commission to evaluate the application of the directive and, where necessary, to put forward proposals for changes to its provisions. It was assumed that the legislation should be revised particularly with respect to technological developments, which, at the same time, would allow evaluation as to whether the EU efficiently supports the actions in this area.

The first report compiled as a result of the review clause was delivered in 2003 (COM(2003)702 final). Despite the short period in which the directive had been in force resulting from the fact that member states had until January 2002 to implement it, a positive and significant influence of the document on e-commerce in Europe was stressed. It was emphasised that the directive referred to a wide variety of services provided online – "information society services."[17] It was found that the short period in which the directive had been in force made it impossible to assess its effects. An action plan was to facilitate drawing more detailed conclusions in subsequent reports, focusing on proper application of the provisions of the directive, enhancing administrative cooperation between member states, raising the awareness of citizens and industry and making them more informed as well as strengthening international collaboration. In the conclusions, the Commission considered that the directive was just a first stage in completing the legislative framework for e-commerce and did not address the essence of information society services in more detail.

In accordance with the directive, the next report should have been published in 2005. Yet, the Commission failed to comply with its duty and the next two reports concerning the economic aspects of the application of the directive were compiled in 2007. Despite the evaluation covering a five-

17 First Report on the application of Directive 2000/31/EC of the European Parliament and of the Council of 8 June 2000 on certain legal aspects of information society services, in particular electronic commerce, in the Internal Market (Directive on electronic commerce), 3-4.

year period, no evidence was found that the directive enhanced the cross-border trade in information society services. This was explained by the short period in which the directive had been in force since its implementation and, as a result, insufficient statistical data that did not allow assessment of the systematic development of these services in e-commerce. The next reports were compiled in 2009 and 2012. In the latter one, the Commission focused on a coherent framework for building trust in the single digital market, strengthening e-commerce and developing online services.[18]

In the report drafted in 2012,[19] the Commission identified five barriers to the development of online services, i.e. inadequate supply of legal cross-border online services, not enough information for online service operators, insufficient protection for internet users, inadequate payment and delivery systems, too many cases of abuse and disputes that are difficult to settle and insufficient use of high-speed communication networks and hi-tech solutions.

An important part of the communication is a definition of online services, which are often considered to be an essential driver for the development of a single digital market and a factor that may speed up European integration. Online services shall be understood as services provided at a distance, electronically, at the request of the person who is the recipient of the service, in return for payment. Thus, this term covers e-commerce in goods and services, but also social networks, vocational training by distance learning, etc. However, this definition was not used in later initiatives of the Commission. In the subsequent communications, terms such

18 Communication from the Commission to the European Parliament, the Council, the European Economic and Social Committee and the Committee of the Regions - A coherent framework for building trust in the digital single market for e-commerce and online services, COM(2011) 942 final/2.

19 Ibidem.

as “digital services”[20], “mobile services”[21], and “Internet services”[22] were used. The above shows that the Commission has not developed a clear position concerning the terms used and that the indicated terms are used interchangeably within one document.[23]

In the literature, the notion of information society services is sometimes used interchangeably with “electronic services” and “services provided electronically” (Zieliński, 2013: 100). Although both these terms relate to e-commerce, considering them as one and the same does not seem to be right.

An electronic communications service means “a service normally provided for remuneration, which consist wholly or mainly in the conveyance of signals on electronic communications networks, including telecommunications services and transmission services in networks used for broadcasting.”[24] Pursuant to Article 2(c) of Directive 2002/21/EC, an electronic communications service does not include information society services which do not consist wholly or mainly in the conveyance of signals on electronic communications networks (Gęsicka, 2014: 183). M. Z. Zieliński adopts a different approach, claiming that information society services are a synonym for electronically supplied services (Zieliński, 2013: 100).

Also the scope of the term of information society services is not clear. Researchers emphasise that it is significantly broader than indicated by the title of the document that regulates it. This term covers namely also information websites, both general and specialised ones, based on provisions

---

20 Communication from the Commission to the European Parliament, the Council, the European Economic and Social Committee and the Committee of the Regions - Single Market Act II. Together for new growth, COM(2012) 573 final, 16.

21 Communication from the Commission to the European Parliament, the Council, the European Economic and Social Committee and the Committee of the Regions - The Digital Agenda for Europe - Driving European growth digitally COM(2012) 784 final, 3.

22 Joint Communication from the Commission to the European Parliament, the Council, the European Economic and Social Committee and the Committee of the Regions - Cybersecurity Strategy…op.cit., 7.

23 More: Communication from the Commission to the European Parliament, the Council, the European Economic and Social Committee and the Committee of the Regions - A Digital Single Market….

24 Art. 2 of Directive 2002/21/EC of the European Parliament and of the Council of 7 March 2002 on a common regulatory framework for electronic communications networks and services (Framework Directive), OJ L 108, 24.04.2002, p. 0033 – 0050.

concerning the media, the access to which is often free of charge (Wróbel, 2007: 2). Annex V to Directive 98/34/EC defined[25] the services excluded from the scope of information society services in a negative way. According to the Commission, the term refers to a wide variety of online services, such as online newspapers, online sale of books, equipment and computer software, including online financial services.[26] Other services that should be included in the list are services offered free-of-charge, professional services and technical support services (Kowalik-Bańczyk, 2006: 174).

A lack of clarity concerning Directive 2000/31 and the unsatisfactory results of the evaluation of its functioning do not make the directive any less a basic act harmonising the provision of information society services in the European Union (Targański, 2010: 64). The added value of the directive lies in the fact that it is not limited to e-commerce. It also seeks to ensure the proper functioning of the internal market in terms of electronic services by harmonising provisions concerning information obligations of electronic service providers, contracts concluded by electronic means, cooperation between member states as regards electronic services and others.

Directive 2000/31 attempts to eliminate legal obstacles that influence the smooth functioning of the internal market in terms of information society services, i.e. disparities in legislation and legal uncertainty with regard to which national rules apply to these services (Kawka, 2015: 223). An important step to support the smooth functioning of the internal market and eliminate obstacles to the implementation of information society services was the adoption of a directive[27] on the transparency of information concerning technical rules and principles as regards information society services in 2015. The definition of the term "service" found in Directive 2015/1535 is the same as in Directive 2000/31. When clarifying the definition, the legislator, however, departed from referring to other acts. Pursuant to Article 1 of Directive 2015/1535, an information society service consists of four elements:

---

25 According to the art. 10 Directive 2015/1535 - Directive 98/34 / EC expired, OJ L 241, 17.9.2015, p. 1-15.

26 First Report on the application of Directive 2000/31/EC of the European Parliament and of the Council of 8 June 2000 on certain legal aspects of information society services…op.cit.

27 Directive (EU) 2015/1535 of the European Parliament and of the Council of 9 September 2015 laying down a procedure for the provision of information in the field of technical regulations and of rules on Information Society services, OJ L 241, 17.9.2015, p. 1-15.

- it is provided for remuneration;
- it is provided without the parties being simultaneously present;
- it is sent and received at its destination by means of electronic equipment for the processing (including digital compression) and storage of data, and entirely transmitted, conveyed and received by wire, by radio, by optical means or by other electromagnetic means;
- it is provided at the individual request of a recipient of services.

Annex 1 to Directive 2015/1535 provides an indicative list of services that fall outside the above definition. In the annex, the legislator referred to particular elements of information society services and, in this way, indicated which services are not covered by the definition.

The directive maintained the notification system for technical regulations at the draft stage. Under this system, the "standstill" principle applies, which is a period of deferment of a particular provision, during which the European Commission and member states may react in a specific form. Furthermore, following the line of Directive 98/48/EC, the directive extended the notification obligation to include information society services, which – this time – was expressed in the very title of the legal act. Information society services are addresses by numerous soft-law acts that refer to them in a more or less detailed way. Soft-law instruments adopted by EU institutions seek to have some legal or political effects (Kurcz, 2012: 618) and may form the basis for future legislative initiatives.

Reference should be made to the i2010 communication from the Commission[28] from June 2005, which presents three main action lines to allow the EU to take advantage of the mass development of ICTs and the latest waves of technological convergence by creating an open and competitive EU single market for information society and media services. In the communication, the Commission highlighted that these services reflect the convergence now taking place between electronic communication services, information society services, broadcasting services and the emergence of new content services resulting therefrom. In this way, the Commission explained the interaction between these services. It emphasised

28 Communication from the Commission to the European Parliament, the Council, the European Economic and Social Committee and the Committee of the Regions "i2010 – A European Information Society for growth and employment", COM(2005) 229 final.

the dependencies arising between them and, at the same time, retained three separate categories of services.[29]

Following the publication of two annual reports in 2006 (COM/2006/0215 final) and 2007 (COM/2007/0146 final), in 2008 the Commission published a communication[30] on the creation of a more coherent, common and efficient approach to e-accessibility, and particularly web accessibility, to hasten the advent of an accessible information society. The Commission refers in this document to ICT-based services and online public services such as e-administration and e-health. It does not use the term of information society services; however, in view of the title of the communication – "Towards an accessible information society" – any doubts as to the type of services covered by the communication are unsubstantiated. Furthermore, the Commission is not consistent in the use of terms and, later on in the communication, it makes reference to information and interactive services such as online banking. This raises doubts because, pursuant to Article 1(4) of Directive 2015/1535, its provisions shall not apply to rules relating to matters which are covered by Union legislation in the field of financial services and distance communication with relatives and friends, which are electronic communications services (Gęsicka, 2014: 183).

Another example of a soft-law act on information society services is a communication from 2009 concerning the Internet.[31] In the communication, the Commission uses the terms "new services" and "proximity services", such as tourism and personal healthcare. In the context of the entire document it can be assumed that the notion of "new services" means information society services as, according to the Commission, they are inextricably linked to the Internet in the context of the evolution of the computer network. This will contribute to the emergence of the so-called Inter-

---

29 More on electronic communications services: Communication from the Commission to the European Parliament, the Council, the European Economic and Social Committee and the Committee of the Regions on the Review of the EU Regulatory Framework for electronic communications networks and services, COM(2006) 334 final.

30 Communication from the Commission to the European Parliament, the Council, the European Economic and Social Committee and the Committee of the Regions "Towards an accessible information society", COM(2008) 804 final.

31 Communication from the Commission to the European Parliament, the Council, the European Economic and Social Committee and the Committee of the Regions - Internet of Things: an action plan for Europe, COM/2009/0278 final.

net of Things, which consists of a network of interconnected objects, from books to cars, from electrical appliances to food. The Internet of Things is a series of new independent systems that operate with their own infrastructures. Its functioning is expected to improve citizens' quality of life, which means that its key element will be electronically supplied services.

In a Digital Agenda for Europe published in 2010, the Commission referred in detail to the development of services in an interoperable and borderless Internet environment. The primary focus is on digital services resulting and benefiting from the development of information society. In particular, public websites and online services in the EU that are important to take a full part in public life should be brought in line with international web accessibility standards. The Commission did not make a direct reference to information society services as such. Special attention was paid in the document to the creation of an environment for their functioning, i.e. conditions, foundations and principles concerning the way they develop and are used by citizens.

Information society services were given the most careful attention by the Commission in a communication on a digital single market in Europe from 2015.[32] The Commission made activities related to Internet services two of the three pillars of a digital single market. Work should focus on providing better access for consumers and businesses to online goods and services. This will allow the elimination of obstacles to cross-border Internet activities and, as a result, to gaining access to online services and to providing them. Also the technical dimension should be addressed by putting in place the right conditions for the development of the Internet and online services. This requires high-speed, secure and reliable infrastructure as well as content services. The Commission also referred to the need to increase confidence in digital services and reinforce security in the context of providers of information society services, who are excluded from the scope of Directive 2002/58/EC on electronic privacy.[33]

---

32 Communication from the Commission to the European Parliament, the Council, the European Economic and Social Committee and the Committee of the Regions - A Digital Single Market Strategy for Europe, COM/2015/0192 final.

33 Directive 2002/58/EC of the European Parliament and of the Council of 12 July 2002concerning the processing of personal data and the protection of privacy in the electronic communications sector (Directive on privacy and electronic communications), OJ L 201, 31.07.2002, p. 0037 – 0047.

The assessment of the Commission's communication on a digital single market strategy in terms of creating conditions for the development of digital services will be possible towards the end of 2016, when the period specified in the schedule annexed to the document ends. However, its importance as the first crucial political document with an integrated character is already being stressed (Lammmerant & Hert 2016: 175).

Summary

The digitalisation process has irrevocably changed the way of life of Europe's citizens and set the direction of the functioning of the European Union. This can be observed at all levels: individual, social, national, local, central and international. The European Union had to address the effects of digitalisation and the ubiquity of information and communication systems. It was very easy to indicate positive changes resulting from the implementation of electronic and digital forms in various economic sectors. What caused more difficulties was the development of legal bases and common standards for the use of new technological opportunities and for the implementation of the objectives set.

An example of effective action is Directive 2015/1535, which removed ambiguity regarding the terms used by taking account of the basic notions. Yet, Directive 2000/31 still makes reference to a document that is no longer applicable. In Article 8 of Directive 2015/1535, the legislator obliged the Commission to report every two years to the European Parliament, the Council and the European Economic and Social Committee on the results of the application of the directive. This is in line with the guidelines on better regulation set by the Commission,[34] which provide for a regular evaluation of legal acts. Similar provisions can be found in Directive 2000/31; however, the Commission has not always taken action to implement them.

The EU's openness and participation is reflected in the Commission acts regarding information society services, which are inextricably linked to the work for a single digital market. The disadvantage of these initiatives is that the terms used are not clear and that their scope has not been

34 Communication from the Commission to the European Parliament, the Council, the European Economic and Social Committee and the Committee of the Regions - Better regulation for better results - An EU agenda, COM(2015) 215 final.

clarified. Yet, introducing new terms such as "new services", "digital services" or "ICT services", though it may be an expression of concern for the editorial aspects, does not help promote cohesion. Moreover, the fact that information society services – as an important element of a digital single market – are referred to in different ways depending on the document, despite there being a legal definition, will negatively influence the effectiveness and efficiency of EU action. When monitoring and evaluating the application of Directive 2015/1535, the Commission must pay more attention to timeliness as well as clarity of terms.

Particular consideration should also be given as to whether the European Commission stands ready to take actions in accordance with the schedule included in the Digital Single Market Strategy. As indicated in a footnote of the strategy, the listed measures that are likely to have significant impacts will be accompanied by a separate impact assessment in line with the Commission's Better Regulation principles. The assessment in this respect will be possible after the expiry of the period set, i.e. after 2016.

References

Fangfei Wang, F. (2009), 'Internet Jurisdiction and Choice of Law: Legal Practices in the EU, US and China', UK: Routledge.

Gęsicka, D.K. (2014), 'Wyłączenie odpowiedzialności cywilnoprawnej dostawców usług sieciowych za treści użytkowników', Warszawa: LEX.

Gołaczyński, J. (2007), 'Umowy elektroniczne w prawie prywatnym międzynarodowym', Warszawa: Oficyna.

Jaroszek, A. (2009), 'Prawo właściwe dla umów konsumenckich zawieranych przez Internet', Warszawa: Oficyna.

Kawka, I. (2015), 'Gospodarcza działalność usługowa w prawie polskim w świetle unijnych swobód przedsiębiorczości i świadczenia usług', Warszawa: LEX.

Kowalik-Bańczyk, K. (2006), 'Sposoby regulacji handlu elektronicznego w prawie wspólnotowym i międzynarodowym', Kraków: Zakamycze.

Kurcz, B. (2012), 'Komentarz do art. 288 TFUE', in: D. Kornobis-Romanowska, J. Łacny, A. Wróbel (eds), *Traktat o funkcjonowaniu Unii Europejskiej. Komentarz. Tom III,* Warszawa: Wolters Kluwer.

Lammerant, H. Hert, P. De. *Visions of Technology* Gutwirth, S. Leenes, R. Hert, P. De (eds) (2016), 'Data Protection on the Move Current Developments in ICT and Privacy/Data Protection', Netherlands: Springer.

Mendes, J. M. Suomi, R.. Passos, C (eds) (2004), 'Digital Communities in a Networked Society e-Commerce, e-Business and e-Government', Springer US.

Nowak, J. S. (2009), 'Społeczeństwo informacyjne – geneza i definicje', in: P. Sienkiewicz, J.S. Nowak (eds), *Społeczeństwo informacyjne. Krok naprzód, dwa kroki wstecz* Katowice: Polskie Towarzystwo Informatyczne - Oddział Górnośląski.

Pietrzak, E. (2013), 'Idea europejskiego społeczeństwa obywatelskiego i jego przeobrażenia', *Przegląd Europejski,* Nr 4 (30) 2013.

Taragański, B. (2010), 'Ochrona konkurencji w działalności platform handlu elektronicznego', Warszawa: Oficyna.

Wegner-Kowalska, J. (2013), 'Administracja w czasach kryzysu', in: J. Zimmermann, P. J.Suwaj, (eds), *Wpływ przemian cywilizacyjnych na prawo administracyjne i administrację publiczną*, Warszawa: Wolters Kluwer.

Wróbel, I. (2007), 'Pojęcie usługi społeczeństwa informacyjnego w prawie wspólnotowym', Wrocław: e-Biuletyn CBKE.

Zieliński, M.Z. (2013), 'Odpowiedzialność deliktowa pośredniczących dostawców internetowych. Analiza prawnoporównawcza', Warszawa: LEX.

Ziemba, E. (2012), 'Miejsce e-administracji w kreowaniu Analysis Annals.społeczeństwa informacyjnego – teoria i praktyka', Katowice: Collegium of Economic

Chapter 5: The good governance rule and balancing the interests of employers and employees in the EU

Piotr Kwasiborski

Key words: social dialogue, employers' interest, balance of interests

The Good Governance rule from employment law perspective

The concept of good governance may be and should be also applied to the area of the employment law decision-making process. From this perspective, the most important is the democratisation aspect. In the view of this aspect engaging society in administrative tasks leads to the accomplishment of the rule of participation which should be treated as one of the most important factors of the good governance concept. Such an approach may be derived from the considerations regarding the issues of constitutionalism and the necessity to involve society in governing measures. Following T. Pogge, everyone should take the responsibility for the effects resulting from the domestic and global governance systems which affect the lives of individuals (de Burca et al., 2012: 210). This call also promotes dispersal of the sovereignty for separate and autonomic legal orders which have a greater ability to provide the observance of the universal individuals' rights of economic or social character. As stressed by U. Karpen, the governance via the operation of democratic principles requires that the individuals have their participatory rights in administrative proceedings guaranteed and protected by the government (Karpen, 2010: 23).

When applying such requirements to the employment law background, one should admit that the above mentioned approach is somehow reflected in the concept of the so called "social dialogue". The social dialogue does not have its one, ever-applicable definition. In general, it relates to the mutual relations between trade unions or other employees' representatives (aiming to protect the interests of employees) and associations of employers, trying to ensure that the voice of employers is also properly heard when it comes to the adoption of employment law[1]. The social dialogue may encompass not only the mutual relations between the above mentioned groups of interests, but also a three-sided relation, including the interaction of the trade unions and employers' associations with the public authorities (at any level of governance), resulting in involving the employees' and employers' representatives in the decision-making process. From this perspective it should be treated as a measure to achieve mutual understanding (by way of compromise) between the above mentioned three main actors to whom the fluctuations on the employment market may have material influence. Such understanding, if the parties succeed in achieving it, enables the finding of comprehensive solutions taking into account the interests of both the employees and employers, and therefore to perform efficient control over the social and economic factors affecting the employment market and the markets on which particular employers perform their business activity.

The social dialogue may in fact be of institutional or non-institutional character (Casale, 1999: 268). The institutional dialogue means that the negotiations between trade unions and employers' associations are performed in a formalized manner, with the use of specific units (such as the commissions, councils, committees) adopted by law with the express purpose of gaining understanding between these contradictory interest groups. Such units operate on the basis of specific legal provisions governing the procedures which must be followed by the participants included in the unit and the unit itself. The participation in such units involves (beside the representatives of the public authority) only the most representative trade unions and employer's associations which have a material and real impact on the activity of their members and therefore may require that the solutions and decisions established by the unit will be truly observed in practice. The non-institutional social dialogue refers to a less formalized procedure of gaining understanding between employees and employers, mainly without the supervision and support of public authorities (which in consequence leads to the adoption only internal and more contractual arrangements between these group interests, having no result in the adopting of statutory law by public authorities).

1 http://www.dialog.gov.pl/czym-jest-dialog-spoleczny/podstawowe-pojecia/ (accessed: 11.2.2016).

The institutional social dialogue may have a national or supranational dimension. An example of the latter is the European social dialogue, i.e. the consultations and undertakings involving the participation of the most representative European social partners (supranational trade unions and employers' associations) within the EU[2]. The European social dialogue is considered as a response to the challenges raised by the operation of the EU internal market based on the rule of competitiveness, due to which the member states cannot conduct their national social policy without respect to their legal obligations resulting from the membership in the European integration.

The European social dialogue has its background in the Treaty on functioning of the European Union ("TFEU") according to which the Commission is obliged to support consultations performed at the EU level by the social partners and adopt any necessary measures which would facilitate such dialogue (Article 154 of the Treaty on Functioning of the European Union). In addition, in event that the Commission intends to prepare the legislation motion within the area of the social policy, it needs to firstly consult the necessity of submitting and the content of such motion with these social partners. At this level one may identify that formally the participation rule being one of the main factors of democratisation and thus the good governance concept as a whole is followed at the European Union level. It has its institutional implications in the form of European sector social dialogue committees[3] being the areas of consultation for EU policies within which social partners may undertake initiatives in their common interest in order to present their mutual approach for the upcoming amendments of the shape of EU employment law. On the other hand, besides that "grassroots movement" the nurturing of the participation rule may be identified by the operation of the European Economic and Social Committee, i.e. the treaty-based EU institution and the advisory unit for EU legislators with respect to, among other things, the employment law. Due to its high position in the EU institutional structure and its treaty-based tasks of assuring a sufficient level of social dialogue (and therefore the good governance standards in the area of employment law), its activity

---

2 http://www.dialog.gov.pl/dialog-miedzynarodowy/dialog-w-ue-komitologia/ (accessed: 11.2.2016).

3 European Commission (2010), *Dokument roboczy służb Komisji w sprawie funkcjonowania i potencjału europejskiego sektorowego dialogu społecznego*, Brussels: SEK (2010) 964.

and practical utility will be examined in subsequent sections of this publication below.

Participation is the main factor contributing to the practical dimension of the democratisation but it would be meaningless if not supported by the transparency factor. In other words, the transparency understood as the open and objective set of administrative procedures is necessary to facilitate the effective use from the right to participate in governance by citizens, private sector and NGO's. The convergence of these two factors makes the democratic fundamentals practical. The same rules apply in the area of employment legislation. If the representatives of the social partners would theoretically be authorized to participate with public authorities in creating the employment legal system without the existence of the transparent rules of such participation, their influence on the final decisions adopted by the public authorities would be false. In fact, this would mean that society would have served the state as the excuse of observing the democratisation requirements. The lack of transparency in the activity of public authorities and adopted legal framework results in no comprehensibility between the government and social partners, which kills the participation initiatives in society. The social partners are simply reluctant to cooperate with the government they do not trust. This outcome confirms that true social dialogue requires the mixture of both the active participation and transparency rules.

The combination of the participation and transparency aspects as described above constitute also the fundamentals of the separate "open government" concept (Supernat, 2009: 645), focused on the achievement of values according to which the organisation and functioning of public institutions should become more reliable by the openness of these institutions and their procedures to the public and their cooperation with the citizens. Therefore one may state that open government is simply a way to respect the good governance concept (one of the good governance components) which is of the wider character and concerns also the other aspects mentioned previously in this publication.

Following U. Karpen, any government must have a strong capacity to react to complex problems in a changing environment (Karpen, 2010: 18). One should note that in order to react to such problems and evolution processes affecting the environment, the participation of the stakeholders in adopting reactive decisions is absolutely indispensable. At the employment background it only confirms that no decisions affecting the employment market can be adopted without hearing both the employees and the employer's approach (especially that any decision regarding the employment market may at the same time affect the entire business of the latter). But calling for participation is not justified only by moral reasons. It also has a practical advantage – the participation simply involves a bunch of experts who deal with the regulated matters every day. That is why their experience gives a material contribution for the identification of and combating the market challenges. The experts do not have legal measures, whereas the government does not have the experience. When both these actors converge and support each other in adopting relevant decisions, the participation rule is triggered in practice.

Beside the participation and transparency contributing to democratisation, the involvement of employees' and employers' representatives in the decision-making process regarding employment law reflects also the other good governance standards. It is also coherent with the rule that the governance performed by public authorities should be responsive, i.e. it should react and correspond to the difficulties met by the participants of the relevant market. It clearly confirms that the trade unions and employers' associations should actively participate in the legislation process so that the adopted law may be effective and efficient (which leads to the achievement of another goal raised by the good governance rule) as it would answer the needs of the market participants. Nevertheless, the participation and transparency aspects are most applicable when analysing the necessity of involving employees' and employers' representatives in decision-making process regarding employment law[4].

The acknowledgement of all these standards at the EU level gives a spark to make the assessment as to whether the good governance concept is also applied in practice in the EU decision-making process and how it actually works – for the purpose of this chapter it will be verified with respect to EU employment legislation and the necessary involvement of employees' and employers' interest groups in this process.

---

4 European Commission (2001), *European governance – a White Paper*, Brussels: COM(2001) 428.

Democratisation and balancing interests of employees and employers

Nevertheless, one may argue that the participation rule (and actually also the other good governance aspects) is truly met in the area of employment law consultations (a social dialogue) only if both the interests of employees and employers are in fact balanced with each other and neither of them is dominant over the other. The balance in this respect should be defined as the situation where there is no abstract preference for one of the above groups from the initial stage of the consultations or negotiations made when working on employment legislation, and the justified interests of each group are respected to the largest possible extent when it comes to their collision. This is a strong display of the general good governance problem of conflict of interests accompanying the participation aspect (Karpen, 2010: 25). Nevertheless, the nature of such conflict is different than in the case of typical competition conflicts between two business entities operating in the same business area. In the case of the employees and employers the conflict results from the existence of quite opposite goals – within one internal organisation, the employer heads towards the income maximisation, whereas the employees concentrate on their individual rights and benefits. These groups are however not competitors in their pure business meaning (to a large extent the situation of employees depends on the situation of their employers). In any case the conflict of interest is a challenge to effectively implement the participation rule involving wider group of participants but in order to reach the good governance standards it must be resolved by the consensus-oriented operation of public authorities. In the area of employment law it means the balancing of employees' and employers' interests.

Additionally, whereas the good governance standards require that decision-making processes involve not only a few participants in a particular market but generally all the stakeholders representing the interests of as large group as possible, it would be inappropriate to rely only on the advice of the one from the two main adversarial interest groups. Furthermore, the true execution of the participation rule requires that the participation of both the employees' and employers' representatives is real, i.e. both of these groups are actually heard in the discussion and that their approach is taken into account by public authorities before initiating or during the legislation stage. Otherwise the participation would be an empty word. That is why one may state that in fact it is about the active participation which counts from the good governance perspective.

One may say that lifting such bar for the non-governmental entities constitutes in fact lobbying. There is nothing wrong about it, since the lobbying has certain advantages. What is most important is that it provides know-how, experience and crucial statistical data of how the regulations work in practice (Joos, 2011: 49). From this perspective it is a material support for making the law effective, which is also one of the fundaments of the good governance concept. Additionally, in the case of the employment law decision-making process such a kind of lobbying seems to be indispensable because employment law is the area where almost each regulation impacts on the position of both the employers and employees at the same time. Besides, as mentioned above, the employees and employers are not true competitors, and these groups are interdependent on each other. Therefore it would be dangerous to create the law *in abstracto* or without the participation of the one of the above mentioned groups. It would make impossible the assessing of what the result of such an action would be for the employers and employees.

Although the lack of transparency is considered to be one of the biggest dangers of lobbying (Karpen, 2010: 28), there are no material reasons to have such fears when it comes to the lobbying of employees' and employers' representatives in the employment law legislation process. Since these groups are the only stakeholders referring to the employment law legislation, their lobbying is actually a proof that the actions taken in this area by public authorities are transparent. In this regard the lack of transparency could occur only when the employees' or employers' representatives invited to the social dialogue would be only governmental facades and would not have a true impact on the employees' or employers' background. In such a case however the active participation requirement would also be not met so that one could not identify the democratisation aspect at all. This shows how the participation and transparency are converged and interdependent on each other in order to talk about nurturing the democratisation in governing activity. There is no better way to assure transparency than by allowing the stakeholders to participate in the relevant decision-making process, especially where such stakeholders form a set of mutual interlinks existing between them and towards the entire state's economy. This is clearly visible in case of employees' and employers' representatives.

Balancing the interests of employees and employers by the public authorities reflects not only the participation and transparency rules being the fundamentals of democratisation and therefore the good governance concept as a whole. It is also an expression of the other factors embedded in the entire institution of democratisation. First of all it assures that the decisions finally adopted are actually an effect of the compromise. In consequence, it also guarantees that the adopted law will be followed by its addressees, which makes it effective. This results in the achievement of high public confidence into the accountability and efficiency of the public authorities. And this is how the good governance concept should be ideally implemented into the decision-making process, i.e. should be a final stop on the way of transition from the government to the governance.

Therefore the active participation of the employees' and employers' representatives in the form of social dialogue accompanying the employment law legislation process grants the legitimacy for good governance of the public authorities in this area. Nevertheless, such a result applies only when both of these interest groups have a feeling that they are treated equally and their justified interests are well respected and balanced by the legislator. Otherwise the good governance concept would be only a theoretical idea having no practical impact on the quality of regulations adopted towards the employees and their employers. Therefore in the latter sections of this chapter it will be assessed as to whether the above mentioned good governance factors are truly followed by relevant authorities when it comes to adopting employment law regulations at the EU level.

The meaning of employer's interest

The necessity of protecting employees' interests is unquestionable. It is also relatively easy to identify what such interest would be composed of. From the employees' perspective the main factors on which they usually concentrate are the adequate remuneration for work, comfortable working conditions, reasonable working time frames and equal treatment with other employees. However, much less is said about the interests of employers and the necessity to protect those of them which are justified and relevant from the perspective of the state's entire economy and not only the employment market. When such a wide background is adopted, one may admit that these interests also deserve reasonable attention.

When it comes to the description of what should be meant as the employer's interest, one may identify a problem with adopting one, clear, ever-applicable definition. Unlike the employees, each employer may have some particular interests which other employers do not share (e.g. due to the competition in the same market with other employers). In general, with reference to employment law an employer's interest should be treated as the conditions of the business (or other) activity which bring the benefits to the employer and contributes to the achievement of the planned income based on the work of its employees (Florek, 2012: 18). What is important, from the perspective of the conflict of interests between employees and employers, a particular employer's interest must expressly appear in its mutual employment relationship with the employees, which always happens in respect of the employees' interests they have against the employer's position. If it is an interest which cannot be confronted with the interests of employees (either to the employees as individuals or assembled in the trade unions), at least in an indirect way, it will not be taken into account by public authorities during the social dialogue and decision-making process.

When describing what the "employer's interest" consists of, one may identify that the employer's interest may in fact be classified from the subjective and objective perspectives (Latos-Miłkowska, 2013: 27). Obviously, the employer's interest in the objective sense i.e. treated as reasonable and justified employer's needs the fulfilment of which is necessary to continue its business activity, is not necessarily in line with what constitutes the employer's interest in its opinion (a consequent fight for the maximization of profits resulting from the operated business). That is why it is the objective employer's interest which deserves protection from the public authorities. Such an approach also has its practical reasons. Generally, as mentioned before, various employers acting in the same market may have some interests which are completely opposite. Therefore, at the level of the social dialogue the employers' representatives must present a consistent standpoint (a "collective" interest), compromising first the particular interests of each separate employers to which the dialogue effects would apply. Otherwise it would not be possible for the employers' representatives to effectively and efficiently participate in the dialogue with trade unions and public authorities. Besides, even if presenting and supporting the subjective interest of a particular employer was possible in practice, it would be completely opposite to the good governance standards according to which the social dialogue should be transparent and consensus-oriented as well as that it should assure the true and active participation of all relevant stakeholders.

Although it is not popular to be in favour of the employers in their conflict of interests with the employees, there are several reasonable and justified arguments supporting a thesis that it is necessary to protect the employers' objective interests. First of all, in the era of capitalism the employment relationship has not the sole social character anymore but instead it also always has its economic use (Latos-Miłkowska, 2013: 38). The employers are business entities and they do not decide to employ individuals due to their sensibility for society's needs or the obligations imposed in this manner by public authorities. Each employment relationship maintained by the employees (especially, but not only from the private sector) must contribute to the proper business performance and the achievement of employers' economic goals (either directly or indirectly). In other words, each employment from the perspective of the particular employer is assumed to support the employer's interest. That is why one cannot expect that the employers do not participate in the legislation process regarding the employment legal framework because, from their perspective, it is one of the backgrounds on which they need to be visible in order to control the organisation of their business.

Following the above, it is a requirement of good governance standards that employment law effectively governs the nature and conditions of employment relationships considered as a form of social relationships. In order to meet this effectiveness requirement the law cannot be adopted *in abstracto*, without reference to the economic situation of the participants of this relationship. If the government cares about the economic situation of the one side of this relationship (employees), the good governance standards (including the equity and accountability factors) require that the economic situation of the other side will be also taken into the account (in the sense that the economic situation of the employer should be confronted with the market conditions being external and independent factors affecting the entire state's economy and not their profit maximization desires). Such an approach is coherent with the tendency to take the economic conditions into account during the legislation process which is visible in the states with a long tradition of relying their economies on the rule of free market (Deakin et al., 1998: 37).

This is all the more significant because, as mentioned before, the situation of employees (and therefore the protection of their interests) is in fact dependent on the protection of the fair employers' interests. If the justified employers' interests are not protected by the legislator in the view of their competitive challenges in the free market (especially in the transnational dimension - within the EU internal market), or the protection granted to them is insufficient in the view of market challenges, such lack of initiative may have its side effects on the situation of employees. No support for employers considered as entrepreneurs, and not only as entities obliged to guarantee certain rights to their employees, may in fact discourage them from continuing their business activity. In consequence the lack of support for the employers may lead to an increase in unemployment and other related effects of the social and economic systems of a particular state. This should be actually treated as the most important argument standing for protection of employers' interests.

In consequence, the state and the employees should also be interested in appreciating the employers' interests wherever it is actually possible (the fair interest requirement should be applicable to the employees as well as it applies to the employers). If such an appreciation is adopted as a one of fundamental factors of the legal framework referring to the mutual relationships between the employees and employers, the employees may perform their business within the system which facilitates their development. In consequence, their business may grow which, after all, will always bear a necessity of creating more job positions and therefore combat unemployment. It is worth emphasizing that such an argument for the protection of employers' interest is strongly raised at the EU level when adopting the policies and legal acts shaping the employment legal framework[5] (Latos-Miłkowska, 2013: 45) – according to this approach the employment law should be construed in such a way that fosters the economic growth in the broader perspective so that each employers' success would result in the development of their work plant.

One could admit that such motivation to protect the employers' interest is not entirely fair towards the employers, since it is only a way to achieve greater protection and comfort of the employees and the price for the appreciation of the employers' interests (which is expected to be paid by the employers) is their permanent pressure to allocate the positive outcome of their economic growth into the creation of additional job positions. This would mean that the protection of employers' interests is only an instrument and not the true goal of public authorities. Yes, it should be acknowledged that employment law has most of all the protective function with respect to the employees, but having in mind its practical correlation with the other disciplines of law, in particular the rules governing the perfor-

5 European Commission (2006), *Green Paper - Modernising labour law to meet the challenges of the 21st century*, Brussels: COM(2006).

mance of the business activity of the employers bound by this employment law, the protection of employers' interest should deserve a similar level of attention as the employees' interest. In the view of EU law such similarity is even based on the fundamentals of European economic integration, which are the freedoms governing the EU internal market. Nevertheless, even the instrumental approach to the employers' interests should be appreciated, if after all it grants them a sufficient level of protection.

Once it is agreed that the employers' interests deserve protection as long as they are fair, objective and common for all interested stakeholders, the good governance standards (especially the active participation factor) require also that such protection is effective. In order to reach such effectiveness, the level and character of protection must correspond to the market conditions these employers face during their regular business. That is why the law-making process, also the one referring to the adoption of the legal provisions which at the first glance govern only certain employment law institutions as such, always needs to bear in mind and foresee the economic outcome of its implementation from the employers' position. Otherwise the adopted law would cause effects which are completely opposite to the goals it was meant to achieve.

Employers' interest in the European Union law

It should be noted that the necessity of granting the protection to the employers' interests may be already recognized in the European Union's *acquis*. In the so called European employment law a number of elements proving the concern for the situation of employers (performing the business activity on the internal market) may be identified. In various documents, policies and papers adopted at the EU level the necessity to facilitate and simplify the rules governing the performance of business activity and to promote the development of entrepreneurship have been outlined from the very beginning of taking initiatives towards the European integration at the economic background. The establishment of the internal free market was one of the fundamental goals of the European integration.

The approach emphasizing the need for nurturing economic growth by caring about the employers' interests may be derived even from the provisions of EU primary law, namely Article 3.3 of the Treaty on European Union ("TEU") which confirms that one of the EU's main tasks is the activity towards the assurance of the highly competitive market. Incidentally, it should be noted that in the EU legal acts reflecting the need to take into account the employers' interests such need is not expressively indicated in the adopted provisions, but it rather may be derived from the meaning of these provisions and the context in which the EU legislator sets the other phrases. The fact that the legislator does not clearly mention the protection of the "employers' interests" does not mean that there is no intention to introduce such protection because all other statements referring generally to the promotion or development of the competitiveness within EU or the activity of the internal market should be interpreted in this way.

In this regard one may identify that a material part of the employment legal framework introduced by the EU secondary law also includes certain references to the protection of employers' interests by increasing their competitiveness ability. This mainly applies to the various European employment law directives, the preambles of which insist on taking into account the market conditions during the adoption of the regulations organising the work and environment of the employees. For instance, such an approach may be recognized in 96/34/EC directive regarding parental leaves, 97/81/EC directive regarding part-time work or 99/70/EC directive regarding work for definite period (Latos-Miłkowska, 2013: 71).

This tendency is still up-to-date, which may be confirmed by the wording of the recently adopted Decision of the Council no. 2015/1848 on guidelines for the employment policies of the member states for 2015. According to this decision, the member states should promote entrepreneurship and support the creation and development of small entrepreneurs (Guideline 5 of the Council Decision). Furthermore, the member states are obliged to facilitate the creation of the attractive job positions and eliminate the barriers that entrepreneurs face when employing the individuals. Additionally, all regulations and policies adopted in this regard should be adopted subject to the strict cooperation with the social partners so that the social dialogue may have an effective impact on the form of these regulations (Guideline 6 of the Council Decision).

Such construction of the guidelines, combining the employees-oriented regulation with the necessity to care about the efficiency of the entrepreneurs in the internal market, reflects the idea of balancing the EU goals of economic growth and the maintenance of a high-level of competitiveness in the internal market (i.e. the fundaments of European integration) with the goals of the social policy mentioned in Article 151 of the TFEU (including the improvement of the living and working conditions of individuals residing in the EU). The existence of such a concept at the EU level has been clearly confirmed by the Court of Justice, especially in the *Viking* and *Laval* judgments concerning the problems of social dumping and the conflicts between the economic freedoms guaranteed by the Treaty and the employees' rights to take collective actions against their employers (ECJ Judgment of 11.12.2007 in case no. C-438/05, *Viking*, and of 18.12.2007, in case no. C-341/05, *Laval*). Such idea may be derived also from the wording of the above mentioned Article 3.3 of the TEU stating that the basis of EU development is among other things the highly competitive social market economy, which should aim at full employment and social progress.

Given the above, one should acknowledge that the balance of the high-level competitiveness in the internal market with the goals of social policy (which is another expression of balancing the employers' and employees' interests) already exists at the EU level. This comes to the conclusion that the demand of such balancing is followed in the EU law. The adoption of such an approach in the European Union clearly corresponds to the good governance standards. Nevertheless, it should be verified whether such compliance is only apparent based on the provisions of EU law and judiciary or whether the EU truly observes in practice the rules it officially follows and requires the member states to follow. That is why the remaining part of this chapter will focus on the activities of the European Economic and Social Committee ("**EESC**"), i.e. the EU institution officially established to answer the necessity of assuring the sufficient level of social dialogue and balancing interests. It will assess whether this institution is given a chance to comply with its formal tasks and duties.

The nature of the EESC and the purpose of its establishment

The EESC is a one of two consultative committees established at the EU level by the Treaties. The EESC considers itself as an exceptional body which is a "forum for consultation, dialogue and consensus between representatives from all the different sectors of organised civil society"[6]. The EESC assembles various interests groups, such as the representatives of employers, trade unions and certain other groups being the experts for the

---

6 European Economic and Social Committee (2015), *Discover what the EESC can do for you*, Brussels: "Visits and Publications" Unit.

operation of the market and social policies in particular areas of their interests (e.g. consumers groups, environmental activists etc.).

The EESC is divided into six sections responsible for certain aspects of the EU's activity. There is a special section for the employment, social affairs and citizenship issues (SOC) which clearly admits that one of the main tasks of this committee is to handle the differentiated interests of employees and employers. Within these sections the opinions on legislation projects prepared by the Commission are drafted. In order to provide the final wording of such opinion, the participants must negotiate in order to reach the consensus. Therefore, in order to make its work productive, the EESC needs to balance the interests of the various groups interested in the specific legislation project.

The purpose of the EESC's existence is to support the assuring that EU policy and legislation is more democratic, more effective and genuinely reflects the needs of EU citizens. It is also said to have three key tasks which are the consequence of the adopted purpose to advise the EU's decision-making bodies: (i) to ensure greater involvement of civil society organisations in the discussion regarding the upcoming legislation projects and therefore (ii) make the EU citizens aware of impact of the EU legislation on their day-to-day activity, and (iii) to support the "organised civil society" (i.e. the various interest groups independent from the government, promoting their common interests by undertaking collective actions, and being therefore the intermediaries between legislators and citizens to make the latter ones engaged in the decision-making process) in its activities both inside and outside the EU[7].

In theory, all these ideas and tasks are a pure reflection of all crucial aspects of good governance concept, which obviously should be appreciated. At first glance, given the organisation and the concept of the EESC, its establishment, ideas and tasks are hopefully contributing to assuring that the voice of both the employees and the employers is heard when adopting the EU legal acts concerning employment law. Especially that, as mentioned above, the goal of protecting the employers' interests (at least for the sake of protecting employees) is visible in EU statutory law, which could make the EESC a field through which such goal may be achieved in practice, since the necessary balance between the employees' and employers' interests may be allocated in the opinion prepared for the EU deci-

7 Ibidem, 1-2.

sion-making bodies. Therefore, the establishment of the EESC in such a form meets, in principle, the calls of the good governance concept to strengthen the transparency of the decision-making process, to promote the involvement of key stakeholders by giving them a chance to express their views and to improve the effectiveness of the adopted statutory law.

Such organisation of the EESC is in line with the postulates included in the Commission's White Paper on good governance where the need for a more proactive role of the EESC in pursuing the good governance standards may be generally derived from[8].

The question is however whether all these ideas and tasks can be and are actually realized in the current organisational form of the EESC's involvement and whether the operation of the EESC provides the results leading to the accomplishment of the said tasks. Searching for the answer to such a question requires looking deeper into the mutual relationship between the EESC and the EU decision-making bodies within the frames of the EU legislative procedures, in order to determine the actual impact of the EESC's activity on the decisions adopted by European Parliament and the Council. In consequence, the actual state of such cooperation and the mutual relationship between the EESC and the EU legislators could be confronted with the thesis of this research project, i.e. the transition from government to governance.

Influence of the EESC on the EU decision-making process

Generally, the formal responsibility of the EESC in the EU decision-making process is to provide expert opinions to the EU legislative bodies (the European Parliament and the Council) with regard to the content of the initial legislation project prepared by the Commission. Depending on the matter a particular legislation project refers to, the EESC may be either required to provide the opinion (the mandatory involvement opinion) or to participate in the decision-making process by voluntary (prepared at the EESC's own initiative) or requested (by European Parliament or Council deciding that they need the expertise of the EESC members) opinions.

In the vast majority of internal market fields the EESC is obliged to provide the opinion to the European Parliament and the Council. This ap-

8 European Commission (2001), *European governance ...op. cit.*, 15.

plies especially to employment policy (Article 148 of TFEU) and social policy (Article 153 of TFEU). In the ordinary legislative procedure, if the legislation project concerns an area where the EESC has a competence to provide the opinion, the Commission sends the project to the EESC at the same time that it is sent to the European Parliament and the Council. In such a case the EESC should provide its opinion to these bodies before they finish the stage of first reading. By its own initiative opinions, the EESC may also additionally raise the need of the EU-level discussion in other areas which are covered by the EU competences. Such actions can be also an instrument to handle the initiatives of citizens and non-governmental organisations calling for respective reaction of the EU to the issues occurring within the course of the EU internal market operation.

Nevertheless, the members of the European Parliament and the Council are not required to follow the EESC's opinion (neither entirely nor at least part of the EESC's recommendations included in its opinion). All of the opinions, regardless of the form and character (mandatory, voluntary, requested) are not officially binding. This is typical for any consultative committees in any legal system since they perform rather an assisting role as advisors and are not true participants of the decision-making process. Therefore the only chance to admit that the EESC has an ability to influence the quality and content of the EU law adopted by the European Parliament and the Council would be the existence of a high level of respect of these bodies for the EESC's role and their willingness (a voluntary acceptance) to follow the EESC's approach.

Such a view may be confirmed by the analysis of the real impact of the EESC's activity on the EU decision-makers. According to the authors of such analysis, the EESC has a "voice yet no vote" in the decision-making process (Panke et al., 2015: 4) and therefore the influence of the EESC over the EU decision-makers depends on the match between the content of the recommendations provided by the EESC and the actual demand for such recommendations from the European Parliament and the Council. In the view of the above mentioned study, the EESC as the advisory body has certain influence on the European Parliament and the Council although its recommendations are not binding, but this influence is very limited. Such limitation is clearly acknowledged by the respondents included in this study, since 40 per cent of them (the members of the European Parliament and the Council) fully ignore the opinions provided by the EESC (Panke et al., 2015: 6).

Of course, according to various reports and standpoints published at the EU level, the EU institutions (in particular the EESC itself) consequently indicate that the EESC plays an important role in the EU legislation process and has a real impact on the decisions adopted by EU decision-makers. For example, following the Commission's report for years 2002-2006 at least one recommendation of each EESC's opinion was implemented by EU legislators in 81 per cent of all opinions, whereas in 56 per cent of all opinions two or even three recommendations were accepted and implemented during the legislation process (Panke et al., 2015: 11).

Nevertheless, one should point out that actually such an evaluation indicates that in almost 50 per cent of cases there is a maximum of one recommendation implemented from the entire opinion (if any). Given that the opinions include usually more than three recommendations; this means that very rarely the entire, comprehensive and adopted as a result of reaching internal consensus opinion of the EESC is taken into account. It should be emphasized that in cases where such opinions are adopted through balancing the differentiated or even contradictory interests of certain interest groups (such as the employees' representatives and employers' representatives), their particular recommendations could make sense and have real influence on the entire legislation project only if they are combined with the others, and therefore a mere partial implementation of a given opinion (one or only some of the recommendations) may have no practical effect on the quality of the decisions adopted by the EU legislators. In consequence, such implementation may not allow assuring that the adopted law is truly effective and corresponds the needs of the market actors.

When indicating the reasons why the EESC does not have that much attention in practice, one may generally emphasize the organisational problems the EESC has during its work within the frame of the EU decision-making procedure. It is visible for its limited administrative capacities in comparison with the European Parliament and the Council resulting in the extremely high workload of the EESC which is very difficult to coordinate with the decision-making procedure in which the EESC needs to provide its opinions very quickly and before the internal decisions are already adopted in the European Parliament and the Council (Panke et al., 2015: 22 and 67). The chances that the EESC's recommendations will be taken into account in the position of these institutions are increased if such recommendations are provided at the very beginning of their first reading stage, before these institutions come up with the results of their internal negotiations on a particular legislation project (since afterwards they are less willing to repeat their work by implementing the recommendations into their already adopted compromise). Due to the high workload of the EESC and its limited administration, it is very difficult to be that much responsive and this problem may also result in the lack of sufficient quality of the opinion in the view of the EU legislators.

Additionally, the question about the pure legitimacy of the EESC should be raised. This might be a problem where apart from the EESC there are also a number of NGO's or other interest groups, associated outside the EESC, which are very active during the EU decision-making process. From this perspective, the EESC is also somehow considered by such interest groups as not being a true social platform reflecting the balanced and fair interests of the stakeholders but as another EU institution which is out of touch with real market challenges concerning the particular interest groups. In such a case, if the EESC is not given with a sufficient level of internal legitimacy, it has also no legitimate influence on the EU decision-makers. Thus, if the particular decision-making process involves many interest groups, the EU legislators seeing the lack of social confidence into the EESC's work may try to negotiate directly with these interests groups and avoiding the EESC (Panke et al., 2015: 57), even if the EESC is also formally involved by providing the opinion under the mandatory procedure.

Another reason may be the nature (a legal basis) of the opinion provided by the EESC. Whereas it is obvious that a particular entity is more willing to take into account the advice when it specifically asks for it (in case of the EU decision-makers – when they initiate the requested opinion procedure towards the EESC), *according to the statistics the EESC is more keen on delivering* opinion in cases including the mandatory procedure, rather than providing the opinion when the European Parliament or the Council actually need such advice. (Panke et al., 2015: 24). Following this research the EESC seems also to be reluctant to use much the own-initiative opinions to be involved in greater number of EU legislation processes. Whereas such an approach to the own-initiative opinions is comprehensible due to the high workload, the preparation of the opinions requested by the EU legislators should be the priority of the EESC since in such cases it has the real chance to be listened to by these bodies, subject to meeting the expectations of the opinion's applicant.

All these negative results are in line with the growing concern for the EESC's utility and the visible calls, even among the members of the European Parliament, for abolishing the EESC as well as the Committee of Regions due to their lack of practical influence over the decisions adopted in the EU legislation process[9].

The above analysis and the practical lack of the EESC's material influence on the EU decision-making process affects the true implementation of the good governance requirements by the establishment and the operation of the EESC. One must acknowledge that the good governance standards requiring in the area of employment law the balancing of employers' and employees' interests may be for sure identified at the level of the EESC's operation and its procedure of adopting relevant opinion. The rules governing its organisation and internal decision-making process are clearly established to balance such interests, through the necessity to reach a consensus between the employees' and employers' representatives when adopting one coordinated standpoint. What is very important from the good governance perspective is that such interest groups need to cooperate with each other at the EESC level because otherwise this body has no possibility of being involved in the EU legislation process.

Nevertheless, it seems that such coordinated work at the EESC level has, after all, little impact on the EU decision-making process due to the non-binding character of any opinions the EESC provides. This means that in general the EESC does not contribute that much to the final wording of the legal acts adopted by the European Parliament and the Council. In that case one should admit that the balance between employees' and employers' interests required for the proper application of the good governance concept in the area of employment law is in fact assured only at the level of the EESC's work and not at the crucial legislation stage where binding decisions are adopted. Whether such necessary balance is provided at the legislation stage depends actually on the genuine motivation and discretion of the EU decision-makers, i.e. the members of the European Parliament and the Council.

As a result of the above, all the efforts made by the relevant employees' and employers' representatives to reach the consensus may become useless at the legislation stage where the respective bodies may decide not to follow the EESC's consensus-oriented opinion. In consequence, if the finally

9 http://www.euractiv.com/future-eu/eu-advisory-committee-defends-role-critics-news-501390 (accessed: 11.2.2016).

adopted EU employment law turns out to be effective, it is usually not a result of the EESC's input.

Therefore, although one may identify that at the EESC level the general assumptions of good governance concept in the area of employment law seem to be followed and implemented in practice on the basis of the treaty provisions (by establishing a treaty-based expertise body assuring the participation of relevant interests groups, imposing their cooperation via a consensus-oriented procedure and resulting in the realization of the transparency rule by showing all relevant projects to these groups), it is not sufficiently linked with the EU legislation stage. Such a link would have been identified if the EESC had a greater influence on the EU decision-making process. This could be achieved for example by the introduction in this area of the rules similar to the comitology procedure, or even by having a greater non-binding respect among the EU legislators. The lack of such a link undermines actually the true effect of the efforts undertaken at the EESC level to comply with the good governance standards.

The above point leads to the conclusion that the pure activity of the EESC is not sufficient to balance the employees' and employers' interests in the form of the European social dialogue, and therefore to truly follow the good governance standards. If nothing else, the EESC's activity contributes only to the provision of the transparency aspect towards the stakeholders who may participate via their representatives in the EESC's mandatory hearings regarding various legislative projects (Joos, 2011: 115). Apart from this aspect there is still a huge need to count on the European Parliament and the Council which decide in their absolute discretion on granting necessary powers to the EESC.

Since when adopting the EU legal acts the members of these legislation bodies tend to heed the political goals of their members' majority or the interests of particular member states instead of having a priority in following the EESC's approaches balancing the employees' and employers' interests, the question about the transition from the government to governance arises. It seems that in this case the governmental entities still play the fundamental role in the EU decision-making process but they actually have the capacity to bring the participation of the market actors (assembled in the EESC) within the EU governance structure to the fore.

This means that the establishment of the EESC is not a solution but only an instrument to comply with the good governance standards in the area of employment law by balancing the employees' and employers' interests, and this is still a challenge to the EU decision-makers as to whether they take that chance to implement such standards and therefore make the EU law sufficiently effective.

Conclusions

The good governance standards should also shape the employment law decision-making process. Such standards, based on the rule of democratisation including the participation, transparency and effectiveness requirements, may be reflected in this area by the institution of the social dialogue. The social dialogue encompasses a set of procedures aimed at achieving mutual understanding between the employees, employers and public authorities who need to adopt fair and efficient law. Thanks to such an understanding, both the interests of the employees and the employers (who are the only actors at the employment market) may be protected to the reasonable extent.

The social dialogue has also its supranational dimension across Europe. The European social dialogue has its background in the TFEU. As regards the efforts to institutionally realise this idea, the EESC as the treaty-based body taking the closest position to the EU legislators is supposed to be a guarantor of the participation rights of employment market stakeholders in the EU decision-making process.

One should admit that the true completion of the democratisation rule in the area of employment law legislation in the form of social dialogue applies when the employees' and employers' representatives are not only official participants, but they actually perform an active role in the decision-making process and their justified interests are balanced by the public authorities. Only in such a case the legitimacy for good governance of the public authorities in the area of employment law may exist and the adopted law may be effective.

It is often questioned as to what is the reason for protecting the interests of employers. Whereas the need of protecting the employees' interests is undisputable, the necessity to protect the employers' interest is underestimated. Such protection is indispensable not only from the perspective of the employees' situation which have their jobs guaranteed only if the employer is able to succeed in the market against the competition (also the foreign one), but also from the perspective of the entire state's economy. Assuring this protection is also necessary to make the employment law effective, since the employers feeling that their voice is ignored would never provide legitimacy for public legislators and would try to circumvent the obligations imposed on them in such manner. Of course, the necessity to grant such employers' protection relates only to their objective and justified interests.

The need for protecting employers' interests is also indicated at the EU level. In various documents, policies and papers adopted at the EU level the voices on facilitating and simplifying the rules governing business activity have been raised. The EU *acquis* reflects the idea of balancing the EU goals of economic growth and the maintenance of the high-level of competitiveness in the internal market with the goals of the social policy according to Article 151 of the TFEU.

Therefore in theory the EU *acquis* acknowledges and follows the rules of good governance concept. Nevertheless, it is important how the provisions reflecting the need of balancing the employers' and employees' interests operate in practice with the use of the EU institutions. To learn about it, one should focus on reviewing the above mentioned EESC's activity and the role it actually performs in the EU decision-making process.

The EESC is an advisory body supporting the EU legislators and the Commission. The purpose for which the EESC has been established is to provide the EU legislation with a decent level of democratic legitimacy and to make the adopted law more effective through the involvement of the EU citizens and stakeholders to be affected by this law. In theory the idea of the EESC's operation is in line with the good governance concept presented above in the area of the employment law decision-making process, requiring the balance in protecting both the employees' and employers' interests.

Nevertheless, the EU legislators are not required to follow the EESC's opinion during the decision-making process. None of the EESC's opinions, regardless of their form and character are officially binding. Therefore the actual influence of the EESC on the EU legislation process depends on its relationship with the European Parliament and the Council, and the willingness of these bodies to take the EESC's opinions on board.

Given the analysis of the EESC's organizational structure, the timing at which it is required to provide the opinions, the problems with its own legitimacy and the significant number of stakeholders which tend to impact the EU legislation process with the avoidance of the EESC, one should admit that the EESC's influence is not sufficient to truly comply with the good governance standards at the EU level which would assure a proper balance between the employees' and employers' interest. This means that the accomplishment of the good governance standards in this matter at the EU level depends in fact on the approach presented by the EU legislators and that is why these bodies are responsible for facing the challenge of the democracy deficit in the European Union.

References

Casale, G. (1999), *'Social Dialogue in Central and Eastern Europe, International Labour Organization'*, Budapest.

De Burca, G. and Weiler, J.H.H. (2014), 'Świat europejskich konstytucjonalizmów', Warsaw: Natolin European Centre.

Deakin, S. and Wilkinson, F. (1998), 'Labour Law and economic theory: a reappraisal, ESCR Centre for Business Research', University of Cambridge Working Paper No. 92.

Florek, L. (2012), 'Interes pracodawcy w prawie pracy', *Państwo i Prawo*, 5: 18-30

Joos, K. (2011), 'Lobbying in the new Europe', Wiley-VCH.

Karpen, U. (2010), *'Good Governance, European Journal of Law Reform'*, 12: 16-31.

Latos-Miłkowska, M. (2013), 'Ochrona interesu pracodawcy', Warsaw: Lexis Nexis.

Panke, D., Hönnige, C. and Gollub, J. (2015), 'Consultative Committees in the European Union: No Vote – No Influence?', ECPR Press.

Supernat, J. (2009), 'Transparentność w funkcjonowaniu instytucji Unii Europejskiej', in: P. J. Suwaj, D. R. Kijowski (eds.), *Patologie w administracji publicznej*, Warsaw: Wolters Kluwer business: 644-649.

Chapter 6: Good Governance thorough Better Regulation. Looking for the impact analysis approach to the proportionality principle

Jędrzej Maśnicki[1]

Key words: good governance, proportionality principle, impact assessment, better regulation

The aim of this paper is to examine the mutual relations between good governance, better regulation and the proportionality principle. Good governance and better regulation are very popular catchwords describing the socio-legal phenomenon . However, the subject of this article is to conceptualize these speculative terms and to find legal implications of the conception of good governance inside the recent Better Regulation package, which was launched by the European Commission (EC) in 2015 and through interpretation of the proportionality principle. The first research question is to address whether the conception of good governance is able to generate any additional value and legal meaning to Better Regulation and what mutual benefits could be recognized by the holistic approach to the both concepts. The second question is focused on the legal node connecting good governance and Better Regulation which could be developed by the proportionality principle.

Searching for the good governance meaning

"Good governance" is a multi-level phenomenon which was accurately described in the foreword to this book. I would like to make some remarks on the "good governance meaning" which will be the most plausible for the following chapter. The need for conceptualization of good governance is broadly recognized by the various scholars who seek to establish their own definitions or who accept the good governance interpretation already

---

1 PhD candidate, University of Warsaw, Faculty of Law and Administration, Department of European Law.

developed for analytical or policy purposes. It is neither possible nor necessary to stress all views on the good governance meaning. In fact, we could briefly classify these considerations in the two good governance concepts.

The first good governance concept refers to the World Bank definition which is based on three overlapping elements. Firstly, good governance requires the institutional system which recognizes the *internal rules and restraints* (e.g. internal accounting and auditing systems, independence of the judiciary and the central bank, civil service and budgeting rules). Secondly, good governance needs *"Voice" and partnership*, which is understood as the deliberative model of public policymaking as well as the client approach engaged to the public services. The third element of the World Bank good governance understanding is *competition*. The competition and market-based approach shall be provided to the private participation in: the public infrastructure, the judiciary (alternative dispute resolution) and privatization of the public services[2]. These elements are not unquestionable and even the World Bank itself sometimes uses other elements to define the good governance concept, e.g. one of the World Bank's definitions of the good governance (Karpen 2010: 16) could be stressed as including: 1) the process by which authority is selected, monitored and replaced; 2) the effectiveness of the government; 3) "the respect of citizens and the state for the institutions that govern economic and social interactions among them". Indeed the World Bank recognizes the respect to the financial institutions as the one of the constitutive elements of the good governance.

It could be doubtful to apply all of the World Bank's good governance criteria to the EU. Good governance at the EU level must be understood in a different manner as than it is adapted for the national level. Otherwise, the good governance concept would be so capacious that it could lose any added value as the appropriate tool to describe either national or the EU actions.

Good governance within the EU policy-making process was broadly recognized by the White Paper on governance (WPG) in 2001[3]. Good governance was indeed characterised as the tool to "boost the effectiveness and enforcement powers of international institutions". Good gover-

2 http://web.worldbank.org/ (accessed:21.2.2016).

3 COM (2001) 428 final, European governance - A white paper (OJ C 287, 12.10.2001, p. 1–29).

nance – as it was described by the EC, should be addressed by the implementation of five principles: *openness*, *participation*, *accountability*, *effectiveness* and *coherence*. These pillars of the EC's view of good governance are focused on the soft law application, rather than undertaking any additional binding measures. Good governance should be provided by e.g.: "language that is accessible and understandable for the general public", "more confidence in the end result and in the institutions which deliver policies" and "political leadership and a strong responsibility on the part of the institutions to ensure a consistent approach within a complex system". It seems that due to its non-binding character and relatively low category (only the communications instead of guidelines) the impact of the European Governance paper is overestimated. However, even within the soft law framework the meaning of good governance has evolved, e.g. good governance in the tax area was defined as "meaning the principles of transparency, exchange of information and fair tax competition"[4].

Currently, the need for a new approach to the EU policymaking is recognized as looking for a more effective and legitimate decision making process. The same need for legitimacy which was described by the Open Method of Coordination (OMC) rules is nowadays addressed by the good governance concept. However, it is evident that the OMC was to address the mutual relationship between the EU as a whole and the Member States (Burca 2003: 824). Good governance could be described as the legitimizing concept, which is in the WPG brought to the technocratic normative vision which "lacks saleability to the European public" (Smith 2010: 74). Non-binding acts referring to the good governance concept appear to be tools which are not clear enough to the EU citizens, however we should take into account that they are not addressed to each one of them. The good governance concept at the EU level is mainly addressed to the professional stakeholders who are already familiar with the current procedures. In my opinion, the only aim of good governance is to facilitate communication between the EU stakeholders and the EU institutions. Good governance urges for clear rules for interest representation within EU decision-making process.

4 COM (2009) 201 final, Communication from the Commission to the Council, the European Parliament and the European Economic and Social Committee - Promoting Good Governance in Tax Matters, Brussels, 28.4.2009.

The good governance legal meaning

The direct usage of the good governance criteria in the regulatory agenda appears to be rather modest. Good governance as a legal term is used in the Article 15(1) TFEU: "In order to promote good governance and ensure the participation of civil society, the Union's institutions, bodies, offices and agencies shall conduct their work as openly as possible". However, the legal meaning of this provision seems to be similar to the policymaking formula which cannot itself create any rights and obligations. References to the term of "good governance" appear to be broadly applied in the recitals of the regulations whose aim is to define the condition of granting financial support or tax relief[5]. However, the statements made in recitals cannot be perceived themselves as legally binding insofar as the reference to good governance made in the above-mentioned regulations seems to be rhetorical rather than creating any new normative standard.

The only one example of the normative definition of the good governance term is the Regulation No 1380/2013 on the Common Fisheries Policy[6] (further as "CFP regulation"). This regulation in article 3 is establishing the principles of good governance, applied to the Common Fisheries Policy. As stated in the recital 14 to the CFP regulation those principles should be the guidance as to how the decision-making process and management within the Common Fisheries Policy should be conducted. The principles of good governance as defined by the CFP regulation shall include various aspects, which are creating the overlapping legal space inhabited i.a. by the terms of: "regionalised approach", "long-term perspective", "cost efficiency", "stakeholders' involvement" and "consistency with other Union policies". Notably, the previous CFP regulation[7] also included the "good governance" principles, but the list was only half as

5 Regulation (EU) No 575/2013, Regulation (EU) No 978/2012, Regulation (EU) No 233/2014, Regulation (EU) No 1288/2013, Regulation (EU) No 230/2014.

6 Regulation (EU) No 1380/2013 of the European Parliament and of the Council of 11 December 2013 on the Common Fisheries Policy, amending Council Regulations (EC) No 1954/2003 and (EC) No 1224/2009 and repealing Council Regulations (EC) No 2371/2002 and (EC) No 639/2004 and Council Decision 2004/585/EC
(OJ L 354, 28.12.2013, p. 22–61).

7 Council Regulation (EC) No 2371/2002 of 20 December 2002 on the conservation and sustainable exploitation of fisheries resources under the Common Fisheries Policy (OJ L 358, 31.12.2002, p. 59–80).

long[8]. Indeed, the good government is an evolving principle, actualized even in the new version of the regulation which is dedicated to the same area.

Revealed in the CFP regulation, the multi-dimension good governance approach is creating a principles-net which is composed of catchy commonly agreed words. However, if we examine the added value of that net, it could be found to be questionable. It is not a matter of legal dispute to stipulate that the stakeholders are involved are "appropriate" or the measures are adopted in line with the "best available scientific advice". The abovementioned dilemmas appear to be matters of political decisions or scientific knowledge, not legal interpretation. However, the interpretation of legal principles, such as the principle of loyalty, proportionality or subsidiarity needs a shift to the more axiological or empirical basis.

Despite the abovementioned good governance definition, which is limited to the scope of the Common Fisheries Policy, there is no legal definition of the discussed term. It opens good governance to more or less speculative assumptions. On the other hand, to construct the legal definition of good governance could be pointless. Good governance is to be described as a policy-making concept rather than a normative issue. Its legal relevance could be seen in the category of an indirect interpretative clause which could guide the actions of the relevant authority. However despite the lack of a well-established legal meaning, good governance could be useful for stakeholders as the policymaking directive as to how the EU institutions could apply their legislative process rules.

The 2015 Better Regulation package

The EU policy cycle requires the ongoing connection of the following components: 1) ex-post evaluation of the existing legislative framework; 2) public consultation; 3) ex-ante impact assessment (IA); 4) draft of the proposal; 5) legislative procedure; 6) transposition and implementation; 7)

8 In its article 2 (2), it had expressed only: "clear definition of responsibilities at the Community, national and local levels, a decision-making process based on sound scientific advice which delivers timely results, broad involvement of stakeholders at all stages of the policy from conception to implementation, consistence with other Community policies, in particular with environmental, social, regional, development, health and consumer protection policies".

enforcement (Luchetta 2012: 561-562). Tools which are provided by the better regulation agenda address all elements of the EU policy cycle. The better regulation agenda, which is based on non-binding (such as communications, guidelines or staff-working documents) or semi-binding (inter-institutional agreements) instruments, is dedicated to the way in which the EC is going to prepare its proposals including, especially, the consultation process and the impact assessment. It is even claimed that better regulation should be perceived as the meta-regulation which "is a fluid and rapidly changing discourse that enables political leaders to address changing priorities in their regulatory reform agenda" (Radaelli 2007: 197).

Despite the fact that the better regulation agenda is implemented by soft law there is a strong voice to treat it as something more than the EC's political strategy. There is a strong belief that the better regulation should be something more than another non-binding instrument which could be ignored by the EU institutions. It should be "owned by the co-legislators to make it stick" (Alemanno 2015: 348). Despite the lack of a legally binding character the better regulation agenda may produce legal effects, by imposing the self-binding requirements such as the equal treatment (Alemanno 2009: 392-394). However, the better regulation agenda does not itself develop self-binding requirements. It is rather the emanation of the general principles or other binding Treaty rules which allows us to find the legal consequences of the better regulation package.

The better regulation agenda is indeed the tool which helps the EC to improve its policymaking, not the tool which is developed to evaluate whether the EC is entitled to undertake certain activities or to grant additional rights to the individual. In fact the better regulation agenda could lead to expand bureaucratic autonomy by limiting the scope of political decisions which should be accompanied by the set of internal staff working documents (Radaelli and Meuwese 2009: 648). As is stated in the general better regulation communicate: "[b]etter regulation is not about "more" or "less" EU legislation; nor is it about deregulating or deprioritising certain policy areas or compromising the values"[9]. The function of the better regulation package is completely auxiliary – "At the end of the day, regulators like to regulate" (Löfstedt 2007: 437). The better regulation agenda is settled by the Commission and is predominantly addressed to its

9 COM (2015) 215 final, Better regulation for better results - An EU agenda, Strasbourg, 19.5.2015, p. 4.

internal units. The better regulation package could have some indirect impact on the other institutions. Especially the CJEU could take into account the better regulation standards connected with consultation process and ex ante impact studies (Keyaerts 2012: 246). Instruments provided by the better regulation agenda could be a useful guidance how to conceptualize the very broad concept of proportionality principle in the judicial review of the EU legislation.

The 2015 Better Regulation package contains not only the Better Regulation Guidelines (BRG), but also: the Regulatory Fitness and Performance Programme Platform (REFIT Platform), the structure of the Regulatory Scrutiny Board (RSB), the draft of Inter-institutional Agreement on Better Regulation (IABB) and Better Regulation "Toolbox" (BRT). These communications and staff working documents are accompanying the general paper: Better Regulation for Better Results[10]. Despite the fact that these documents do not directly refer to good governance, it is self-evident that the realization of the aims provided by these instruments is indeed coherent with the good governance principles. Finding indirect connections between good governance and the better regulation package should be preceded by a brief description of its content.

The Regulatory Fitness and Performance Programme Platform

The main task of the REFIT Platform[11] is to gather the various suggestions from the stakeholders and any other participants (legal or natural person). Everyone is entitled to bring a submission which could be further examined by the REFIT Platform. These opinions should be concentrated on the question as to which areas of the EU legislation could be deregulated

10 COM(2015) 215 final, Communication from the Commission to the European Parliament, the Council, the European Economic and Social Committee and the Committee of the Regions Better regulation for better results - An EU agenda, Strasbourg, 19.5.2015.

11 SWD(2015) 110 final, Commission Staff Working Document Regulatory Fitness and Performance Programme (REFIT): State of Play and Outlook. Accompanying the document Better Regulation for Better Results – An EU Agenda, Strasbourg, 19.5.2015, C(2015) 3261 final, Commission Decision of 19.5.2015 establishing the REFIT Platform, Strasbourg, 19.5.2015, C(2015) 3260 final, Communication to the Commission The REFIT Platform Structure and Functioning, Strasbourg, 19.5.2015,.

in order to minimize the regulatory burden. The REFIT Platform as a constant body will consist of two types of experts[12]. The first group of members of the REFIT Platform includes 28 "high-level experts" from Member States (the "government group"). The second group consists of 20 experts representing the business sector, NGOs and other social partners, representatives of the European Economic and Social Committee and the Committee of the Regions ("stakeholder group").

These diverse bodies will be operating in working groups which: "will invite and analyse suggestions on regulatory and administrative burden reduction arising from Union regulation and its implementation and application in Member States". The first meeting of the REFIT Platform was held on the 29th January 2016, however it should be borne in mind that the REFIT Programme itself was introduced in 2012[13] and evolved from the "fitness check" which was introduced in 2010[14]. The EC is still in the process of making sure that the EU law is fit for its purpose and have decided to transfer that function to the semi-independent body chaired by the Commission's First Vice-President. The establishment of the REFIT Platform is also in line with the technocratic concept of democracy in which legitimization is provided by the stakeholders' participation evaluated by the more or less objective experts. Despite the fact that the REFIT Platform recommendations are not binding themselves, the EC will probably take into account the REFIT Platform outcomes. In terms of the good governance agenda the task and structure of the REFIT Platform refers to the accountability principle. The decision-making process could be perceived as being accountable due to the fact it is ex post evaluated by a semi-independent body (Grzeszczak 2012: 54). It is also reflecting the coherence principle as the part of the good governance requirements. The REFIT Platform needs to evaluate the possible deregulation taking into account the holistic approach which reflects to the EU legislation as a coherent system.

---

12 C(2015) 3260 final, p. 2.

13 COM (2012) 746 final, Communication from the Commission to the European Parliament, the Council, the European Economic and Social Committee and the Committee of the Regions. EU Regulatory Fitness, Strasbourg, 12.12.2012.

14 COM(2010) 543 final, Communication from the Commission to the European Parliament, the Council, the European Economic and Social Committee and the Committee of the Regions. Smart Regulation in the European Union, Brussels, 8.10.2010.

The Regulatory Scrutiny Board

The other institutional body which was established by the better regulation package is the Regulatory Scrutiny Board[15] (RSB). The main task of the RSB is to "scrutinise the quality of all impact assessments, major evaluations and fitness-checks of existing legislation and issue opinions on the draft of the related reports in line with the relevant guidelines"[16]. It should be underlined that the RSB is not competent to evaluate already existing legislation, its competences are predominantly limited to giving "opinions on impact assessment reports". Its function is clearly auxiliary: "the Board gives advice and opinions to the political level of the Commission".

Contrary to the REFIT Platform, the RSB is not an entirely new body. It is the personal and organizational successor of the Impact Assessment Board (IAB) which was established in 2006. Competences which were prescribed to the RSB in comparison with the IAB are widened by the "major retrospective evaluation and fitness checks of existing Union policies and legislation". It will be interesting to find how these competences will be examined with the respect to REFIT Platform prerogatives, especially when the REFIT Platform and RSB come to the different conclusions and would recommend different action to the same piece of legislation. Probably the further co-existence of the REFIT Platform and RSB would develop in some cooperation way, or the RSB would be self-restrained in the examining overlapping competences.

However, the major changes are connected with changing the status of the working staff. The RSB is composed of the six permanent members and a chair person. They should be experts in different policy areas adequate for the scope of the impacts assessment results. Three members will be provided from EC staff and others will bc thc employed only for the RSB. External experts will be selected "on the basis of their proven academic expertise in impact assessment, ex-post evaluation and regulatory policy generally". The three year cadence of the RSB member cannot be renewed or extended. Moreover, the RSB may rely on other EC units or experts "for ad hoc advice".

---

15 C(2015) 3263 final, Decision of the President of the European Commission on the establishment of an independent Regulatory Scrutiny Board, Strasbourg, 19.5.2015, C(2015) 3262 final, Communication to the Commission Regulatory Scrutiny Board Mission, tasks and staff, Strasbourg, 19.5.2015.

16 C(2015) 3262 final, p. 2.

It is too early to evaluate whether the RSB changes indeed enhanced the function which was previously played by the IAB. However, the gradual emancipation of the RSB is in the right direction. In the terms of the good governance requirements the tasks conducted by the RSB best fit in the accountability which is provided by the internal assessment of the other administration units working.

The draft of Interinstitutional Agreement on Better Regulation

The most important part of the better regulation package and the major novelty in the better regulation agenda as well (Alemanno 2015: 346) is the draft of the Interinstitutional Agreement on Better Regulation[17] (IABR). The legal character of the interinstitutional agreements may vary and depends on their content (Senden 2004: 202). However, it is justified to seek that the IABR could have semi-binding character due to the fact it has a self-limiting effect on the institutions which were willing to adopt it (Alemanno 2009: 391). The new IABR is to replace the current agreement on policymaking which was concluded by the EC, the Council and the European Parliament in 2003[18] and the common approach to the impact assessment (2005)[19]. The provisional text of the IABR[20], which was adopted in December 2015 by the Council, probably will be soon published in the Official Journal. Taking into account the semi-binding institutional agreements character it is of significant importance to examine what kind of duties will be placed on the abovementioned institutions on its basis.

First of all, the IABR will ensure that the EC work programme will be prepared in the multi-annual perspective. The annual programming will no longer be the unilateral EC decision; it will engage co-legislators as well. Three institutions will be obliged to reach the "joint declaration on the inter-institutional programming", which shall be accepted by the Presidents of the EC, the EP and the Council respectively. The declaration will have

17 COM(2015) 216 final, Communication from the Commission to the European Parliament and the Council Proposal for an Inter-institutional Agreement on Better Regulation, Strasbourg, 19.5.2015.

18 Inter-institutional agreement on better law-making (OJ C 321, 31.12.2003, p. 1–5).

19 http://ec.europa.eu/, 2016-02-21.

20 http://ec.europa.eu/, 2016-02-21.

to confirm "broad objectives and priorities" and identify "items-of major political importance" which should be the subject of "priority treatment" by the co-legislators[21]. The abovementioned joint declaration appears to be the triumph of the EP and the Council, which shall have a political influence on the FC's exclusive right to set up legislative proposals. However, the EC gains something of significant value the declaration that the co-legislators will not delay the flag-initiatives. Even if the meaning of the joint declaration will be more of political than legal importance it is worth noting that the signature made by the President of the Council and the President of the European Parliament could provide some expectation on the future effective legislative process timeliness in the case of most important proposals.

Secondly, the IABR will enhance the control over the procedure of adopting the delegating and implementing acts. The IABR includes the "Common Understanding on Delegated Acts" (CUDA) which aim is to introduce more transparency to the process of adopting the delegated acts provided by the consultation with Member States experts and other stakeholders[22]. It will be conducted usually prior to the adoption of delegated acts and occasionally ("whenever the broader expertise is needed") in the draft of implementing acts. As is stated itself in the IABR, the CUDA shall establish only non-binding criteria. However, as was stated above, as long as the CUDA is the part of the inter-institutional agreement it should be perceived as establishing the self-limitation on the EC.

Last but not least, the IABR introduces some new duties connected with the preparing of the Impact Assessment (IA). Firstly, it recalls the provision which was introduced to the previous Better Regulation Guidelines that the IA will carry out of the EC's legislative and non-legislative initiatives which are "expected to have significant economic, environmental or social impacts". It does not imply a strictly new approach to the criteria

21 The declaration is not the same as the annual Commission Work Programme The annual Commission Work Programme, which will be extended by including not only legislative but also the non-legislative proposals it shall include repeals, recasts, simplifications and withdrawals.

22 The detailed description of the CUDA is not the aim of this article. It provides two major innovations to the adoption of delegation acts: the mandatory consultation with the experts who will be designated by the each Member State and the compulsory consultation with the experts representing other stakeholders. Moreover, to the EC experts meeting may be attended by experts from the EP and the Council.

which are adopted by the EC in the decision as to whether the IA is necessary to be carried out. However, including these criteria in the IABR has a more strict character than was in the last 2003 Interinstitutional Agreement on better law-making (IABL)[23]. Moreover, it could be claimed that this provision will impose the duty to prepare the IA by the co-legislators. It is worth citing clearly this provision: "The European Parliament and the Council will, when they consider it to be appropriate and necessary for the legislative process, carry out impact assessments in relation to their substantial amendments to the Commission's proposal". In my opinion, the above cited provision itself does not have such an effect, as was emphasized by the flexible terms such as *appropriate* and *necessary*. Moreover the subject of how to classify the "substantial amendment" will be "for the respective Institution to determine". What is indeed new in the regulatory assessment is the possibility of updating the IA or undertaking other analytical work, which may be necessary due to the amendments or because of the time which has passed since the proposal was adopted and sent to the co-legislators. The result of the complemented IA and additional analytical work should be fully taken into account by the EP and the Council.

It is worth noting that the IABR will not provide any new approach to the stakeholder's consultation. Especially it is not clear if the consultation will be focused only on the pre-decision policy making process. Nowadays, consultations conducted by the EC are focused only on general policy issues, not the particular provisions, which are formulated in the final proposal. Sometimes it is hard to see any connection between these broad questions and any particular legal provisions which could be an unsuspected jack-in-the-box for the stakeholders. However, despite the abovementioned disadvantages the IABR is a significant step forward in the application of openness and could possibly more deeply engage the stakeholders (i.a. on consultation of the future EP and Council impact assessments) in

23 In the section 29 the 2003 IABL states that: "The Commission will continue to implement the integrated advance impact-assessment process for major items of draft legislation, combining in one single evaluation the impact assessments relating inter alia to social, economic and environmental aspects. The results of the assessments will be made fully and freely available to the European Parliament, the Council and the general public. In the explanatory memorandum to its proposals, the Commission will indicate the manner in which the impact assessments have influenced them", source: Inter-institutional agreement on better law-making, OJ C 321, 31.12.2003, p. 1–5.

the EU lawmaking process. To this extent it also reflects the good governance principles.

The Better Regulation Guidelines and the Better Regulation "Toolbox"

The most detailed parts of the 2015 Better Regulation package are the Better Regulation Guidelines[24] (BRG) and the Better Regulation "Toolbox"[25] (BRT). It is not possible to give here a complete description of the abovementioned tools. However, I would like to provide some remarks which are crucial to understand the scope of application declared by the EC instruments and mark the line between the BRG and the BRT and the concept of good governance.

The role of the BRG and the BRT should not be overestimated. The BRG itself limits its scope of application: "the aim is not to respect procedural requirements per se but to ensure that the Commission is equipped with relevant information on which to base its decisions in a timely manner". Moreover, the EC has provided a flexible clause which states that: "there may be a political imperative to move ahead quickly, an emergency that requires a rapid response or a need to abide to specific timeframes set in legislation which cannot be simply respected on the basis of proper planning" (BRG 2015: 4). Most of the requirements are also shaped by the very broad terms and in a non-decisive spirit (*may* or *could*). It led to the conclusion that the EC applies the BRG and BRT when it is willing to do so.

The second myth connected with the BRG and the BRT is that they are designed to deregulate the EU legislation or reduce the burden which is imposed on enterprises and citizens. The aim of the evaluation of the EU legislation and formulating the suggestions on the deregulation is conferred to the REFIT Platform. The BRG: "is not about regulating or deregulating. It is a way of working to ensure that political decisions are prepared in an open, transparent manner, informed by the best available evidence and backed by the comprehensive involvement of stakeholders" (BRG 2015: 5). The tools discussed are developed to give the answer to

24 SWD(2015) 111 final, Commission Staff Working Document Better Regulation Guidelines, Strasbourg, 19.5.2015, further as "BRG 2015".

25 http://ec.europa.eu/ (accessed:21.2.2016).

the question: "how to legislate?", not to deliver an answer to the question: "to legislate, or not to legislate?".

Taking into account above-mentioned limitations, the BRG and the BRT could be very useful as guidance as to how the EC will be drafting legislative proposals, traditionally claimed to be the subject of its own discretionary power. The BRG and the BRT alongside with other better regulation package instruments are providing the feeling which could be developed in certain cases to the belief that "the EU has the best regulation possible". In fact the BRG and the BRT provides to the stakeholders some information on that how the process of the policymaking is formulated and how the strategic decisions (e.g. about the preparing IA) are made. The content of BRG and the BRT cover key issues of the legislative process: planning, stakeholder consultation, impact assessment, preparing proposals, implementation, monitoring and evaluation. I would like to turn our attention to the issues which will be crucial to the further evaluation of the proportionality principle[26]. To optimize the proportionality principle it is very important to gather information and data which could be helpful to deliver justification as to the choice of measure which is the most adequate and how to develop its merit. Great significance in achieving these aims should be prescribed to the two external sources of information: stakeholder's consultation and impact assessment.

The stakeholder's consultation is an obligatory part of the consultation strategy for initiatives subject of impact assessments, evaluation and Fitness Checks as well as for Green Papers. The consultations should be held over a 12-week period on the internet platform. Stakeholders are also free to express their views on each roadmap, legislative and policy proposals and draft implementing and delegated acts (BRG 2015: 63). The function of the wide and relatively early consultation is clearly pragmatic, due to the consultation the EC can: "avoid problems later and promote greater acceptance of the policy initiative/intervention" (BRG 2015: 64). Consultations should be governed by the principles of the: participation, openness and accountability, effectiveness and coherence. However, the meaning of these principles is not as inclusive as it could be perceived. First of all – the participation principle means that the consultation is conducted "as widely as possible". Taking into account the fact that the consultations are

26 The examination of the application of the proportionality measures will be conducted in the next part of the chapter.

made over the internet platform it is hard not to guarantee the fulfilment of this principle. Openness and accountability involve the question as to how the consultation process "has affected policy making transparent to those involved to the general public" (BRG 2015: 65). The tool which could be helpful to evaluate whether these principles were fulfilled is the consultation report which is very general and hardly verifiable. Of course, the stakeholders' consultation submissions are available at the EC website and one could say that it is enough to satisfy the accountability requirement. However, it is not easy to find a direct reflection of the stakeholders' input in the further legislative proposals.

This leads us to two assumptions. In the first one, the stakeholders' consultation has a strictly legitimatizing character. It is necessary to provide the stakeholders' consultation to strengthen the acceptance of the further norms and to envisage that the EC is interested in the views which are expressed by the interest groups. However, this point of view reduces the meaning of the consultation to an activity which could have only a ritual character. The ritual questions are placed to receive answers which have been already determined by the EC's officials. It is contrary to the theoretical assumptions on the consultations as the form of reflexive government in which all involved parties are equal and could mutually learn their preferences from each other (Brown and Scott 2011: 479).

The second, more realistic approach is based on the assumption that the stakeholder consultations should provide specific information which is not shared with the EC (Meuwese 2011: 529). This second assumption is more convincing than the first one. The EC cannot possess all necessary information to address complex regulatory issues. It needs external inputs which could be provided by the wide stakeholders' consultation. The usage of the information provided by the various lobbyist groups depends on the EC's own judgment. The abovementioned information-oriented approach shifts the stakeholders' consultation from a legitimacy tool to a prosaic additional information source. Irrespective of my opinion it should be noted that the above-described consultations rules could guarantee the openness and participation which also refers to the crucial good governance principles.

The information provided by the consulted stakeholders is always based on the selection which is most preferable for the particular lobbyist groups. Indeed the EC cannot always justify its policymaking on the basis of information provided only by the stakeholders' consultation. In such a case there is a need to develop a more professional information tool which is indeed the impact assessment (IA) accompanying the final legislative proposal. The scope of the IA analysis is well defined in the EC's guidelines[27]. It should cover economic, environmental and social impacts of the proposed regulation. The tool which is helpful in estimating these impacts could be the cost-benefit analysis which is in line with the approach that all impacts should be measured in the most quantifiable way and monetarised if possible[28]. The IA is itself the subject of a 12-week consultation, which strengthens the acceptance and improves the quality of this policymaking instrument. However, the overall role of the IA appears to be overestimated. The abovementioned broadly consulted IA is not about deciding to legislate in certain areas (it is the task of the Inception Impact Assessment).The decision on legislation in the area analysed in the impact assessment was made prior to the IA preparation. It is emphasized directly in the BRG: "IA is only an aid to policymaking/decision-making and not a substitute for it" (BRG 2015: 17). It means that the results of the IA cannot make the particular decision, because it was already made before the official IA was prepared. The IA conducted within the EU policymaking decision process has post-decision effect, it is used by the EU institutions after the decision to initiate proposal made (Dunlop and Radaelli 2015: 31).

Therefore the preparation of the IA is not mandatory itself. The BRG states that: "[a]n IA is required for Commission initiatives that are likely to have significant economic, environmental or social impacts" (BRG 2015: 17). However, the decision on the preparation of the IA is clearly discretionary. It is envisaged by the BRT which claims that the: "IA should be carried out only when it is useful" and reveals it is very unlikely to prepare the IA when *inter alia* "the Commission is implementing previous policy decisions already subject to an IA" or "impacts cannot be clearly identified ex ante"(BRT 2015: 33). Moreover, the only survey which addresses the EC's practice on this subject shows that the each of directorates has its own practice on defining the need to prepare the IA and indeed this decision is the subject of wide discretion which is granted to the leading DG[29]. The insufficient coordination in the preparation of the IA

27 SEC(2009) 92, Impact Assessment Guidelines, 15 January 2009.
28 Centre for European Policy Studies, *Assessing the Costs and Benefits of Regulation. Study for the European Commission*, Brussels, 10 December 2013, p. 202-204.
29 The Evaluation Partnership, *Evaluation of the Commission's Impact Assessment System. Final Report*, April 2007, p. 32.

(i.a. in undertaking decision on its providing) should be perceived as a very negative factor which could lead to “a single sector ‘chimney’ approach” (Torriti and Löfstedt 2012: 176).

However, conducting the IA is not only a matter of public communication. Referring to some elements of the ‘speaking truth to power’ typology the IA should deliver relevant data which are essential to the further evaluation of the EU measure (Meuwese 2008: 42-44). This effect is on the significant importance in the post-Lisbon period, since the *Protocol on the application of the principles of subsidiarity and proportionality*[30] emphasizes that: “Any draft legislative act should contain a detailed statement making it possible to appraise compliance with the principles of subsidiarity and proportionality. This statement should contain some assessment of the proposal's financial impact” (Article 5). Taking into account that the protocol has the same legal importance as the TFEU it could be borne in mind that the reliance in the EU legislative process on the detailed and verified empirical data which could be provided by the IA should be qualified as the vivid operational part of the application of the proportionality principle.

The practical application of ex ante e.g. cost/benefit analysis to the each of the proposals is not possible, even it could “lead to the false sense of certainty” (Radaelli 2007: 203). Moreover it should be noted that the narrow perspective which limits the IA to the cost/benefit analysis is broadly criticized and should be replaced by the holistic approach which should refer also to the policy analysis and public administration disciplines (Torriti 2007: 247). I do not claim that the analysis provided by the IA should replace the other factors which should be taken into account in the application of the proportionality principle it only gives an additional argument which is a very persuasive and could be the subject of the further control concerning the methodology and assumptions which were taken to prepare the impact analysis.

30 Protocol (No 2) on the application of the principles of subsidiarity and proportionality, annexed to the Treaty on European Union and the Treaty on the Functioning of the European Union by the Treaty of Lisbon of 13 December 2007 (OJ C 83, 30.3.2010, p. 206-209).

The adoption of the proportionality principle to the EU policy measures

The proportionality principle is one of the general principles of the law, which has a broad scope of application. Its importance is especially visible in the sphere of the administrative and constitutional law. The very meaning of the proportionality principle refers to the philosophical concepts which are connected in modern times with German liberal thought and the continental conception of the constitutional state (Danwitz 2012: 369). For further considerations it is enough to state that the modern proportionality principle consists of three elements, which could be adopted to the EU respectively.

To satisfy the proportionality principle criteria it is crucial to answer the questions: 1) whether the action undertaken by the EU institutions or other (e.g. national) authority is adequate (appropriate) to the aim of the result to be achieved and 2) whether the measure which was chosen to realize the aim of the legislation does not go beyond what is necessary to achieve that aim and 3) how to establish the correlation between burdens which are imposed by the regulations and expected outcomes (proportionality *stricto sensu*). It is disputed if the third element is in the CJEU practice recognized as being the separate part of the proportionality principle (Gordon and Moffatt 2014:345) or if it is applied as the part of adequacy test (Tridimas 2006: 139) which examination requires the lawful benefit ratio as well as if the appropriateness should include also the consistency requirement (Danwitz 2012: 372). Craig claims that the proportionality *stricto sensu* is applicable only if the measure was recognized as being "both suited and necessary" but the burden caused by the measure is more onerous than the benefits which are the added value of the regulatory measure (Craig 2012: 602). It leads to the conclusion that the proportionality *strico sensu* is the latest and eventually final step of the full test application.

Within the EU law the definition of the proportionality principle has two different scopes of application and meanings (i.a. AG opinion in case C-293/12 and C-594/12, ECLI:EU:C:2013:845, paragraph 89). The first one is partially settled in the Article 5(4), paragraph 1 TEU: "Under the principle of proportionality, the content and form of Union action shall not exceed what is necessary to achieve the objectives of the Treaties". In fact this provision does not go beyond the already established case-law standard, (Gordon and Moffatt 2014: 343). It refers to the actions undertaken by the EU institutions, which is (together with the principle of subsidiarity) verified *ex ante* by the national parliaments and could be evaluated *ex post* by the judicial control of the validity of the EU measures by the action for annulment or by the preliminary rulings. This version of the proportionality test is indeed self-limited by the CJEU judiciary to the extent that it enables us to mark it as the "weak version" of the proportionality test (Pirker 2013: 249) or "low intensity review" (Craig 2012: 595).

The second approach is applied to the evaluation of the national measures which are evaluated by the national courts and occasionally could be the basis for the preliminary reference to the CJEU. The justification of national measures which are the subject of review by the proportionality principle standard seems to be a crucial task. The standard which is developed to evaluate the member states measures is very high and usually leads to questioning the national legislative instrument which is in dispute. However, the case-law review standard which is applied to the EU measures has a very limited scope of approach.

On the review of the EU-measures ECJ has declared that the principle of proportionality requires that the means should be appropriate for attaining the pursued objectives (i.a. case C-339/92, ADM Ölmühlen, ECLI:EU:C:1993:917, paragraph 15) and it must not go beyond what is necessary to achieve it (i.a. case C-293/12 and C-594/12, Digital Rights Ireland and Others, ECLI:EU:C:2014:238, paragraph 46). However, the practical implementation of these two assumptions is very flexible. The legality of the EU measure could be successfully questioned only if it is *manifestly* inappropriate having regard to the objective which the competent institution is seeking to pursue (i.a. case C-331/88, Fedesa, ECLI:EU:C: 1990:391, paragraph 14). This point is justified by the broad discretion in areas which entail political, economic and social choices, and in which it is called upon to undertake complex assessments (i.a. case C-157/96, National Farmers' Union and Others, ECLI:EU:C:1998:191, paragraph 61). Beyond the separation of powers, this statement has a more prosaic background – the need to avoid "endless challenges by applicants who sought to argue an alternative balancing of potentially conflicting factors" (Gordon and Moffatt 2014: 346). It is enhancing the applicant's obligation to provide sufficient evidence to demonstrate the manifestly inappropriate nature of the measures adopted by the EU legislature (case C-508/13, Estonia v Parliament and Council, ECLI:EU:C:2015:403, paragraph 37). Indeed this approach should be applied only to the non-rights based claims (Craig 2012: 606). However, the necessity requirement also seems to be rather hard to overrule (case C-101/01, Lindqvist, ECLI:EU:C:2003:596, paragraph 41).

The most discretionary element of the proportionality test is the balancing of different principles, objectives and interests which are revealed in the questioned regulation. However, in the third element of the proportionality test the CJEU has also limited its review to the question whether the EU institutions committed a *manifest error* of appraisal (case C-284/95, Safety Hi-Tech, ECLI:EU:C:1998:352, paragraph 37). This qualified form of proportionality *stricto sensu* evaluation is justified by the mixed values which are reflected in the provisions which establish the legal basis of the questioned act, e.g.: "in view of the complexity of implementing the criteria which the Community legislature must observe in conducting environmental policy" (case C-86/03, Greece v Commission, ECLI:EU:C: 2005:769, paragraph 88). Moreover, the point of balance between different objectives and interests reflected by the EU legislation refers to the generalized situation among all EU countries. The specific situation in the applicant's country cannot itself be sufficient to declare the annulment of the EU measure (case C-508/13, Estonia v Parliament and Council, ECLI: EU: C: 2015:403, paragraph 39). The CJEU declared in well-established case-law that the point of balance cannot abuse the very substance of the balanced rights (i.a. case C-544/10, Deutsches Weintor, ECLI:EU:C: 2012:526, paragraph 54). The concept of the very substance abasement reflects to the assumption that principles are being applied gradually and we could apply plenty of them to some extent simultaneously. The extent to which one principle or objective which is reflected in the EU legislation cannot abuse another which also must be reflected in the overall EU law to the extent in which the limited right is restricted in a disproportionate and intolerable manner (i.a. case T-614/13, Romonta v Commission, ECLI:EU:T:2014:835, paragraph 59). It reveals the liberal concept of the individual autonomy in which the possible freedom limitations may be made, as is stated in the Charter of Fundamental Rights of the European Union[31]: "only if they are necessary and genuinely meet objectives of general interest recognised by the Union or the need to protect the rights and freedoms of others" (Article 52). However, within the EU policy measures review, the CJEU is undertaking this balancing in order to preserve the individual's freedom "within the confines of the broad discretionary powers

---

31 OJ C 326, 26.10.2012, p. 391–407.

of the institutions inherent in the exercise of legislative power" (Tridimas 2006: 163).

As is depicted by the above mentioned CJEU judiciary, the preparation for a decision-making process could be the subject of independent judicial review. The CJEU does not evaluate the merits of the factual basis which lays behind the legislative decision but reserves the right to decide whether the EU institutions were well enough prepared to execute their powers. However, how to define if the socio-economic circumstances lying behind the legislative proposal were recognized as being satisfactory by the EU institutions at least? This is the field of the judicial discretionary power which could be limited by the concept of the good governance at the theoretical level and by the better regulation package on the pragmatically side. It should be recalled that the legality of the act cannot depend on retrospective assessment of its efficacy (case C-189/01, Jippes and Others, ECLI:EU:C:2001:420, paragraph 84) and should be based on the facts which were available when the decision was made. If the retrospective assessment and effectiveness could not be taken into account due to the proportionality principle evaluation, there is a fair question – how could the CJEU possibly reveal the disproportionate character of the EU policy measure? The clue could be found in the judiciary in which the CJEU had to challenge the EU legislation related to the highly economic issues (e.g. medicaments). In several judgments (case T-13/99, Pfizer Animal Health, ECLI:EU:T:2002:209, paragraph 410, case T-70/99, Alpharma, ECLI:EU:T:2002:210, paragraph 323) the CJEU has stated that in case involving risk management the "cost/benefit analysis is a particular expression of the principle of proportionality". It is worth recalling the Asso's considerations on the interpretation of the Community law, who stressed that: "the Community Court which is essentially a court dealing with economic interests, should interpret the Community norms on the basis of economic considerations" (Emiliou, 1996: 175). The inclusion of economic elements into the grounds of the legal interpretation could be the first step to perceive the impact analysis (in particular IA) as a practical tool to apply the proportionality principle. However, it is necessary to underline that the increasing role of economic considerations and analysis provided i.a. by the IA was to only a small extent developed by the CJEU itself (Tridimas 2006: 145-146). It is rather a reverse process – the administrative tools such as IA's are finding some reflections through the CJEU judiciary simultaneously to their wider development by the soft law measures.

The impact analysis as the tool of the proportionality principle

An IA is often invoked by the parties and participants, but the CJEU judiciary does not often refer to the IA as the grounds for legal considerations. However, in a well-established judiciary the CJEU recognizes the importance of the impact analysis which could be conducted by the EU institutions (especially by the EC as the author of the proposal) and tends to evaluate whether or not the analysis refers to the relevant facts or even methodology.

The most important case for the impact assessment proportionality approach was the action for annulment the part of the Regulation 1782/2003 on common rules for direct support schemes under the common agricultural policy[32] (case C-310/04, Spain v CouncilECLI:EU:C:2006:521). The compliant was submitted i.a. on the basis that the measures adopted to facilitate the new cotton support scheme were manifestly inappropriate. The plea was justified by the two studies which claimed that the adopted measures were counter-effective. The proceeding revealed that the proposal of the contested measure was accompanied by the EC's "comparative study of the foreseeable profitability of cotton growing under the new support scheme" which in the EC's view should be enough to satisfy the requirements of the proportionality principle based duty to take into account relevant socio-economic circumstances. As was noted by the AG it was only a comparative table showing the relative profitability of wheat, maize and cotton at particular levels of world prices prepared during the legislative procedure not primarily accompanying the proposal.

The CJEU has avoided evaluation of the figures which were submitted by the parties, however they contested the methodology which was adopted to the EC's study. Judges were focused on the fact that the EC's study was too optimistic because it has omitted certain labour costs (as was shown by the Spanish government) and examination of the consequences the reform is liable to produce for ginning undertakings situated in the production regions. It was precisely stated that: "even though such judicial

32 Council Regulation (EC) No 1782/2003 of 29 September 2003 establishing common rules for direct support schemes under the common agricultural policy and establishing certain support schemes for farmers and amending Regulations (EEC) No 2019/93, (EC) No 1452/2001, (EC) No 1453/2001, (EC) No 1454/2001, (EC) 1868/94, (EC) No 1251/1999, (EC) No 1254/1999, (EC) No 1673/2000, (EEC) No 2358/71 and (EC) No 2529/2001 (OJ L 270, 21.10.2003, p. 1–69).

review is of limited scope, it requires that the Community institutions [..] must be able to show before the Court that in adopting the act they actually exercised their discretion, which presupposes the taking into consideration of all the relevant factors and circumstances of the situation the act was intended to regulate. It follows that the institutions must at the very least be able to produce and set out clearly and unequivocally the basic facts which had to be taken into account as the basis of the contested measures of the act and on which the exercise of their discretion depended" (paragraph 123). Alemanno claims that the above mentioned sentence, which comes from the previous Jippes case (case C-189/01, Jippes and Others, ECLI:EU:C:2001:420) is a remarkable step forward to find the legal effects of the better regulation agenda by engaging judicial scrutiny of the basic facts by the proportionality principle control (Alemanno 2015: 398-399).

This case is considered to be the most vivid evidence of the exercising the proportionality control over the EU measures in which the proper analysis of the facts examined by the EU institutions was indeed decisive (Meuwese and Popelier 2011: 462-463). It is worth noting that the CJEU did not state that the lack of formal IA accompanying the proposal was evidence to state that the regulation was contrary to the proportionality principle. The manifest inappropriateness was stated only after examination the general content of the impact study. The form of this study was irrelevant to the CJEU however it could have had some influence on the study methodology. Probably it would have been easier to defend the regulation if the formal AI could be provided. If the Commission had decided to provide a detailed IA it would have included the elements (especially the labour cost), the omission of which was invoked before the CJEU as the evidence of the insufficient factual basis for the exercise of discretionary legislative power.

As long as the preparing of an IA is optional, as is confirmed by the latest better regulation package, the lack of an IA could not be itself the reason for annulment. However, Eleanor Sharpston AG has stated that the lack of "any preliminary study to examine the likely socio-economic impact" led to the omission of various factors which should be addressed by the EU institutions during the decision-making process (AG opinion in case C-310/04, ECLI:EU:C:2006:179, paragraph 82). It had led to the raising of questions whether the EC and the Council were informed enough to prepare and conduct the legislative action. From the external perspective "[i]n the absence of any impact study, certain choices made by the Commission and the Council appear arbitrary". Predominantly, the added value of the eventual preliminary impact study is performing the well-grounded base for further policy formulation and legislative process. The preliminary impact study is also the part of legitimization of the EU measures which are additionally justified not only by the legal arguments (which are not very difficult to satisfy) but also by the empirical evidence which allows answering the question on the non-legal reason of the regulation (Voermans and Schuurmans 2011: 514). This point is of significant importance, taking into account that the duty to give the reasons is interpreted by the CJEU in the current judiciary with a very limited and formalistic scope. The matter of justification becomes the more or less the part of the third part of the proportionality test to the scope which non-legal arguments were excluded from the duty to give the reasons.

In the widely discussed Vodafone case the CJEU has examined i.a. the infringement of the proportionality principle. It was stated that even though the EU institutions has a broad discretion: "the Community legislature must base its choice on objective criteria. Furthermore, in assessing the burdens associated with various possible measures, it must examine whether objectives pursued by the measure chosen are such as to justify even substantial negative economic consequences for certain operators" (case C-58/08, Vodafone and Others, ECLI:EU:C:2010:321, paragraph 53). It should be noted that the CJEU and other EU institutions during the judicial proceeding referred several times to the EC's impact assessment. In the Vodafone case to the some extent, the legal reasoning was in fact driven by the numbers provided by the IA. The comprehensive study which was prepared by the European Commission in accordance with the impact assessment was taken by the CJEU as the basis of the findings of facts necessary to state that the community measure which has introduced the retail price control (the roaming Eurotariif) was appropriate for the purpose of the Regulation No 717/2007[33], the purpose of which is to protect consumers against high levels of charges imposed by the mobile operators. Probably without evaluation of the prices it could be very difficult to challenge the disproportionality plea (Keyaerts 2012: 245).

---

33 Regulation (EC) No 717/2007 of the European Parliament and of the Council of 27 June 2007 on roaming on public mobile telephone networks within the Community and amending Directive 2002/21/EC (Text with EEA relevance) (OJ L 171, 29.6.2007, p. 32–40).

In the next case the proportionality principle plea was in fact based on the cost-benefit analysis which was provided to examine whether the additional burden caused by the directive on airport charges[34] is too high for the Luxembourg-Findel airport (case C-176/09, Luxembourg v Parliament and Council, ECLI:EU:C:2011:290). The plea was based on the estimation that the requirements provided by the directive would result in a 16% increase in passengers charges. On the contrary, the Commission has stated that the IA led to the rejection of the most restrictive regulatory option which was considered when the directive proposal was drafted. The CJEU has invoked the EC's impact assessment to stipulate that the measure which was chosen to be included in the directive proposal was the least restrictive regulatory option. It is apparent from this case that the CJEU does not only evaluate whether the EU institutions had the sufficient knowledge while the contested measure was adopted in the discussed case, but also that the CJEU has itself decided if the EU measure was the most appropriate option.

The abovementioned cases have revealed the importance of the EC's impact assessment to the proportionality principle judicial review of the EU measures. The acceptance of the data provided by the EC's impact study is based on the presumption on its correctness. However, how to evaluate the EC's impact assessment? In the Jippes judgment the CJEU has stated that: "[w]here the Community legislature is obliged to assess the future effects of rules to be adopted and those effects cannot be accurately foreseen, its assessment is open to criticism only if it appears manifestly incorrect in the light of the information available to it at the time of the adoption of the rules in question" (case C-189/01, Jippes and Others, ECLI:EU:C:2001:420, paragraph 84). This statement does not refer directly to the impact assessment in the meaning provided by the Better Regulation package but it could be applied to it. In the light of this statement the CJEU is even obliged to evaluate the methodology which is applied to the IA study.

In the Jippes case it was stated that the measure was not manifestly inappropriate due to the "global assessment of the advantages and drawbacks of the system to be established and that that policy, corresponding to the recommendations of the IOE and the practice followed by numerous

34 Directive 2009/12/EC of the European Parliament and of the Council of 11 March 2009 on airport charges (Text with EEA relevance) (OJ L 70, 14.3.2009, p. 11–16).

countries worldwide" (paragraph 95) provided by the EC in its IA. However, even if the data provided by the Commission could be perceived as being insufficient to evaluate the situation in the each of the Member States, it is necessary to put these considerations in the context of the judicial proceeding in which the other party should be obliged to prove its contention on the disproportionality of the EU measures. In the IATA and ELFAA case the parties complained that the cost of the contested measure was disproportionate, however, were not capable of providing its own data which could counter the EC's estimations. It resulted in the rejection of the disproportionality plea: "the theoretical costs which those measures involve for airlines, as put forward by the parties concerned, do not in any event enable it to be regarded as established that those effects would be out of proportion to the interest in the measures" (case C-344/04, IATA and ELFAA, ECLI:EU:C:2006:10, paragraph 89). The requirement of providing an alternative cost-benefit analysis places a significant advantage in the favour of the EU institutions which are taking decisions based on the IA.

However, providing the impact study does not itself result in the automatically stated compatibility with the proportionality principle. In the Pfizer Animal Health case the CJEU was faced with errors in the cost-benefit analysis provided by the EU institutions. In accordance with the applicant's submission the Community institutions made errors in the cost-benefit analysis, in which the costs and benefits to society are compared with the costs and benefits which would apply if no action were taken. In the applicant's view it could be seen that the cost-benefit analysis is based on the manifest error because it is hard to believe that the new EU legislation does not cause any additional costs. Pfizer has additionally held that the providing of the cost-benefit analysis of the banning of the product (*virginiamycin*) will cause a broad loss of revenues which could be harmful not only for the enterprises which were directly distributing the product, but also for those associated with these enterprises services. The CJEU has admitted that the impact analysis (the EC did not carry out the formal impact assessment) was based upon the errors when the EU institutions were deciding upon the choice of the regulatory options. However: "the legality of the contested regulation could be called into question only if the institutions had made a manifest error of assessment in deciding upon their policy" (case T-13/99, Pfizer Animal Health v Council, ECLI:EU:T:2002:209, paragraph 470). Only the qualified form of the error made by the EC in the preparation of the impact study could be enough to open the way to declare the disproportionality of the EU measure. It would be very challenging to justify the plea. The manifest error is also a broad concept which includes both error of law and error of fact (Emiliou, 1996: 185). Due to the professionalism of the EC legal service the error of law is hard to imagine, but the error of fact could be based on economic considerations, especially if the IA preparation was omitted.

The lack of the cost-benefit analysis was also the subject of the consideration in the Alpharma case. The applicant claimed that the cost-benefit analysis should: "include a comparison between the most likely positive and negative consequences of the proposed action and those which would follow if no action were taken, in terms of the overall short-term and long-term cost for the Community, and that the analysis must also include non-economic considerations" (case T-70/99, Alpharma v Council, ECLI:EU:T:2002:210, paragraph 359). Irrespective of the amount of time since the Alpharma judgment, these requirements are very similar to the function of the current IA which is stated in the better regulation package. However, the ECJ has revealed that the impact study was made due to : "several of the reports by international bodies which had been submitted to the institutions during the procedure culminating in adoption of the contested regulation". The CJEU has recalled the reasoning which was presented in the Pfizer case and has upheld the legality of the contested measure.

The two-steps impact analysis approach to the proportionality principle

The evaluation of the impact study is surely the essential part of the proportionality principle. The impact analysis, e.g. provided by the formal IA or other analytical data, is necessary to quantify costs and benefits and to establish whether the contested measure is necessary (least onerous) and satisfies the stricto sensu proportionality test. However, as follows from the CJEU judiciary the evaluation of the assessment studies usually does not result in the annulment of the contested EU measure.

The CJEU attitude to the impact studies prepared for proposals of the further questioned acts could lead to the two step proportionality check formula. In the first step the CJEU is evaluating whether or not the EU institutions were sufficiently informed when they were adopting the contested measure. The administration should have known "its exact motifs and the facts in the light of which it reached its decision" before the act was adopted (Emiliou 1996: 183). Preparing of the impact study is usually treated as being enough to satisfy the proportionality requirements. It is worth noting that this step could be satisfied not only when the formal IA was prepared but also when the other analysis formula was applied. The CJEU does not see the difference between the IA in the meaning of the better regulation package and any other quantified form of the preliminary assessment.

The second step requires that the analysis which accompanied the decision-making process was made in the right way. It means that it included the most important factors, such as the all serious costs or it was based on accurate data. However, when the second step is applied the CJEU has developed the self-limiting doctrine of the *manifest error*, as was depicted the CJEU is occasionally finding violations "only in cases where it becomes virtually impossible to asses the reasons that led to the conclusion of legislation" (Pirker 2013: 250). In my opinion, the new approach to the proportionality principle requires that the manifest error concept should be abandoned, because its successful application seems to be the barrier which cannot be challenged by the applicants and is the final weakness of the judicial application of the proportionality test to the EU measures.

The two-step application of the above described proportionality formula is partly dependent on the internal EC decision on the providing of an IA for each regulation. As it was stated in the first part of this paper, these decisions seem to be completely discretionary. The discretionary sphere of the internal decision-making process could be the subject of the judicial review only to the extent in which it concerns the rights of individuals (i.a. case C-129/96, Inter-Environnement Wallonie, ECLI:EU:C:1997:628). The preparation of the IA does not directly refer to the rights or freedom of the other parties. The internal decision on providing the IA does not appear to be actionable. It could be basis for the further legal provisions, which may be the subject of the action for annulment but it cannot impose on the EC the legal duty to provide the IA itself. To establish the duty to provide the IA it is necessary to refer to the soft law requirements, namely the better regulation package and to the good governance principle as decisive to the application of the abovementioned rules governing the technical way of the IA preparation.

Conclusions - the additional impact of the good governance principle

As was described, the legal status of the good governance principle is uncertain itself. Despite the lack of well-established good governance meaning, the CJEU occasionally refers to good governance. These references are very rare and it is doubtful if they indeed drive the legal reasoning. In the Gabi Thesing case the right to the access to the ECB documents was justified by the wording of the Article 15(1) TFEU, in which the wording refers i.a. to governance in order to promote the openness and transparency of the EU institutions, bodies and agencies (case T-590/10, Gabi Thesing, ECLI:EU:T:2012:635, paragraph 39). However in the abovementioned case the CJEU did not conclude any finding on the basis of the good governance mentioned in the article 15(1) TFEU and has limited itself to recapitulating the wording of this provision. The good governance principle was discussed in this respect in the opinion to the Sophie in't Veld case. Eleanor Sharpston AG has invoked the good governance principle as one of the principles governing the taxation regime (AG opinion in case C-350/12 P, ECLI:EU:C:2014:88, paragraph 58-59). The approach revealed in the abovementioned opinion does not allow us to claim that the new legal meaning of good governance has been discovered. Good governance was presented as being the part of the rhetorical phase of argumentation, which could enhance the already stated considerations, but does not itself provide any significant added value.

Quite different consequences could be revealed if we follow the approach presented in the joined cases C-120/06 P and C-121/06 opinion. In regard to the good governance meaning the Poiares Maduro AG has noted that the additional argument for the principle of no-fault liability of the EU institutions are the requirements of good governance. It would be especially important in the cases where other instruments (action for annulment, preliminary ruling) are not admissible (AG opinion in joined cases C-120/06 P and C-121/06 P, ECLI:EU:C:2008:98, paragraph 59). It means that the good governance principle was presented as the tool which could affect the sphere of discretionary power of the EC institutions which are not the subject of direct judiciary control. If we assume that point is justified by the wording of the Article 15 (1) TFEU it could be also applied to the drafting of legislative proposals and the decision on the preparing impact assessment study.

Although the requirements imposed by the soft law (BR and BRT) precisely refer to the content of the IA, the better regulation package does not answer the question of whether or not to provide the IA. In fact, this pre-decision on the IA preparation should be the subject of the good governance principle which could be verified by the conducted by the CJEU ex post control of the subsidiarity principle by the action for annulment. This could be an additional impact of the good governance principle as the tool which limits the internal EU intuitions discretionary power in order to maintain their decisions in a more rational analysis, based on the quantified cost-benefit analysis.

This approach is envisaged by the two-step formula in which the CJEU verifies whether the competent institutions were sufficiently informed and could have had the sufficient knowledge about the basic facts when the act was adopted. This formula requires not only whether or not the EU institutions were sufficiently informed (first step) but also engages the evaluation of the methodology which was applied to the impact studies accompanying the legislative process (second step). To this extent the soft law rules imposed by the better regulation package (e.g. on the IA minimum content) should be recognised further by the CJEU judiciary as establishing the guidelines on that how the proportionality *stricto sensu* should be conceptualised. It is necessary to enhance the EU measures of judicial review by the impact analysis approach to the justification of the exercising the EC and co-legislators powers.

References

Alemanno, A. (2015), 'How Much Better Is Better Regulation? Assessing the Impact of the Better Regulation Package on the European Union – A Research Agenda', *European Journal of Risk Regulation*, 3: 344-357.

Alemanno, A. (2009), 'The Better Regulation Initiative at the Judicial Gate: A Trojan Horse within the Commission's Walls or the Way Forward?', *European Law Journal*, 15(3): 382-401.

Burca, G. De (2003), 'The constitutional challenge of new governance in the European Union', *European Law Review*, 28 (6): 814-836.

Brown, C. and Scott, C. (2011), 'Regulation, Public Law, and Better Regulation', *European Public Law*, 17 (3): 467–484.

Craig, P. (2012) ,'EU Administrative Law. Second Edition', Oxford: Oxford University Press, 591-615.

Danwitz, T. von (2012), 'Thoughts on Proportionality and Coherence in the Jurisprudence of the Court of Justice', in: P. Cardonnel, A. Rosas, N. Wahl (eds), *Constitutionalising the EU Judicial System. Essays in Honour of Pernilla Lindh*, Oxford: Hart Publishing, 367-382.

Dunlop C.A. and Radaelli, C.M. (2015), 'Impact Assessment in the European Union: Lessons from a Research Project', *European Journal of Risk Regulation*, 6(1): 27-34.

Emiliou, N. (1996), 'The Principle of Proportionality in European Law. A Comparative Study', London: Kluwer Law International.

Gordon, R. and Moffatt, R.(2014), 'EU Law in Judicial Review', Oxford: Oxford University Press, 340-365.

Grzeszczak, R. (2012), 'Accountability and Legitimacy of Executive to the Succession of States', *Studia Iuridica*, 54: 45-58.

Karpen, U. (2010), 'Good Governance', *European Journal of Law Reform*, (12) 1-2: 16-31.

Keyaerts, D. (2012), 'The Impact of Better Regulation in the Case Law of the European Court of Justice', *European Journal of Risk Regulation*, 3 (2): 241-247.

Luchetta, G. (2012), 'Impact Assessment and the Policy Cycle in the EU', *European Journal of Risk Regulation*, 3: 561-575.

Löfstedt, R. (2007), 'The 'Plateau-ing' of the European Better Regulation Agenda: An Analysis of Activities Carried out by the Barroso Commission', *Journal of Risk Research*, 10 (4): 423-447.

Meuwese A. (2011), 'Embedding consultation procedures: Law or Institutionalization', *European Public Law*, 17(3): 527-538.

Meuwese A. (2008), 'Impact Assessment in EU Lawmaking', London: Kluwer Law International.

Meuwese A. and Popelier, P. (2011), 'Legal Implications of Better Regulation: A Special Issue', *European Public Law*, 17(3): 455–466.

Pirker, B. (2013), 'Proportionality Analysis and Models of Judicial Review. A Theoretical and Comparative Study', Groningen: Europa Law Publishing, 235-276.

Radaelli, C.M. (2007), 'Whither better regulation for the Lisbon agenda?', *Journal of European Public Policy*, 14 (2): 190-207.

Radaelli, C.M. and Meuwese, A. (2009), 'Better regulation in Europe: between public management and regulatory reform', *Public Administration*, 87(3): 639-654.

Senden, L. (2004), 'Soft Law in European Community Law', Oxford: Hart Publishing.

Smith, M. (2010), 'Centralised Enforcement, Legitimacy and Good Governance in the EU', New York: Routledge.

Torriti, J. (2007), 'Impact Assessment in the EU: A Tool for Better Regulation, Less Regulation or Less Bad Regulation?', *Journal of Risk Research*, 10(2): 239-276.

Torriti, J. and Löfstedt, R. (2012), 'The first five years of the EU Impact Assessment system: a risk economics perspective on gaps between rationale and practice', *Journal of Risk Research*, 15(2): 169-186.

Tridimas, T. (2006), 'The General Principles of EU Law. Second Edition', Oxford: Oxford University Press, 2006: 136-192.

Voermans, W. and Schuurmans, Y. (2011), 'Better Regulation by Appeal', *European Public Law*, 17(3): 507-525.

Chapter 7: The access to e-justice and its benefits for citizens and business environment

Jagna Mucha

Key words: European e-Justice System, access to justice, judicial system, information and communication technologies

Introduction

The right to effective access to justice constitutes one of the fundamental pillars of a democratic legal order. The contemporary interpretation of this right to such access must not be limited solely to the national level (Mucha, 2015). As the number of cases with a cross-border component increases, a full guarantee of transnational access to justice has become an indispensable requirement. This is because one cannot speak of effective access to justice if the access is limited only to solving domestic legal problems.

Taking the above into account, the European Union has introduced a tool to facilitate the easier management of cross-border cases. It is the European e-Justice system, an electronic tool based on information and telecommunication technology aimed at facilitating comprehensive access to justice across the EU. The key task for the system is to convey relevant information concerning EU and member state legislation to EU citizens, businesses and legal professionals. The entities interested in e-Justice can use the tool to find information concerning access to trade registers, land and mortgage registers or insolvency registers both at the EU and at the national (member state) level – among other information. The solution enables its users to learn about the systems of courts in particular member states as well as verifying which court has jurisdiction over the case at hand. E-Justice also facilitates cooperation between judicial authorities in particular member states.

Contrary to popular perception, the scope of e-Justice does not only encompass the legal sector. It is part of a broader concept of e-Government that refers to the application of information and communication methods across the entire public administration. For this reason, the European Union's e-Justice system also covers non-legal areas of application. An example here may include administrative activities consisting in the issuance of transcripts from land registers or informing citizens about alternative dispute resolution measures through persons from outside of the legal professions. The existing literature on the subject also indicates that launching e-Government (including e-Justice) is a means of achieving good governance. By implementing e-Government, central government authorities respond to the citizen's need for a broader access to public services (Kettani, Moulin, 2009).

In this chapter, I will attempt to verify whether the European e-Justice system actually provides an easier access to justice for the EU's citizens and entrepreneurs, and whether the system, in fact, facilitates the cooperation of lawyers and judicial authorities in cross-border matters. In order to verify this I will refer to the legal framework of e-Justice and conduct an analysis of the system's formation starting from 2007. I will also pay particular attention to the Internet portal that operates as part of e-Justice. Subsequently, I will analyse the portal's scope of functionality and later assess its effectiveness.

Legal background of the European e-Justice System

An analysis of the EU e-Justice system must take into account the role played in its formation by the European Council (in its Justice and Home Affairs configuration, hereafter referred to as the "JHA Council") and the European Commission. The idea to create the system first appeared in 2007 within the JHA Council. The general concept consisted in creating a European e-Justice web portal that would broaden access to justice thanks to information and communication technologies.

a) Communication of the European Commission "Towards a European e-Justice Strategy" (2008)

The initial outline suggested by the JHA Council was later developed by the European Commission, which issued a Communication entitled "Towards a European E-justice Strategy" (hereafter referred to as the "Communication").[1] The document's authors proposed that an electronic tool be created to facilitate modernisation of the EU's justice systems as well as introducing closer judicial collaboration thanks to information and communication technologies.

According to the Communication, the system had the following objective and target users: "(...) e-Justice's primary objective is to help justice to be administered more effectively throughout Europe, for the benefit of citizens. The first hallmark of priority projects should be that they help legal professionals work more effectively and citizens obtain justice more easily."[2] The quotation suggests that from the perspective of the subject of law, e-Justice was initially intended as a two-layer structure. On the one hand, the portal's objective was to provide information for stakeholders seeking to solve their cross-border legal issues, and on the other hand it also aimed at facilitating the resolution of the cases for the relevant judicial authorities.

From the perspective of the stakeholder, the system's value consisted in the fact that it collected in one place information such as the course of legal proceeding, court activities, court rulings and acts of law across the entire EU and, if necessary, referred the user to the relevant databases.[3] The intention was also for the portal to become highly applicable – it was meant to enable the stakeholders to take part in electronic legal proceedings (Kotecka, 2011) and perform the related actions including payment of court fees or testifying.

On the other hand, from the point of view of judicial authorities, e-Justice was intended to facilitate collaboration between courts from particular member states. The project consisted in creating a network of national criminal registers and a secure information exchange network for judicial authorities, as well as by promoting the use of tele- and video-conferencing as part of court proceedings. Due to the European Union's linguistic

1 Communication from the Commission to the Council, the European Parliament and the European Economic and Social Committee „Towards a European e-Justice Strategy" dated 30 May 2008, COM(2008)329final.

2 Communication COM(2008)329final, *op. cit.*, p. 3.

3 Primarily, the information available via the e-justice system was to be accessible by the victims and those who were accused with committing the trans-border offences so that they could find out – via the portal - about their rights in the individual member states. Additionally, the portal was to give access to the practical guidelines for the entities which plan to initiate the court proceedings in another member state.

diversity policy, translation services for the cooperating entities are of key importance. This is why the Commission (in its Communication) devoted much space to the need for development of appropriate translation tools (Więcławska, 2014). Consequently, the e-Justice platform is intended to include, among other things, a database with court translators and interpreters in particular member states as well as on-line forms for automatic translation.

Fig. 1: Diagram representing e-Justice and its functionality as proposed by the European Commission in 2008

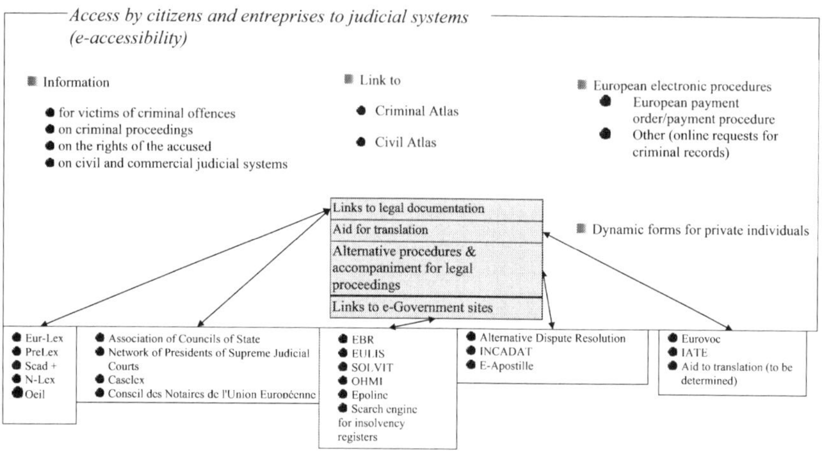

Source: Communication from the Commission to the Council, the European Parliament and the European Economic and Social Committee "Towards a European e-Justice Strategy" dated 30 May 2008, COM(2008)329final, p. 7.

b) The first multiannual European e-Justice action plan (2009-2013)

The solutions proposed in the Communication were then approved by the JHA Council, which subsequently drafted "The first multiannual European e-Justice action plan (2009-2013),"[4] hereafter referred to as the "First Plan". The document included a schedule of activities for the years 2009-2013 aimed at creating an e-Justice for the following four groups of

4 The first multiannual European e-Justice action plan (2009-2013), Official Journal of European Union no. C-75/1 dated 31 March 2009.

stakeholders: citizens, entrepreneurs, legal professionals and judicial authorities. According to the First Plan, the system's core was the European e-Justice portal. Among the many tasks specified in the Plan for the European Commission collaborating with member states the most important ones were launching and providing public accessibility to the portal's basic version by the end of 2009. According to the First Plan, the first version was to be supplemented with additional functionalities in the following years.[5]

The First Plan divided the efforts aimed at creating e-Justice in the years 2009-2013 into four categories. The first category of activities concerned the implementation of acts of law adopted with a view to create a European judiciary domain. These activities included, among others, projects aimed at implementing a prototype of an automated European payment order, creating European small claims forms, or creating on-line payment functionality for court fee payments. The second category included endeavours aimed at combining the national registers into one network, encompassing the national criminal registers, insolvent debtor registers, real estate registers, trade registers and land registers. The third category concerned implementation of cross-sectoral projects linking different legal domains (in particular, civil law, criminal law and administrative law).[6] Apart from the basic task of launching European e-Justice and its subsequent extension as well as development through the remaining activities, the cross-sectoral activities also included electronic signature projects and translation projects (including the development of a multilingual dictionary of legal terms, provision of the funding for translation tools, merging translator and interpreter databases, and compiling a glossary of legal terms). The last category of the proposed activities focused on further development of the solutions, and the training of legal professionals. This category included on-line training projects organised as part of the European judicial personnel training network as well as organising annual meetings of the European Justice Forum – a platform devoted to the EU's justice system.

Studies show that from the moment of adoption of the First Plan until its completion the e-Justice system developed in many member states. However, not all of the planned activities were timely implemented. For

5 The first multiannual European e-Justice action plan… *op. cit.* point 63.

6 For more on the cross-sectoral projects see: The first multiannual European e-Justice action plan… *op. cit.* point 15.

example, the merging of national registers into one network did not succeed, first of all because of the fact that these registers did not exist in an electronic format in many member states. Consequently, the implementation of unsuccessful activities was moved down in the schedule. The priority endeavour of launching the European e-Justice Portal was completed with a delay: the portal was officially launched on the European Commission's server in July 2010. In subsequent years the website was gradually extended by addition of new functionalities and content.

c) The first multiannual European e-Justice action plan (2014-2018)

In order to improve e-Justice's functionality both at the EU and member state levels, the JHA Council developed the second multiannual action plan for the years 2014-2018,[7] hereafter referred to as the "Second Plan". The Plan included a list of actions that were deemed necessary in order to ensure e-Justice's development. The actions are now divided into the following domains: access to justice-related information, access to court and out-of-court procedures in cross-border cases and communication between judicial authorities.

The first category includes activities related to gathering information and publishing justice-related information on e-Justice portal. The portal's existing body of information is to be complemented with data on minors taking part in court proceedings and information on the capacity and location of penal institutions, as well as information about legal professionals who deal with criminal law. This category also encompasses the pending task from the First Plan i.e. merging the national registers of relevant data into a single European register – including registers of entrepreneurs, registers of insolvent businesses, registers of last wills or land registers. The second group of activities to be implemented in the years 2014-2014 focuses on ensuring access to court and out-of-court proceedings in cross-border situations by creating a register of courts and mediators and by introducing the possibility to resolve disputes via electronic means. The third category of endeavours is aimed at streamlining communication be-

7 The second multiannual European e-Justice action plan (2014-2018), Official Journal of the European Union, no. C-182/2 dated 14 June 2014.

tween judicial authorities through the organisation and facilitation of cross-border video conferences and secure electronic data exchange.

The implementation of both multiannual plans is overseen by the Working Group on e-Law at the Council, which prepares the Council's decisions necessary to reach the objectives of the Plans as well as supervising the e-Justice portal.

The scope of European e-Justice Portal

As prescribed in the First Plan, the European e-Justice Portal is currently composed of four modules that correspond to the four categories of entities to which the portal is directed countries, citizens, enterprises, legal professionals and the judiciary. Each of the modules is divided into sections corresponding to the needs of the users. The list below presents the contents of the particular modules.

Module 1: Citizens

Section	Content
1. Find a lawyer	A search engine which facilitates finding lawyers across the EU
2. Find a notary public	A search engine which facilitates finding notaries across the EU
3. Filing a case to a court	Guidelines and information concerning cross-border proceedings: from initiation to enforcement
4. Rights of victims in criminal proceedings	Information sets concerning the rights of victims in criminal cases
5. Family cases	Information on legal provisions concerning divorce, parental duties and alimony payment claims
6. Costs of proceedings	Information about costs of legal proceedings at both EU and member state levels
7. Rights of defendants in criminal proceedings	Information sets concerning the rights of defendants in criminal cases across all EU member states

Source: Own analysis based on: https://e-justice.europa.eu/home.do?action=home&plang=pl

Module 2: Enterprises

Section	Content
1. Combined insolvency registers – search engine functionality	A search engine that enables the user to find insolvent companies in selected member states
2. Trade registers	Information about trade registers at both EU and member state levels
3. Forms for the European order for payment	The on-line forms contained in the Regulation of the European Parliament creating a European order for payment procedure.[8]
4. Land and real estate registers	Information about land and real estate registers both EU and member state levels
5. Filing a case to a court	Guidelines and information concerning cross-border proceedings: from initiation to enforcement
6. Monetary claims	Information about financial matters that may appear in cross-border cases
7. Legal professions	Information on the organisation of legal professions at EU and member state levels

Source: Own analysis based on: https://e-justice.europa.eu/home.do?action=home&plang=pl

Module 3: Legal professions

Section	Content
1. Law	General information about EU law, member state laws and international law
2. Court rulings	General information about EU and member state rulings
3. Legal professions and judicial networks	Information on the types and organisation of legal professions at EU and member state levels; information about different judicial networks
4. EJN in civil cases and court proceedings	Information about the European Judicial Network and its role in resolving cases under civil and commercial law
5. Court systems	General information on the organisation of the judiciary at EU and member state levels
6. Registers	Information about trade, land and real estate registers as well as insolvency registers at both EU and member state levels
7. European training courses for the employees of the judiciary	General information concerning training activities for legal professionals in EU law and the relevant programmes/solutions at both EU and member state levels

Source: Own analysis based on: https://e-justice.europa.eu/home.do?action=home&plang=pl

8 Regulation (EC) No 1896/2006 of the European Parliament and of the Council of 12 December 2006 creating a European order for payment procedure, Official Journal of the European Union no. L 399/1 dated 30 December 2006.

Module 4: The Judiciary

Section	Content
1. Law	General information about EU law, member state laws and international law
2. Tools for courts and lawyers	Information concerning tools and other solutions aimed at streamlining the work of courts and lawyers within the judiciary
3. The EJN in commercial cases and court proceedings	Information about the European Judicial Network and its role in solving civil and commercial law cases
4. European training courses for the employees of the judiciary	General information concerning training activities for legal professionals in EU law and the relevant programmes/solutions at both EU and member state levels
5. Video-conferences	General introduction to video conferences, including a list of the appropriate strategies, information on the available possibilities as regards organisation of video conferences, information on interactive forms
6. Examination of evidence in commercial cases and court proceedings: forms	The on-line forms contained in the regulation of the Council on cooperation between the courts of the member states in the taking of evidence in civil or commercial matters.[9]

Source: Own analysis based on: https://e-justice.europa.eu/home.do?action=home&plang=pl

Apart from the four modules directed to the particular groups of users, there is also a generic module composed of about a dozen sections. The content of these sections is briefly presented below.

General module:

Section	Content
1. Law	General information about EU law, member state laws and international law
2. Court rulings	General information about EU and member state rulings
3. Court systems	General information on the organisation of the judiciary at EU and member state levels
4. Legal professions and judicial networks	Information on the types and organisation of legal professions at EU and member state levels; information about different judicial networks
5. The role of the EJN in commercial cases and court proceedings	Information about the European Judicial Network and its role in cases under civil and commercial law

9 Council Regulation (EC) no. 1206/2001 of 28 May 2001 r. on cooperation between the courts of the Member States in the taking of evidence in civil or commercial matters, Official Journal of the European Union no. L 174/1 dated 27 June 2001.

Section	Content
6. Filing a case to a court	Guidelines and information concerning cross-border proceedings: from initiation to enforcement
7. Legal assistance	General information on the system of legal assistance in civil and criminal proceedings
8. Mediation	General information about mediation at both EU and member state levels
9. Inheritance Law	General information about inheritance law at both EU and member state levels
10. Victims of crimes	General information on the rights of victims of crimes
11. Rights of defendants in criminal proceedings	General information on criminal proceedings and its stages, with particular attention paid to the rights and obligations of the defendant
12. Tools for courts and lawyers	Information concerning tools and other solutions aimed at streamlining the work of courts and lawyers within the judiciary
13. Registers	Information about trade, land and real estate registers as well as insolvency registers at both EU and member state levels
14. How do I find...	Tips for finding lawyers, notaries, sworn translators/interpreters, and mediators
15. Glossaries and terminology	An overview of existing EU-level glossaries and multi-language thesauruses
16. European training courses for the employees of the judiciary	General information concerning training activities for legal professionals in EU law and the relevant programmes/solutions at both EU and member state levels
17. Interactive forms	Easy-to-use on-line forms related to civil law and commercial law legislation
18. Access to the judiciary in environmental law cases	General information on the rights of citizens who have been victims of actions harmful to the environment or citizens who wish to protect the natural environment
19. The European Judicial Atlas of civil cases	A user-friendly repository of information about judicial cooperation in civil cases

Source: Own analysis based on: https://e-justice.europa.eu/home.do?action=home&plang=pl

The Assessment of the European e-Justice Portal and its functionality

As the European e-Justice Portal has been functioning for over five years now, it seems that enough time has passed to perform a preliminary assessment of its functionality based on the experience gathered so far. When one enters the portal's website, it may make an impression of being highly comprehensive. The site's structure seems well designed and clear, and the division into modules matching the users' needs is a functional and user-friendly solution. What adds to the portal's comprehensive nature is the fact that it is available in 23 languages.

After a more detailed analysis, it turns out, however, that apart from its undeniable advantages, the European e-Justice Portal also has a few shortcomings that need to be improved upon. One of drawbacks is that there are a few imprecise pieces of information in it and many redundancies, which makes it more difficult for the user to access the required information quickly. For example, the data contained in the particular modules are, in my opinion, unnecessarily repeated also in the general module. This creates an impression of chaos and doubt as to the scope of information in both modules. After entering particular sections with the same titles but from different modules (e.g. law, court rulings, and court systems) it turns out that their content is identical, regardless of the target user of the module.

The portal's part devoted to registers also raises doubt: in some modules it contains generic references to all registers (it is the case in the general module and the module for legal professionals), while in other modules it is split into particular registers i.e. insolvency, trade, and land/real estate registers (in the module for enterprises it is also unclear why the lawyer and notary search engine is only linked to the citizen module and not linked to the module for enterprises.

It must also be emphasized that the modules and sections are complemented with information from particular member states. Consequently, many shortcomings of the portal stem from the fact that some data is not provided by member states, or the data provided may be incomplete. This is to be noticed in the register of insolvent entities which only covers 7 member states (the Czech Republic, the Netherlands, Slovenia, Germany, Austria, Estonia and Romania) – the only countries which have shared information on insolvent natural persons and legal entities.

Finally I can also remark that the literature devoted to this subject has already drawn attention to the problem of inconsistency within the portal, its internal redundancy and the need to align the contents of the modules (Łuczak, 2013). Unfortunately, the current shape of the portal suggests that not all comments reported as early as 2013 have been taken into account. Therefore, the European e-Justice Portal is still in need of content elaboration and expansion. Time will show whether the portal will in fact become a universal electronic point of contact for all EU stakeholders interested in the judiciary.

Conclusions

The European e-Justice system and its key instrument, the European e-Justice Portal is most definitely an important source of information about the functioning to the judiciary in the European Union and all its member states. Although one may have certain doubts as to the current structure of the portal and criticise incomplete contents of some of the portal's modules, it must be noted that the instrument is still being dynamically developed. Its ongoing modifications and improvements mean that we can be hopeful as to future elimination of the portal's current shortcomings. The portal's electronic format, its availability in all EU official languages and its free-of-charge nature mean that it could potentially be taken advantage of by a very wide group of users. Still, however, not many potential users are aware of the fact that there is such a tool as the European e-Justice Portal that facilitates an easy and free-of-charge access to basic information and assistance in solving cross-border legal matters – i.e. matters that seem complicated while in fact they are fairly easy to resolve. Consequently, apart from further development and optimization efforts, it is indispensable to conduct promotional campaigns directed to the portal's potential users: citizens, legal professionals, and businesses. The European e-Justice system is only likely to facilitate access to justice if it is able to reach a broad group of users.

References

Kettani D., Moulin B. (2014), 'E-government for good governance in developing countries. Empirical evidence from the eFez Project', London: Anthem Press.

Łuczak L. (2013), 'Portal e-Justice jako element budowy społeczeństwa informacyjnego Unii Europejskiej', in: *e-mentor. Dwumiesięcznik Szkoły Głównej Handlowej w Warszawie*, 4(51): 81-89, http://www.e-mentor.edu.pl/artykul/index/numer/51/id/1051 (accessed: 9.2.2016).

Kotecka S. (2011), 'E-government and e-justice', in: A. Brudziak [et al.], *Technologia informacyjna dla prawników*, Wrocław: Prawnicza i Ekonomiczna Biblioteka Cyfrowa: 51-77.

Mucha J. (2015), 'Nowe spojrzenie na *access to justice* w świetle najnowszych legislacji unijnych w sprawie ADR', in: *Prawo Europejskie w Praktyce*, 9: 18-23.

The Subcarpathian Studies in English Language, Literature and Culture. T. 1 Linguistics:

Part Three:
The practice of good governance at the EU and national level

Chapter 1: Initiatives supporting the internal and external security of the EU and its member states

Anna Kańciak

Key words: Area of Freedom, Security and Justice, external and global security, threats to internal security

Introduction

The evaluation of good governance in the European Union in the context of freedom, security and justice requires a two-step approach. In order to assess the effectiveness and efficiency of the activities of the EU, it is essential to determine the EU's tasks and competences regarding security. In the first step of the evaluation, a theoretical framework of the area under consideration will be established. This will allow analysis of specific initiatives and, in this way, to verify to what extent the EU meets its obligations within the AFSJ.

Security is a broad concept which can be interpreted very differently. In political science, security[1] is understood as the freedom of entities – individuals, socials groups, states and organisations – from threats to their fundamental values, accompanied by effective measures aimed at preventing and eliminating such threats. A high level of security, which the EU is obliged to ensure under Article 67(3) TFEU, means achieving a low level of risk. The EU's commitment to a high level of security can be a manifestation of good governance if it is effective, transparent and compatible with the rules of law as well as if it contributes to mitigating risks – in other words, if the risk of threats to security is low and the sense of security of EU citizens is high.

1 More: chapter 6 part II.

In 2014,[2] 49% of Europeans considered terrorism to be the most dangerous threat to the EU's security. In November 2015, despite terrorist attacks in Paris, for almost 60% of Europeans the biggest threat to security was illegal immigration, which is a 20% growth since spring 2015. Crime ranked lower on the list of threats, right after the threats to state's financial security.

Contrary to the feelings of European citizens, in 2015, the Commission decided to stick to the catalogue of the three main threats to EU's security: terrorism, cyber-crime and organised crime. Due to political decisions, the issues concerning migration are presented as a challenge and an urgent need to meet EU's Treaty commitments rather than as a threat.[3]

Tools supporting EU's internal security

The European Union constitutes an area of freedom, security and justice (Article 67(1) TFEU) as well as an area of cooperation in the fields of justice and home affairs (Miąsik, 2012: 1021). Moreover, the AFSJ forms the backbone of EU's activities taken as a response to long-term global problems.[4]

Accomplishing this task requires four types of method, as specified in Article 67 TFEU.[5] The activities in this area are followed up with strategic guidelines for legislative and operational planning laid down by the European Council (Article 68 TFEU). This institution guides the planning of law-making and action-taking within the AFSJ. Strategic guidelines set the directions of cooperation and pan-European goals. They also influence the work of other EU institutions and relevant agencies. However, they are just policy papers and not legal instruments of a binding nature. The guidelines set forth by consensus of the European Council pave the way for more detailed documents containing practical suggestions along with

2 European Commission, Security and Justice, http://ec.europa.eu/priorities/justice-fundamental-rights/docs/security-justice-1-year_en.pdf?foodoc=0 (accessed: 15.1.2016).

3 Ibidem.

4 Communication from the Commission to the European Parliament, the Council, the European Economic and Social Committee and the Committee of the Regions - Delivering an area of freedom, security and justice for Europe's citizens - Action Plan Implementing the Stockholm Programme, COM (2010) 171.

5 More: Chapter 6: The high level of security.

timetables for their implementation. The documents specified by the EU legislator in Article 68 TFEU include the conclusions of the European Council regarding the programmes intended to enhance the creation of the AFSJ (Nilsson&Siegel, 2010: 70), such as the Tampere Programme (1999), the Hague Programme (2004)[6] and the Stockholm Programme (2010).[7] The next, fourth programme was discussed by the Ministers of Interior in December 2015 in the context of the Council Conclusions on the Renewed European Union Internal Security Strategy 2015-2020 adopted in June 2015.[8] The document provided for a complex set of rules in full respect of the exclusive competence of member states (Article 4(2) TEU) and the principles of subsidiarity and proportionality (Article 5 TEU, Article 69 TFEU). The renewed strategy, as a multiannual programme, is addressed to the Council, Commission and Parliament, which should develop an appropriate approach when implementing its provisions. The document sets out three priorities for the EU in the years to come concerning combating and preventing terrorism, radicalisation and the financing of terrorism, serious and organised crime as well as cyber-crime. When implementing the priorities set out by the EU, member states should avail themselves of the exchange of information and operational cooperation, including investigation of criminal activities and a system of trainings and exercises, as well as developing and promoting the use of secure information and communication technology systems in order to enhance cyber-security.

The tools shaping EU's internal security in the context of the assessment as to what extent the EU meets the obligation imposed by Article 67(3) TFEU should be presented in a complex and coherent manner. This means that the programmes shaping the area where the values of freedom, security and justice are fostered should be addressed along with other strategic guidelines in this area. Particular attention should be drawn to strategies related to internal security. The first strategy devised in February

6 The Hague Programme: strengthening freedom, security and justice in the European Union, OJ C 53, 3.3.2005, p. 1–14.
7 The Stockholm Programme — An open and secure Europe serving and protecting citizens, OJ C 115, 4.5.2010, p. 1–38.
8 Draft Council Conclusions on the Renewed European Union Internal Security Strategy 2015-2020, doc. 9798/15.

2010[9] outlined a European security model to be pursued by means of specific measures laid out in the next communication of the European Commission: "The EU Internal Strategy in Action: Five steps towards a more secure Europe."[10] The European security model encompasses actions related to preventing threats to security and overcoming their impact as well as designing security policies founded upon shared values. Referring to the five steps towards a more secure Europe mentioned in the title, the Commission set five strategic goals for internal security, i.e.: dismantling international criminal networks; preventing terrorism and addressing radicalisation and recruitment; raising the levels of security for citizens and businesses in cyberspace; strengthening security through border management; and increasing Europe's resilience to crises and disasters.

Within this area, the measures key to strengthening freedom, security and justice in the European Union that were defined for the period of 2010-2014[11] remained fundamentally unchanged in the strategy for the next five-year period. The EU approach to the security of the AFSJ was clearly confirmed in the Commission communication entitled "The European Agenda on Security" (hereafter: Agenda on Security, EAS).[12] As an expression of a renewed approach to internal security, the Commission replaced the word "strategy" with "agenda."[13] This, however, did not change the nature of the document, which continued to set strategic goals in the AFSJ for a period of five years (2015-2019). The Agenda on Security is based on the assumption that threats are becoming increasingly diverse as well as international, cross-border and multi-sectoral in scope. This challenge requires a coordinated European-level response of all EU

---

9 Council Document, 5842/2/2010, Internal Security Strategy for the European Union: Towards a European Security Model.

10 Communication from the Commission to the European Parliament and the Council - The EU Internal Security Strategy in Action: Five steps towards a more secure Europe, COM/2010/0673 final.

11 Council Conclusions of 25.2.2010 on the Internal Security Strategy for the European Union: Towards a European security model, COM(2014) 154 final of 11.3.2014.

12 Communication from the Commission to the European Parliament and the Council - The European Agenda on Security, COM(2015) 185 final.

13 European Council Conclusions, 26/27 June 2014 EUCO 79/14; European Parliament Resolution 2014/2918 of 17.12.2014, Council Conclusions of 4.12.2014 on the development of arenewed EU Internal Security Strategy.

institutions.[14] The renewed strategy implies cooperation focused on three priorities: terrorism, organised crime and cyber-crime.

This communication is an initiative that sets strategic objectives for the AFSJ from a multi-annual perspective. It confirms the list of three main priorities in the field of European security: terrorism, organised crime and cyber-threats. Also the legal basis for the actions within the AFSJ should be mentioned here, particularly the improved protection of fundamental rights and democratic control over the Union's policy concerning internal security. The Commission emphasised the importance of the Treaty of Lisbon, which strengthened the role of the European Parliament with respect to police and judicial cooperation in criminal matters. Moreover, reference was made to the changes covering police and judicial cooperation in criminal matters that became effective on 1 December 2014 after a five-year transition period[15] As a result of the changes, the Court of Justice assumed full judicial control and the right of the Commission to exercise its competence under Article 258 TFEU with respect to the relevant EU legislation adopted before the entry into force of the Treaty of Lisbon was restored. In the context of the existing strategic documents in this area, this is undeniably a change in the quality of the work of the Commission. Another clear progression is the introduction of performance indicators for key EU instruments to the Agenda on Security by the Commission. They will be used to compile reports to the European Parliament and the Council on up-to-date information regarding the implementation of the Agenda on Security.

In the context of good governance in the EU with respect to the AFSJ, the interdependence between relevant actors at different levels should be strengthened. The tools devised in this area since 1999 are based mostly on the concepts of shared responsibility, mutual trust and effective cooperation between all interested parties: UE institutions and agencies, member states and national bodies. This is a revival of the concept of multi-level governance (MLG) set out by the Commission in the White Paper on

---

14 Communication from the Commission to the European Parliament and the Council - The European Agenda on Security, COM(2015) 185 final, 2.

15 Subject to the specific terms of Protocol 22 as concerns Denmark and Protocol 21and 36 as concerns the United
Kingdom and Ireland. Communication from the Commission to the European Parliament and the Council - The European Agenda…, 3.

European Governance.[16] The activities based on this model should revolve around five principles:

- full respect for fundamental rights;
- better transparency and accountability as well as greater democratic control in order to reinforce citizens' confidence;
- better application and implementation of existing EU legal instruments;
- coordinated cooperation between agencies and a multi-sectoral approach;
- combining the external and internal dimensions of security.

This means that the cooperation at all levels will also be scrutinised in order to ascertain that it is effective, efficient and coherent. Growing interconnection between different kinds of security threats requires the coordinated action of all EU agencies competent in the field of judiciary and home affairs and their cooperation with national law-enforcement authorities.

The above indicates that the implementation of good governance in the AFSJ in the context of the European Agenda on Security will encompass not only the literal meaning of the Treaty concept of a "high level of security" understood as a low level of risk. It should be noted that this reflects the Commission's maturity in the interpretation of Treaty rules that govern the AFSJ. The Commission no longer implements the priorities of security policy from an operational perspective – an approach which created the erroneous impression that the EU was obliged to provide member states with physical protection. This resulted from referring to individual provisions of Title V of the TFEU, without taking into account the powers of the EU within the AFSJ.

The Agenda on Security clearly states that the Commission takes action within the EU competences regarding security. This was expressed by Jean-Claude Juncker,[17] who stressed that the Treaty allows for "bringing

16 European Governance – A White Paper, COM (2001)) 428, 25.7.2001.

17 A New Start for Europe: My Agenda for Jobs, Growth, Fairness and Democratic Change. Political Guidelines
for the next European Commission Opening Statement in the European Parliament Plenary Session President-elect of the European Commission Strasbourg, Strasbourg, 15 July 2014 Jean-Claude Juncker http://www.eesc.europa.eu/resources/docs/jean-claude-juncker---political-guidelines.pdf (accessed: 27.1.2016).

added value" by supporting member states in ensuring security. This seems to be the Commission's interpretation of Article 3(2) TEU and Article 67(1) TFEU – the provisions concerning the EU's actions aimed at providing citizens with a high level of security within the areas of freedom, security and justice. Furthermore, in the EAS, the Commission explains that Europeans need the confidence that when they move throughout Europe, their freedom and security are well protected, with full respect for the EU's values such as the rule of law and fundamental rights.

To sum up, the EU complies with the provisions related to ensuring security through the support EU institutions and agencies provide to member states. However, it is only member states that can ensure complete security. As a result, the assessment of the compliance with the conditions concerning the efficiency and effectiveness of actions promoting security in the EU should consist in evaluating the results achieved by member states. The European level, in turn, may be assessed it terms of whether it is coherent, consistent, open and participatory. This confirms the need for a bi-directional assessment of good governance in the EU within the AFSJ, resulting from the interrelationship between the EU and member states in this area. In practice, this should be reflected in better cooperation between relevant EU and national bodies.

The initiatives should take into account the obligations of the parties involved and should focus on three priorities, i.e. protection of security by member states, implementation of UE goals whilst respecting its values, and observation of the rule of law and fundamental rights. The need for synergy, coordination and closer cooperation in pursuing these goals should concentrate on the implementation of the priorities set in the programmes and strategic guidelines. Terrorism, organised crime and cyber-crime, which pose the greatest threat to security, are inter-related areas with a clear cross-border dimension. They require an initiative of member states and the support of the EU, which is reflected in detailed strategy papers.

Terrorism

Member states have developed a common position on combating and preventing terrorism and presented it in the European Union Counter-Terrorism Strategy.[18] The EU strategy based on four pillars (prevention, protection, prosecution and responding) provides for concrete actions in specific areas related to combating terrorist activities in the EU. The first pillar is of a preventive nature and entails recognising and combating factors contributing to terrorist radicalisation and recruitment. The Strategy for Combating Radicalisation and Recruitment to Terrorism describes this phenomenon and provides recommendations in this area.[19] The emergence of new trends and the constantly changing *modus operandi* of terrorists has led to the strategy being revised twice, in 2008[20] and 2014.[21]

The second pillar provides for actions aimed at protecting citizens and infrastructure, particularly through the improved protection of external borders and transport as well as the protection of strategic objectives and the reduction of vulnerability of infrastructure. Under this pillar, initiatives are undertaken in order to regulate the use of passenger name record (PNR) data captured and stored by air carriers. In 2011, the Commission submitted a proposal for a Directive on the submission of Passenger Name Record data to member states and the processing of this data for law-enforcement purposes.[22] In 2012, the Council made a few amendments[23] and the negotiations with the European Parliament are currently underway.

The third pillar provides for improving practical cooperation and information exchange between police and judicial authorities, with a particular role for Europol and Eurojust, preventing the financing of terrorism and cutting off terrorists' access to funds that allow them to stage attacks and communicate. To this end, in May 2015, the Council and the Parliament

18 Council of the European Union, 30 November 2005: The European Union Counter-Terrorism Strategy, doc. 14469/4/05.

19 The European Union Strategy for Combating Radicalisation and Recruitment to Terrorism, doc. 14781/1/05.

20 Revised EU Strategy for Combating Radicalisation and Recruitment to Terrorism, doc. 15175/08.

21 Communication from the Commission to the European Parliament and the Council, the European Economic and Social Committee and the Committee of the Regions – Preventing radicalization to terrorism and violent extremism: Strengthening the EU's Response, COM(2013) 941 final.

22 Proposal for a Directive of the European Parliament and the Council on the use of Passenger Name Record data for the prevention, detection, investigation and prosecution of terrorist offences and serious crime, doc. 6007/11.

23 Proposal for a Directive of the Council and the European Parliament on the use of Passenger Name Record data for the prevention, detection, investigation and prosecution of terrorist offences and serious crime, doc. 8916/12.

adopted the Directive on the prevention of the use of the financial system for the purposes of money laundering or terrorist financing.[24] The last pillar is related to responding to and minimising the consequences of terrorist attacks. Priority initiatives encompass crisis coordination of the EU, revision of the EU Civil Protection Mechanism, as well as building risk assessment and sharing best practices with regard to assistance to victims of terrorism. UE's activities in the field of anti-terrorism encompass also recognition and reduction of risks related to CBRJ material and explosives,[25] protection of critical infrastructure,[26] and security of trading with explosives.[27]

Organised crime

Since the 1990s, the European Union has taken a number of measures to improve the effectiveness of combating organised crime. In 2010, the EU adopted a methodology of policy cycles in order to eliminate the most serious criminal threats. In serious crime and organised crime prevention, the EU endeavours to mobilise all the instruments of police and judicial cooperation and strengthen the role of Europol and Eurojust. In its conclusions on setting 11 priorities of the EU for the fight against serious and organised crime between 2014 and 2017, the Council addressed operational activities related to preventing and combating serious and organised crime.[28]

A phenomenon that falls under the area of fighting organised crime is illegal migration. However, the migration crisis moved this issue to the

24 Directive (EU) 2015/849 of the European Parliament and of the Council of 20 May 2015 on the prevention of the use of the financial system for the purposes of money laundering or terrorist financing, amending Regulation (EU) No 648/2012 of the European Parliament and of the Council, and repealing Directive 2005/60/EC of the European Parliament and of the Council and Commission Directive 2006/70/EC, OJ L 141, 5.6.2015, p. 73–117.

25 EU Action Plan on Enhancing the Security of Explosives, doc. 8311/08.

26 Communication from the Commission on a European Programme for Critical Infrastructure Protection,
COM(2006) 786 final.

27 EU Action Plan on Enhancing the Security of Explosives, doc. 8311/08.

28 Council conclusions on setting the EU's priorities for the fight against serious and organised crime between 2014 and 2017, doc.12095/13.

top of EU's agenda for 2015. The EU responded to the uncontrolled influx of immigrants to Europe with multiple-stage actions. As a first step, in April 2015, the Extraordinary European Council committed to strengthen EU's maritime operations, combat human smugglers in accordance with international law, prevent irregular migration flows as well as enhance solidarity and responsibility sharing within the EU. In May 2015, the European Commission adopted the European Agenda on Migration.[29] In this document, the Commission reiterated the need to manage migration more effectively and placed special emphasis on the joint responsibility of all member states. As another step, in May 2015, the Commission proposed the first package of measures aimed at dealing with the migration crisis,[30] and, four months later, the second package of measures was proposed concerning the refugee crisis.[31] In November 2015, the Conclusions on securing the functioning of the Schengen area and alleviating migratory pressures were adopted.[32] Finally, in December 2015, the Commission presented a package of legislative measures aimed at securing EU's external borders and the more effective management of migration.

Cyber-security

Under the third priority, in 2013, the Cyber-security Strategy of the European Union was published in the Joint Communication by the Commission and the High Representative of the European Union for Foreign Affairs and Security Policy.[33] The strategy lays down the scope of the EU's

29 Communication from the Commission to the European Parliament and the Council, the European Economic and Social Committee and the Committee of the Regions - A European Agenda on Migration, COM(2015) 240 final.

30 More: http://europa.eu/rapid/press-release_IP-15-5039_en.htm (accessed: 16.1.2016).

31 More: http://ec.europa.eu/dgs/home-affairs/what-we-do/policies/european-agenda-migration/background-information/index_en.htm (accessed: 16.1.2016).

32 http://www.consilium.europa.eu/press-releases-pdf/2015/11/40802204716_pl_635828367000000000.pdf.

33 Joint Communication from the Commission to the European Parliament and the Council, the European Economic and Social Committee and the Committee of the Regions - Cybersecurity Strategy of the European Union: An Open, Safe and Secure Cyberspace, JOIN(2013) 1 final.

security policy in cyberspace in the form of five strategic goals[34] aimed at achieving resilience in the area of cyberspace, significant reduction of cyber-crime, developing cyber-defence capabilities related to the framework of the Common Security and Defence Policy, developing industrial and technological resources for cyber-security, establishing a coherent cyber-policy for the European Union, and promoting the EU's core values. The cyber-security strategy, which serves as a strategic paper, complements legal acts in the field of combating cyber-crime, i.e. the Directive on attacks against information systems,[35] the Directive on combating the sexual abuse and sexual exploitation of children and child pornography,[36] the Directive concerning the processing of personal data and the protection of privacy in the electronic communications sector,[37] and the Decision combating fraud and counterfeiting of non-cash means of payment.[38]

The assessment of the implementation of good governance within the domain of internal security in terms of its effectiveness, efficiency, coherence and consistency should be based on the adopted security concept. The role of the EU is to provide support as regards ensuring security to the member states that are not able to ensure security on their own. The assessment should not be based on risk level indicators. What should be assessed is the extent to which the objectives set in the strategic guidelines relevant to the EU's internal and external security are met.

---

34 Joint Communication from the Commission to the European Parliament and the Council, the European Economic and Social Committee and the Committee of the Regions - Cybersecurity Strategy… 5.

35 Directive 2013/40/EU of the European Parliament and of the Council of 12 August 2013 on attacks against information systems and replacing Council Framework Decision 2005/222/JHA, OJ L 218, 14.8.2013.

36 Directive 2011/92/EU of the European Parliament and of the Council of 13 December 2011 on combating the sexual abuse and sexual exploitation of children and child pornography, and replacing Council Framework Decision 2004/68/JHA, OJ L 335, 17.12.2011, p. 1–14.

37 Directive 2002/58/EC of the European Parliament and of the Council of 12 July 2002 concerning the processing of personal data and the protection of privacy in the electronic communications sector, OJ L 201, 31.7.2002, p. 37–47.

38 Council Framework Decision 2001/413/JHA of 28 May 200 combating fraud and counterfeiting of non-cash means of payment, OJ L 149, 2.6.2001, p. 1–4.

Tools supporting the EU's external security

According to the Commission, security threats result from the lack of stability in the immediate neighbourhood of the EU and changing forms of radicalisation, violence and terrorism.[39] Threats are becoming increasingly diverse, which creates a need for a closer link between the external and internal aspects of EU's security and the promotion of initiatives aimed at strengthening third countries' ability to act. In the European Agenda on Security, the Commission emphasised that security threats do not stop at the EU's borders. Internal security of the EU and global security are interrelated and interdependent.

The Commission's position on connecting the external and internal aspects fits in with the ideas behind the concept of the EU's security[40] and supports the view of Advocate General Yves Bot[41] and the Court of Justice of the EU.

In accordance with Article 18 TEU, the High Representative of the Union for Foreign Affairs and Security Policy (hereafter: HR / High Representative) undertakes initiatives promoting the external dimension of security. Following the provisions of the Treaty, the HR shall conduct Union's common foreign and security policy, coordinate Union's external action and ensure its consistency.

The first external security initiative was the European Security Strategy (ESS)[42] adopted by the European Council in December 2003. It sets three strategic goals for the EU: the active contribution to stability and security in the Union's neighbourhood, the creation of an international order based on effective multilateralism, and the prevention of traditional and new forms of threats. These objectives should be pursued in relation to the threats to the EU's security, such as regional conflicts, terrorism, proliferation of weapons of mass destruction and the possibility that they will be used against the EU, failing states and the conflicts arising there and in

39 Communication from the Commission to the European Parliament and the Council - The EU Internal Security Strategy in Action: Five steps towards a more secure Europe, COM/2010/0673 final.

40 More: Chapter 6: The high level of security.

41 Opinion of Advocate General Bot delivered on 8 June 2010, Case C-145/09 Land Baden-Württemberg, 2010 I-11979.

42 European Security Strategy, Brussels, 12 December 2003, http://www.consilium.europa.eu/uedocs /cmsUpload/78367.pdf (accessed: 6.1.2016).

neighbouring countries, as well as organised crime. During the French Presidency of the Council, the document was assessed and, as a result, the Report on the Implementation of the ESS was compiled in December 2008.[43] However, the results were not considered to be positive. Moreover, on top of adding new security threats, the report reiterated the issues already addressed in the ESS. As the report was not seen as bringing any added value, it was quickly forgotten and was never followed by in-depth analyses (Norheim-Martinsen, 2013:39).

In December 2013, the European Council authorised the High Representative to draw up a report on a changing global environment in order to identify areas where a change in action is required as well as to determine growth possibilities for the EU.[44] In June 2014, the HR presented a report on the position of the EU in a changing global environment.[45] An analysis of the global security situation was performed in the context of geographic areas of cooperation of the EU, i.e. its nearest neighbourhood, north Africa, Middle East, the transatlantic partnership and Asia. The EU's activities in each of these areas require evaluation and redefinition of priorities and the action plan. The conclusions show that the advance in globalisation brought about economic growth and the development of freedom in the broadest sense but, at the same time, it resulted in growing risks and challenges for regions and states. The paper concluded that the European Union needs a common complex and coherent global strategy. This position was upheld by the High Commissioner, who saw it as a way to determine priorities and develop the ability to make decisions concerning the choice of partners for cooperation and the tools for its implementation (Aggestam, 2015:30).

The Council endorsed this approach in June 2015 and authorised the High Representative to continue to work to develop a new foreign and security policy strategy of the EU in cooperation with member states. The strategy should be presented to member states for approval in June 2016.

---

43 Report on the Implementation of the European Security Strategy - Providing Security in a Changing World, doc. S407/08, https://www.satcen.europa.eu/pdf_key/report%20on%20the%20implementation%20of%20the% 20ess.pdf (accessed: 17.1.2016).

44 Conclusions European Council 19/20 December 2013, doc. EUCO 217/13.

45 The European Union in a Changing Global Environment. A more connected, contested and complex world http://eeas.europa.eu/docs/strategic_review/eu-strategic-review_strategic_review_en.pdf (accessed: 17.1.2016).

The EU's new foreign and security policy strategy will have to meet high expectations. The decision to draw up the next strategic guidelines in this area was taken 12 years after the publication of the ESS. If the new guidelines to any extent draw on the ESS, this will equal stagnation, especially as the implementation of the goals of the ESS failed. It set the strategic goal of the protection of the EU, which can be achieved through good democratic governance. This will be fostered by promoting good governance, supporting social and political reforms, fighting corruption and protecting human rights. Although the challenges addressed in the ESS in 2003 still remain, they require a new approach and modus operandi. The new strategy should, above all, give high priority to the geopolitical situation and the most urgent threats to the interests of the EU (Biscop, 2015: 14).

Conclusion

Strategic guidelines in the AFSJ and common foreign and security policy (CFSP) of the EU, although very diverse and more visible in the context of security at internal level, are an example of good governance within the EU. The assessment of the EU's actions can be performed by referring to the principles of good governance, i.e. cohesion, participation, responsibility, effectiveness and consistency (Ruszkowski, 2015: 256). The provisions of the Treaty approve the approach taken by the Commission in the European Agenda on Security and emphasise the support role of the EU and the exclusive competence of member states as regards ensuring security. The EU is obliged to ensure a high level of security (Article 67(3) TFEU), brings added value through strategic guidelines (Article 68 TFUE) and coordinates the measures at European level. Thus, the EU fulfils the criterion of participation. With full regard to the provisions of Article 4(2) TEU, the EU endeavours to establish guidelines concerning the EU's security.

The EU's activities in the AFSJP were subject also to a qualitative change. The EU departed from explaining the concept of security in terms of the lack of threats (in the context of political science) and put emphasis on achieving the objectives enshrined in the Treaties, including the rule of law and fundamental rights. It would be a mistake to evaluate the EU's counter-terrorism policy through the attacks in Paris in 2015. The attacks were not targeted at the European Union as an international organisation but were an example of the policy of the so-called ISIS towards the counter-terrorism coalition comprising approximately 60 states. In view of the events that took place on its territory and affected its members directly, the EU took vigorous measures aimed at preventing and combating terrorism. This was reflected in a legislative package submitted by the Commission in December 2015 in order to step up the fight against terrorism and the illicit trade of firearms and explosive materials. It encompasses a proposal for a Directive on combating terrorism[46] and an action plan on stepping up the fight against criminals and terrorists using firearms and explosive materials through tightening controls of the illicit possession and import of firearms and explosive materials into the EU.[47] The presented package is part of implementation of the European security strategy. The actions, though taken under pressure of terrorist attacks, are an example of good governance in terms of participation, responsibility, consistency and cohesion. The conclusions are also consistent with the implementation of Commission's agenda in 2016.[48]

The initiatives taken in 2015 in order to overcome the migration crisis are also part of participation and responsibility components. Attention should also be drawn to the European scheme on migration and a package of legislative proposals presented in December 2015 on securing the external borders of the EU and more effective migration management. Despite the fact that, at this stage, it is hard to assess the efficiency and effectiveness of these actions, they are proof of the EU's consistency.

It is more difficult to assess the initiatives focused on security at the external level. The work is slow and its quality meets with scepticism (Biscop, 2016). The evaluation of measures, particularly with respect to the global strategy, will be possible in June 2016 after its publication by the High Commissioner. However, good governance is manifested in another dimension. The European Agenda on Security, which replaced the EU Internal Security Strategy adopted in 2010, marks a clear change in the ap-

46 Proposal for a Directive of the European Parliament and of the Council on combating terrorism and replacing Council Framework Decision 2002/475/JHA on combating terrorism, COM(2015) 625 final.

47 http://europa.eu/rapid/press-release_IP-15-6218_en.htm (accessed:17.1.2016).

48 Communication from the Commission to the European Parliament and the Council, the European Economic and Social Committee and the Committee of the Regions Commission Work Programme 2016 - No time for business as usual, COM(2015) 610 final.

proach to the EU's security policy. This time, the Commission chose the term "agenda", which is broader than "strategy". Although this may seem a mistake, the content of the paper, which presents demands and objectives, justifies this choice. External security constitutes an essential part of the EAS, and stressing its internal nature would be in contradiction with the content of the paper. This should be viewed as a turn by the EU towards the concept of security governance (Webber, 2014:17). This concept provides for the creation of a political area of cooperation in terms of internal security, also taking into account external threats and the geopolitical situation (Sperling, 2014:10). Such a multidimensional approach to security would allow to better implement the principles of good governance.

References

Aggestam, L. (2015*)*, 'Transformative Power or Political Dwarf? European Leadership and Global Imbalances', in: A., Mårtensson, M. Oxelheim L. Persson, T. (eds) *The EU's Role in Fighting Global Imbalances*, UK: Edward Elgar.

Biscop S., (2015), 'Global and Operational: A New Strategy for EU Foreign and Security Policy', Italy: IAI-CSF.

Biscop S., (2016), 'Brexit and defence: where is the strategy?', European Geostrategy http://www.europeangeostrategy.org/2016/01/brexit-and-defence-where-is-the-strategy/ (accessed: 16.1.2016).

Miąsik, D. Półtorak, N. Wróbel, A. (eds) (2012) 'Traktat o funkcjonowaniu Unii Europejskiej. Komentarz.', Vol. I, Warszawa: Wolters Kluwer.

Nilsson, H. G, Siegl, J. (2010), 'The Council in the Area of Freedom, Security and Justice', in: Monar, J. (eds) *The Institutional Dimension of the European Union's Area of Freedom, Security and Justice,* Brussels: Peter Lang.

Norheim-Martinsen, P.M. (2013), 'EU strategic culture: when the means become the end' Schmidt P. & Zyla, B. (eds), London: Routledge.

Sperling, J. (2014), 'Governance and security in the twenty-first century', in: Sperling J. (eds) *Handbook of Governance and Security*, USA: Edward Elgar.

Webber, M. (2014), *'Security governance'*, in: Sperling, J. (eds) *Handbook of Governance and Security,* USA: Edward Elgar Pub.

Chapter 2: Into the light of good governance – what is the role of transparency in health law?

Atina Krajewska[*]

Key words: EU health law, global health law, international law, transparency, transnational law

Introduction

This chapter seeks to investigate the underlying reasons for the lack of transparency in the area of global health law[1] (Rowson et al. 2012, Koplan et al. 2009) and to evaluate the proposals for remedying the current situation through traditional public international instruments, such as the Framework Convention of Global Health. The connection between good governance, EU health policies, and global health law is not self-evident and one might wonder how the problem of transparency in global health law has made its way into a volume on good governance in the EU. After all, since the establishment of the European Communities, the delivery of health care and the design of health policies have remained predominantly within the remit of member states (MS). Even now, after the Lisbon Treaty, Art. 168 TEU provides the EU only with supporting competence in this area and exceptions to this rule remain very limited. And yet, there are strong reasons for including a discussion of the development of global health law in a collection analyzing the scope and limits of good governance in the EU.

---

* Dr Atina Krajewska, Senior Lecturer at Sheffield Law School, University of Sheffield, UK. Email: a.krajewska@sheffield.ac.uk.

1 Global health is understood as 'a field of practice, research and education focussed on health and the social, economic, political and cultural forces that shape it across the world...[and a] discipline (...) concerned with health-related issues that transcend national boundaries and the differential impacts of globalisation.' (Rowson et al, 2012). Global health includes issues that directly or indirectly affect both health prevention in populations and clinical care and treatment of individuals. (Koplan et al., 2009).

First of all, the EU Treaties contain provisions that affect the area of global health. Most importantly, according to Article 21.2 TEU on EU external action, the Union shall define and pursue common policies and actions, and shall work for a high degree of cooperation in all fields of international relations, in order to (…) (d) foster the sustainable economic, social and environmental development of developing countries (…); (f) help (…) to ensure sustainable development; (g) assist populations, countries and regions confronting natural or man-made disasters; and (h) promote an international system based on stronger multilateral cooperation and good global governance. This commitment is further developed in Article 208 TFEU, which states that the Union development cooperation policy shall have as its primary objective the reduction and, in the long term, the eradication of poverty. Poverty is widely seen as one of the most important health determinants (Daniels, 2008: 145). Critics notice that today the provision of and access to health care[2] in the low- and middle-income countries and health inequities continue to cause 20 million deaths annually, mostly among the world's poor.[3]

Second, regardless of formal commitments and the EU's development agenda, the challenges faced in the area of global health require the EU's attention. Although, historically, the global health has been associated with low-income countries, today its scope is much broader. Thus, it now encompasses a very wide variety of issues, ranging from the well-publicised emerging and re-emerging epidemics (HIV/AIDS, SARS, 'swine flu') and other diseases affecting mostly low- and middle-income countries (tuberculosis, malaria), to non-communicable diseases (obesity, heart disease or dementia), which receive much less attention and resources, but which affect both, the 'developed' and the 'developing' world (Aginam, 2005; Gostin/Mok, 2009; Prah Ruger, 2008). In addition, globalisation,

2 The distinction between "health care systems" and "global health" adopted in this paper follows the differentiation made by N. Daniels between the right to health care and the right to health. According to Daniels "the right to health care" includes both the right medical services and public health measures, whereas "the right to health" is defined more broadly as a way to characterise functionally the relevant, socially controllable actions that affect population health and its distribution. Due to the fact that the field of global health clearly exceeds health care services which are predominantly delivered at the national level, this papers refers to health care systems at the national level and global health system at the international/global level.

3 WHO, World Health Statistics Report, November 2012, at: http://www.who.int/healthinfo/EN_WHS2012_Full.pdf (accessed 1.4.2016).

underpinned by unparalleled scientific and technological advances and digitisation in medicine and healthcare – particularly prominent in high-income countries – has undermined the autonomy of national healthcare systems. All these developments have clear implication for EU MS and the EU itself. The EU has already taken control over the regulation of substantive parts of data protection, patients' rights and mobility, organ and blood donation, the use of medical devices, or embryo research. The system of intellectual property rights co-created by the EU, MS, and other international organisations (IO) transcends these areas and has strong influence on global health.

Furthermore, although the recognition of the need for policy coherence and strategic direction of global health is only just beginning to emerge in Europe, health goals have formed an integral part of the EU development agenda for over a decade (Kickbusch, 2008). In 2005 the European Commission issued a Communication on the support for the Millennium Development Goals.[4] The engagement specifically with global health issues was later confirmed in the Health Strategy of the European Commission, which introduced 'Strengthening the EU's voice in global health' as one of the four basic principles of its approach.[5] In 2010 both the Commission and the Council confirmed the role of the EU in global health governance and the 'importance to take action to improve health, reduce inequalities and increase protection against global health threats.' They acknowledged that the 'EU has a central role to play in accelerating progress on global health challenges, including the health MDGs and non-communicable diseases, through its commitment to protect and promote the right of everyone to enjoy the highest attainable standard of physical and mental health.'[6] In order to achieve those aims the Council called the MS to support the WHO in its normative and guidance functions at global, regional and national level and establish a single coherent EU position in the

4 Commission of the European Communities Communication. Accelerating progress towards attaining the Millennium Development Goals: financing for development and aid effectiveness. Brussels(April 12, 2005) http://eur-lex.europa.eu/LexUriServ/LexUriServ.do?uri=CELEX:52005DC0133:EN:HTML (accessed 1.4.2016).

5 Commission of the European Communities White paper: together for health: a strategic approach for the EU 2008-2013. Brussels, Oct 23, 2007: http://ec.europa.eu/health/ph_overview/Documents/strategy_wp_en.pdf (accessed 24.4.2008).

6 Commission Communication on Global Health COM(2010)128 Brussels, 31 March 2010 and Council conclusions on the EU role in Global Health 3011th FOREIGN AFFAIRS Council meeting Brussels, 10 May 2010.

WHO. At the same time, the Council highlighted the EU's engagement with other global health multilateral processes in particular the UN Human Rights Council, the UN General Assembly initiative on Non-Communicable Diseases, the health related Millennium Development Goals (MDGs), the Framework Convention on Tobacco Control, as well as the Post-2015 development agenda. With regard to access to medicines, it has been announced that the EU is committed to preserving access and affordability to essential medicines in line with the principles of the Doha Declaration.[7] Consequently, the EU is aiming to become yet another important player in the already crowded field of global health governance.[8] (Gostin, 2013)

One of the key ways in which the EU carries out its development policy in this area is by increasing its budgetary contribution to the Global Fund to fight HIV/AIDS, Tuberculosis and Malaria (ATM). In 2013 this commitment exceeded 1M euros. According to Tamara Hervey and Jean McHale, this is an example of a more general phenomenon in terms of how the EU has become involved in global health. 'The EU embeds itself in, and contributes (human and financial resources) to, global governance institutions and activities that have a reputation for success. At least, arguably, the possibility of reputational gain, and the pursuit of an efficiency agenda, related to the idea of value for public money, rather than, for instance, a desire to improve global health equality, is a primary driver of the EU's policy choices.' (Hervey/McHale, 2015: 492) This observation finally makes clear why questions concerning the conditions of good governance for global health should be of interest to EU specialists and experts.

For the purposes of this volume good governance refers to, for example, the efficient functioning of administration, particularly with respect to the ability to absorb funds effectively and to address collective issues.[9] Good governance contains a multitude of elements. In 2001 the European Commission famously identified five principles of 'good governance': openness, participation, accountability, effectiveness and coherence.[10]

---

7 Ibidem.

8 Global governance for health is understood as 'the collection of rules, norms, institutions, and processes that shape the health of the world's population' (Gostin, 2013).

9 Introduction to this Volume, p. 11.

10 Communication from the Commission of 25 July 2001 "European governance - A white paper" COM(2001) 428 final - Official Journal C 287 of 12.10.2001.

However, as noted in Chapter 1 of this book, good governance goes beyond these principles and encompasses 'respect for the principles of democracy and the rule of law, a well-functioning administration, transparency of activities and efficiency, responsiveness and responsibility, ownership and accountability, legitimacy and democracy, and respect for human rights.'[11] According to the Venice Commission, accountability, transparency and participation are the most frequently mentioned elements.[12] Alas, global health is often seen as ineffective, increasingly chaotic, and highly dysfunctional (Gostin, 2008; Kickbush et al. 2013). Despite the WHO reforms and the new post-2015 global health agenda, almost all depictions of global health bear a sense of failure and continuous crisis.[13] This crisis is often associated with lack of legitimacy, accountability, and the rapidly decreasing transparency of the global health system. Traditionally, transparency was considered at odds with the purpose and function of health law, due to the paramount role of confidentiality and privacy for the functioning of the healthcare system. In recent years, however, the principle of transparency has become particularly important in the field of global health governance. This is due to the fact that global health is closely linked to the law regulating health emergencies (epidemics), which require openness and public health measures, such as monitoring and notifications. Also, with time it became clear that the global health system struggles to maintain legitimacy of its decisions and to provide accountability of its actors. Thus, between the three principles of accountability, transparency and participation, transparency seems to be the easiest to obtain.

The paper first notices that the 'obscurity' of the system is caused by both: abundance *and* scarcity of normative responses to global health challenges at different levels. On the one hand, global health is characterised by growing institutional, normative, and thematic plurality. On the other hand, what can be observed is a general lack of legally binding norms

11 Introduction to this Volume, p. 11.

12 Venice Commission, *Stocktaking on the notions of good governance and good administration*, 2009.

13 Global Health and Foreign Policy, United Nations res. 63/33, United Nations A/RES/64/108 (Jan. 27,
2009). The future of financing for WHO: World Health Organization: reforms for a health future: World
Health Assembly A64/INF.DOC./5 (May 12, 2011).

alongside an overwhelming proliferation of soft law instruments. The institutional and normative fragmentation leads to lack of transparency that hinders the creation and sustainment of unified, coherent responses to the global health challenges. However, this chapter proposes an additional line of enquiry elaborated in the last section of the analysis. It argues that the lack of transparency is exacerbated by the difficulties in setting the semantic and normative boundaries of the fundamental notion of 'global health', which has expanded dramatically in recent years. Bearing on systems theoretical approaches that view global health as a functional regime of global society (Teubner, 2012), it suggests that the impossibility to define 'global health' stems from the intrinsic characteristics of the system itself.

Having outlined different aspects of fragmentation and expansion of global health law, the paper goes on to analyse the main proposals for remedying the lack of transparency. A closer look at the proposal for the Framework Convention of Global Health suggests that such a treaty would aim to perform a constitutionalising function within the global health system. In this respect it might indeed enhance visibility of global health as a subsystem of international law and provide the adequate and necessary structure that will establish and/or strengthen coordination, collaboration and enforcement mechanisms. However, the paper importantly argues that the inner complexity and obscurity of the system might also be seen as its intrinsic feature, present in modern global law. According to some accounts originating in systems theory global law is not based on consistency of legal norms, structurally secured by the hierarchy of courts (D'Amato 2005:335), but it constitutes a legal reproduction of collisions between the diverse rationalities within global society itself. This approach provides a new lens through which recent developments and debates in the field of global health can be viewed, not necessarily as yet another crisis or a systemic failure, but on the contrary, as a new stage in the growing constitutional autonomy and organization of global health law. Thus, any aspirations to a normative unity of a global law are doomed from the outset. (Fischer-Lescano/Teubner, 2004) Establishing all of these issues is far from straightforward. The paper does not offer unity, uniformity, or even harmonisation of global health law, but it is an attempt to construct a conceptual framework that offers a more precise model of analysis of global health law and governance and at the same time accommodates its complex and dynamic development at supranational and global levels of lawmaking.

Abundance and scarcity: two faces of global health law's opacity

This section focuses on the institutional and normative proliferation and fragmentation of global health law, as the most obvious causes of the lack of transparency in the field. Since the adoption of the WHO Constitution ('*Magna Carta* of Health'[14]) in 1948, global health has been usually associated with the World Health Organisation as the undisputed leader in the field. As stated in its Constitution the WHO is destined to 'act as the directing and co-ordinating authority on international health work'[15]. It is often claimed that it would act as an umbrella health agency convening legal and non-legal activities of different organisations providing thereby a more effective collective management (Buse/Walt, 2000). The Constitution was intended to set out formal foundations for the operation of the WHO and guarantee coherency of the global health system. However, the internal coherency turned out to be illusory. With advancing globalisation the incoherencies have been growing rapidly. They have been accompanied by a progressing lack of transparency. This lack of transparency of global health law is a result of two interwoven processes. The first one involves institutional and normative proliferation resulting in an abundance of global health actors and legal instruments of different binding force. The second process is linked to the persistent scarcity of traditional public international law responses resulting in a: a) lack of an international legally binding treaty concerning health, b) lack of reflexive (second-level) norms guiding normative conflicts, and c) lack of an adjudicative body – in other words, a lack of a global health constitution. What follows is a detailed analysis of these elements.

The fragmentation of global health law has been closely linked to the increasing dominance of new actors in international health policy, including governmental and non-governmental organisations, philanthropic foundations, professional networks, religious groups, private-public partnerships, and private companies, accompanied by a simultaneous dramatic

14 WHO, Chronicle of the World Health Organization 1. Geneva: WHO, 1947, at: http://www.who.int/library/collections/historical/en/index3.html (accessed: 1.4.2016).

15 Art. 2 (a) of the Constitution of the World Health Organization as adopted by the International Health Conference, New York (19-22 June 1946) (Official Records of the World Health Organization, no. 2, p. 100), entered into force on 7 April 1948.

decline of the WHO leadership (Buse/Walt, 2000). The WHO which would traditionally be the *de facto* leader of any international cross-border response to a public health emergency no longer possesses unquestioned control over international health issues. This has contributed to increased fragmentation of legal instruments and norms, which in turn obscures the normative character of global health law. (Fidler, 2010)

First of all, the emergence of global health has been marked by structural changes in stakeholders involved in the field. New governmental and non-state actors have emerged and have become significantly involved in the sector. Some, like the Joint United Nations Programme on HIV/AIDS (UNAIDS), operate under the aegis of the UN, but are distinct from WHO. Other organizations like the World Bank or the Global Fund to Fight AIDS, Tuberculosis, and Malaria (Global Fund), also independent from WHO, have adopted health concerns as central to their mission and operations. Others, like the Gates Foundation or the Treatment Action Campaign (TAC), exist wholly outside official government structures. This wide range of agencies, foundations, professional networks, religious groups, and for-profit organisations such as pharmaceutical companies, have an increasingly powerful influence on international health policy and global law-making. (Buse/Walt, 2000) For instance, the WHO and the EU work together in the Codex Alimentarius Commission. Although the CAC works through guidelines, codes and standards, which are technically voluntary and non-binding, in practice, these are referred to and embedded in binding national (and EU) laws concerning food safety, including the CJEU's case law. Legal, political, and various other forms of decision-making result in regulatory instruments of contrasting normative status. Instead of reforming and strengthening existing organisations with explicit health mandates, greater energy has gone into creating new actors and expanding the mandates of others (Sridhar, 2010: 462). In addition, the health sector has resisted attempts to measure its efficiency and effectiveness, avoiding close monitoring and accountability. As a result of this deep fragmentation, 'there is vast duplication of effort (…). Priorities are badly skewed, such that funding and programs are disproportionately targeted to politically popular programs and the latest high profile disease (think of SARS, influenza, and bioterrorism) rather than the global burden of disease (think of cancer, heart disease, mental health, and injuries).' (Gostin/Mok, 2009)

Simultaneously market-driven global economic policies, notably those associated with extended intellectual property rights and structural adjustment programmes implemented by the World Bank and the International Monetary Fund have gained unprecedented prominence. They have been pointed as reasons for increased commercialization in health care systems and trade openness, which could hinder health reforms in particular in low-income countries. (Labonte et al., 2011:263) Consequently, the law created in this heterogeneous environment has been said to be developing in a uncoordinated and amorphous manner. What exacerbates the problem is the extraordinary proliferation of soft-law instruments and other forms of regulation, accompanied by perhaps comparatively modest and latent process of juridification.[16] (Teubner, 2012; Krisch, 2010)

Thus, secondly, global health law remains fragmented and lacks a common legal point of reference to appeal to for resolving its internal or external conflicts. Despite the WHO's astounding normative powers, modern international health law is remarkably thin. There currently exist three legally binding international health instruments the International Classification of Disease 1948, International Health Regulations (IHRs) (Fidler/Gostin, 2006), and the WHO Framework Convention on Tobacco Control 2003 (FCTC)[17]), and two of them predate the WHO[18]. These instruments are often characterised by 'structural weaknesses – e.g. vague standards, ineffective monitoring and weak enforcement – and a "statist" approach that insufficiently harnesses the creativity and resources of non-state actors and civil society.' (Gostin, 2008: 240) Their impact is severely weakened by the fact that they provide no financial or technical support to do so, member states may reject or submit reservations to their provisions, and most importantly they lack enforcement mechanisms for addressing compliance failure. (Prah Ruger 2008) For instance, one analysis of the IHRs effectiveness over their 56-year history concluded that, due to poor national surveillance systems and protection measures, they had been relatively ineffective in achieving their main goals (Fidler/Gostin 2006). The FCTC, to which the EU is a signatory, remains the first and only legally

---

16 "Juridification" is a term used by Teubner and it seems to be tantamount to "legalisation" used by Krisch to describe proliferation of treaties and the creation of ever more courts and tribunals. Despite subtle differences they will both be used interchangeably.

17 WHO Framework Convention on Tobacco Control (WHO FCTC) adopted by the World Health Assembly (21 May 2003) , entered into force on 27 Feb 2005, at: http://whqlibdoc.who.int/publications/2003/9241591013.pdf (accessed: 1.4.2016).

18 Depending on the scope of the definition of health it is possible to include also the UN Convention of the People with Disabilities 2006.

binding global health treaty and it was criticised with regard to its formation and content (Mason Meier/Shelly, 2006). Together with other WHO instruments it still neglects rights-based terminology (Kuppuswamy, 2009) and it covers an extremely limited subject matter, which prevents it from being a centre of an emerging self-contained regime[19].

Consequently, some argue that despite the legislative attempts the WHO has been reluctant to pursue international law and human rights approaches to public health issues. (Fidler, 1998) This standpoint can be supported by the fact that it was UNESCO, and not the WHO that adopted the three most important international human rights acts in the area of biomedicine and bioethics[20] (Andorno, 2007). The latter acts, especially the UNESCO Declaration on Human Genome and Human Rights (1997) and the UN Declaration on Reproductive Cloning (2005) are sometimes seen as emerging international customary law. (Francioni, 2006) However, there still seem to be little evidence that either of the declarations has actually affected the *opinion juris* of the international community. This is especially true of the UNESCO Declaration on Bioethics (2005). Despite its extremely broad scope encompassing issues such as biodiversity, equality, social responsibility and justice, it has been so far almost completely ignored in the discussions about global health law and a global health treaty. Therefore in general, international health law has been viewed as ineffective in at least two ways. First, in a legal sense, due to the states' failure to comply with stipulated legal rules and second, in a behavioural sense, due to states' failure to change their behaviour as a result of a treaty or a declaration. (Prah Ruger, 2008: 438)

---

19 The ILC preferred the term 'special regime' over 'self-contained regime', since no evidence is found supporting a full exclusion from general international law. However, as the latter notion has been adopted in case law and scholarship it will be used here. For detailed definition see: Report of the Study Group of the International Law Commission finalized by Martti Koskenniemi, *Fragmentation of International Law: Difficulties arising from the Diversification and Expansion of International Law*, 13 Apr 2006, UN Doc. A/CN.4/L.682 p. 1-256 and 18 July 2006, UN Doc. A/CN.4/L.702 1-25.

20 Universal Declaration on the Human Genome and Human Rights (11 Nov 1997), International Declaration on Human Genetic Data (16 Oct 2003), Universal Declaration on Bioethics and Human Rights (19 Oct 2005), at: http://www.unesco.org/new/en/social-and-human-sciences/themes/bioethics/about-bioethics/ (accessed: 1.4.2016).

There are very few other candidates that could potentially fulfil the role of a founding treaty at a global level. These are the Convention on the Rights of Persons with Disability (2006), the TRIPS Agreement signed under the auspices of the WTO and the Convention on Biological Diversity[21] accompanied by the Cartagena Protocol on Biosafety[22]. However, their subject matter is clearly distinctive and they are usually seen as central to other regimes such as human rights (anti-discrimination) law, global trade law or environmental law. Several disputes before the WTO Dispute Settlement Body concerning public health involved the EU. However, the approach of the to the health policy exceptions has been criticized for being unprincipled, inconsistent and unworkable. Therefore, the WTO is almost never seen the primary decision-maker or even arbiter in the field of global health.

Interestingly, it is not the WHO instruments, but the International Covenants on Civil and Political Rights and Social Economic and Cultural Rights[23] that so far seems to have had the biggest impact on the development of the system. The right to health, stipulated in Art. 12 ICCSEC, has been often proclaimed to be a well-established part of international law and has been reproduced in different 'shapes and forms' in numerous documents, some of which certainly carry a constitutional status (Wolff, 2012). The right to health has constituted the basis for most global health actions at the global and national level (e.g. in disputes with WTO about TRIPS Agreements, or in access to medicines and health care services litigation in South Africa, India, Brazil, Columbia, etc…). Nevertheless, the attempts to define the semantic and normative boundaries of the global health regime through the right to health have not always been successful and the latter constitutes one of the most controversial human rights developed in the post-war order. In addition, the UN Special Rapporteur on the Right to Health noticed that duties of pharmaceutical companies with regard to access to medicines (based on the right to health) were not artic-

21 The Convention on Biological Diversity (CBD) adopted 22 May 1992 at the Conference for the Adoption of the Convention on Biological Diversity, Nairobi, Kenya, entered into force on 29 Dec 1993.

22 The Cartagena Protocol on Biosafety adopted at First Extraordinary Meeting of the Conference of the Parties, Cartagena, Colombia 22 - 23 Feb 1999 and Montreal, Canada, 24 - 28 Jan 2000, entered into force 11 Sep 2003.

23 International Covenants on Civil and Political Rights and International Covenant on Social Economic and Cultural Rights, adopted by General Assembly resolution 2200A (XXI) of 16 Dec 1966, entered into force 3 Jan 1976.

ulated as peremptory duties (Yamin/Gloppen, 2011). As will be argued later, it is the interpretation of the 'right to highest attainable standard of health' defined as 'a state of complete physical, mental and social well-being and not merely the absence of disease or infirmity' that contributes to these problems.

Furthermore, what has been acutely missed in the field of global health, are the secondary legal norms prescribing 'how the identification, setting, amendment and regulation of competences for the issuing and delegating of primary norms are to occur'. (Teubner, 2012: 106) There are still no visible and clear rules defining authority, competences, and mechanisms for the global health law-making. It is uncertain how violations should be handled, and how third parties should be included. Secondary rules enclosed in the WHO Constitution concerning its interpretation and dispute resolution have never been enforced. The interpretative role has been partially taken over by the UN Committee on Economic, Social and Cultural Rights that issued the General Comment No. 14: The Right to the Highest Attainable Standard of Health, and it is now the Office of the High Commissioner for Human Rights, that adopts Reports on various aspects of the right to health prepared by Special Rapporteurs on the right of everyone to the enjoyment of the highest attainable standard of physical and mental health, which aim to advance clarity regarding the scope and content of the right.[24] However, as the Human Rights Council mechanisms are predominantly soft and spread across a whole range of areas, a question arises to what extent the Council can and will assume mediating authority in the crowded global health landscape. These concerns are particularly relevant in light of the fact that, despite its efforts to clarify and apply the WHO definition of health[25], there are still serious definitional problems and academic debates concerning the nature and the conceptual boundaries of global health (Fried at al., 2010; Rowson et al., 2010; Bozorgmehr, 2010).

---

24 See: http://www.nesri.org/resources/general-comment-no-14-the-right-to-the-highest-attainable-standard-of-health#sthash.deGP2egv.dpuf and http://www.ohchr.org/EN/Issues/Health/Pages/AnnualReports.aspx (accessed: 1.4.2016).

25 'Health is a state of complete physical, mental and social well-being and not merely the absence of disease or infirmity.' See: Preamble to the Constitution of the World Health Organization as adopted by the International Health Conference, New York, 19-22 June, 1946; signed on 22 July 1946 (Official Records of the World Health Organization, no. 2, p. 100) and entered into force on 7 April 1948.

The third face of global health law's opacity: a troublesome definition

This section investigates the definitional problems permeating the field of global health. It proposes to view these difficulties as an important factor contributing to the lack of transparency accompanying the development of global health law. First of all, there have been efforts to define global health as an area derived from, and yet distinctively separate from more established disciplines of *public health* and *international health*.[26] International health is usually understood as a field developed already in the late 19th and early 20th century focused primarily on the control of epidemics across the boundaries between nations or on problems concerning the developing world (Kickbusch et al., 2013). Global health on the other hand: a) refers to the problems which are global in scope and transcend the north-south division in their interdependence; b) emphasises transnational health issues, determinants, and solutions; c) encompasses prevention, treatment, and care; d) and is a synthesis of population based prevention with individual-level clinical care (Koplan et al., 2009). Its goal is the equitable access to health across the globe (Kickbusch et al., 2013). Both terms are not always seen as mutually exclusive and in fact can be understood as complementary. At a different level, some authors still maintain global health is tantamount to public health in that 'both view health in terms of physical, mental and social wellbeing, rather than mainly absence of disease. Both focus on population-level policies as well as individual approaches to health promotion. And both address the root causes of ill-health through a broad array of scientific, social, cultural, and economic strategies.' (Fried et al., 2010: 536)

These attempts to define global health signify the increasing relevance of the system. They aim to capture the developments that have been recently taking place in the field of health (care), including globalisation, market liberalisation, and technological innovations. However, the struggle to produce a uniform and precise definition of global health (law and governance) lie at the root of the difficulties of achieving transparency of the system. Some theoretical explanations of the definitional and regula-

26 All three entities share the following characteristics: priority on a population-based and preventive focus; concentration on poorer, vulnerable, and underserved populations; multidisciplinary and interdisciplinary approaches; emphasis on health as a public good and the importance of systems and structures; and the participation of several stakeholders.' (J. P. Koplan et al., 2009).

tory challenges point to an inherent problem in the area of global health system. Here, approaches based on systems theory, developed by Niklas Luhmann seem particularly illuminating.

According to Luhmann, medicine and health care[27] clearly constitutes a separate functional system despite the fact that it is often coupled with other systems including science, economy, and law. (Luhmann, 1983) The criterion for differentiation is its code ill/healthy or health and illness, which is used in the communication between the doctor and the patient, with illness being the value side of the distinction. Only illness is instructive for the doctor, as he can only act when the latter is identified. Health gives nothing to work with, as it only describes what one feels in the absence of illness. Consequently, there are many illnesses and only one health. This is why the notion of health poses so many difficulties and it is both, problematic and empty. From medicine's point of view, healthy people are those who are not yet ill, or not ill anymore, or those who are ill, but asymptomatic. Thus, the main aim and function of medicine is to free from disease, the move from positive towards the negative value (Luhmann, 1990). Once this aim (i.e. the reflexive value of health) has been achieved, there is nothing more, upon which to reflect. All the communication between the doctor and the patient is about present illness and, hence, unnecessary when the illness disappears and the patient is cured. No second-order observation is necessary; the absence of illness speaks for itself (Luhmann, 1990). For Luhmann (and later also for J. Bauch) this explains why, in contrast to other function systems, medicine and health care has developed neither a specific generalized symbolic means of communication, nor a complex theory of reflection based purely on its function (Bauch, 1996). However, this is not to say that there is no communication at all. It just observes that the system has so far not developed a reflection theory, although this is changing with the expansion of the notion (and positive value) of illness, which focuses on the different classifications of disease and discovery (distinction) of ever new conditions. Luhmann has been criticised by J. Bauch and J. Pelikan[28] for his narrow (al-

27 To define a specific function system dealing with health in modern society Luhmann interchangeably used different terms: "treatment of disease", "treatment of ill persons" or "medicine", "health care", not carefully distinguishing between the three terms (Luhmann, 1983).

28 Bauch criticized Luhmann for not taking into account newer health related developments and therefore proposed a much wider binary code; that of hindering

most biomedical) understanding of health as the absence of health. (Bauch, 1996; Pelikan, 2007) Nevertheless, Luhmann's analysis has been taken up by P. Fuchs who described the development of medicine and health care as expansionist and hence typical to functional systems. The expansion stems from the fact that illness is seen not simply as disturbance of the body (and more recently also of 'consciousness'), which constitutes a necessary environment for all communication systems in society, but as an immediate threat to every 'virtual full inclusion', a threat that the system tries to stabilise, eliminate or prevent through anticipatory means of health care. (Fuchs, 2006) As a result, over the years the health care system has proliferated so massively that it has not only identified illnesses of the body, but also 'created' new diseases, to which it can react, which in turn led to even more proliferation of diagnostic, therapeutic, and prophylactic procedures, medicines, and treatments. This vision coincides and explains the process of 'medicalization' that refers to the increasing dominance of medical experts over the way in which health and illness are defined, approached and treated in society. (Scambler, 2001)

Therefore, Luhmann's vision, as refined by Bauch and Fuchs, not only provides an explanation for a relatively scarce reflexive theory of medicine and health care, but also opens up the possibility of a definition. This definition understands global health as a system operating on the basis of the code: promoting health of the global population /hindering health of the global population. This definition of global health would include considerations about future generations, which have an increasingly prominent place on the global agenda. It would also mean that promoting/ hindering equitable access to health falls within, but does not necessarily exhaust, the function of the global health system. Of course, a flexible and precise definition does not prevent the global health regime from paradoxes occurring in the process of its excessive expansion. It is at that moment that the pressure for global self-foundation (and autonomisation) increases and reveals its 'jurisgenerative potential', and it is then that subsystems of world society are beginning to develop their own constitutional legal norms (Scambler, 2001). Therefore, proposals have been formulated for more effective separation (Williams, 2005), coordination (Prah Ruger, 2008; Taylor 2004), or subsumption (Ashcroft, 2010) of different regula-

health vs. promoting health. The reformulation of the code in this way enables the inclusion of public health into the health system.

tory remits. Indeed, claims have been made that a formalised, centralised, institutionalised, and legalised system would help address existing and new health challenges. Most importantly, that it would help increase transparency of the global governance for health.

False promise of harmonisation and transparency?

Many prominent voices call for more unity through harmonisation, co-ordination, and synchronisation and constitutionalisation via codification of the area. In April 2011, the United Nations General Secretary, Ban Ki Moon, asked political leaders 'to commit to global solidarity, built on the tenets of shared responsibility, true national ownership and mutual accountability....and set the stage for a future *United Nations Framework Convention on Global Health.*'[29] The main objective of the FCGH is to reimagine global governance for health through setting priorities so that international assistance is appropriately directed at meeting basic survival needs. It also aims to coordinate and harmonize the activities among the current proliferation of global health actors which would augment the existing diversity of approaches. (Gostin, 2013).

The Framework Convention on Global Health, originally proposed by L.O. Gostin, would provide some of the missing elements of a *global health constitution*, although the proposal avoids such terminology. Academic commentators have noted that such a convention could be an appropriate instrument to (co-)create a sustainable funding mechanism, coordinate stakeholders, control the allocation of aid, define basic survival needs, and provide access to health services. It would have the potential to ensure compliance if it was indeed based on reciprocity (mutual advantages), transparency, legitimacy, social learning, mobilization through the negotiation process, and integration of treaty rules into states' legal systems and bureaucracies (Haffeld, 2010: 616). It would certainly facilitate the creation of communicative platform between different global health

29 UN Secretary-General, *Uniting for universal access: towards zero new HIV infections, zero discrimination and zero AIDS-related deaths: Report of the Secretary-General*, U.N. Doc A/65/979 (Mar. 2011), § 73, at: http://www.unaids.org/en/media/unaids/contentassets/documents/document/2011/A-65-797_English.pdf (accessed: 1.4.2016).

care actors. Such communication could strengthen the position of global health in the global arena.

Nevertheless, recent discussions on fragmentation (Koskenniemi, 2007; Teubner, 2012), pluralisation (Twining, 2000), privatisation (Slaughter, 2004; Tully, 2007) and constitutionalisation (Walker, 2002; Krisch, 2010; Thornhill, 2011), pervading international law and global (dis)order (Delmas-Marty, 2009) have shed some doubt that introducing international hard law instrument, constitutes a perfect remedy to deal with the challenges of global health law. According to Gunther Teubner an autonomous network of legal communications has arisen at the global level that produces its inventory of norms primarily from a plurality of transnational processes of rule-making. In his account more communication does not necessarily bring unity or even harmonisation. On the contrary, seen from a systems-theoretical perspective 'communication produces volatile situations of complexity and contingency from which decisions are continuously made.' (Sand, 2011). The predominant 'softness' and fragmentation of global health law should not be seen as deficiency, but as its typical characteristic. It compensates for the lack of global enforceability, rendering it suited to a global unification of law, remaining at the same time relatively resistant to symbolic destruction in the case of deviance (Teubner/Korth, 2012). The abundance of soft law instruments may actually be identified not only as a phase in the process of legalisation, but also as an alternative, to more formal sets of law. In the age of uncertainty (Bauman, 2007: 16), in the epoch that has witnessed the collapse of the grand 'metanarrative' schemas that once promised truth or justice at the end of the inquiry (Lyotard, 2006), it may be in the interests of the parties to keep to a less legalized relationship, providing for the possibility of compromise in terms of cost-effectiveness, pluralism and flexibility (Abbott/Sindal, 2000). Global health law remains fragmented and lacks a common legal point of reference to appeal to for resolving disagreements, but this feature complies with the pluralist vision of the law proposed above. According to Teubner we must grapple with 'new confusigness in the legal in-between-worlds of global society' (Teubner/Korth, 2012) that has to live with contradictory individual case decisions, with colliding settings of rules governing the same social field with masses of laws that do not give rise to a single 'ultimate rule of recognition' and decisions, which are only "final" within the meaning of each specific system (Fischer-Lescano/Teubner, 2004: 1008). In the pluralist world conflicts are solved through convergence, mutual accommodation or not at all (Krisch, 2010: 69). Viewing law in functional terms as a system stabilising normative counterfactual expectations over time (Luhmann 1988), rather than a set of norms adherent to a particular form of international law, makes it possible to include in the analysis the variety of activities concerning global health, thus defining global health law more widely and yet, more precisely.

Seen from this perspective, we may conclude that in recent years some aspects of global health have undergone considerable process legalization and "autonomisation", albeit perhaps still scarce and latent in comparison to other regimes. This process can be divided into three 'constitutional moments'. First occurred at the aftermath of the Second World War and was linked to the emergence of the post-war international health law order. The second was driven by the HIV/AIDS crisis and was marked by the emergence of the global health paradigm. The third, and most recent one, coincided with the biotechnological revolution (Krajewska, 2015). Analysis of these moments highlights that recently constitutional global health norms have been developing incrementally, remaining embedded in the ensemble of legal norms, forming the global health constitution in long concealed evolutionary processes. In a nation state as well as on a global scale they also exist latently and are peculiarly invisible. They are 'hidden' in transnational medical practice and may be found in particular treaty provisions, codes of practice, or even research agreements and consent forms. They are latent in the sense that to date they have not been incorporated in any national or global constitutional texts. Nevertheless, it is arguable that these redefined rights and principles can acquire constitutional status, especially that they will be followed as binding by the different global players and will form the basis of their actions and transnational agreements.

This conclusion is only possible if we adopt a functional vision of (constitutional) law and accept that that contractual rule-making and intra-organizational norm production is not necessarily only delegated law-making which requires recognition by the official legal order. We have to accept that sanction is losing the place it once held as the central concept for the definition of law and legal validity – for the delineation of the legal from the social and the global from the national (Teubner, 1997). Norms predominantly belong to soft law and take the form of declarations, guidelines, codes of practice, committees' decisions, public-private partnership programmes and commercial, private law contracts and agreements. This decentralized and non-harmonized body of norms is further complemented by other forms of governance, such as standardization through regulations and data sharing. This softness should not be seen as a deficiency, but as a typical characteristic of global law, an alternative to more formal sets of law (Teubner/Korth, 2012), which provides for the possibility of compromise in terms of cost-effectiveness, pluralism and flexibility (Abbott/ Sindal, 2000). This vision sounds very appealing as it allows the domain of global health law to include all health programmes, agendas and global partnerships, as well as (health care) professional codes of practice. It enables a theorisation of global health law as a societal autonomous regime, a transnational regulatory regime, a functional order, or a global fragment.

However, this means that the boundaries between law and non-law are inevitably blurred. At the national level, it is courts that take up the function of ascribing a binding force to particular normative rules at a particular point in time. However, at the global level, their capacity is considerably restricted.[30] The question thus remains, who holds the authority to interpret and reveal constitutional norms from different legal instruments. Transparency of the global health law might be a distant and unachievable goal. In operational and dynamic vision of a global law an attempt to provide a definitive answer to this question is doomed from the outset. Nevertheless, the question of what could and what could not amount to global health law, and where the limits of global health regime are, certainly requires further analysis.

Conclusions

The underlying and primary reason for this study is linked to the difficulties that arise in all areas of global health law and governance today, starting from the lack of leadership and coherence, and finishing with the lack of equality and justice. The analysis presented in this Chapter revealed 'concealed' mechanisms and characteristics of global health law that need reconceptualization. First of all, bearing diversely on approaches rooted in systems theory, the chapter traced back the growing lack of transparency of the system to its fragmentation, proliferation, but more importantly to intrinsic characteristics of global health as a functional regime. According

30 A positive example of a court's involvement in settling a claim with a transnational element is the Judgment of the High Court of Kenya in Nairobi: PETITION NO. 409 OF 2009, 20. 04.2012, at: http://kelinkenya.org/wp-content/uploads/2012/04/Judgment-Petition-No-409-of-20092.pdf (accessed:1.4.2016).

to the systems-theoretical vision of global society regimes are not founded by anyone or anything, and they are a sum of communicative operations of different actors. The same can be said of the emerging system of global health law. At the same time, the application of systems-theoretical lenses to global health law and governance sheds doubt on the effectiveness of the Framework Convention on Global Health as the best remedy for lack of coherency and transparency of global health law. In light of theories of global constitutionalism and societal fragmentation any promise of coherency or transparency is just an illusion. At the same time, Teubner's highly operative vision of regime formation helped to reveal processes of constitutionalisation that have been taking place in the area of global health law. Seen from this perspective, constitutional norms are not captured in one document or a treaty, but that they are hidden in different international and transnational acts and legal instruments.

This finding could have potentially significant consequences. It could shift the pressures to legalise certain issues at the international level in a top-down manner, and redirect the efforts towards attempts to reveal self-founding and self-limitative rules that already exist within the system. What is paramount is the progressive establishment of 'secondary rules' that show how to identify the foci of decision-making in a particular situation and moment in time. Establishing these rules could indirectly contribute to the solution of two difficult problems in the area of global health: legitimacy and effectiveness. Creation of institutional structures that would help resolve conflicts between rules and organisational and professional rationales – rather than adoption of more primary rules in international treaties – should be the next priority for the global health law and governance. This gradual and systematic 'unconcealment' of the global health law system might be one of the most important tasks for future scholars, lawyers, and policy-makers in the area of global health. EU scholars and regulators should not shy away from this task either, for the EU has an important role to play in shaping the future of global health.

References

Abbott, K.W. and Sindal, D. (2000), 'Hard and Soft Law in International Governance', 54 *International Organization* 3, 421-456.

Aginam O. (2005), 'Global health governance: international law and public health in a divided world', Toronto: University of Toronto Press Inc.

Andorno, R. (2007), 'Global Bioethics at UNESCO: in defence of the Universal Declaration of Bioethics and Human Rights', *Journal of Medical Ethics*, 33: 150-154.

Ashcroft, R. (2010), 'Could Human Rights Supersede Bioethics?', *Human Rights Law Review*, DOI: 10.1093/hrlr/ngq037.

Bauch, J. (1996), 'Gesundheit als sozialer Code. Von der Vergesellschaftung des Gesundheitswesens zur Medikalisierung der Gesellschaft', Weinheim, Munchen: Juventa.

Bauch, J. (2000), 'Selbst- und Fremdbeschreibung des Gesundheitswesens', in H. de Berg and J. Schmidt (eds), *Rezeption und Reflexion. Zur Resonanz der Systemtheorie Niklas Luhmanns außerhalb der Soziologie,* Frankfurt/Main: Suhrkamp.

Bauman, Z. (2007), 'Liquid Times: Living in an Age of Uncertainty', Cambridge: Polity Press 2007.

Bozorgmehr, K. (2010), 'Rethinking the 'global' in global health: a dialectic approach 6', *Globalization and Health* 19.

Buse, K. Walt, G. (2000), 'Global public–private health partnerships: Part II — what are the issues for global governance?' 78 *Bulletin of the World Health Organization*, 699–709.

D'Amato A. (2005), 'International Law as an Autopoietic System', in: R.Wolfrum, V.Roeben (ed), *Developments of International Treaty Making*, Springer.

Daniels N. (2008), 'Just health', Cambridge: Cambridge University Press.

Delmas-Marty M. and Izorche M-L., (2000), 'Marge nationale d'appréciation et internationalisation du droit. Réflexions sur la validité formelle d'un droit commun pluraliste', *Revue internationale de droit comparé* 4, 52: 753-780.

Delmas-Marty, M. (2009), 'Ordering Pluralism: A Conceptual Framework for Understanding the Transnational Legal World', London: Hart Publishing.

Fidler, P. (1998) 'The Future of the World Health Organization: What Role for International Law?', *Vanderbilt Journal of Transnational Law*, 31:1079.

Fidler, D. and Gostin L.O. (2006), 'The New International Health Regulations: An Historic Development for International Law and Public Health', *Journal of Medicine and Ethics*, 34: 85-94.

Fidler, D.P. (2010), 'Challenges to Global Health Governance', Council of Foreign Relations Working Paper. New York: Council of Foreign Relations.

Fischer-Lescano, A. Teubner, G. (2004), 'Regime collisions: the vain search for legal unity in the fragmentation of global law', *Michigan Journal of International Law,* 25: 999-1045.

Francioni, F. (2006), 'Genetic Resources, Biotechnology and Human Rights: The International Legal Framework', *EUI Working Paper* LAW No. 2006/17, at: http://cadmus.eui.eu/handle/1814/6070 (accessed: 1.4.2016).

Fried, L.P. et al. (2010), 'Global health is public health' *Lancet*, 375(9714): 535-537.

Fuchs P. (2006), 'Das Gesundheitssystem ist niemals verschnupft.' in J. Bauch (ed.) *Gesundheit als System. Systemtheoretische Betrachtungen des Gesundheitswesens,* Konstanz: Hartung-Gorre-Verlag, 21–38.

Gostin L.O., (2008), 'Public Health Law: Power, Duty, Restraint', Berkley, Los Angeles, London: University of California Press.

Gostin L. O. and Mok E. A. (2009), 'Grand challenges in global health governance', *British Medical Bulletin*, 90: 7–18.

Gostin L.O. and Mok, E.A. (2010), 'Innovative Solutions to Closing the Health Gap Between Rich and Poor: A Special Symposium on Global Health Governance', *Journal of Law Medicine, and Ethics,* 34: 451.

Gostin L.O. (2013), 'Global Health Justice: Towards a Framework Convention on Global Health—A Transformative Agenda for Global Governance for Health', 13 *Yale Journal of Health Policy, Law, and Ethics* 1, at: http://digitalcommons.law.yale.edu/yjhple/vol13/iss1/1http://digitalcommons.law.yale.edu/yjhple/vol13/iss1/1 (accessed: 1.4.2016).

Haffeld, J. B. et al. (2010), 'Examining the Global Health Arena: Strengths and Weaknesses of a Convention Approach to Global Health Challenges', *Journal of Law Medicine, and Ethics, 38:* 614.

Hervey T. and McHale J. (2015), 'European Union Health Law', Cambridge: Cambridge University Press.

Kickbusch, I. (2008), 'A European Council on Global Health', 371 *The Lancet*, 24 May 2008.

Kickbusch I. et al. (eds.) (2013), 'Global Health Diplomacy: Concepts, Issues, Actors, Instruments, Fora and Cases', New York: Springer.

Koplan J. P. et al. (2009), 'Towards a common definition of global health', *The Lancet*, 373: 1993-95.

Koskenniemi, M. (2007), 'The Fate of Public International Law: Between Technique and Politics', 70 *Modern Law Review*, 1-30.

Krajewska, A. (2015), 'Bioethics and Human Rights in the Constitutional Formation of Global Health', 4 *Laws Special Issue: Bioethics, Law and Human Rights: Global Intersections* 4, 771-802; http://www.mdpi.com/2075-471X/4/4/771 (accessed: 1.4.2016).

Krisch, N. (2010), 'Beyond Constitutionalism. The Pluralist Structure of Postnational Law OUP'.

Kuppuswamy, Ch. (2007), 'The Role of International Institutions in the Formation of International Bioethical Law: UNESCO and the United Nations General Assembly Attempt to Govern Human Cloning', *Journal international de bioethique*, 18: 1-2.

Kuppuswamy, Ch. (2009), 'The International Legal Governance of the Human Genome', London: Routledge.

Labonté, R. et al. (2011), 'The growing impact of globalisation for health and public practice', *Annual Review of Public Health*, 32: 263.

Luhman, N. (1988-89), 'Law as a Social System', *Newark University Law Review,* 83: 136.

Luhmann, N. (1983), 'Medizin und Gesellschaftstheorie' *8 Medizin Mensch Gesellschaft,* 3: 168–175.

Luhmann, N. (1990), 'Der medizinische Code' in Niklas Luhmann (ed). *Soziologische Aufklärung 5. Konstruktivistische Perspektiven,* Opladen: Westdeutscher Verlag, 1176-188.

Lyotard, J-F. (2006), 'The Postmodern Condition: A Report on Knowledge', in K. Crome & J. Williams (eds), *The Lyotard Reader and Guide*, Edinburgh: Edinburgh University Press, 84-85.

Mason Meier, B. Shelley, D. (2006), 'The Fourth Pillar of the Framework Convention on Tobacco Control: Harm Reduction and the International Human Right to Health', *Public Health Report* 5, 121: 494–500.

Pelikan, J.M. (2007), 'Understanding Differentiation of Health in Late Modernity - by use of sociological system theory', in D.V. McQueen, I.S. Kickbusch (eds.), *Health and Modernity: The Role of Theory in Health Promotion* New York: Springer, 74-102.

Prah Ruger J., (2008), 'Normative Foundations of Global Health Law', *Georgetown Law Journal*, 96: 423-443.

Rowson, M. et al. (2012), 'Conceptualising Global Health: Theoretical Issues and their Relevance for Teaching', *Globalization and Health,* 8: 36.

Sand, J-I. (2011), 'Niklas Luhmann´s Theories of Law in the Twenty-first Century', in: K. Papendorf, S. Machura, K. Andenes (eds.), *Understanding Law in Society: Developments in Socio-Legal Studies,* Society and Law Series Vol. 7, LIT Verlag, Berlin.

Scambler, G. (2001), 'Habermas, Critical Theory and Health', London: Routledge.

Slaughter, A.M. (2004), 'A New World Order', Princeton, NJ: Princeton University Press

Sridhar, D. (2010), 'Seven challenges in international development assistance for health and ways forward' *Journal of Law, Medicine and Ethics* 3, 38: 459-69, 462.

Taylor, A. (2004), 'Governing Globalization of Public Health', *The Journal of Law, Medicine and Ethics* 3, 32: 500-508.

Teubner, G. (1997), 'Global Bukowina: Legal Pluralism in the World Society', G.Teubner (ed.), *Global Law Without a State,* Aldershot: Dartmouth Publishing, 3-28.

Teubner, G. and Korth, P. (2009), 'Two Kinds of Legal Pluralism: Collision of Laws in the Double Fragmentation of World Society', in: M. Young (ed), *Regime Interaction in International Law: Theoretical and Practical Challenges*, available at: SSRN: http://ssrn.com/abstract=1416041. (accessed 1.4.2016).

Teubner, G. (2012), 'Constitutional Fragments. Societal Constitutionalism and Globalisation', Oxford: Oxford University Press.

Thornhill, C. (2011), 'A Sociology of Constitutions: Constitutional and State Legitimacy in Historical-Sociological Perspective CUP'.

Twining, W. (2000), 'Globalisation and Legal Theory', London: Butterworths.

Walker, N. (2002), 'The Idea of Constitutional Pluralism', *Modern Law Review*, 65: 317-359.

Walker, N. (2008), 'Beyond Boundary Disputes and Basic Grids: Mapping the Global Disorder of Normative Orders', *International Journal of Constitutional Law,* 6: 373-96.

Williams, J. (2005), 'UNESCO's proposed declaration on bioethics and human rights: A bland compromise', 5 *Developing World Bioethics. Special Issue: Reflections on the UNESCO Draft Declaration on Bioethics and Human Rights*, 210-5.

Wollf, J. (2012), 'The Human Right to Health', New York, London: W.W Northon and Company.

Yamin A.E., Gloppen, S. (2011), 'Litigating Health Rights: Can Court Bring More Justice to Health', Harvard: Harvard University Press.

Chapter 3: The impact of the informatisation of the judiciary on the efficiency and effectiveness of public duties – case study.

Kamil Mroczka

Key words: informatisation, efficiency, effectiveness, public duties, judiciary system

Introduction

There is no doubt that the development of information technologies decisively influences the functioning of public sector in Poland, in particular public administration, whose main goal is to provide public service to citizens and other stakeholders. This trend is delayed with respect to the developed administrative systems of Western democracies; however, recently taken actions tend to rely on best practices. The development of digitalisation in the sector of private companies is also not without influence, providing newer and more efficient electronic services. In this context a good example is provided by electronic banking and the undoubted success of the mBank in the first decade of the twentieth century. As emphasised in the literature, "citizens and businesses, that are using modern information technologies in everyday life, will expect that the administration will meet their needs and allow handling of official matters by electronic means" (Ganczar, 2011: 11).

The aim of this chapter is to reflect on solutions related to the impact of computerisation on efficiency and effectiveness of the judiciary system as a part of the broadly understood public sector. The author based his reflections on particular implementation within the Ministry of Justice. Thus, this paper analyses the specific IT project regarding computerisation of the Land and Mortgage Registry. Source materials used in this presentation, regarding implementation and the conclusions drawn, come from the Ministry of Justice and other public bodies. It should be emphasised that due to assumptions taken and the form of presentation, most of this paper refers to the analysis of the implementation in the context of theoretical assumptions set in the introduction.

The author leads this paper on the basis of proposed and accepted terminology and definitional convention. For the purpose of this research it is therefore assumed, that the key determinant of good governance is respecting the rules and principles of the democratic state of law, and, especially, the functioning of an efficient (good) administration, transparency of activities, responsibility and accountability, legitimacy and democracy and, finally, respect for human rights (Farrall and Rubenstein, 2009: 191-213; Farrall, 2014: 389-408). What is particularly important, in context of this paper, is the efficient functioning of administration with regard to the computerisation of public services and its impact on the efficiency and effectiveness of providing services to citizens. Efficiency defined through the prism of funds absorption is one of the key assumptions of the concept of good governance, whereas the computerisation of the public administration is a determinant of the level of civilisation development with its practical consequence of increased efficiency and transparency of the public sector (Kowalczyk, 2008). The efficiency of actions refers, in turn, to the time of providing specific services to specific stakeholders.

What is expected of this paper is a thorough theoretical basis for discussion, since the main aim of the author is to show how good governance is realised in practice. Theoretical considerations on changing paradigms in public management, key determinants and the role of public administration in the concept of good governance are presented in other parts of this work. This chapter does not present, otherwise interesting, legal aspects of the functioning of the Land Register and security in the form of mortgages and computerisation of processes provided by public service.

The author claimed his right to choose the form of presentation, focusing his observation on the analysis of the impact of computerisation of land registry on the efficiency and effectiveness of public services provided to citizens and other stakeholders.

Conceptualisation of research terms

Conceptualisation is the process of creating concepts on the basis of general knowledge about the world by establishing the problem and the definition of the given term. The main purpose of conceptualisation is therefore to clarify abstract concepts and establish their meaning in the context adopted by a given scientific work (Mroczka 2015: 23). In this paper, the process of conceptualisation of concepts was carried out as a result of the analysis of the scientific literature, Polish and foreign, and laws. Concepts such as computerisation, efficiency and effectiveness were defined on the basis of above sources.

The term informatisation, with regard to Polish public sector, is used both in government documents and rules of law. The Law on Government Administration created public branch of informatisation[1]. It comprises of, among others, computerisation of public administration and entities performing public tasks; communication and information systems of public administration; encouraging investments in the field of computerisation and the development of services provided electronically.

In government documents it is stressed that "the informatisation of the state is to support the creation of the optimum state model through creation and development of public services - central and local, and monitoring and improving their quality – by including new possibilities that appear in connection with the rapid development of digital technologies and the expansion of digital resources and digital content" (Program, 2013: 5). Problems with introducing modern solutions to public administration gave rise to creation of the five principles of the digital state.

The efficiency of public administration systems is one of the conditions for the stability of the state. Problems in computerisation appearing in recent years, including the lack of tangible effects despite huge expenditures significantly undermining citizens' trust in public institutions. Implementation of efficient public services requires determination, concentrated actions and - most importantly - the participation of the whole government and support for all stakeholders. Achieving the above-mentioned target requires joint implementation of a number of strategic changes concentrated in 5 basic areas:

- the state should serve the citizen. Thanks to digital technology it should connect dispersed institutions and change entangled procedures into consistent and simple services;
- access to the public network and services must be safe for our data and all kinds of transactions conducted in the network;

1 The Government Administration Departments Act of September 4, 1997, Dz.U. 2015.812 j.t.

- to pursue e-administration targets, but above all, to achieve social and economic aims- it is necessary to accelerate the development of a modern telecommunications infrastructure;
- development of innovative economy needs permanent, easy access to data gathered by public services;
- we need to constantly - regardless of age - improve our digital competences to effectively use the benefits of digitisation and compete on the global market (*Directions* 2016: 3-4).

According to dictionary definition, informatisation is a process of introducing computer solutions to assist functioning of enterprises or the institutions. It is a quality development of computerisation process by the human-organisational sphere, characterised by technical and technological advancement. Its effective implementation is conditioned by applying proven methodologies and treating the entire operation as a complex IT enterprise, i.e. with budget, schedule and effects (Adamczewski, 2005: 11).

Informatisation is often erroneously described as computerisation, that is introducing computers into a chosen destination (e.g. schools, offices, agencies), replacing paper databases with digital databases equipped with engines for searching, sorting and storing, electronic forms, communication based on system cooperation or instant messengers etc. Whereas, informatisation relates to transformation whether of economies or societies of a given area into an information economy or society, that is based on information as a main good. Informatisation comes, for example, as an increase in the number of information systems, financial contributions to projects based on IT technologies in general it is a turn from an industrial economy towards an economy based on knowledge/information. Processes of informatisation and computerisation are fundamental to the establishment of the European Union as a modern frame of governance eg. e - administration[2].

2 Project of „eAdministracja". The program of „eAdministracja" is executed by Preparatory Center of Informatics of CompLearn in cooperation with State Scientific Network of KBN LFPPI (Laboratory of Physical Grounds of Processing of Information) in accordance with the Strategy for the Development of Information Society in Poland until 2013, under the Human Capital Operational Program (Subaction 5.2.1 "Modernisation of management processes in local administration" implemented by The Ministry of Internal Affairs and Administration.

For the functioning of entities forming the broadly defined public sector what becomes increasingly common and natural is the belief that efficiency and effectiveness are one of the major prerequisites for providing public services to citizens and other stakeholders. Modernisation, including more flexible action mechanisms are the effect of such an approach. They are aimed at assuring professional, and on quality (also technical), and quantitative measures (Grotkowski, 2014: 274). The second important factor shaping functioning of public administration is the effectiveness of activities.

In the literature it is assumed that "effectiveness is a relationship between results, results and/or influences and costs, mainly financial, incurred for achieving them". Effectiveness compares what has been done with what was originally planned, i.e. it compares actual with expected or estimated outputs, results, and/or impacts (The New Programme, 1999: 9). Effectiveness is also sometimes referred to as a fact of achieving results at anticipated costs, conversion of activities into results and the quality of results achieved (Aid Delivery Methods, 2004: 139). Additionally, apart from financial costs, there can be, for example, human resources and administrative expenditures (Jeruzalski, 2009: 99).

Efficiency looks at the ratio between the outputs, results, and/or impacts and the inputs (particularly financial resources) used to achieve them. Efficiency is the contribution made by the project's results to the achievement of the project purpose.

Effectiveness and efficiency ratios can thus be calculated for each stage of the programme or measure, i.e., in terms of output, result, and impact. They allow comparisons of what has been achieved with what was planned (effectiveness) or with the resources used (efficiency). These indicators can provide useful information for programme managers and evaluators, assisting them to make better (re)programming decisions.

Legal conditioning of the Land and Mortgage Registry proceedings

This part of the study presents basic issues regarding legal conditions for land and mortgage proceedings in Poland. The most important legal act regulating issues related to the Land and Mortgage Register is the Act of 6 July 1982 on Land Books and Mortgage[3].

According to art. 1 the Land books are kept in order to establish the legal status of the given real estate. Land registers are public, and parties can not plead ignorance of the entries in the land registry or applications, which are remarked in it. What is important (especially in the case of keeping books in electronic form), is that there is the presumption of land register credibility, that is the presumption that the legal entry to the land register is made according to the actual legal status.

Maintenance of land register stays in the jurisdiction of regional courts. In keeping land and mortgage registers, court can use registrars to perform activities of the court in this matter. In particular, art. 251 is essential for deliberations of this chapter, as it states that Land Books are established and run in electronic form. Introduction of this provision was forced by the need to improve the process of Land and Mortgage registration, which will be discussed later.

Informatisation of the Land and Mortgage Registry - implementation analysis

Before discussing basic assumptions regarding the project of the New Electronic Land Book (implemented between 2002-2014) and the Electronic Land and Mortgage Register (2012-2015), the author will briefly present the stages of the system creation. This presentation will be embedded in a historical and socio-economic context. The first years of political transformation restored due meaning to many civil law institutions, which in the period of Polish People's Republic were treated in an instrumental way. It is important to emphasise that restored institutions stayed in close relationship with law of the private property. Undoubtedly, land registers are included among such institutions, as they are crucial to the safety of real estate trading and security of real estate mortgage credit (Rudnicki, 2011).

The first work related to informatisation of Land Registry begun in 1995, when the group of experts from Norway and Poland worked out the

3 Act of 6 July 1982 on land and mortgage registers (Consolidated text: Dziennik Ustaw 2013, item 707, item 830, item 941).

grounds for creation of the Centre of National Court Registers (Bogucki, 2010: 36). Creation of the working group for the informatisation of the state registers, which remained an exclusive responsibility of the Minister of Justice, arose in 1991 out of the practical problems associated with entrusting common courts with duty to keep Land books. As pointed out in the literature, these problems resulted mainly from the lack of preparation of judicial staff and associated personnel, as well as improper storing conditions (Borys, 1998: 35).

The second category of problems with land and mortgage proceedings, resulted from dramatic increase in the number of applications, in connection with complicated and outdated system of filling forms manually and the need to carry out an "entire sequence of laborious duties" (Rudnicki, 1998: 31). Workforce, organisational, legal and procedural problems resulted in the creation of backlog in dealing with applications to land registry.

Delays in Land Registry proceedings didn't remain without the reaction of legislator, who decided to improve proceedings by implementing the electronic database of the land register. It was aimed at improving the efficiency and effectiveness of public services.

Also in 1995, the Department of Organisation and Information of the Ministry of Justice welcomed the creation of a working group for Land registers (Kołodziejska, 1998: 49). From January 1997 informatisation of the land registry became the responsibility of the newly created Bureau of Project Implementation of the Centre of National Court Registers (CNCR)[4]. Also that year witnessed presentation of basic assumptions for the process of informatisation of the land registry. Two years later, it was decided to prepare and submit an application to the European Commission for funding the project "Construction of the Integrated Cadastral System". The system assumed, among other things, the informatisation of processing and circulating data regarding real estates.

Formally, the process of land registry informatisation was initiated by Act of 14 February 2003 on the content transfer of land and mortgage register to structures of electronic land books[5]. This act amended the Act of 1982 on land registers by adding art. 363^3. That provision obliged the Mi-

4 Para 1 of Regulation of the Council of Ministers on organizational changes in the Ministry of Justice, Dz.U.1996.147.689.

5 Act 14 February 2003 on Migration of Land Book Contents to the Structure of Land and Mortgage Register, Dz.U.2003.42.363.

nister of Justice to create and maintain the central database of land registers. This database was to be a collection of national land registers. Also, the Ministry of Justice was obliged to ensure the safety of the central database of land registers, in particular protection against unauthorized access by third parties, destruction and loss of data. The legislature obliged district courts, which established and kept land registers in a computer system, to carry out activities related to keeping land registers in a central database of land registers.

Legislator, being aware of a revolutionary nature of the changes to be implemented, decided to implement the project in stages. The pilot programme for the project of the *New* Land and Mortgage Register was launched on 1 October 2003. Pursuant to the Directive of the Minister of Justice of 20 August 2003 on the schedule of performing tasks of land registers migratory centres, migration of land registers was performed in the district courts of Plock, Bytom, Olsztyn, Warsaw and Wejherowo[6]. Migration of data from the existing land registry to the electronic land registry engaged specially designated migratory centres of land registers. Obviously, migration employed a computer system (Gryszczyńska, 2009: 43). Completing implementation in pilot form resulted in positive consequences. As Grażyna Kołodziejska, representative from the Ministry of Justice, describes "pilot works enabled to test basic system functions and its suitability for full implementation. It eliminated many faults associated with technical matters (Sopyło, 2010: 36)." In subsequent years, the process of land registry computerisation included other courts.

Summarising, it should be emphasised that project of the New Land Register, aimed at complex computerisation of land registry, that is to transfer all land registers to electronic form, create a central database of land registry and computerise regional courts' Land and Mortgage Registry Divisions. The project was fully implemented on December 2, 2014, marking the end of the land registers migration process. It was implemented in several stages, each stage being a separate project with separate funding and its own aims and indicators. As a general rule, indicators related to the number of digitised land registers and the date of migration completion.

The next step in computerisation of land registry was marked by the project of the New Electronic Land Book. Its implementation started in

6 See Dz.Urz.MS. 2003.4.15.

January 2012. The general objective of the project was to facilitate access of citizens, companies and other entities to information and services provided by judiciary system[7]. Specific objectives of the project were divided into the following blocks:

- e-services facilitating access to land registry:
    - acquiring via e-mail electronic copies from the registry, excerpts from the registry and certificates of closing the land registry, with the possibility of self printing a document validated as a legal document issued by the court;
    - verification of authenticity and up-to-dateness of copies from the registry, excerpts from the registry and certificates of closing the land registry;
    - searching the register by entities named in the Act (mainly bailiffs and notaries);
    - granting entitled entities named in the Act with a direct access to the central database of the registry, with ability to search them according to set criteria - access via tele- transmission, web-services (mainly tax institutions, special forces, police, enforcement bodies and others);
    - enabling courts that keep land registries to accept electronic notices regarding data changes in registry of land and buildings, and mailing electronic information on data changes made in a land book via an integrated Real Estate Cadastre to organs that keep registers of land and buildings
- implement provisions of the Land and Mortgage Registry electronic proceedings
    - electronic submission of an application for registration, with the automatic mention of temporary entry in the book;
    - enabling persons submitting an application for registration to receive notification on registration in land registry via e-mail;
    - enabling interested parties to receive information via IT system about matter in question;
- improvement in quality of data stored in land register by automatic verification of entries introduced to the land registry with other national registers. [8].

---

7 Source documents of the Ministry of Justice provided for the author, Warsaw 2016.
8 Ibidem.

The project assumed the following indicators

- share of copies from Land registry generated electronically in the total number of copies generated (target value of 2015 - 10%; in 2015 reached 21%, in December 2015 - 30%)
- share of applications for registration in the Registry submitted electronically in the total number of applications (target value of 2%, indicator not yet measured as regulations will come into effect in 1 April 2016). [9].

Specific costs of the project are as follows:

- system creation: 6 447 540 PLN;
- equipment purchase 652 266 PLN;
- license purchase : 996 615 PLN;
- expert support: 167 238 PLN.[10].

As presented above, the project's costs did not exceed 10 million PLN, which should be emphasised, since as a rule any IT implementations in Poland absorb significantly higher amounts. According to information provided by the Ministry of Justice, the project was successfully implemented within the scheduled period of time.

To sum up, the project, due to the complicated subject matter and legal consequences was rightly divided into stages. The implementation of all activities within one project could result in irreversible errors. What seems especially important is the adoption of the project's specific operational objectives and indicators for implementation assessment. It should be noted, however, that the implementation of the first stage of the New Land Registry was not devoid of problems. As stated in control results by Supreme Chamber of Control, although the implementation "significantly enhanced and accelerated the issuance of copies of land registers, and improved access to them" it did not result in "the expected elimination of backlog cases in the departments of land and mortgage registries." The auditors also highlighted the weaknesses in project management, which lacked complete information on incurred expenditure and reliable indicators regarding completion of specific objectives of the project's stages (Informacja, 2009: 7-8).

9 Ibidem.
10 Ibidem.

What is becoming increasingly common and natural in the functioning of entities forming the broadly defined public sector, is the belief that efficiency and effectiveness are some of the major prerequisites for the provision of public services for citizens and other stakeholders. This approach results in modernisation including more flexible action mechanisms. They are aimed at providing professional, quality and quantitative based indicators (Grotkowski, 2014: 274).. Another important factor influencing the functioning of the public administration is effectiveness.

Impact of project's implementation on efficiency and effectiveness of public services

As mentioned above, the purpose of the project of land registry computerisation was to digitalise paper versions of land registers into a central system managed by the Ministry of Justice. According to data provided by this institution as of 31 January 2016 central land register database consists of 20 755 626 books[11].

The impact analysis of implementation of the electronic land register and electronic land proceedings on efficiency and effectiveness of public services proved that implementation undoubtedly contributed to increase in efficiency and effectiveness for several reasons.

Firstly, as a result of the implementation and modernisation of IT solutions related to land and mortgage proceedings, the national average rate of efficiency of land and mortgage proceedings fell from 3.40 in 2001 to 1.06 in 2015. In 2002, just before pilot implementation of new land registry indicator reached a value of 2.77. The lowest level of the index was recorded in 2012 (0.60). From the perspective of citizens this significant decline in indicator value results in shorter time of delivering public service, which consequently reduces implementation cost.

It should also be noted that over the last 15 years there has been a significant increase in the number of proceedings. In 2000 land registry departments dealt with approx. 2.1 million cases, and in 2015 with nearly 3.4 million.

11 Source documents of the Ministry of Justice provided for the author, Warsaw 2016.

It is also necessary to draw attention to the average duration of land registry proceedings completed in accordance with methodology of the Council of Europe Commission for the Evaluation of the Efficiency of Justice. As a result of the computerisation process of the Land Register, the average duration of proceedings has been reduced by several dozen days. In 2001 the average proceedings duration totalled more than 103 days, whereas in 2012 it fell to an average of 19.2 days.

Table 1. Registration and management of cases related to land books between 2000-2015

Year	Incoming	Resolved	Number of pending cases	Clearance rate (in months)*	Indicator of disposition time (in days) **
2000	2 107 207	2 203 178	577 011	3,29	95,59
2001	2 065 228	2 054 924	584 633	3,40	103,84
2002	2 034 999	2 166 783	470 052	2,77	79,18
2003	2 301 161	2 417 441	359 119	1,87	54,22
2004	2 493 833	2 533 420	324 032	1,56	46,68
2005	2 438 726	2 473 150	295 374	1,45	43,59
2006	2 637 036	2 603 568	333 908	1,52	46,81
2007	3 270 225	3 026 587	577 593	2,12	69,66
2008	3 559 659	3 572 875	564 377	1,90	57,66
2009	3 405 233	3 522 405	448 751	1,58	46,50
2010	3 135 675	3 297 665	287 311	1,10	31,80
2011	3 195 986	3 279 579	203 773	0,77	22,68
2012	3 193 012	3 020 764	158 906	0,60	19,20
2013	3 213 073	3 168 434	203 574	0,76	23,45
2014	3 244 280	3 246 650	201 206	0,74	22,62
2015	3 363 422	3 266 246	298 382	1,06	33,34

* clearance rate - ratio of the number of all unresolved cases over the number of average incoming cases per month.

**indicator of disposition time (in days) - number of unresolved cases that remain for a next statistical period in relation to an average disposition time of resolved cases (365 days).

Source: statistical data of the Ministry of Justice, Warsaw 2016.

What should be pointed out is that positive aspects of the computerisation of public services are noticed by international institutions. According to data related in Doing Business 2012, report by the World Bank, the average duration of proceedings in the case of land books registration (registration of ownership) was 152 days. In 2013 the average duration of proceedings decreased to 54 days. According to the latest report of 2015, the average duration of proceedings is 40 days.

As Melissa Johns and Marcin Piatkowski from the World Bank emphasised, significant acceleration in property registration has been achieved "through the introduction of new cases load system for the courts dealing with real estate registers and by continuing digitisation of documentation of these units" (Johns and Piatkowski, 2012: 6).

It should also be noted that from 1 July 2014, copies of land registers, extracts from land registers and certificates to close the land registry are issued electronically - 52 654 electronic documents were issued in 2014 and 150 179 in 2015[12]. As this shows, we are dealing with an increasing trend, which the author believes to be likely to continue in the coming years. This is mainly due to the ease of access and significantly shorter waiting time which is still the case when doing business in traditional form connected with a visit in the competent court.

In order to present positive aspects of the implementation we should also recall data relating to the use of the public database of land registers. Since the launch of the service, in the period of June 2010 to 31January 2016, land registry has been viewed through a special portal more than 263 000 000 times. It is an indicator of interest in this project's result. In 2010 the portal was visited by 9.7 million users, in 2011- 21.4 million, in 2012 - 57.2 million, in 2013 - 66.4 million, in 2014 - 45.4 million, and in 2015 - 56.7 million[13]. It proves that interest in using this tool is significant, and, in author's opinion, is becoming more widespread.

While analysing the project's results one should also refer to the stability of the IT system supporting land registers. According to data from the Ministry of Justice, in recent years there has been no serious system failure. Temporary unavailability was due to planned technical work in Ministry's data centre. It should be noted, however, that there were some temporary technical problems with system performance caused by periodic, sudden increase in inputs (robots) to land registers browser and with technical infrastructure. These problems, however, are typical to any IT tools irrespective of the sector in which they are used.

---

12 Source documents of the Ministry of Justice provided for the author, Warsaw 2016.

13 Ibidem.

The author believes that while discussing this project, additional aspects related to the increase in efficiency and effectiveness of public service should also be highlighted. Firstly, the possibility of remote viewing of land registry contributed to a significant reduction in access time to the desired official document. With the number of the land and mortgage book, the user can instantly browse its contents. In this context, it is also necessary to emphasise that user is able to print land book legitimately as any public document. Secondly, such a possibility has helped to reduce the user's cost of obtaining information. Currently, there is no need to engage the appropriate department of the district court, because land registry content is in the central database. Thirdly, standardisation of data input and its presentation reduces possibility of clerical error practically to a minimum. This, in turn, generates savings in terms of ensuring an adequate number of clerical and judicial officials. Fourthly, there is no doubt that computerisation of public services increases the ability of the state to implement public policies in a fair and economical (thrifty) way. According to the Central Statistical Office, the vast majority of entrepreneurs (92.7%) and households (75.8%) have Internet access. Potential critics of the low level of household Internet availability should be aware that 63% of households in 2015 indicated as the main reason for not having Internet access at home no need to use it[14].

With regard to the cited report, however, what is disturbing is a very low level of e-government services use by households (ie citizens). Less than 30% of them used e-government services. In this context, the result achieved in 2014 of 92.4% by entrepreneurs is impressive. Individuals using e-government services most commonly searched administration sites, and the least sent completed on-line forms. More than 90% of entrepreneurs communicated with public administration by sending appropriate forms and applications, while less than 75% used the Internet to download relevant forms and documents[15]. The author believes, that the

---

14 *Społeczeństwo informacyjne w Polsce w 2015 r. Opracowanie sygnalne,* Główny Urząd Statystyczny, Warszawa, 20.10.2015, s. 1, źródło: http://stat.gov.pl/download/gfx/portalinformacyjny/pl/defaultaktualnosci/5497/2/5/1/spoleczenstwo_informacyjne_w_polsce_2015_-_notatka.pdf (accessed: 22.1.2015).

15 *Społeczeństwo informacyjne w Polsce w 2015 r. Opracowanie sygnalne,* Główny Urząd Statystyczny, Warszawa, 20.10.2015, s. 2-6, źródło: http://stat.gov.pl/download/gfx/portalinformacyjny/pl/defaultaktualnosci/5497/2/5/1/spoleczenstwo_informacyjne_w_polsce_2015_-_notatka.pdf (accessed: 22.1.2015).

low level of public interest in e-government services results from the complicated and time-consuming authentication process (compared eg. to the banking sector), low level of citizens' trust in the state and its institutions and habits that paper and direct contact with an official provide a sense of security in conflict situations.

Summary and conclusions

A high degree of standardisation and computerisation of the judiciary and the use of "Rechtspfleger", especially in the branches with a high numbers of cases (land registry, business registry, family law, enforcement cases, and payment orders), enable courts to keep the costs low and allow the revenue (derived from court fees) to be distributed to other parts of the court system (for example, criminal proceedings)[16].

References

Aid Delivery Methods. Project Cycle Manageent Guidelines (2004), Europe Aid Cooperation Office, Brussels.

Bogucki, D. (1998), 'Projekt Nowa Księga Wieczysta a reforma ksiąg wieczystych', *Rejent*, 6 (86): 13-22.

Borys, G. (2009), 'Funkcjonowanie elektronicznej księgi wieczystej – zarys problematyki', in: G. Tylec, J. Misztal-Konecka (eds.), *Elektroniczne aspekty wymiaru sprawiedliwości,* Bydgoszcz-Lublin: Oficyna Wydawnicza Branta.

'Directions of Strategic Actions of the Minister of Digital Affairs in the field of computerization of public services', Ministry of Digital Affairs, Warsaw 2016.

Farall, J. (2014), 'Rule of Accountability or Rule of Law? Regulating the UN Security Council's accountability deficits', *Journal of Conflict Security Law,* 19(3): 389-408.

Farrall, J., Rubenstein, K. (eds.) (2009), 'Sanctions Accountability and Governance in a Globalised World', Cambridge: Cambridge University Press.

Ganczar, M. (2009), 'Informatyzacja administracji publicznej. Nowa jakość usług publicznych dla obywateli i przedsiębiorców', Warszawa: CeDeWu.pl.

Grotkowski, M. (2014), 'Zmiany podmiotowe jako element modernizacji administracji publicznej we współczesnej Polsce', praca doktorska, Warszawa.

---

16 Report on "European judicial systems – Edition 2014 (2012 data): efficiency and quality of justice", p. 85, http://www.coe.int/t/dghl/cooperation/cepej/evaluation/2014/Rapport_2014_en.pdf (accessed: 22.1.2015).

Gryszczyńska, A. (2009), 'Migracja ksiąg wieczystych', in: G. Tylec, J. Misztal-Konecka (eds.), *Elektroniczne aspekty wymiaru sprawiedliwości,* , Bydgoszcz-Lublin: Oficyna Wydawnicza Branta.

'Informacja o wynikach kontroli rozpoznawania przez sądy spraw wieczystoksięgowych oraz realizacji projektu Nowa Księga Wieczysta' (2009), Najwyższa Izba Kontroli, Warszawa.

Jeruzalski, T. (2009), 'Efektywność i skuteczność wdrażania systemów IT w administracji publicznej. Wspomaganie procesów podejmowania decyzji', Warszawa,: CeDeWu.

Johns, M., Piątkowski, M. (2012), 'Doing Business 2013 w Polsce', Warszawa 23 października 2012 r.

Kołodziejska, G. (1998), 'Problemy występujące w funkcjonowaniu wydziałów ksiąg wieczystych w przededniu informatyzacji', *Rejent*, 6(86): 34-49.

Kołodziejska, G., Kapusta, W., Bogucki, D. (1998), 'Informatyczna księga wieczysta – omówienie wstępnych założeń systemowych (Warsztaty – Popowo w dniach 20-21 grudnia 1997 r.)', *Rejent*, 6(86): 49- 88.

Kowalczyk, L. (2008), 'Elektroniczne Usługi Publiczne (Zarys problemów)', Wrocław.

Mroczka, K. (2015), *Wpływ polityki zarządzania zasobami ludzkimi w służbie cywilnej na funkcjonowanie państwa,* Warszawa.

Program zintegrowanej informatyzacji państwa, Ministerstwo Administracji i Cyfryzacji, Warszawa, listopad 2013.

Rudnicki, S. (1998), 'Polski system ksiąg wieczystych na tle regulacji państw europejskich – członków UE – wady i zalety tego systemu, ocena stanu obecnego i wnioski na przyszłość', *Rejent*, 6(86): 29-33.

Rudnicki, S. (2011), 'Ustawa o księgach wieczystych i hipotece. Przepisy o postępowaniu w sprawach wieczystoksięgowych. Komentarz', Warszawa: Lexis Nexis.

Sopyło J. (2010), 'Nowa jakość księgi wieczystej', „Na wokandzie", http://www.ebos.pl/wiadomosci/988_nowa_jakosc_ksiegi_wieczystej (accessed 22.1.2016).

'The New Programming period 2000-2006: methodological working papers. Working Paper 3. Indicators for monitoring and Evaluation: An indicative Methodology' (1999), European Commission, Directorate-General XVI, Brussels.

Chapter 4: The impact of the principles of good governance on the EU Investment Law

Jagna Mucha

Key words: investment promotion, EU investment law, FDI, BITs

Introductory remarks

Foreign investors are encouraged by those jurisdictions in which there exists a stable and transparent legal framework for the investments. The EU wants to be perceived as such a jurisdiction. In the recent years the EU legal system has been creating a new legal order which aims at regulating the issue of foreign investments. The framework for creating such law was introduced already in the Treaty of Lisbon by virtue of the legal provision setting forth the exclusive competence of the EU over foreign direct investment (hereinafter referred to as "FDI") of the Member States. By covering FDI within the framework of the common commercial policy, the European Union became authorised to exercise its policy and legislate in this field. Therefore, the European Commission launched its active policy aiming at creation of a stable, fair and properly regulated environment in which the EU investors may conduct their business.

By implementing its policy the European Commission drew attention to the principles of the concept of good governance. Being aware of the fact that investment law protects the investors more effectively if it makes use of the concept of good governance, the European Commission referred to these principles while proposing a regulatory framework for the EU investments. In this context, it emphasised the meaning of legal stability and transparency, as well as the existence of an effective dispute resolution system in the effective investment protection. Pursuing these principles the European Commission presented its vision of a comprehensive, international, European investment policy and proposed the new piece of legislation aiming at establishing the transitional arrangements for bilateral investment agreements and the framework to manage financial responsibility linked to investor-state dispute settlement.

In the following it will demonstrated that the concept of good governance has a significant influence on the directions of EU investment policy and EU law. Such interrelation will be firstly justified by the fact that the rate of the direct investments, desired for EU economic growth, depends on the application of good governance principles. Then, for the purpose of clarity of the discussion, the definition of FDI against the EU law background will be presented, and this will be followed by the interpretation of this notion by the Court of Justice of the European Union. Further, the Chapter analyses the EU competence over FDI and the related issue of the so called extra- and intra-EU bilateral investment treaties (hereinafter referred to as "the BITs"). Last but not least, the Chapter discusses the influence of good governance on the current EU investment policy and the emerging EU investment law.

The significance of good governance for the amount of the direct investments

In the context of EU investments, good governance gained significance in the 90's since at that time a lot of European countries were experiencing the transition process towards political transformation. The investors coming from the old Member States were interested in investing in these emerging markets and they researched the quality of the public services in the host states in order to decide whether they should locate the investments outside the old EU. For the potential investors it was vital to acknowledge that the legal systems of the emerging markets were transformed to fit in the image of the legal institutions characteristic for developed countries. Although such a legal framework was created, foreign investors were still uncertain on how the new institutions operate in the free market reality and therefore they were reluctant to invest in the Central and Eastern Europe.

Nowadays, with the benefit of hindsight, public authorities from this region aim at maintaining such institutional framework which enables: (1) to decrease the costs of the trade exchange, (2) to reduce uncertainty connected thereto, (3) to minimalise the risk of corruption and finally (4) to increase the transparency of the functioning of public authorities (Wilkin 2008: 15). However, the most recent research shows that there are still many obstacles which slow down the rate of investments. It has been demonstrated that such factors as the lack of transparency in public procurement, low predictability of the commercial policy and ineffective fight against corruption still discourage foreign investors coming from the old EU to invest in the Central and Eastern Europe (Charatynowicz et al 2015: 49). Taking Poland and Germany as examples, one may notice that although Poland is a forefront location for the German investments from the region in question, German investors complain that the Polish public administration operates ineffectively and that the tax system is complicated and full of contradictory legal interpretations (Forbes, 2015). This situation may be attributed to the effects of poor governance.

It emerges from the relevant literature on the subject that the way and the effects of governance affect the investment-related attractiveness of the EU (Oman, 2000: 11; Mucha, 2015: 47-52). The quality of public administration has direct influence on the economic environment and therefore it is essential for stimulating economic growth. Also effective public administration is a key factor to ensure a country's long term competitiveness as regards foreign investments. As was demonstrated by the OECD study "(…) many of the governments that are most successful in attracting FDI are also among those that the best meet requirements of good governance (…)" (Oman, 2000:11). These requirements include, among others, the absence of corruption, transparent proceedings based on the high-quality legislation, the reduction of the administrative burden and existence of an independent, efficient judicial system which enables fair dispute resolution[1].

On the other hand, deficiency of good governance limits the state's possibility of economic growth which is fostered, among other things, by the income from investments. It emerges from the relevant literature on the subject that "(…) without proper-functioning institutions of governance based on the rule of law that promote social stability and legal certainty, there cannot be investment and assumption of risk that form the basis of market economy development, let alone sustainable development" (Sachiko, Durwood, 2005: 16). Deficiency of good governance has devastating consequences both for the state's and the market players' confidence. It discourages investors from making investments and consequently it deprives the states of foreign capital.

1 European Commission (2014), „Promoting good governance. European Socioal Fund Thematic Paper", EU, 2014.

The definition and interpretation of FDI in the EU Law

For the purpose of clarity of the discussion on the impact of the good governance on the European investment law it seems to be indispensable to clarify what the notion of FDI means. Although this term is explicitly included in the Treaty on the Functioning of the European Union (hereinafter referred to as "the TFUE") [2] [3], neither the TFUE, nor the Court of Justice of the European Union (hereinafter referred to as "the Court") provide a legal definition of this term. Therefore, in order to determine what FDI means, it may be useful to refer to the notion of "direct investment", which was widely interpreted by the said Court with reference to free movement of capital and payments and in the light of the Nomenclature of the capital movements annexed to the Directive 88/361/EEC.[4]

In line with the said Directive 88/361/EEC, direct investments involve "investments of all kinds by natural persons or commercial, industrial or financial undertakings, and which serve to establish or to maintain lasting and direct links between the person providing the capital and the entrepreneur to whom or the undertaking to which the capital is made available in order to carry on an economic activity. This concept must therefore be understood in its widest sense".[5]In the relevant literature on the subject special emphasis is placed on the "lasting links" in relation to the investment, which excludes from this group the investments with solely financial aims (Strik, 2015: 29).

In the context outlined in the Directive 88/361/EEC, the term "direct investments" was also subject to the interpretation of the Court. In a wide range of judgements the Court agreed that direct investments include "investments of any kind undertaken by natural or legal persons and which serve to establish or maintain lasting and direct links between the persons providing the capital and the undertakings to which that capital is made available in order to carry out an economic activity (…)" (Case C-194/06, *Staatssecretaris van Financiën,* ECLI:EU:C:2008:289, para 100; Case

---

2 Consolidated version of the Treaty on European Union, Official Journal the European Union no. C-326/13, dated 26 October 2012.

3 See point 4 of this Chapter.

4 Nomenclature of the capital movements referred to in Article 1 of the Council Directive 88/361/EEC of 24 June 1988 for the implementation of Article 67 of the Treaty, Official Journal L 178 dated 8 July 1988 p.5-18.

5 Explanatory note to the Annex to the Council Directive 88/361/EEC, *op. cit.*

C-326/07, *Commission v. Italian Republic* ECLI:EU:C:2009:193, para 35; Case C-101/05 *Skatterverket*, ECLI:EU:C:2007:804, para.46).

This coherent interpretation of the notion of "direct investments", as presented by the Court was subsequently shared by the European Commission which adopted it in relation to the FDI.[6] At the same time, the European Commission emphasised that it opts for very broad and general definition of FDI, saying that "it consists in making capital available from one country for carrying out an economic activity in another country with a view to exercising a form of control, such as ability to influence business decisions."[7]

The EU competence over FDI and BITs

By 2009 the European Community did not have exclusive competence to execute agreements in the field of investment. Therefore, such agreements were concluded by the Member States with third countries, independently of the EU. In order to protect their investors outside the EU and attract foreign investments, Member States executed BITs, which according to the European Commission are "the most visible manifestation of the Member States' policies on investments".[8] A lot of them were executed before the subsequent EU enlargements between the old Member States and those countries which became Member States after later accessions. Therefore, nowadays there are many intra-EU BITs inside the single market, which gives rise to doubts of legal nature, as will be discussed in what follows.

In brief, the main goal of BITs is to encourage foreign investments by strengthening the level of investor protection in two states. The contents of BITs are in general standardised (Słok-Wódkowska, Śledziewska, 2014: 36). They typically include provisions regarding the scope of the investments, the protection against expropriation and legal discrimination. In line with BITs, the states-signatories are often obliged to ensure fair and equitable treatment to the investors, which in the broad sense means that

6 Communication from the Commission to the Council, the European Parliament, the European Economic and Social Commitee and the Committee of the Regions entitled "Towards a comprehensive European international investment policy" COM(2010)343 final dated 7 July 2010 p.2.

7 http://ec.europa.eu/trade/policy/accessing-markets/investment/.

8 Communication COM(2010)343… *op. cit.*, p.4.

they shall "(...) act consistently, transparently, reasonably, without ambiguity, arbitrariness or discrimination, in an even-handed manner, to ensure due process in decision-making and respect investor's legitimate expectations."[9] Furthermore, one of the most common instruments provided by BITs is the dispute resolution system which enables investors to enforce their rights outside the national court system by submitting the given case to the arbitration proceedings.

The legality of the intra-EU BITs was questioned when the Treaty of Lisbon came into being. The said Treaty provided frameworks for establishing EU investment law. Article 207 of TFEU is treated as the foundation here, since it puts FDI on the list of the issues falling under the common commercial policy. This new scope of the said legal provision caused a fundamental change, as since 2009 FDI has been within the scope of the exclusive competence of the European Union. Consequently, only the European Union may legislate and adopt legally binding acts in this field, whereas the Member States are able to do so themselves only if they are so empowered by the Union or in case of implementation of the Union acts.[10]

In view of the above, there emerged an issue of conformity of the existing intra-EU BITs with the EU law. In line with EU law, all Member States are subject to the same rules (also with regard to the investment protection) and none of them shall be discriminated against, or in favour of, on grounds of nationality.[11] Therefore, the European Commission claims that intra-EU BITs, which grant the same level of protection to the investors coming from two Member States only, may fragment the single market and infringe the principle of non-discrimination on grounds of their nationality.[12] Due to the fact that some outcomes of the proceedings based on the intra-EU BITs were incompatible with EU law, the European Commission, by letter of formal notice, requested five Member States (Austria, the Netherlands, Romania, Slovakia and Sweden) to terminate their intra-EU BITs. [13]

---

9 UN Conference on Trade and Development, 'Fair and equitable treatment', UNCTAD Series on Issues in International Investment Agreements II, New York, 2012, p. 13.

10 Article 2 paragraph 1 of the TFEU.

11 Art. 18 of the TFEU, *op. cit.*

12 http://europa.eu/rapid/press-release_IP-15-5198_en.htm.

13 http://europa.eu/rapid/press-release_IP-15-5198_en.htm.

Good governance in EU investment policy

With reference to the current status of BITs, the European Commission issued a Communication "Towards a comprehensive European international investment policy".[14] In this document one may find a lot of references to the principles of the concept of good governance, such as predictability, legal framework and transparency. Materialisation of those principles is particularly visible in the need for the creation of a stable, sound and predictable environment for investment, since the national law, policy and economy affect the rate of the investments. Applying the concept of good governance, the European Commission emphasises that EU investment policy aims at ensuring investors' open, properly and fairly regulated business environment.

Accordingly, the main consideration of the European Commission in this field is to provide appropriate legal framework for the BITs. Such an idea is drawn from the OECD research regarding the influence of the investment law on regional trade agreements (hereinafter referred to as "RTAs"), which confirms that "(…) substantive investment provisions in RTAs impact trade and FDI flows more profoundly, or that the combination of substantive investments rules and provisions liberalising other parts of the economy come together to more significantly impact trade and investment flows"[15] (OECD, 2006: 5).

Being aware of the above mentioned interplay, the European Commission proposed a system governing BITs which will support legal certainty and transparency. According to this system, in the long run BITs will be executed between the EU and respective third countries.[16] Thus, foreign investors will not need to rely on the BIT entered by individual Member States. However, there is no plan for the creation of a one-sized-fits-all model for BITs to be entered by the EU. On the contrary, they will be negotiated separately with special consideration of the interest of the stakeholders and level of development of the third country.

There are many requirements which the emerging EU legal framework for investments involving the rules on BITs shall have to comply with.

---

14 Communication COM(2010) 343… *op. cit.*

15 OECD (2006), "Analysis of the economic impact of investment provision in regional trade agreements", OECD Trade and Policy Working Paper no. 36 dated 11 July 2006.

16 See point 6 of this Chapter.

According to the European Commission, it shall include substantive rules of the EU law, such as a principle of non-discrimination, which shall constitute a key ingredient of the EU investment negotiations. Furthermore, the BITs shall be consistent with the chapter on capital and payments included in TFUE, which prohibits all restrictions on payments and capital movements, including those involving investments. Nevertheless, also typical standards of investment protection used by Member States, such as a fair and equitable treatment clause or a guarantee of compensation in case of expropriation shall be also employed in BITs executed by the EU.

Last but not least, in the EU legal framework all of the investment provisions shall be effectively enforceable through a binding dispute resolution system, as is usually set forth in BITs executed by Member States. Including this enables the investors to bring a claim against a state to the binding international arbitration. This means that in a case in which a conflict between the foreign investor and government of the host Member States arises, the latter will be represented by the EU. Here we can see influence of the concept of good governance particularly vividly, and it is illustrated by the requirement of transparency of investor-state dispute settlement as well as by the consistent and predictable interpretation of law made by the quasi-permanent arbitrators and also by clear rules for the conduct of arbitration.

Good governance in the emerging EU investment law

The framework establishing the EU investment law, as was mentioned above was created by the Treaty of Lisbon which included the FDI in the list of issues falling under common commercial policy. In view of the above mentioned change, there emerged a need for clarification of the status of the existing BITs executed by Member States with third countries ("extra-EU BITs") and verification of the provisions included therein. Thus, the EU legislator used its newly-gained exclusive competence over FDI and introduced some legislation in the field of BITs and in reference to the specific issues related to the investor-state dispute resolution included in BITs. Following the concept of good governance, the EU legislator aimed at guaranteeing legal certainty and transparency as regards the conditions under which investors shall operate and resolve their disputes.

a) Regulation no. 1219/2012

In order to clarify the status of the existing BITs, the regulation no. 1219/2012 establishing transitional arrangements for bilateral investment agreements between Member States and third countries was enacted.[17] The said regulation uses a broad definition of BIT, saying that BIT means any agreement with a third country that contains provisions on investment protection.[18] BITs defined in such a way should remain binding in the Member States. However, in light of the exclusive competence of the EU in this field, they will be progressively replaced by the BITs relating to the same subject matter executed by the EU, providing for high standards of investment protection. In line with the regulation no. 1219/2012, the existing extra-EU BITs are notified to the European Commission. The BITs which in any part are incompatible with EU law are required to be amended in order to ensure their compliance with EU law (Kleinheisterkamp, 2011). Interestingly, in spite of the exclusive competence of the EU in this field, the Member States themselves are authorised to enter into negotiations with a third country in order to amend the existing BIT or to conclude a new one.[19] However, the intention to enter into negotiations shall be notified to the European Commission, which - under certain conditions - may forbid such negotiations[20] or it may participate in this proceedings.[21] Superficially, such twofold entitlement of both the EU and Member States may seem to contradict the exclusive competence granted by the Treaty of Lisbon to the EU. However, this construction proved to be indispensable in order to ensure legal certainty until the respective BITs which shall be concluded by the EU come into force.

---

17 Regulation (EU) no 1219/2012 of the European Parliament and of the Council of 12 December 2012 establishing transitional arrangements for bilateral investment agreements between Member States and third countries, Official Journal of the European Union dated 20 December 2012, L 351/40.

18 Art. 1 para. 2 of the Regulation (EU) no 1219/2012…, *op. cit.*

19 Art. 7 of the Regulation (EU) no 1219/2012…, *op. cit.*

20 Art. 9 of the Regulation (EU) no 1219/2012…, *op. cit.*

21 Art. 10 of the Regulation (EU) no 1219/2012…, *op. cit.*

b) Regulation no. 912/2014

The exclusive competence of the EU over FDI forced changes as regards the third country investor-state dispute resolution system. Due to the fact that such a system is a central feature of BITs and in view of that the extra-EU BITs concluded by the Member States will be progressively replaced by those concluded by the EU, there emerged a need to regulate the issue of financial responsibility linked to the investor-state dispute settlement. Bearing this in mind, the regulation no. 912/2014 establishing a framework for managing financial responsibility linked to investor-state dispute settlement, tribunals established by international agreements to which the EU is party was legislated.[22] In brief, the regulation in question clarifies to whom the third country investor shall direct his claim and who would pay compensation if the Member State acts inconsistently with the provisions of the investment agreement. In line with the central principle of this act, financial responsibility should be attributed to the actor who is involved in the treatment in dispute. It means that the EU is responsible if the treatment is afforded by the EU institutions, while the responsibility rests with the Member State if it has afforded the concerned treatment. However, the EU (and not the Member State) would not bear responsibility when the undertaken actions are required by the EU law.[23] Quite in the same spirit, the entity involved in the violation of the agreement - a Member State or the EU institution - shall act as the respondent. As a matter of exception, the EU and not the Member State will act as the respondent when the latter does not intend to act as respondent or when the European Commission decides that the EU shall bear the financial responsibility for the afforded treatment.

22 Regulation (EU) no. 912/2014 of the European Parliament and of the Council of 23 July 2014 establishing a framework for managing financial responsibility linked to investor state dispute settlement tribunals established by international agreements to which the EU is party, Official Journal of the European Union dated 28 August 2014, no. L 257/121. Regulation (EU) no. 912/2014 of the European Parliament and of the Council of 23 July 2014 establishing a framework for managing financial responsibility linked to investor state dispute settlement tribunals established by international agreements to which the EU is party, Official Journal of the European Union dated 28 August 2014, L 257/121.

23 Art. 3 para. 1 of the Regulation (EU) no. 912/2014, *op. cit.* Regulation (EU) no. 912/2014, op. cit.

As illustrated by the examples of the above mentioned piece of legislation, the EU does not aim at creating any mechanisms in a manner reflecting a strict application of the rules of its exclusive competence in the field of FDI. Such approach is confirmed, *inter alia*, by the provisions of the regulation no. 1219/2012, according to which the Member States retain the right to conclude extra-EU BITs, as well as by the provisions of the regulation no. 912/2014, which still enables the Member State to act as the respondent in the investor-state disputes arising out of the BITs concluded by the EU. Instead of such strict application of EU exclusive competence, the EU introduces some practical solutions, based on the current experiences of Member States which ensures legal certainty and transparency for investors as regards operating and resolving disputes. Such an attitude demonstrates a clear influence of the concept good governance on the EU investment law.

Conclusions

It emerges from the discussion included herein that the use of the concept of good governance is of utmost importance for the amount of the investments made, since the investors locate their capital in these countries where there are stable legal frameworks regulating the working of the transparent public administration. In view of this fact the influence of good governance is particularly noticeable and to be maintained in the newly created branch of the EU law, that is investment law. The application of the concept of good governance is particularly noticeable in the attitude of the EU institutions towards BITs and the financial issues related to the investor-state dispute resolution. In spite of the fact that EU has been granted the exclusive competence to legislate on foreign direct investments, the Member States are still in the position to have influence on this. It is the very fact that with the exclusive character of the EU competence in the field under discussion and in the name of securing legal certainty in the legal trade in the scope discussed above the Member States have preserved specific instruments to act, which may be treated as the manifestation of the concept of good governance. The example in point here is that the Member States can still execute BITs with the third countries and act as respondent in the investment-state dispute resolution.

References

Charytonowicz J., Modzelewska A., Strojny M., Trusiewicz M., Żuchowski F. (2015), 'Perspektywiczne sąsiedztwo. Polsko-niemieckie relacje gospodarcze', KPMG, http://ahk.pl/fileadmin/ahk_polen/OA/Raport_KPMG_i_AHK_Perspektywiczne_sasiedztwo._Polsko-niemieckie_relacje_gospodarcze.pdf (accessed: 4.2.2016).

Kleinheisterkamp J. (2011), 'The next 10 year ECT investment arbitration: a vision for the future – from a European law perspective', http://sccinstitute.com/media/61991/jan_kleinheisterkamp_report-ect-eu-law.pdf (accessed: 31.1.2016).

Mucha J. (2015), 'Wpływ good governance na procesy inwestycyjne w Unii Europejskiej', *Prawo Europejskie w Praktyce,* 3: 47-52.

Oman C. (2000), 'Policy competition for Foreign Direct Investment. A study of competition among governments to attract FDI', http://www.oecd.org/mena/investment/35275189.pdf (accessed: 4.2.2016).

'Polska najlepszym krajem pod niemieckie inwestycje' (2015), *Forbes* 24.06.2015, http://www.forbes.pl/polska-najlepszym-krajem-pod-niemieckie-inwestycje,artykuly,196362,1,1.html# (accessed: 4.2.2016).

Sachiko M., Durwood Z. (2005), 'Rule of law, good governance and sustainable development', http://www.inece.org/conference/7/vol1/05_Sachiko_Zaelke.pdf (accessed: 4.2.2016).

Słok-Wódkowska M., Śledziewska K. (2014), 'Umowy inwestycyjne Unii Europejskiej i jej państw członkowskich- porównanie BIT i RTA', *International Business and Global Economy,* 33: 33- 46.

Strik P. (2014), 'Shaping the Single European Market in the Field of Foreign Direct Investment', Oxford and Portland: Hart Publishing.

Wilkin J. (2008), „Badanie dotyczące stworzenia systemu wskaźników dla oceny realizacji zasady good governance w Polsce. Raport końcowy", Warszawa: ECORYS Polska.

Chapter 5: Good governance at the local level. The EGTC as a tool for cross-border cooperation

Elżbieta Opiłowska

Key words: EGTC, cross-border cooperation, cohesion policy, European Territorial Cooperation, good governance

Introduction

Since the implementation of the Lisbon Treaty, territorial cohesion has become one of the main objectives of the European Union. In this respect, cross-border cooperation plays an important role. Since the early 1990s cross-border cooperation has transformed from a marginal issue into a significant aim of the EU's regional policy (Harguindéguy and Hayword, 2012). It functions as a mediator between global markets and national states and provides an overreaching framework within which European borders are transforming (O'Dowd, 2003: 14). The European Commission underlined, in its White Paper on European Governance of 2001[1], the importance of local and regional authorities as channels for interaction with citizens and identified five principles supporting good governance, specifically: openness, participation, responsibility, effectiveness and coherence. Decentralisation and multi-level governance performed due to the subsidiarity rule may guarantee the implementation of these principles. The conditions for good multi-level governance depend to a large extent on the Member States; how they apply the mechanisms of consultation, coordination, cooperation and evaluation recommended at the Community level.[2]

The European Commission arranges regular consultations with sub-national units when developing policy proposals (Grazi, 2013: 92). This dia-

1 European Commission White Paper (COM (2001) 428 final, http://aei.pitt.edu/1188 / (accessed: 16.01.2016).

2 The Committee of the Regions' White Paper on Multi-Level Governance 2009, http://web.cor.europa.eu/epp/Ourviews/Documents/White%20Paper%20on%20ML G.pdf (accessed: 16.01.2016).

logue of the European Commission, at both regional and local level, was confirmed in the Treaty of Lisbon. Under the principle of subsidiarity, not only the Member States, but also regional and local level authorities, were mentioned. Indeed, for the first time the principle of subsidiarity was considered below the state level, where subsidiarity, implying multi-level governance, should be exercised in a spirit of cooperation amongst the various levels of power (Grazi, 2013: 93).

Further, the Lisbon Treaty reflects that "in order to promote good governance and ensure the participation of civil society, the Union institutions, bodies, offices and agencies shall conduct their work as openly as possible" (art. 15)[3]. Decentralisation of power and the practice of good governance are important drivers for the fulfillment of the European Territorial Cooperation programmes. Moreover, the Europe 2020 Strategy emphasises the role of territorial cooperation for sustainable and inclusive growth.[4] Carlos Santiso argues that well-institutionalised democracies, and thereby well-institutionalised cross-border cooperations, are more likely to "produce over the long run, effective, efficient and sustainable economic and social policies, because they provide effective and stable institutional and procedural mechanisms to represent interests, arbitrate disputes, provide checks and balances, and negotiate change" (Santiso, 2001: 7).

As an institutionalised form of cooperation in border regions, Euroregions have been developed throughout Europe. The first; the Dutch–German EUREGIO, in the area of Enschede (NL) and Gronau (DE), was established in 1958 with its own cross-border office (1971) and close links to German and Dutch state agencies. It later provided a model for the development of cross-border policy throughout the European Union. Nowadays, there are about seventy cross-border regions which operate within Euroregions or Euregios. However, apart from undeniable achievements, Euroregions have not automatically provided trans-border cooperation and alliances. The framework of Euroregions proved to be insufficient in developing trans-border structures. Although they created joint Euroregional institutions such as a council, joint programmes, committees and imple-

3 http://www.lisbon-treaty.org/wcm/the-lisbon-treaty/treaty-on-the-functioning-of-the-european-union-and-comments/part-1-principles/title-ii-provisions-having-general-application/157-article-15.html (accessed: 19.1.2016).

4 http://eur-lex.europa.eu/LexUriServ/LexUriServ.do?uri=COM:2010:2020:FIN:EN:PDF (accessed: 19.1.2016).

mentation documents, each side usually receives and coordinates its own money from the programme. In order to overcome these obstacles, in 2006 the European Grouping for Territorial Cooperation (EGTC) with a legal personality was introduced. The EGTC is designed to enhance trans-border cooperation between local and regional authorities and administrations at different levels to collaborate and promote common interests by improving living conditions for the populations concerned and pooling resources and know-how. The Committee of the Regions (CoR) collaborates with local and regional stakeholders, the European Commission, the European Parliament and Member States to optimise the potential of this tool and facilitate the creation of a public space for communication, information, analysis, research and the pooling of expertise (Committee of the Regions' White Paper on Multi-Level Governance 2009).

The aim of this chapter is to analyse the EGTC as a tool for improving the effectiveness of the cross-border cooperation and for implementing the principles of good governance by reducing the difficulties encountered by Member States and by regional and local authorities in carrying out and managing cooperation activities in the context of differing national laws and procedures.

Creating the EGTC instrument in the EU

The European Union created the European Grouping for Territorial Cooperation legal instrument with the adoption of the EU Regulation 1082/2006 on the 5th of July 2006[5]. The Regulation had to be authorised by the national law of Member States. The EGTC allows public institutions to develop cooperating structures across national borders and to act with one name. In contrast to Euroregions, EGTCs are provided with an extensive legal capacity including a legal personality (Regulation (EC) No 1082/2006 2006: art. 1 par. 3) that aims at overcoming barriers for territorial cooperation. According to the Regulation, potential members of the EGTC could be EU Member States, local and regional authorities of EU Member States, other public bodies and associations of stakeholders

5 Regulation (EC) No. 1082/2006 (2006) of the European Parliament and of the Council of 5 July 2006 on a European grouping of territorial cooperation (EGTC), http://eur-lex.europa.eu/legal-content/EN/TXT/?uri=celex:32006R1082 (accessed: 16.1.2016).

whose members belong to one of the aforementioned categories. The instrument was introduced in order to carry out the following tasks – managing the Structural Funds, carrying out strategic cooperation and acting as a vehicle for the operational implementation of a cooperation project. Thus, thanks to this Regulation, territorial cooperation should move from being a marginal, specialised activity to being at the heart of the process of European integration. Furthermore, the flexibility to define the arrangements for the cooperation of stakeholders should allow for diversity in types of cooperation, reflecting the diversity of the stakeholders and their expectations.[6]

The EGTC instrument allows members to create a single legal body, using a single set of rules to implement joint initiatives in two or more Member States. This means a single staff employment contract, and common procedures for procurement. The legal stability, as Spinaci and Vara-Arribas point out, "reinforces decision-making among the partners, their position in interaction with the EU institutions, their possibilities for launching or improving their international position and the effective management of cooperation programmes and projects" (Spinaci and Vara-Arribas, 2009: 6).

Further, EGTCs are able to respond directly to calls for projects launched by EU territorial programmes and to act as the single managing authority for them. Thereby they give a clear political signal that cooperation with partners in other Member States is supported at the highest political level (Ładysz, 2011: 181-82).

However, the project of the regulation was criticised by sub-national actors, EU Member States and associations. Some of the regions that are members of the Assembly of European Regions found the regulation as unnecessary bureaucracy und accused the Commission with not respecting the principle of subsidiarity. They were afraid the regions would have to create the EGTC in order to apply for the Structural Funds. In opinion of the European Economic and Social Committee an important shortcoming of the new instrument was the impossibility of economic and social actors

6 The European Grouping of Territorial Cooperation. Study carried out by GEPE under the supervision of Professor Nicolas Levrat in the context of the CoR's research programme, 2007, http://cor.europa.eu/en/documentation/studies/Documents/The%20European%20Grouping%20of%20Territorial%20Cooperation%20%20EGTC/The%20European%20Grouping%20of%20Territorial%20Cooperation%20-%20EGTC%20-%20EN.pdf (accessed 16.1.2016).

as well as civic organisations, which are driving forces for development, to join the EGTC (Dumała, 2009: 58). However, there were also a lot of proponents of a new instrument who saw in it new opportunities for European integration and decentralised cooperation between regional and local agencies.

Lately Regulation No 1302/2013[7] has tended to clarify, simplify and improve the legal framework governing these groupings. The main goals were to make the constitution of the EGTC easier and more transparent, to reduce bureaucracy and to enlarge the scope of participation in these groupings, allowing certain private entities and entities from outside the EU to be part of them (Alcolea Martinez, 2014).

In 2014 there was a discussion between EGTCs and Member States regarding the implementation of the revised Regulation of 2013. The European Parliament, the Commission and the Council issued three joint statements that consisted in engagements to make the EGTC visible and to ensure clear, efficient and transparent procedures (CoR, EGTC monitoring report 2014).

Using the EGTC instrument following objectives of good governance can be achieved: creating a strategic approach for integrating several actions under the framework of mutual policy, stabilising cooperation structures and continuity of actions, participation of the partners in decision-making processes and creating ownership, transparency and visibility of the structure, improving the efficiency when using public funds, better democratic legitimisation due to the general assembly, easier access to tendering and acquisition procedures, improved possibility to participate in EU programmes as a single beneficiary, achieving more democratic legitimacy or public responsiveness through an enhanced participative approach (Zillmer and Toptsidou, 2014: 6-7).

EGTCs may be used for different tasks and thereby satisfy specific needs in border regions that depend on local geographic, economic, social and cultural conditions. Usually, they are created for the integrated management of the territory or of cross-border infrastructures; for the promo-

7 Regulation (EU) No 1302/2013 of the European Parliament and of the Council of 17 December 2013 amending Regulation (EC) No 1082/2006 on a European Grouping of Territorial Cooperation (EGTC) concerning the clarification, simplification and improvement of the establishment and functioning of EGTCs, http://eur-lex.europa.eu/legal-content/EN/TXT/?uri=CELEX%3A32013R1302 (accessed: 16.1.2016).

tion of an economy based on knowledge, of entrepreneurship and innovation economy; for the protection and valorisation of the environment; the provision of cross-border specific services of general interest, such as health care or for fund raising at a European and national level to finance programmes or projects (Ładysz, 2011: 182). Further, joint services can be agreed without the need to sign an international agreement needing ratification it by national parliments. The EGTC is governed by EU Regulations, conventions and statutes, which are its constitutive documents, and by the law applicable in the Member State in which the official EGTC headquater is located. It should have at least one assembly consiting of representatives of its members, and a director, who represents the EGTC and acts on its behalf.

Zillmer and Toptsidou (2014: 4) distinguish different types of EGTCs according to the four following perspectives:

- Financial differentiation. An EGTC may be founded for cooperation that is co-financed by European Territorial Cooperation (ETC) as well as for general cooperation without financial contributions of the EU.
- Territorial differentiation. The EGTC regulation includes all three types of territorial cooperation – cross-border, transnational and interregional. They may either be supported by the EU or be part of the general cooperation.
- Institutional differentiation. Within the territorial cooperation supported by the EU the EGTC regulation explicitly differentiates between EGTC dealing with programmes and projects.
- Thematic focus. This goes along with different degrees of thematic specifications.

The following section focuses on the implementation of the EU Regulations on EGTC providing an overview of the established EGTC in Western and Eastern Europe, their potentials and shortcomings.

Implementing the EGTC as a new formula of cross-border cooperation

The location on the border has an enormous impact on the adjacent areas and living communities. Thereby the border can present a barrier or a bridge for cross-border contacts and interactions, is a line of inclusion and exclusion and determines the difference between "us" and "them". However, there are many problems such as environmental pollution or organised crime that do not end at the frontier and require joint treatment. Cross-border cooperation is established in order to create cross-border development strategy, to use better resources of both sides of the border and to solve efficiently problems that occur in different fields such as in the environment, urban planning, transport, labour market, tourism, security, education and culture without having to appeal to state actors and turning the issue into an international affair. Moreover, within the proces of European integration and the creation of a common market national borders were seen as obstacles to the free movement of people, goods, services and capital.

Since the establishment of the European Regional Development Fund in 1975, the European Commission provided financial support for the cross-border activities. Introduced in 1990, the INTERREG programme provided a framework for the cross-border relations that has gradually been transformed from a strict neighbourhood focus to interregional and transnational cooperation. The cohesion policy of the EU encourages different regions of Member States to cooperate and to learn from each other best practices.

The Schengen Agreement was the next step in abolishing the national borders and creating a common European space. As a result, private actors could develop and locate their activities throughout the Schengen area, whereas regional and local authorities were confined to national spheres. Thus, the increase of economic, social and cultural activities of European citizens across the national borders, created the need for enhanced cooperation between public authorities in order to provide public services for the citizens.

The programming period of Interreg 2007-2013 had a total budget of EUR 8.7 billion (2.5 % of the total 2007-13 allocation for cohesion policy). The European Territorial Cooperation focused on three types of programmes: 60 cross-border cooperation programmes along 38 internal borders, 13 transnational co-operation programmes addressed to larger areas such as the Baltic Sea, Alpine and Mediterranean regions and interregional co-operation programme (INTERREG IVC) and three networking programmes (Urbact II, Interact II and ESPON) that provided a framework for exchanging experience between regional and local bodies in different countries. The cross-border cooperation programmes gained the most part of the Interreg budget – 5.6 billion EUR.

The fifth programming period (2014-2020) has a budget of EUR 10.1 billion, from which 6.6 billion EUR will be allocated to 60 cross-border programmes.

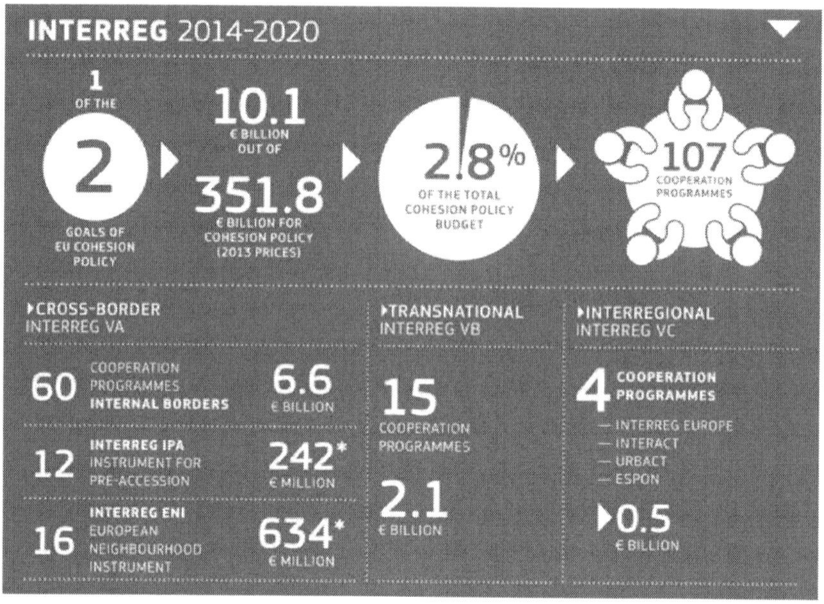

Chart 1: Interreg and inter-regional cooperation 2014-2010, source: www.ec.europa.eu

The targets of the fifth period of Interreg (2014-2020) have been reshaped according to the Europe 2020 strategy for smart, sustainable and inclusive growth. Stronger governance that is based on partnership agreements is one of the means to achieve the goal:

> "All national, regional and local authorities should implement the partnership, closely associating parliaments, as well as social partners and representatives of civil society, contributing to the elaboration of national reform programmes as well as to its implementation. By establishing a permanent dialogue between various levels of government, the priorities of the Union are brought closer to citizens, strengthening the ownership needed to delivery the Europe 2020 strategy. [...] Exchange of good practices, benchmarking and

> networking [...] has proven another useful tool to forge ownership and dynamism around the need for reform."[8]

However, for a long time period an adequate legal and institutional framework for a joint transborder management structure has been lacking. Therefore, the need to establish a suitable tool put pressure on the European Commission to propose a regulation at the EGTC. The EGTC is like the Euroregions a border entity, but unlike the latter, the group has legal personality recognized both at EU Member State and EU level. According to Article 1, paragraph 4, Regulation (EC) No 1082/2006 it may acquire or dispose of movable and immovable property and employ staff and may be a party to legal proceedings. It is a legal instrument under Community law, not under international law as is the Madrid Framework Convention. It is binding and directly applicable in all Member States and does not require ratification and allows local and regional authorities to establish common legal personality to implement programmes and projects of cooperation. In particular, the EGTC has the most extensive legal capacity accorded to legal entities within Member States through national legislation (Toca and Popoviciu 2010: 91). Furthermore, the important difference between Euroregion and an EGTC is that the latter has a common budget and access to EU funds and not, as Euroregions used to have, only access to micro-projects in Interreg programme and nationally divided budgets.

The EGTCs created at the Western European borders focus considerably on scientific and research dialogue, educational programmes and energy policy. Whereas the EGTCs in Eastern and Central Europe develop cooperation in the fields of infrastructure, tourism and education (Grosse, 2011).

On the 21st of January 2008 the first EGTC was established in Kortrijk (Belgium) as Eurometropolis Lille-Kortrijk-Tournai. It was founded by 14 institutions. From France there were state, the Nord-Pas-de-Calais Region, the Department du Nord, Métropole européenne de Lille and from Belgium – the federal state, the Region and Community of Flanders, the Province of Western Flanders, Kortrijk district, Roeselare, Ieper and Tielt districts, Wallonia, the French Community of Belgium, the Hainaut Province, districts of Tournai and Ath, communes of Lessines, Silly and

8 Europe 2020. A strategy for smart, sustainable and inclusive growth. COM(2010) 2020 final, http://eur-lex.europa.eu/LexUriServ/LexUriServ.do?uri=COM:2010:2020:FIN:EN:PDF (accessed: 25.1.2016).

Enghien, district of Mouscron and commune of Estaimpuis. Eurometropolis is a hub for all cross-border information, activities and services. It aims to promote and support efficient and coherent cross-border cooperation within its territory to progressively erase administrative, political and cultural borders. One of the ways to achieve this is the *adapted governance* that is realised through involvement and consideration of the interests of the 14 member institutions, development of legislation, regulations and actions with a view to the ongoing improvement of quality of life within the territory. In Curtrai the cross-border agency was established with the aim to coordinate the work of 14 members. It prepares and implements the decisions made by the assembly following proposals by the board. It coordinates the thematic working groups and organises the conference of mayors, which is held once a year. Moreover, in 2009 the Civil Society Forum was founded to guarantee the representativeness of civil society voice in the decision making process.[9] Besides, the Eurometropolis belongs to European networks and participates in the development of cross-border governance in Europe. Thus, taking advantage of good practices worked out on the European level, the Eurometropolis can adapt them to the own structure and requirements.

The second EGTC and the first in the Central Europe was the Hungarian-Slovakian Ister-Granum that was established on the 6th of May 2008. It unites 86 municipalities from both sides of the border. The highest decision making body of the EGTC is the General Assembly of mayors, which meets twice a year. The operational work is carried out by the director who is elected by the General Assembly for two years. The aim of the EGTC is to create and realise common development projects. Therefore they plan to build up common institutions – a regional tourist destination management organisation, a common energy agency, an enterprise-logistic zone, cross-border service provided to the NGOs, integrated health systems, Ister-Granum EXPO. Business Support System, integration of public transport and regional solidarity-development fund.[10] All the planned institutions should contribute to create a united, cross-border space in different areas as business, health, energy, tourism and transport. In view of the benefits for both sides of the border that could bring coordinated actions, the EGTC seems to be a proper tool to reach the ambitious goals. In

9 http://www.eurometropolis.eu/areas-focused-on/overview.html (accessed: 19.1.2016).

10 http://www.istergranum.hu (accessed: 22.1.2016).

order to get public support for the actions and increase of public awareness of the EGTC, the stakeholders plan to found a common news agency with an on-line radio transmission, bilingual television and weekly newspaper.

Since the establishment of the EGTC instrument, 59 EGTCs have already been founded by January 2016.[11] Most of them were created for the purpose of cross-border cooperation. The large majority of existing EGTCs can be assigned to cross-sector EGTCs that focus on more than one theme of regional development and build on general cooperation. They also develop new strategies of governance that are realised by political debates between stakeholders in order to overcome merely local interests and to contribute to a broader regional development strategy (Zillmer and Toptsidou, 2014: 6). Two types of EGTC-partnership are dominant – the first group consists of local authorities and is managed by local stakeholders and the second group is composed of regional authorities. Besides, there exist multi-level or inter-regional networks (CoR, EGTC monitoring report 2014).

Thirty of all of the EGTCs were created with the participation of institutions from East-Central Europe. So far, Hungarian stakeholders seem to be the most active in founding the EGTCs. Hungarian agencies have established 23 EGTCs with partners from Slovakia, Romania, Slovenia, Poland, Croatia and Ukraine. One of the groupings – European Urban Knowledge Network Limited (EUKN) – consists of partners from nine countries, from both East as well as West Europe. The EUKN is a network of national governments and knowledge institutes, deeply involved in EU policy-making. The aim is to generate a professional community that shares expert urban knowledge and best policy practice and to inspire policy makers, practitioners and researchers. It is associated with European, national and regional governmental authorities and responds to the knowledge demands of its users while connecting urban stakeholders to policy, practice and research.[12]

11 Committee of the Regions: List of European Groupings of Territorial Cooperation, https://portal.cor.europa.eu/egtc/Register/Pages/welcome.aspx (accessed: 19.1.2016).

12 http://www.eukn.eu/about-the-eukn/ (accessed: 19.1.2016).

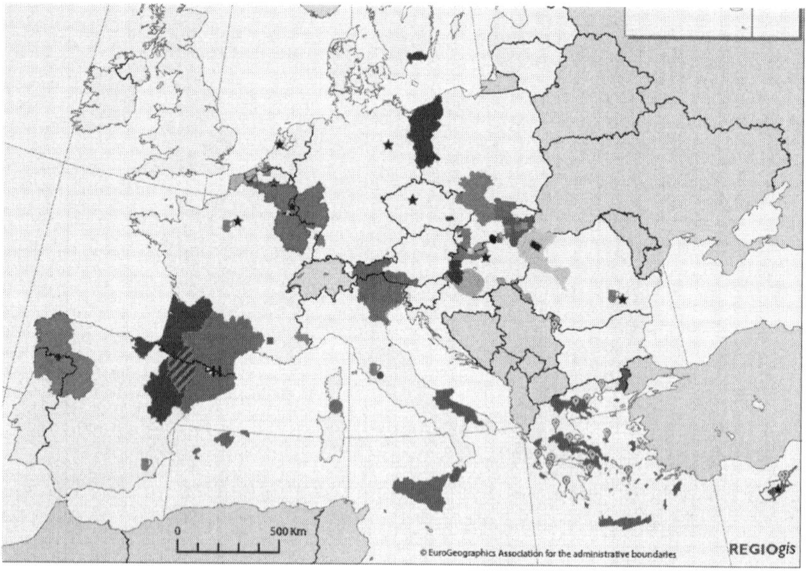

Map 1: EGTC Setups, source: www.cor.europa.eu

According to the EGTC monitoring report (CoR, EGTC monitoring report 2014) the year 2014 constituted a difficult transition period for many EGTCs, because funds from the financing period 2007-2013 have already been allocated to projects and programmes for the new period had not yet begun. In general, regular membership fees are an essential component of an EGTC budget. By and by EGTCs are more actively involved in the programming process for the European Territorial Cooperation programmes.

The purpose to establish an EGTC is often, as Elisabeth Winkel claims, the "will to create a visible and permanent structure of cross-border or territorial cooperation, to design joint growth strategies, to generate economies of scale, and to manage joint projects, infrastructure or environmental resources" (Winkel, 2011). Reports from Member States, regional and local authorities and EGTCs demonstrate that the decision to set up an EGTC often depends on the previous history of cooperation between the partners. Partners emphasised that the EGTCs were established in order cooperate in a better way. Reaching an agreement on the role and tasks of the EGTC is an important stage of the construction process (Winkel, 2011).

In the last two years, as the chart below illustrates, thirteen EGTC have been created. They define their purpose in general meaning as developing territorial or cross-border cooperation in order to strengthen economic and social cohesion. However, some of the EGTCs were established for specific goals to carry out projects and services for the ceramics sector, to protect the environment, to stimulate cross-border tourism as well as to promote cultural heritage and architecture. Moreover, a further thirteen EGTCs are in the construction process, from which two await approval, three have undertaken actions to set up EGTC and eight are in preparation (they officially communicated their willingness to establish an EGTC). Among them are groupings narrowly focused on cross-border health (Hôpital de Cerdagne) or with cross-border protected natural areas (joint alpine park Italy-France: Parc National Mercantour and Parco Regionale Alpi Marittime).

No	Name	Goals	Countries	Date of foundation
1.	AEuCC Cities of Ceramics, AECT limitada	The mission of AEuCC is to develop territorial and transnational cooperation in the field of ceramic art and craft, mainly to create social and economic cohesion, by developing projects and services for the ceramic sector stakeholders.	ES, FR, IT, RO	07/01/2014
2.	Central European Transport Corridor EGTC Ltd.	The Grouping has been established to facilitate and promote cross-border, transnational and transregional cooperation within the framework of the Central European Transport Corridor (Skåne-Rijeka) in order to strengthen economic and social cohesion, particularly through the implementation of projects and programmes of territorial cooperation.	PL, HU, SV	24/03/2014
3.	Huesca Pirineos – Hautes Pyrénées(HP-HP)	The EGTC HP-HP helps stimulating the development of a sustainable model of cross-border tourism, through a series of actions to streamline, consolidate and promote the tourism sector in both territories, by bringing added value to natural resources and shared heritage.	ES/FR	11/11/2014

No	Name	Goals	Countries	Date of foundation
4.	AECT Faja Piriítica Ibérica	The EGTC aims to develop relations currently existing between the municipalities of the Iberian Pyrite ensuring structural cooperation and fostering relationships of territorial cooperation. This follows the explicit aim to achieve the maximum economic, social and territorial cohesion as proposed by TFEU. Furthermore the Grouping aims to consolidate fluid and cordial relations between the municipalities of the EGTC.	ES/PT	14/10/2014
5.	European Border Cities European Grouping of Territorial Cooperation Limited Liability (European Border Cities EGTC)	No information available	HU/RO	20/11/2014
6.	ESPON EGTC – European Node for Territorial Evidence (ESPON EGTC)	The EGTC aims to support the reinforcement of the effectiveness of EU Cohesion Policy and other sectoral policies and programmes under European Structural Investment (ESI) funds as well as national and regional territorial development policies, through the production, dissemination and promotion of territorial evidence covering the entire territory of the 28 EU Members States, as well as 4 Partner States of Iceland, Liechtenstein, Norway and Switzerland.	LU/BE	19/1/2015
7.	AECT País d'Art i d'Història Transfronterer Les Valls Catalanes del Tec i del Ter	Its mission is to facilitate and promote territorial cooperation to strengthen economic and social cohesion. The EGTC aims to develop a cultural and tourism policy in regard to awareness of residents and professionals of their environment and architectural quality and landscape; heritage presentation and promotion of the architectural quality and initiation of the young audience to architecture, urban planning, landscape and heritage.	FR/ES	28/1/2015 (R)

No	Name	Goals	Countries	Date of foundation
8.	Interregional Alliance for the Rhine-Alpine Corridor EGTC	The main objective of the EGTC is combining and focusing the joint interests of its members towards national, European and infrastructure institions; evolution of the joint development strategy for the multimodal Rhine-Alpine-Corridor; directing funds to corridor related activities and projects; providing a central platform for mutual information, exchange of experience and encounter; improving the visibility and promotion of the corridor.	DE/NL	27/5/2015 (P)
9.	Mura Region European Grouping of Territorial Cooperation Limited Liability	No information available	HU/HR	28/05/2015 (R)
10.	MASH European Grouping of Territorial Cooperation	No information avaiable	HU/SL	16/06/2015 (R)
11.	GECT-Autorité de gestion programme INTERREG V A Grande Région	The EGTC aims at intensifying cross-border cooperation. This goal is to be achieved by means of local and regional projects between partners from the various areas in the Greater Region in order to enhance and promote the competitiveness of the interregional economy; improve the quality of life, increase the attractiveness of the individual areas and protect the environment and to support the acquisition and dissemination of knowledge, using cultural resources and strengthening social cohesion.	LU/FR	19/10/2015
12.	Tisza European Grouping of Territorial Cooperation Limited Liability	No information available	HU/ Ukraine	26/10/2015

No	Name	Goals	Countries	Date of foundation
13.	European Grouping of Territorial Cooperation NOVUM Limited (EGTC NOVUM Ltd.)	The EGTC aims at increasing, facilitating and promoting Polish-Czech border cooperation to strengthen economic and social cohesion by developing collaboration and joint use of human resources and infrastructure, in particular in sectors such as tourism, culture, education and health care, as well as research and technology. Further it focuses i.a. on supporting and improving joint protection of natural and cultural resources; reducing isolation through improved access to services and transport and supporting and promoting effective and consistent cross-border cooperation, including legal and administrative cooperation.	PL/CS	16/12/2015

Chart 2: EGTCs established in 2014 and 2015, source: Own compilation on the base of data of Committee of the Regions and EGTCs monitoring report 2014.

Most of the EGTCs are considered by institutional stakeholders as vehicles of cooperation in order to jointly manage short-term action plans or to discuss long-term development strategies. They undertake initiatives working towards exploring and consolidating new ways of governance and cohesion. EGTCs as broad partnership "contracts" reveal a willingness to improve political cooperation and multilevel governance across borders and beyond, promoting the external representation of shared interests (Spinaci and Vara-Arribas, 2009).

Continuous efforts to increase territorial cohesion is an implicit key objective of the groupings (CoR, EGTC monitoring report 2014). Further, implementing territorial cooperation programmes funded by the EU belongs to their primary goals. Scrutinising the last activities, at the start of 2015 the major cooperation fields of EGTCs were transport and infrastructure, enterpreneurship, rural development, culture, sport, education and training as well as environmental and strategy development. Moreover, many groupings emphasised in their mission statements the need for raising the awareness of common goals, managing of public discourse on development strategies and thereby enhancing the involvement of citizens.

In opinion of Spinaci and Vara-Arribas (2009: 9-10), in order to increase the level of cohesion and the performance of cooperation, EGTC should undertake the following activities:

- integrated territorial planning and the targeting of relevant basins of intervention, including interconnection with those territories neighbouring the cooperation area;
- focusing on policies with a clear impact on citizens and for which the constituent members have substantial competences, e.g. infrastructure and provision of services of general interest;
- rationalisation and the pooling of initiatives, human and financial resources;
- a sustainable financial framework, through adequate modelling of a mix of members' fees, service revenues, loans, fund-raising, and public-private partnerships;
- proper "association" of economic and social partners;
- interaction with other (EGTC) cooperation initiatives within the same territory or in the neighbourhood.

As a result, EGTC can become a significant platform of cooperation tackling the local problems from below as closely as possible to citizens' needs.

Conclusion

With the Schengen treaty and introduction of freedom of movement the EU aims at creation of the united territory for economic, social and cultural transfers, while being still governed by national institutions. Environmental, social and economic problems require joint actions and policies. The territorial cohesion is one of a new main objectives of the EU. Cross-border cooperation between different territories and various tiers of governance offers both a significant opportunity and a challenge to multi-level governance. The EGTC is becoming an important tool for managing the regional and local transborder governance.

The overall objective of the most EGTCs is to strengthen the territorial cohesion and ensure sustainable development. Local stakeholders aim to realise the goals through the exchanging of information, experiences, promotion and practices among its members ensuring the access to knowledge and thereby contributing to a coherent and efficient cross-border cooperation. Regular consultations and dialogue assure political representation within the area and joint representation vis-à-vis external bodies. Thus, common management and implementation of projects are enhanced.

A further purpose is the reinforcement of participation of citizens and agencies of local societies. As a result of removing barriers and obstacles, encouraging bilingualism and supporting their initiatives the day-to-day lives of citizens should be improved. By these means an intercultural dialogue and the attractiveness and European character of a concerned territory may be enhanced.

Summing up, it can be claimed that the EGTC instrument can be an effective tool to enhance cross-border cooperation by fulfillment the principles of good governance. It may provide an operative instrument towards the harmonisation and unification of cross-border cooperation in the EU. Furthermore, the institutional relations between local stakeholders can be facilitated and in consequence they may gain more competence in representing the interests of considered area. The possibility to manage EU-projects within the framework of EU cohesion policy 2014-2020 can lead to implementing of large projects and investments.

Nevertheless, there are still some challenges and shortcomings to be faced by local authorities. Differences in national and regional competences may complicate the construction process of the grouping and slow-down the functioning of projects in areas, which are handled by different levels across EU. The further institutionalisation of the relations between local authorities bears the risk that decisions will be taken over the heads of citizens (Lewkowicz 2013). Therefore, the next challenge is the visibility of EGTC and the guarantee of citizens' participation. According to the results of the Flash Eurobarometer survey the majority of interviewed EU citizens (68%) living in cross-border areas are unaware of EU-funded cross-border areas activities in their region. Only 31 % of Europeans have heard about EU funded projects (Flash Eurobarometer 422, June 2015). However, only the public dialogue and engagement of civil society can provide a successful fulfillment of good governance principle and thereby of cohesion policy.

According to the first appraisal of the implementation of EU Regulations on the EGTC so far the instrument has shown more potential than achievements. It has created a new dynamism that could be beneficial for territorial cooperation as well as European integration. Further, stable cooperation requires strong political commitment and institutional recognition (Spinaci and Vara-Arribas 2009). However, there is a lack of an in-depth analysis of the effectiveness of EGTCs that could provide significant conclusions and contribute to formulation of some recommendations.

References

Alcolea Martinez, A. (2014), 'Towards a New Generation of European Groupings of Territorial Cooperation?' *European Structural & Investment Funds Journal*, Vol. 2 (2): 89-100.

Committee of the Regions (2014), 'EGTC monitoring report 2014. Implementing the strategy Europe 2020', http://cor.europa.eu/en/documentation/studies/Documents/EGTC_MonitoringReport_2014.pdf (accessed: 18.1.2016).

Dumała, H. (2009), 'Europejskie Ugrupowanie Współpracy Terytorialnej. Nowe możliwości dla polsko-niemieckich euroregionów', in J. Jańczak, M. Musiał-Karg (eds), *Pogranicze polsko-niemieckie po 2004 roku. Nowa jakość sąsiedztwa?*, Toruń: Adam Marszałek, 55-73.

Flash Eurobarometer 422 (2015), 'Cross-border cooperation in the EU', http://ec.europa.eu/COMMFrontOffice/PublicOpinion/index.cfm/Survey/getSurveyDetail/instruments/FLASH/surveyKy/1565 (accessed: 18.1.2016).

Grazi, L. (2013), 'EU Cohesion Policy: A Tool for Constructive Neighbourhood Relationships via Subnational Actors. Lessons from the Eastward Enlargement', *Eurolimes* Supplement: 87-105.

Grosse, T. (2011), 'Uwarunkowania wykorzystania nowego europejskiego instrumentu prawnego i rozwojowego', *Opinie i Ekspertyzy* 171, Warszawa: Kancelaria Senatu.

Harguindéguy, J.-B. and Hayword K. (2012), 'The Institutionalization of the European Internal Cross-Border Co-operation Policy: A First Appraisal', *European Planning Studies:* 1-20.

Lewkowicz, Ł. (2013), 'Europejskie ugrupowania współpracy terytorialnej – nowa jakość polsko-słowackiej współpracy transgranicznej?' *Studia Regionalne i Lokalne,* 1 (51): 45-70.

Ładysz, J. (2011), 'EGTC as a tool of cross-border cooperation management', in P. Jedlička (ed.) *The International Conference Hradec Economic Days 2011, Economic Development and Management of Regions,* Hradec Králové, February, 179-183.

O'Dowd, L. (2003), 'The Changing Significance of European Borders', in J. Anderson et.al. (eds) *New Borders for a Changing Europe. Cross-border Cooperation and Governance*, London: Routledge, 13-36.

Santiso, C. (2001), 'Good Governance and Aid Effectiveness: The World Bank and Conditionality', *The Georgetown Public Policy Review*, Vol. 7 (1), Fall: 1-22

Spinaci, G. and Vara-Arribas, G. (2009), 'The European Grouping of Territorial Cooperation (EGTC): New Spaces and Contracts for European Integration?' *EIPASCOPE* 2: 5-13.

Toca, C.-V. and Popoviciu, A. C. (2010), 'The European Grouping of Territorial Cooperation (EGTC), Instrument of Cross-border Cooperation. Case Study: Romania – Hungary', *Eurolimes. Journal of the Institute for Euroregional Studies*, Vol. 10, ed. by Dolghi, D. I. et. al. The Geopolitics of the European Frontires, Oradea University Press.

Winkel, E. (2011) , 'The application of a European Grouping of Territorial Cooperation', http://www.eukn.eu/e-library/project/bericht/eventDetail/the-application-of-a-european-grouping-of-territorial-cooperation-egtc/ (accessed: 18.1.2016).

Zillmer, S. and Toptsidou, M. (2014), 'Potential and Limits of the EGTC Instrument for Enhancing Integration across Borders', *Spatial Foresight Brief* 5: Luxembourg, www.spatialforesight.eu (acceded: 15.1.2016).

Chapter 6: Mutual recognition of official documents as an example of an initiative that brings the European Union closer to its citizens

Ewelina Tomczak / Michalina Szpyrka

Key words: free movement of citizens, mutual recognition, official documents, European Certificate of Succession

Open borders and the freedom of movement

The development of a common area of freedom, security and justice has become one of the key activities for the European Union. The scope and dynamism of this activity is delineated in the EU's multiannual programmes. At the same time, the EU's citizens are now taking advantage of quicker and simpler means of pursuing their legal claims, both the small and the more complicated ones. So far the European Union has contributed, among other things, to harmonising the applicable law regulations concerning accountability under civil law and contracts, and has optimised judicial collaboration by revising the regulations on service of documents (Lewandowski, 2014:51-52).

Moreover, thanks to the Union's open borders and freedom of movement, currently 12 million EU citizens live, study or work in a member state other than their state of origin. These opportunities result, among others, from the provisions of the Charter of Fundamental Rights (hereafter referred to as ChFR), whose Article 45 stipulates that the right to travel freely is one of the fundamental rights of the citizens of the EU, and one that is very frequently taken advantage of. Unfortunately, as with many rights, the right to freedom of movement is also subject to many limitations. One of the key hindrances that citizens must face when exercising the right is a number of administrative regulations concerning the use and receipt of official documentation. According to Article 41 of the ChFR, every person has the right to have his or her affairs handled impartially, fairly and within a reasonable time by the institutions and bodies of the Union, and official documents issued by institutions of one member state must be automatically recognised in another member state. Through mutual recognition, this significantly influences the creation of the relationship between a citizen and administrative bodies.

Currently EU law lacks a legal and doctrinal definition of mutual recognition. This contributes to an unlimited capacity to argue for an extended interpretation of law (Barwina, 2012:56), especially in light of mutual recognition of freedom, security and justice in the EU. According to *M. Ortino,* mutual recognition is not a compensation rule – both from the point of view of public and private law. The rule imposes an obligation upon the recipient state to take into account foreign regulations, but it does not create any obligation or right for the state where such a regulation originated (Ortino, 2007:319). Moreover, mutual recognition is also of huge importance for the domain of the internal market. Thanks to mutual recognition, a foreign country recognizes professional qualifications, diplomas, certificates or driving licenses issued or obtained in compliance with the provisions of law binding in another member state (Ouwerker, 2011: 68).

Mutual recognition of official documents

Mutual recognition in the EU is undoubtedly a manifestation of the right to good governance. The need to take action in order to optimize the flow of official documentation in the EU results to a large extent from the fact that EU citizens exercise their right to free movement, which in turn leads to the necessity of proving their rights or obligations as stated in their official documents. The adoption of a unified system of mutual recognition of official EU documentation would have a very significant impact as it would shorten the duration of the authentication procedures as well as significantly reducing the cost of such procedures. It seems that due to the advancing integration of EU member states and the introduction of new technical solutions, the postulate of the mutual recognition of official documents is most definitely feasible, and its realisation can lead to elimination of one of the largest barriers to the free movement of EU citizens.

Definition of official documents

It is important to note at this point that the term 'official documentation' has not yet been legally defined by either EU law or national (member state) laws. In the EU, mutual recognition is defined for the purpose of particular acts of law, but for the sake of this chapter it is reasonable to adopt a simplified approach to recognition of documentation and provide the understanding of mutual recognition contained in the Proposal for a Regulation of the European Parliament and of the Council on promoting the free movement of citizens and businesses by simplifying the acceptance of certain public documents in the European Union and amending Regulation (EU) No 1024/2012.[1] Article 3 of the proposed regulation defines official documentation as documentation issued by authorities of member states and having a formal evidence value as regards the following: 1) birth, 2) death, 3) name and surname, 4) marriage and registered civil partnership, 5) country of origin of the child, 6) adoption, 7) place of residence, 8) citizenship and nationality, 9) real estate, 10) legal status and representation of a company or an enterprise, 11) intellectual property rights, 12) lack of criminal records.

Barriers to the unrestrained flow of official documents

Owing to a noticeable growth in overall internal migration figures within the EU, the "migration" of official documentation also increases to a significant extent. There are several key aspects to be considered here. One of them is the necessity to authenticate official documents in order to prevent document abuse. The basic means of document authentication is legalisation consisting in confirming the document in question via consular legalisation. Through consular legalisation, all the stamps and signatures on the document are authenticated, as well as confirming the fact that the document was prepared by an authorized official. In its broad sense, legalisation can also mean confirmation that the person who drafted the document was duly authorised to do so, and that the document is compliant

1 Proposal for a Regulation of the European Parliament and of the Council on promoting the free movement of citizens and businesses by simplifying the acceptance of certain public documents in the European Union and amending Regulation (EU) No 1024/2012 (COM(2013)228) final).

with the applicable law of the place of issuance (Czubik, 2004: 27-32). Unfortunately, legalisation is a very time-consuming, arduous and costly process.

The necessity of the simplification of authentication procedures has led to international and regional initiatives aimed at shifting away from legalisation and, instead, opting for easier solutions. The legalisation requirement has been replaced by the mechanism of certification of the document in question through the *apostille* clause as stipulated in the Hague Convention of October 5, 1961[2], with reference to the parties to the Convention. *Apostille* is a type of an authenticity certificate issued by the country where the original was issued upon request by the signatory of the document or the person in possession of the document. A document certified through *apostille* may be presented to the relevant authorities and institutions of the states party to the Convention, without the necessity to perform further consular legalisation or legalisation through diplomatic representatives. It must be emphasised that *apostille* does not certify the compliance of the document with the law of the country of issuance. Therefore, as stipulated by Article 12 of private international law, it does not certify that the juridical act certified by the document was performed "in compliance with the form prescribed by the law of the country where the act was performer."[3]

At EU level there have also been initiatives aimed at simplifying the flow of documents between the EU's member states and its institutions. On May 25, 1987, the Brussels Convention was adopted which abolished the necessity of legalising official documents applied between the member states. The Convention, however, did not enter into force as it was not ratified by all of the EU member states. Several provisions relating to the functioning of the judiciary were later introduced by the Lugano Convention on jurisdiction and the enforcement of judgements in civil and commercial matters (September 16, 1988),[4] Council Regulation (EC) No 44/2001 of 22 December 2000 on jurisdiction and the recognition and en-

2 Convention of 5 October 1961 Abolishing the Requirement of Legalisation for Foreign Public Documents (Dz. U. 2005 nr 112 poz. 938).

3 Private international law of 4 February 2011 (Dz. U. 2015 r., No. 1792).

4 Convention of 16 September 1988
on jurisdiction and the enforcement of judgments in civil and commercial matters (Dz. U. 2000., No. 10/132).

forcement of judgments in civil and commercial matters,[5] Regulation (EC) No 1393/2007 of the European Parliament and of the Council of 13 November 2007 on the service in the Member States of judicial and extrajudicial documents in civil or commercial matters (service of documents), and repealing Council Regulation (EC) No 1348/2000 (1393/2007/WE),[6] as well as Council Regulation (EC) No 1206/2001 of 28 May 2001 on cooperation between the courts of the Member States in the taking of evidence in civil or commercial matters.[7] So far however, no single act of law has been issued in the EU with a comprehensive and unified definition of the conditions of the use of official documents issued by one member state in another member state. Owing to the previously mentioned increased migration rates within the EU, the necessity to authenticate official documents (in particular, vital records and business activity records) must be seen as a major obstacle to free movement, and a significant economic burden.

The second highly important aspect of the mutual recognition of documents concerns the language of the original version. In order to streamline the procedure of document recognition, the entity or person who wishes to use the document must present the relevant authorities with a translation of the document that meets certain quality criteria. This brings about significant costs that will have to be borne by the person or entity who wishes to use the document in a different member state. In the case of vital records it is possible to use multilingual documents which constitute a transcript of the record in question and a confirmed authentication of the document at the same time. The challenges surrounding the issuance of multilingual vital records were addressed by the International Commission on Civil Status on 27 September, 1956 when the Commission adopted its Convention No. 1 on the issue of extracts of vital records to be used

5 Council Regulation (EC) No 44/2001 of 22 December 2000 on jurisdiction and the recognition and enforcement of judgments in civil and commercial matters (OJ L 12, 16.1.2001).

6 Regulation (EC) No 1393/2007 of the European Parliament and of the Council of 13 November 2007 on the service in the Member States of judicial and extrajudicial documents in civil or commercial matters (service of documents), and repealing Council Regulation (EC) No 1348/2000 (OJ L 324, 10.12.2007).

7 Council Regulation (EC) No 1206/2001 of 28 May 2001 on cooperation between the courts of the Member States in the taking of evidence in civil or commercial matters (OJ L 174, 27.6.2001).

abroad.[8] The Convention stipulates that multilingual extracts from civil status records shall have the same status as extracts issued in compliance with the law of the country of the document's origin. So far the Convention has been ratified by only sixteen member states, and Poland is not one of them. The legal basis for the issue of multilingual extracts from civil status records in Poland is another convention by the International Commission on Civil Status, namely Convention No. 16 on the issue of multilingual extracts of vital records drafted and adopted in Vienna on 8 September, 1976, and ratified by Poland on 2 October 2003.[9] The states party to Convention no. 16 undertook to recognise the vital records covered by the Convention without the necessity of authentication. However, attention should be paid to the fact that although Convention No. 16 has been ratified by many countries, still not all EU member states are party to the Convention. For example, in the United Kingdom it is not possible to use the multilingual forms offered by Convention No. 16 without authentication, as the UK has not ratified the Convention.

Mutual recognition of official documents in the EU: A vision for change

The work aimed at optimising the use of vital records in cross-border cases has inspired the institutions of the European Union to make efforts to abolish the existing barriers in this area. As previously mentioned, the first activities to meet the objective were performed by the EU in 1987 with the adoption of the Brussels Convention abolishing the obligation to legalise official documents. The Convention, however, did not enter into force as it was not ratified by all EU member states.

The need to simplify the process of recognition of official documents across the EU was also postulated by the European Commission, and finally it became part of the Stockholm Programme of 2009[10] and was un-

8 Convention (No 1) of 27 september 1956, on the issue of certain extracts from civil status records for use abroad http://ciec1.org/SiteCIEC/PAGE_Principale/5BkAAJclQQ93RXpqb3BLQVVlBAA (accessed: 20.1.2016).

9 Convention (No 16) of 8 September 1976 on the issue of multilingual extracts from civil status records, (DZ. U. 2004., No. 166/173).

10 *The 2009 Stockholm Programme "An open and secure Europe serving and protecting citizens"* (OJ C 115, 4.5.2010, p.1.).

derlined in the Commission's report of 2010.[11] The policy of promoting EU citizenship adopted in the Stockholm Programme, and the European Commission's activities in the field have contributed to forging a vision for change leading to streamlined flow of official documents, as outlined in the green paper entitled *"Less bureaucracy for citizens: promoting free movement of public documents and recognition of the effects of civil status records"*.[12] The authors of the green paper extensively presented the status quo regarding the flow of official documentation and specified the key improvement areas. First and foremost, they underlined the necessity of abolishing the obligation to authenticate official documents. Secondly, they pointed to the need to improve collaboration between the administrative bodies of all member states in the case of discrepancies between the documents issued, or in the case of non-existence of particular types of official documents in particular member states. The authors also stressed the necessity of the application of the most modern technologies in order to optimise the flow of official documents and reduce the need for translations that could be replaced by standardised multilingual forms resembling the forms for the European driver's licence or passport.

The need to optimise the flow of documents has also been recognised by the Court of Justice of the European Union: in the Dafeki case it ruled that the authorities of particular member states are obliged to recognise official documents confirming an individual's status (Case C-336/94, *Dafeki*, ECLI:EU:C:1997:579).

The proposed regulation

The necessity of facilitating the mutual recognition of documentation within the EU as expressed by the Union's bodies and institutions has also been reflected in the proposal for a regulation of the European parliament and of the Council promoting the free movement of citizens and businesses by simplifying the acceptance of certain public documents in the European Union and amending Regulation (EU) No 1024/2012 no. 1024/2012 (hereafter referred to as the proposal). The proposal provides for the ex-

11 The EU Citizenship Report 2010. Dismantling the obstacles to EU citizens' rights. (COM(2010) 603 final).

12 *"Less bureaucracy for citizens: promoting free movement of public documents and recognition of the effects of civil status records"*. (COM(2010) 747 final).

emption from all forms of document legalisation, including *apostille*, by deeming such legalisation mechanisms obsolete and contrary to the principle of proportionality. The scope of Article 3 of the draft regulation defines official documentation as documentation issued by authorities of member states and having a formal evidence value. The scope of application of the regulation excludes private documents and documents issued by the states which are not part of the EU.

It must be underlined that the proposed regulation clearly indicates that it will not affect the national laws of the member states, and it does not impose the recognition of the contents of documents – it only concerns the authenticity of the documents and their compliance with the law of the place of issuance.

The proposal also introduces the exemption from the obligation to obtain a certificate for the true copies of the original document in situations where it is indispensable to present the document and its copy. Furthermore, the document proposes that standardised EU multilingual forms be introduced for birth, death, marriage, civil partnership and legal status as well as the representation of companies or other enterprises – whose evidence capacity and character is to be identical with the documents used so far. According to the proposal, a member state will be obliged to issue a standardised form if an equivalent official document is also used in the member state. Moreover, electronic versions of the standardised forms are also being planned by the European Commission. As regards documents with no equivalents in standardised forms the proposal introduces the obligation to ensure a translation; however, apart from the exceptions (also presented in the proposal) it will not have to be a sworn (certified) translation.

It is also important that Article 7 of the proposed regulation introduces the presumption of the authenticity of official document. The article stipulates that in the case of reasonable doubt as to the authenticity of the document (a list of situations of doubt is contained in the Article), the authorities of the member state where the copy is presented may request the authorities of the member state where the document was issued to provide relevant information; therefore, the proposal has shifted the burden of proof of authenticity of the document from the citizen to the administrative authority.

Although some elements of the proposal can be criticised, (e.g. the lack of standardised forms for real estate or adoption, imperfect forms for companies and their legal status/representation or the recurring problem of the necessity of presenting translations), it is clear that the adoption of the proposal can eliminate a few significant barriers to the free movement of EU citizens. The adoption would also constitute a proof of the implementation of the principle of good governance through a simplification of procedures and reduced costs of verification of official documents that citizens or entities wish to use in cross-border matters.

Recognition of official documents in light of the succession regulation

It has already been underlined (at the beginning of this article) that the times of, for example, Poles living exclusively in Poland and Germans living exclusively in Germany are over. Citizens residing outside of their countries of origin purchase real estate enter into marriages and die in their new country of residence, which leads to the need for the mutual recognition of vital records. Such real-life situations have contributed to the introduction of unified legal regulations and the recognition of official documents, as well as establishing the European Certificate of Succession.

The idea to create a European inheritance law first appeared in the 1990s, but the law was finally introduced on 4 July 2012 thanks to the regulation (EU) No 650/2012 on jurisdiction, applicable law, recognition and enforcement of decisions and acceptance and enforcement of authentic instruments in matters of succession and on the creation of a European Certificate of Succession[13] (hereafter referred to as the succession regulation). The succession regulation has become part of the legal orders of the majority of member states. The United Kingdom, Ireland and Denmark did not participate in the adoption of the document and are therefore treated by the regulation as third countries.

The succession regulation is an initiative that brings the EU closer to its citizens because of its legal form and direct application (with no need do be implemented at the national level) in alignment with Article 1 point 1 and Article 83 point 1 referring to succession on 17 August 2015, whereby, if the person selected the applicable law in accordance with the provi-

13 Regulation (EU) No 650/2012 of the European Parliament and of the Council of 4 July 2012 on jurisdiction, applicable law, recognition and enforcement of decisions and acceptance and enforcement of authentic instruments in matters of succession and on the creation of a European Certificate of Succession (OJ L 107–134 27.7.2012).

sions of the regulation or based on Private International Law (binding on the day of selection) in the place of their residence or in any of the countries whose citizenship the person held, such a selection shall be deemed as legally valid (Orecki 2013: 82).

The succession regulation in Article 3 point 1 letter i requires that two criteria be jointly met in order to recognise a document as official. Firstly, an official document is a document that has been officially drafted or registered as a state document in a member state; it is also a document with authentic signatures and contents, whose authenticity has been certified by a public authority or another entity authorised by the state of origin of the document.

The recognition of documents that meet the criteria listed above means that such documents will provide the same or comparable evidence as in the state where the document was originally issued. Moreover, the recognition also makes it possible to pronounce the document enforceable in a different member state, without the necessity of prior legalisation. The solutions indicated above facilitate the creation of unified and common solutions across the entire European Union.

European Certificate of Succession

Another initiative that constitutes an example of the EU working more closely to its citizens is the creation of the European Certificate of Succession (hereafter referred to as the ECS). The ECS is a unified document to be used by heirs, legatees, executors of wills and administrators of the estate to prove their status and exercise their rights to the succession across all member states. It has already been mentioned that the right to free movement may lead to, for instance, citizens of one member state purchasing real estate in a different member state(s). If an EU citizen who owns estate in different EU member states dies, the case acquires a cross-border character. As the evidence of being an heir or legatee is regulated differently in different countries, a unified regulation was necessary. The succession regulation was mostly intended to introduce harmonised norms leading to the optimization and unification of legal outcomes across the entire European Union. The ECS facilitates a more efficient (i.e. faster and more effective) management of cross-border inheritance cases. Additionally, the entity holding the ECS will not be required by the relevant authority to present any other documentation proving the ECS holder's right to inheritance (Załucki, 2015: 286- 287). Additionally, the ECS is used to indicate the legal status of the person claiming succession and constitutes the basis for making the relevant entries in the registers kept by particular member states, e.g. land and real estate registers. Also, the subject scope of the ECS is broader that that of a certification of confirmation of inheritance acquisition or a registered certification of the deed of succession. It also encompasses the rights of the executor of the will and estate manager.

As with anything, however, the ECS also has its limitations. The basic limitation is that it can only be drafted in an uncontested situation. Whenever there are any doubts as to the scope of the ECS, the relevant authorities should refuse to issue the document without any delay. Another problem is associated with the ECS colliding with national documents. If a document certifying the right to inheritance was issued by the relevant authority previously or subsequently in its currently binding form, there are no obstacles to the issuance of the ECS. Otherwise, the issuance is unwarranted.

In summary, the ECS, despite its shortcomings, is a huge leap forward for European inheritance law. In the past, the cross-border characteristics of a case often translated into many complications and therefore extended the duration of succession cases with cross-border features. Moreover, the application of the ECS enables its users to avoid the procedure of authentication or legalisation of certificates of entitlement to inheritance, and the succession regulation itself abolishes the necessity of authentication of both Polish and foreign documents. This significantly contributes to reducing the limitations to free movement of citizens between the EU's member states.

References

Barwina Z., 'Zasada wzajemnego uznawania w sprawach karnych', Warszawa: Wolters Kluwer Bussines.

Czubik P. (2004), 'Konwencja Haska o zniesieniu wymogu uwierzytelniania zagranicznych dokumentów publicznych', Bydgoszcz- Kraków: Oficyna Wydawnicza Branta: 27-32.

Lewandowski M. (2014), 'Wspólnotowe instrumenty prawa cywilnego – wykonanie programu haskiego', in: A. Całus , M. Lewandowski, M. Zachariasiewicz, M. P. Zachariasiewicz, J. Pazdan, J. Ciszewski, *Problemy Prawa Prywatnego Międzynarodowego*, Katowice: Wydawnictwo Uniwersytetu Śląskiego: s. 51-52.

Orecki M. (2013), 'Jurysdykcja, prawo właściwe oraz uznawania i wykonywania orzeczeń w sprawach spadkowych w świetle rozporządzenia (UE) nr 650/2012 z 4 lipca 2012 r.', *Przegląd Sądowy* 1: 79-98.

Ortino M. (2007), 'The Role and Functioning of Mutual Recognition in the European Market of Financial Services', *International and Comparative Law Quarterly* 56(2): 309- 338.

Ouwerker J. (2011), 'Quid pro quo: a comparative law perspective on the mutual recognition of judicial decisions in criminal matters', Antwerp: Intersentia.

Załucki M.(ed.)(2015), 'Unijne rozporządzenie spadkowe nr 650/2012. Komentarz', Warszawa: C. H. Beck.

Chapter 7: Good governance at the metropolitan level. Examples of institutional practice in selected Polish metropolitan areas[1]

Aldona Wiktorska-Święcka

Key words: good governance, metropolitan governance, metropolitan areas, Poland, metropolitan institutions

Introduction

The question of *good governance* is important in the context of the quality of the functioning of public institutions as well as other entities carrying out public tasks, and to the quality of conditions in which citizens live and act, and enterprises operate. It is crucial not only to the pursuit of sectoral policies but also to *territorial governance*. The aim of the study is to provide an in-depth reflection on institutional practice in Poland in the context of the implementation of *good governance* standards in selected metropolitan areas. The paradigm adopted by the author reflects the approach whereby cities should develop not only in order to support the economy but also to be able to meet people's aspirations to a better quality of life. Such an approach is accompanied by a presentation of arrangements relating to *governance* in selected metropolitan areas in Poland as well as reflection as to the extent to which they contribute to better quality democracy. The objective defined above can be achieved with the help of a descriptive method on the basis of an overview of the literature and various documents as well as analyses of issues relating both strictly to metropolitan areas and to the concept of *good governance*. In the chapter the author examines the basic issues concerning metropolitan areas as well as their governance with regard to *good governance* standards. She discusses the question of innovation associated with the paradigm in question

1 This part of the book is a result of research conducted under a project financed by the National Science Centre, on the basis of agreement no. UMO-2013/09/B/HS5/04522.

as well as the directions and challenges connected with metropolitan governance in Poland, including its institutional dimension. In the empirical portion the author presents a model on the basis of which she analyses examples of institutional practice in selected metropolitan areas (Wrocław, Łódź and Tri-City: Gdańsk, Sopot, Gdynia) with regard to the implementation of *good governance* standards.

Metropolis – a few conceptual remarks

A metropolis can be a specific form of an urbanisation, although there is no agreement in the literature on the subject as to whether a metropolis is still a city or some other form of settlement (Jałowiecki, 2009: 7). According to N. Brenner, sources of metropolitanisation as a consequence of globalisation lie in two location-related advantages of big cities: concentration of well-qualified labour and strategic position they owe to their communication and transport capacities (Brenner, 2003: 18). Metropolitanisation processes lead to changes in the inner structure of cities and transform the relations between cities and the regions that surround them. The sprawl of a metropolis in the region leads to the emergence of a metropolitan area, in which links to the metropolis are very strong and profound (Wiktorska-Święcka, 2013a). On the other hand the economic links between the city, its metropolitan area and the surrounding region get weakened (in favour of links within a global or continental network of cities). A metropolis has high a functional potential and as a centre maintains strong relations with other territorial entities, which very often are distant, because they are part of the international metropolitan network. Metropolitan areas transform themselves into a network of strongly interlinked, specialised regions, which perform international, European, national, regional and local functions. As a result of the rise of the significance of the international functions, there are also increasing differences within regions in the levels of economic growth. This is accompanied by an expansion of the territory performing international functions and the metropolitan sprawl into the surrounding region (Kunzmann, 1998). To illustrate the position of Polish metropolitan areas in Europe and the world, it is worth referring to the typology of metropolitan growth in the MEGA network, which is based on four criteria: size of the metropolitan area, competitiveness, connectivity and knowledge base. In Poland, only Warsaw can be regarded as a continental metropolis in Europe (potential

MEGA); the number of Polish regional metropolises (weak MEGAs) is very limited: Kraków, Katowice, Gdańsk-Gdynia-Sopot, Poznań, Wrocław, Łódź, Szczecin (*Interim Territorial Cohesion Report* 2004).

Good governance in the context of metropolitan governance

The concept of *governance*, developing since the mid 1990s, has contributed to the formulation of a new framework for further development of participatory democracy, which takes into account the civil, horizontal, pluralist and productive dimensions of politics. What have become key words in this approach are relations associated with control, coordination networks, participation of stakeholders, partnership, strategic alliances, network economy, network society and civil society as the "effects of new forms of coordination" (Jessop, 2007: 6). A pragmatic and analytical-descriptive approach associated with *governance* is linked to normative trends in the public administration which are characterised by the concept of *good governance*. Its features include the participation of all stakeholders, efforts to build a consensus, a strategic vision of development, response to needs, productivity and effectiveness, accountability transparency, justice and the rule of law. This approach is connected with a belief in the necessity of respecting democratic values and standards as guarantees of the social order, especially when pursuing such universal standards as professionalism, political neutrality, honesty and avoidance of conflicts of interest. A translation of this concept into practice requires respect for the principle of transparency, personal honesty, high ethical standards, respect for the law, accountability, accessibility, openness and solidarity with citizens. Effective implementation of the principle of good governance is key also from the point of view of building the state's capacity to create conditions favourable to the growth of civil society and enterprise.

This principle determines desirable directions of change in decision-making and the exercising of authority. It points to areas for necessary reforms of the state and defines instruments that should be created for this concept to be implemented and put into practice. In addition, it matters for territorial governance, especially in the context of the contemporary trends the metropolitan area are facing. They provoke questions about the directions in which these areas will develop given the current and future challenges. These processes have an objective global reach, though their nature is by no means uniform; they undergo constant modifications and generally stem from the fact that today the political role of the state is changing as is thus the political role of local governments (Wiktorska-Święcka, 2010a). This redefines territorial governance as it stands now and contributes to highlighting *metropolitan governance* as a special approach dedicated to this level of governance. *Metropolitan governance* is an attempt to imagine possible scenarios for the development of metropolitan areas in a rapidly changing reality and formulate recommendations for a more efficient provision of public services as well as implementation of policies stimulating social and economic development. In the case of *metropolitan governance* there has been a shift of focus: from a policy referring to the entire territory (of a region or state) to what is key to subregional development, i.e. urban centres and the functional areas around them (metropolitan areas). According to this concept, what is needed is the inclusion of normative premises referring to *good governance*, which means that forms of action to be implemented should focus on:

a) ensuring democratic legitimacy through cooperation mechanisms;
b) systemic inclusion of social actors (participation in management and governance);
c) systemic and regular communication and information as a central function of governance (Wiktorska-Święcka, 2010b).

Important features of the approach to *good metropolitan governance* include a new political culture making flexible governance possible, the structural participation of citizens (clients, city users) and decentralised decision-making mechanisms in accordance with the principles specified in the *White Paper on European Governance* in which the European Commission proposed five main criteria of *good governance*. They refer primarily to the functioning of European policies, but also concern the improvement of governance in the member states, also on subnational levels, including metropolitan areas. These principles are: openness, participation, accountability, effectiveness and coherence[2]. Thus *good metropolitan governance* denotes an approach which focuses on the inclusion of various stakeholders in making decisions about directions of development. Jointly defined projects are implemented – as far as possible – through the existing institutional structures. What remains a challenge, however, is a practi-

2 *White Paper European Governance* (2001) COM (2001) 428, Brussels.

cal implementation of these premises, i.e. creating the right governance framework that will optimise the potential of a given metropolitan area. It should be flexible enough to adapt to rapid economic and social changes as well as future developmental trends.

Good metropolitan governance as an innovation in public governance

Today *good metropolitan governance* means maximising the assets of a metropolitan area. In addition to traditional assets like location, the financial situation, the level of the inhabitants' formal knowledge, the technical-logical development of the technical infrastructure, the structure of the urban economy, or those stimulating economic growth (e.g. taxation level, situation on the labour market, municipal services, the image of the city), of key importance also are the people who live in that metropolitan area. The implementation of the concept of *good metropolitan governance* in institutional practice determines the creation and co-creation of innovation by the public sector. It should become a source of new motivations, both for the participation of citizens in the pursuit of public goals and for the efforts of public sector representatives to improve its policies and services. The new paradigm of the relations with citizens is based on the process of mutual learning, which is linked to the problem of open membership and, hence, the acknowledgement of the special role/roles of citizens/residents as participants in the process of *public governance* (principle of openness in *good governance*).

Practical application is a process of continuous improvement by public entities of their organisational capacity to change and learn from each other, based on the right attitudes and relations (principle of participation in *good governance*). It can become a process of creation in the public sector of an innovative environment and a culture of innovation drawing on the knowledge of various partners, especially when public institutions are confronted with budget cuts, but citizens demand high quality public goods at the current level (principle of effectiveness in *good governance*). That is why public institutions are becoming more and more open to innovation and the co-creation of goods in collaboration with private enterprises, social enterprises and citizens, and the innovations generated in the metropolitan environment offer new possibilities for the production of public goods without the key involvement of public administration and for goods and services valuable to society, without being dependent only on market mechanisms (principle of openness in *good governance*).

Today *metropolitan governance* may offer optimistic prospects concerning more room for innovation, including the ability to choose between alternative scenarios and variants of action, set the right course of action, and, consequently, more efficient and effective ways of solving problems occurring in the socio-economic space. A normatively viewed concept of *metropolitan governance* indicates new kinds of contacts between the state and society and recommends forms of cooperation that involve various levels (principle of coherence in *good governance*). Such a way of regulating common affairs provides for citizens' involvement in the creation of public goods and the delivery of services, and thus creates an opportunity for signalling individual needs and problems as well as responding to them, creating various forms of citizens' mutual support (principle of effectiveness in *good governance*).

This approach is inextricably linked to the culture of participation and involvement, which in its very essence displays a high innovation potential, because it creates and strengthens social capital in individuals: openness to cooperation, mutual trust, readiness to help, involvement in common causes, going beyond vested interests (principle of openness in *good governance*). Since social capital is a product of the interdependency and mutual impact of economic and social phenomena, it must be stressed that its intangible values (i.e. factors influencing the quality of human relations, present in individuals and their interactions with others, binding them to each other, facilitating cooperation) boost competition, enterprise and thus have a positive impact on the competitiveness of individuals and cities in which they function (principle of effectiveness in *good governance*). However, the growing role of citizens in public governance (*empowerment*) and the treatment of citizens as those who create prosperity (*co-production*) cause tensions between the individualisation of needs, and the maintenance and strengthening of social cohesion. This requires a number of untypical arrangements which, on the one hand, respond to the expectations and needs of citizens and, at the same time, potential users, and on the other take into account the requirements of efficiency and effectiveness of proposed public interventions (principles of effectiveness and accountability in *good governance*).

What constitutes a response to this call is precisely innovation in *good metropolitan governance*, which usually takes the form of social innovation (Wiktorska-Święcka et al., 2015), or tailor made solutions satisfying the user's need, which are also accepted by society. Social innovations, given their essence and characteristic features such as an intersectoral approach, openness and cooperation, grassroots actions, prosumption and co-production, mutualism, creation of new roles and relations in society as well as the better use of capital, resources and the development of capacities (Caulier-Grice et al., 2012), can be viewed as a response to the current challenges and limitations. If we want to generate, design, implement, disseminate, scale up and consolidate social innovations, we need to link public policies to a democratic renewal (Windrum, Koch, 2008), as a result of which they will contribute to more effective and rational:

a) economic and social development (ensuring better quality of life for citizens thanks to a guaranteed economic growth);
b) psychosocial development (increasing people's identification with their community, which consequently may boost their activity);
c) cultural development (cultivation of social identities);
d) innovative and technological development (improving the system of networks providing services for citizens);
e) political development (broader participation in the local governance system, creating democratic power and leadership structures) (Starosta, 1995: 216-217).

In *good metropolitan governance*, which can stimulate social innovations and thus speed up and improve the development of metropolitan areas, we can point to:

a) development of a participatory political culture: a key role in this respect is played by the public administration; without it, the state cannot function, it determines the legal, institutional and organisational conditions of economic and social development. An appropriate, participatory political culture focused on the collaboration with various stakeholders is required not only from the citizens, political and economic elites, but, above all, from individuals exercising power: central, regional and local government officials;
b) innovative local governments, which, in seeking prosperity for their citizens, should make sure that their employees are responsible and accountable, their procedures transparent and their public consultations correct: in the long-term all these elements build citizens' trust, prevent social exclusion and, as a result, strengthen social capital. To this end

we need to disseminate organisational innovation in local governments so that their functioning could meet the highest possible standards;

c) intensification of cooperation with various public actors, including strengthened cooperation with non-governmental organisations, which carry out important public tasks;
d) initiation of public-private partnerships and public-social partnerships and the strengthening of clusters: cooperation should be based on partnership understood as a platform bringing together various social and economic actors, which – acting together in a systematic, permanent manner, using innovative methods and resources – plan, design, implement and carry out specific actions and initiatives aimed at developing the socio-economic environment and building regional identity;
e) competent formulation of strategic developmental goals taking into account the dynamics of geopolitical, social and economic change: the ability to use the available expertise and translate experts' opinions into political goals;
f) continuous improvement of institutional arrangements and increasing of the capacity of administration on the local government level: e.g. decentralisation, optimisation of procedures, introduction of modern management methods;
g) building of a real and electronic platform for public debate enabling actors to engage in efficient dialogue and exchange information and opinions about proposed regulations: expanding social dialogue to include a dialogue involving citizens and non-governmental organisations as well as other organisations protecting the rights of individuals and groups of citizens;
h) significant increase of the effectiveness of the operations of state administration through improvement of the mechanisms of rapid operational decision-making: introducing instruments of social and market verification of programme and legislation proposals from the administration; introducing mechanisms of on-going efficiency monitoring;
i) standardisation of the administration's communication with regard to goals, strategy and annual action plans: consistent public communication methods used by institutions to inform people about proposed programmes or other important initiatives requiring public debate and regulation (Wiktorska-Święcka, 2011a: 115).

In *metropolitan governance* innovation can be used as a tool to achieve social cohesion, transmit values, and maintain balance between tradition and modernity. It is a constant search for ways to improve the quality of governance. *Metropolitan governance* serves development in the long-term as well as constant renewal. It is a process that demands openness and flexibility in adapting to the changing socio-economic conditions, in a situation where old solutions have ceased to work.

Metropolitan governance in Poland – dimensions and challenges

The current challenges associated with the development of metropolitan areas in Poland include a number of objective phenomena (globalisation, Europeanisation, demography, gentrification, migration pressures, social diversity) as well as specific phenomena depending on local contexts and determinants (level of socio-economic development, geographical and spatial determinants etc.). These challenges differ in their nature (environmental, social, economic, spatial) (Table 1) and correlate with the way in which they are managed.

When it comes to political-institutional and administrative changes, it can be said that metropolitan issues have two basic dimensions in Poland, which demand debate and reform (Hausner, 2013: 23): objective and subjective. The former include challenges facing national public authorities: country-wide development and integration of the metropolitan network, which should strengthen the creative and innovative developmental potential of the country, and, consequently, improve Poland's position in the globalised world. Another aspect is the organisation of the development of the various metropolitan areas, which – in a technical and social sense – are in themselves multifunctional settlement networks. With regard to the subjective dimension, researchers see the metropolitan issue with respect to the organisation of government administration at the central and regional levels, since they construct legislative acts and government documents of a strategic nature. Another subjective aspect is the existence of a metropolitan government entity within the structure of regional government that would be a partner for the central and local governments (Hausner, 2013: 23-26).

Table 1. Current developmental challenges in metropolitan areas in Poland

Aspect	Challenge
environmental	ensuring high standards of the quality of the natural environment; rational water management; rational waste management, rational energy management and supply; maintaining a balance between urbanised and green areas
social	eliminating disproportions in development and living conditions; counteracting negative demographic trends; stopping the deepening social stratification; stopping the spread of pathological phenomena and then introducing reforms; preventing the rise of the diseases of civilisation; ensuring security for citizens; ensuring proper sanitary conditions; ensuring safe and accessible travel
economic	dealing with growing international competition; developing new areas of social and economic life; organising an effective and economically efficient public transport system; solving financial problems caused by rising costs of living; pursuing active labour market policies; improving the status of Polish metropolitan areas in Europe
spatial	taking care of proper spatial planning: seeking spatial order, rational land management; stopping the urban sprawl; uniform architectural style; increasing land functionality; raising the level of cleanliness and aesthetics; reurbanisation and rehabilitation of degraded areas; stopping the increasing decline of the most valuable parts of the urban fabric; revival of dysfunctional parts of inner cities; partial gentrification of inner-city areas
political-cultural	effects of system transformation strengthening the individualist approach and concurrent aversion to collective attitudes; wide-spread belief in privatisation and the market as the basic remedies for inefficient delivery of municipal services; fetishisation of property rights, which results in the disappearance of the public sphere; lack of the ability to cooperate, which limits participation in joint actions; lack of trust in public institutions and fellow citizens, which results in lip service to involvement in public causes
institutional-governmental	delimitation of metropolitan areas; globalisation and Europeanisation; rise of technology and IT, change of developmental paradigms: knowledge, creativity, innovation as standards in developmental policies and strategies; new type of leadership; "co-decision making"; low democratic capital measured by the number of non-governmental organisations, partnerships, people committed to civil society

Source: Author's own analysis

Institutional aspects of metropolitan governance in Poland

The transformations of Polish metropolitan areas demand a redefinition of the concept of managing such structures. It is worth stressing, however, that the Polish public policy concerning the development of metropolitan areas has not been autonomous or systemic so far, nor has it been treated as a priority. It has failed to take into account model EU standards of *multilevel governance* whereby public policy concerning metropolitan areas should be implemented at all levels of government: from the EU, through the national to the regional and local levels, which would enhance the effect of public interventions.

In national policies the *good governance* dimension was recognised relatively late. It is understood as an "exercise of public authority within the mutual relations between the government, administration and society characterised by openness, partnership, accountability, effectiveness, efficiency and coherence. This definition takes into account participation in the exercise of authority by three groups of entities: government, administration and society, because only their harmonious cooperation can ensure efficient functioning of the state" (*Koncepcja good governance* 2008). This principle also appears in the document *Polska 2030. Wyzwania rozwojowe* [*Poland 2030. Developmental challenges*] (*Polska 2030* 2009). It contains ideas and norms concerning the strategic perspective of Poland's development. The principle of *good governance* is defined explicitly under Priority 9: *Efficient state.* According to the authors, a strategic orientation in government should consist in:

- modernisation of the public sector;
- deregulation;
- democracy, participation, advocacy, dialogue and cooperation in the strengthening of civil society.

In addition, the document for the first time notes the significance of urban and metropolitan areas to Poland's continued development. The authors of the report call for a strengthening of large cities; they believe that Poland's development should conform to the polarisation-diffusion model. This means that in addition to supporting growth centres, we should also create conditions for a diffusion of developmental impulses from metropolises to the regions surrounding them. The state's economic policy should focus on catching up and supporting new competitive advantages of these centres. The advantages stem from the growth of the knowledge-based economy, the availability of transport as well as internal and external functional connectivity (*Polska 2030* 2009). Moreover, in recent years regional policy has increasingly focused on supporting the metropolitan structure of the country, particularly taking into account the links between its main elements. This policy, at least in its declarative layer, has abandoned compensatory approaches, adopting instead a functional approach to cohesion, including territorial cohesion (*Strategia Rozwoju Regionalnego* 2010).

In 2012 the Ministry of Administration and Digitisation published a *Green Paper on Metropolitan Areas.* It called for the creation in the administrative structure and policy of the state of metropolitan (and urban) areas, in addition to rural areas, which would lay the groundwork for a sustainable development policy. During public consultations the document was criticised for its fairly narrow scope of administrative matters concerning mainly local government, which had little to do with metropolitan questions (*Green Paper* 2012). Consequently, the Ministry of Administration and Digitisation published a *White Paper on Metropolitan Areas*, proposing a range of solutions to improve the functioning of metropolitan areas[3] (*White Paper* 2013).

With regard to the institutional dimension it must be said that the documents in question contained proposals and recommendations which were not transformed into any binding legal instruments. Yet between 2001 and 2008 six drafts that could be termed metropolitan bills were produced. In mid-2009 there emerged another draft, *Act on the state urban policy and cooperation of local and regional governments* (Knosala, 2010). As with all subsequent documents, it was not accepted; in 2010 the Ministry of Internal Affairs and Administration proposed that Polish cities draft their own bills regulating the formalisation of the cooperation between municipalities within functional unions. Independently of this proposal, work continued on the national level, producing in 2011 a bill on cooperation of local and regional governments for local and regional development (referred to as the cooperation bill). The bill drafting "craze" continued in the following years (e.g. a bill on "cooperation of local and regional governments for local and regional development and amending certain acts of parliament" was submitted in late 2012). It took three more years for a bill regulating the metropolitan question to be finally adopted. It happened in October 2015 and the new law entered into force on 1 January 2016. Significantly, the new law does not comply with the requirements of *good metropolitan governance.* It does not include normative premises and is decidedly functional. It regulates only a limited range of tasks of metropolitan unions. They include spatial planning and development of the territory of a metropolitan union, cooperation on national and regional roads running through that territory and promotion of the metropolis. The new law limits the governance aspect to a possibility of establishing metropolitan unions, i.e. territorially cohesive spheres of influence of

3 *White Paper, Biała Księga obszarów metropolitalnych* (2013) Warszawa: Ministerstwo Administracji i Cyfryzacji.

cities in which governors or regional assemblies reside. Under the new law, a metropolis should have strong functional links and be characterised by advanced urbanisation processes[4].

As we analyse the current institutional arrangements concerning metropolitan areas in Poland, we have to conclude that they do not take into account the concepts, standards, criteria and principles of *good metropolitan governance*, neither those formulated by international institutions and the European Union, nor those adopted on the national level.

Assumptions of an analytical model of good metropolitan governance in Poland

Noting the problem of the underdevelopment of metropolitan areas in the case of Polish cities, Jałowiecki (2002: 32) listed among cities with the biggest metropolitan potential:

- Warsaw;
- Poznań and Kraków;
- Wrocław, Łódź and Tri-City: Gdańsk-Sopot-Gdynia.

Among Poland's metropolitan areas only Warsaw is mentioned among those of European significance. The others are – or can be – of local significance. This applies to the last three areas. They will be analysed in the context of the implementation of *good metropolitan governance* standards. In order to make such an analysis possible, the author has constructed a research model taking into account the *good governance* criteria formulated by the European Commission. Possible institutional arrangements are marked either 0 or 1, with 0 denoting "such an arrangement does not function", and 1 – "arrangement is present". An ND (no data) answer can also be indicated – it is treated as having the value of 0. The assumption is that one of the principles of *good governance* is transparency and open communication. This means that information about the institutional foundations of metropolitan area management should be publicly available. If they cannot be found in open sources, they have to be treated as non-existent. The analysis is to determine and then provide an overview of the existing arrangements in the context of the above listed criteria. Given the

4 Ustawa from October 9, 2015 DzU 1890.

framework of this chapter, it was not possible to carry out an in-depth qualitative analysis **(Table 2).** Owing to a lack of clear-cut delimitations of these areas, in the definitions of the various metropolitan areas the following has been assumed:

- with regard to the Wrocław area: signatories of the agreement establishing the Integrated Territorial Investments of the Wrocław Functional Area as an institutional-organisational-legal form of implementing the new EU mechanism of regional development, comprising Municipality of Wrocław, Town and Municipality of Jelcz-Laskowice, Town and Municipality of Kąty Wrocławskie, Municipality of Siechnice, Municipality of Trzebnica, Town and Municipality of Sobótka, Town Oleśnica, Municipality of Długołęka, Municipality of Czernica, Municipality of Kobierzyce, Municipality of Miękinia, Municipality of Oleśnica, Municipality of Wisznia Mała, Municipality of Żórawina, Town and Municipality of Oborniki Śląskie;
- with regard to the Łódź area: Łódź Metropolitan Area Association comprising 31 local government entities from five districts: City of Łódź, Brzeziny, Lódź East, Pabianice and Zgierz. One of the main goals of the Association is to support social and economic development of the Łódź Metropolitan Area; the Association serves as the so-called Integrated Territorial Investment (ITI) association;
- with regard to the Tri-City area: Gdańsk Metropolitan Area (currently: Gdańsk-Gdynia-Sopot Metropolitan Area) is a local government association established on 15 September 2011 to boost cooperation and harmonious development of the entire metropolitan area around Gdańsk through the best possible use of the potential of its member cities, towns and municipalities, respecting their distinct nature and specificity; the area comprises 54 local government entities; Integrated Territorial Investments are implemented in the area.

Table 2. Good metropolitan governance in selected Polish metropolitan areas

Criterion of *good governance*	**Features of the criterion**	**Possible institutional arrangements**	**Metropolitan areas**		
			Wrocław	**Łódź**	**Tri-City: Gdańsk-Sopot-Gdynia**
openess	assumes, that metropolitan institutions should be fully transparent to the public	publication of contracts	1	1	1
		facilities for citizens in the process of complaints and appeals	0	0	0
		making public expenditure and revenue visible	1	1	1
		access to public information as broad, as deep and as simple as possible	0	1	0
		information about planned actions	1	1	1
		information about the results of initiatives	0	0	0
		anti-corruption mechanisms supporting administration transparency	0	0	0

Criterion of *good governance*	**Features of the criterion**	**Possible institutional arrangements**	**Metropolitan areas**		
			Wrocław	**Łódź**	**Tri-City: Gdańsk-Sopot-Gdynia**
participation	means broad public participation in metropolitan governance, at all levels, as well as at all major stages of implementation of public policies (ie. in programming, implementation and monitoring); participation of NGOs in the work of the administration (civil dialogue) and representatives of employers and trade unions (social dialogue); equal access of individuals and groups to the possibility of creating of the initiative in the metropolitan area, the real impact on its implementation, the right to be heard effectively	civic groups involved in the decision-making process	**0**	**1**	**0**
		the amount of funds dedicated for civic initiatives	**0**	**0**	**0**
		manner and quality of cooperation with local NGOs	**0**	**0**	**0**
		cooperation with minority groups	**0**	**1**	**0**
		cooperation (not: declaration of cooperation) with business organizations	**0**	**0**	**0**
		Chartas and Civil Agreements	**0**	**0**	**0**
		presence of women in decision-making bodies	**0**	**1**	**0**
		friendly solutions for persons with low income	**0**	**1**	**0**
		support for informal enterprises (citizens' initiatives)	**0**	**1**	**0**
		participation of minority groups in creating of public policies	**0**	**1**	**0**
		adherence to the principle of empowerment	**0**	**1**	**0**
		open and comprehensive communication	**0**	**1**	**0**

Criterion of *good governance*	Features of the criterion	Possible institutional arrangements	Metropolitan areas		
			Wrocław	**Łódź**	**Tri-City: Gdańsk-Sopot-Gdynia**
		building the capacity of institutions seeking to create partnership mechanisms	**0**	**1**	**1**
		developing the capacity of administration to cooperate with society in the performance of public tasks	**0**	**1**	**0**
		stimulating the potential of social actors to cooperate with the administration and government	**0**	**1**	**0**
accountability	means a precise definition of the responsibilities of the various actors involved in the metropolitan area, including in particular standards and norms promoted by the public sector	guaranteed protection of the initiative and its sustainability through higher levels of public administration (region, state)	**1**	**1**	**1**
		codes of conduct for policy makers and senior officials	**0**	**0**	**0**
		commissions and anti-corruption panels	**0**	**0**	**0**
		independent audits	**0**	**0**	**0**
		norms, values and standards institutionalized in policies	**0**	**0**	**0**
		possibility of objective evaluation of action effectiveness and efficiency	**1**	**1**	**1**

Criterion of *good governance*	**Features of the criterion**	**Possible institutional arrangements**	**Metropolitan areas**		
			Wrocław	**Łódź**	**Tri-City: Gdańsk-Sopot-Gdynia**
effectiveness	refers to the improvement of the „state capacity" in terms of efficient, effective (i.e . acting without delay) public administration to pursue the objectives of public policies. The criterion includes two additional principles: the principle of proportionality (which assumes that the instruments of service delivery and public policy should be proportionate to the objectives pursued, and thus implemented in an optimal and cost-effective way); the principle of subsidiarity (whereby the higher-level administrative actions are merely ancillary to the activities carried out at lower levels of management, so they do not replace them)	diverse sources of funding (sources mix)	**0**	**0**	**0**
		predictability of the flows of local budgets	**0**	**1**	**0**
		open and publicly available performance standards of services offered	**0**	**0**	**0**
		customer/users satisfaction survey	**0**	**0**	**0**
		precise definition of vision, and then construction of a plan and its implementation	**0**	**1**	**0**
		evaluation of implemented and completed tasks in the context of moving towards a certain vision	**0**	**0**	**0**
cohesion	assumes integrating the management of various public policies, both European and national ones, as well as between the various levels of public authorities in the framework of multi-level governance and the integration of sectoral and territorial policies	mechanisms of coordination in all dimensions in which metropolitan areas function	**0**	**1**	**0**
		existing arrangements comply with the standards of *good governance* included in the EU *White Paper* of 2001	**0**	**0**	**0**

Criterion of *good governance*	Features of the criterion	Possible institutional arrangements	Metropolitan areas		
			Wrocław	Łódź	Tri-City: Gdańsk-Sopot-Gdynia
		existing arrangements comply with the standards of *good governance* included in the Ministry of Regional Development's *Concept of good governance* of 2008	0	0	0
		existing arrangements comply with the standards of *good governance* included in the Prime Minister Office' *Poland 2030* of 2009	0	0	0
		existing arrangements comply with the standards of *good governance* included in the Ministry of Administration and Digitalisation' *White Paper* of 2013	0	0	0
		own arrangements comply with the standards of *good governance*	0	0	0

Source: Author's own data based on: White Paper 2001, http://www.wroclaw.pl/zit-wrof, http://lom.lodz.pl/, http://www.metropoliagdansk.pl/ (retrieved: 20.01.2016), *Strategia ZIT WrOF* 2015, *Strategia Rozwoju* ... 2014, *Strategia ZIT OM GGS* 2015.

The examples presented above of the most recent arrangements introduced in the Wrocław, Łódź and Tri-City metropolitan areas confirm the problem of weak institutionalisation of the concept of *good metropolitan governance*. The practices that have been adopted are generally imitative and consolidate the existing system. An opportunity for a positive change can be seen in the Łódź area, which in its key policy paper, *Strategia Rozwoju Łódzkiego Obszaru Metropolitalnego 2020+* [Development Strategy for the Łódź Metropolitan Area 2020+], has introduced a number of elements that in the future can adopt the *metropolitan governance* paradigm. Unfortunately, in this case, too, there are no elements that would testify to an understanding of the specificity of the *good metropolitan governance* approach. In principle, the authorities of the analysed metropolitan areas do not encourage stakeholders to become involved: the analysed case studies lack arrangements constituting a platform for communication between members of the public and the public administration. There are no systems that would encourage or improve dialogue, no infrastructure facilitating smooth communication between various stakeholders, no mechanisms providing incentives to become actively involved in the development of metropolitan areas (e.g. the quality of public information). The biggest weakness of the adopted arrangements is a lack of regulations preventing or limiting corruption, introducing ethical standards in public governance as well as transparency of procedures and open participation in decision-making. Moreover, no appropriate tools have been generated to create civil society, as a result of which the quality of the infrastructure of civil public spaces – fundamental to *good governance* – hampers the development of the basic arrangements stimulating metropolitan governance, e.g. multi-sectoral partnerships, entrusting public tasks to non-public entities. Responsibility for such a state of affairs lies not only with the existing legal system in Poland, but also with the passive attitudes of the public administration in the analysed metropolitan areas – the public administration not only fails to implement the existing institutional arrangements concerning *good governance* already functioning at the international, European and national levels, but also fails to formulate its own.

Towards good metropolitan governance? Conclusions

Metropolitan governance should in principle be perceived as an institutional response to the failings of the market and the state, and an attempt to go beyond the pattern of dealing with the problem by shifting between market and imperative coordination. We need to bear in mind, though, that *metropolitan governance* is not a guarantee of success. Success or lack thereof can be linked to both objects and subjects. If an object is complex and the subjects do not have sufficient knowledge of the relations that constitute it, guaranteed success is questionable. As the current institutional practice in the selected metropolitan areas shows, Polish local governments are not yet able to effectively put the normative idea of *metropolitan governance* into practice. Weaknesses concern both the object – owing to the problem of establishing and formally delimiting a metropolitan area – and the subjects, which in general have not acquired the capacity to engage in participatory governance constituting the foundation of *metropolitan governance*. There are many complex causes of such a state of affairs: from the low quality of democratic political culture in Poland to a deficit of civil and managerial competence of people responsible for decisions and actions associated with the governance of metropolitan areas. Although we need an in-depth analysis of the problem in question, the quick overview of the problem presented in this chapter is sufficient to formulate an assertion that the idea of *good metropolitan governance* translated into institutional practice in Poland still remains a slogan which is not reflected in reality. Current practice cannot be regarded as *good*, because it lacks openness, participation, coherence, accountability and effectiveness. Nor has it become more *metropolitan* in recent years, given the status of the Polish metropolitan areas in Europe. It is even further away from *governance*, if we take into account how metropolitan areas are managed in Poland. This means that Polish metropolitan areas are in the embryonic stage of the implementation of the *good metropolitan governance* concept. Desirable changes – if they do occur – will be slow to come. What should be an important catalyst of institutional change are the authorities as the entities serving as coordinators and motivators, and facilitating access to information about possible new arrangements as well as creating an atmosphere of joint decision-making. However, the ability of local governments to take up this challenge remains a matter of guesswork.

References

Brenner, N. (2003), 'Standortpolitik, State Rescaling and the Metropolitan Governance in Western Europe', *DISP*, 152: 15–25.

Caulier-Grice, J., Davies, A., Patrick, R. and Norman, W. (2012), 'Defining Social Innovation. A deliverable of the project: The theoretical, empirical and policy foundations for building social innovation in Europe (TEPSIE)', Brussels: European Commission, DG Research.

'Green Paper Metropolitan areas, Zielona Księga obszarów metropolitalnych (2012)' Warszawa: Ministerstwo Administracji i Cyfryzacji, Warszawa.

Hausner, J. (ed.) (2013), 'Narastające dysfunkcje, zasadnicze dylematy, konieczne działania. Raport o stanie samorządności terytorialnej w Polsce', Kraków: Uniwersytet Ekonomiczny w *Krakowie.*

'Interim Territorial Cohesion Report' (2004), Luxembourg: European Commission.

Jałowiecki, B. (2002), 'Zarządzanie rozwojem aglomeracji miejskich', Białystok: Wyższa Szkoła Finansów i Zarządzania.

Jałowiecki, B. (ed.) (2009), 'Czy metropolia jest miastem?', Warszawa: Wydawnictwo Naukowe Scholar.

Jessop, B. (2007), 'Promowanie „dobrego rządzenia" i ukrywanie jego słabości: refleksja nad politycznymi paradygmatami i politycznymi narracjami w sferze rządzenia', *Zarządzanie Publiczne,* 2(2).

Knosala, E. (2010), 'Metropolie w świetle projektów ustaw', A. Lutrzykowski and R. Gawłowski (eds.) *Metropolie. Wyzwania polskiej polityki miejskiej,* Toruń: Wydawnictwo Adam Marszałek.

'Koncepcja good governance. Refleksje do dyskusji' (2008), Warszawa: Ministerstwo Rozwoju Regionalnego.

Kunzmann, K. R. (1998), 'World city regions in Europe: Structural change and future challenges', F. Y. Lo (ed.) *Globalisation and the World Large Cities,* Tokyo, New York, Paris: UN University Press.

'Polska 2030. Wyzwania rozwojowe' (2009), Warszawa: Kancelaria Prezesa Rady Ministrów.

Starosta, P. (1995), 'Poza metropolią. Wiejskie i małomiasteczkowe zbiorowości lokalne a wzory porządku makrospołecznego', Łódź: Wydawnictwo Uniwersytetu Łódzkiego.

'Strategia Rozwoju Łódzkiego Obszaru Metropolitalnego 2020+' (2014), część II: Strategia Rozwoju. Łódź: Polskie Towarzystwo Ekonomiczne. Oddział w Łodzi.

'Strategia rozwoju regionalnego 2010 – 2020. Regiony, miasta, obszary wiejskie' (2010), Warszawa: Ministerstwo Rozwoju Regionalnego.

'Strategia Zintegrowanych Inwestycji Terytorialnych Obszaru Metropolitalnego Gdańsk – Gdynia – Sopot do roku 2020' (2015), Gdańsk.

'Strategia Zintegrowanych Inwestycji Terytorialnych Wrocławskiego Obszaru Funkcjonalnego' (2015), Wrocław.

Wiktorska-Święcka, A. (2010a), 'Europejskie miasto w erze global cities', *Transformacje. Pismo interdyscyplinarne,* Warszawa: Centrum Badań Ewaluacyjnych i Prognostycznych: 142 – 151.

Wiktorska-Święcka, A. (2010b), 'Identyfikacja głównych trendów zarządzania w odniesieniu do wytycznych unijnych', A. Wiktorska-Święcka et el., *Analiza określająca wpływ zintegrowanego zarządzania obszarem metropolitarnym na region,* Wrocław: Dolnośląska Agencja Współpracy Gospodarczej: 166-175.

Wiktorska-Święcka, A. (2011), 'Koncepcja governance jako nowy paradygmat zarządzania rozwojem regionalnym', *Transformacje. Pismo interdyscyplinarne*, Warszawa: Centrum Badań Ewaluacyjnych i Prognostycznych. Akademia Leona Koźmińskiego: 98 – 119.

Wiktorska-Święcka, A. (2013a), 'Badania nad jakością i efektywnością zarządzania rozwojem obszarów metropolitalnych w Polsce w kontekście założeń koncepcji metropolitan governance', J. Juchnowski and R. Wiszniowski (eds.) *Współczesna teoria i praktyka badań społecznych i humanistycznych,* Toruń: Wydawnictwo Adam Marszałek: 434 – 456.

Wiktorska-Święcka, A., Moroń, D., Klimowicz, M. (2015), 'Zarządzanie innowacjami społecznymi. Trendy, perspektywy, wyzwania', Warszawa: Difin.

Windrum, P. and Koch, P. M. (eds.) (2008), 'Innovation in Public Sector Services: Entrepreneurship, Creativity and Management', Cheltenham: Edward Elgar.

About the Authors

Gniadzik, Magdalena is a PhD candidate at the Chair of European Law, Institute of International Law, Faculty of Law and Administration, University of Warsaw. Her scietific interests focus on issues concerning right to free movement and protection of fundamental rights of EU citizens and their family members.

Grzeszczak, Robert – is Professor of European Law, Faculty of Law and Administration University of Warsaw; His interests are in public European law and he has published extensively in these areas. Member of the Committee of Legal Sciences of the Polish Academy of Sciences; Member of the Programming Board of the Strategic Litigation Program of the Helsinki Foundation for Human Rights.

Kańciak, Anna - is PhD candidate at the Chair of European Law, Institute of International Law, Faculty of Law and Administration University of Warsaw. She graduated law at the University of Warmia and Mazury in Olsztyn. She is the employee of the public administration, interested in the issues related to the area of freedom, security and justice as well as the cyberspace protection. The winner as well as the contractor of the scientific grants funded by the National Science Centre.

Karolewski, Ireneusz P. - is Associate Professor of Political Science, Willy Brandt Centre for German and European Studies, University of Wrocław, Poland. He received his PhD in political science from the University of Potsdam, Germany. He is the author of *Citizenship and Collective Identity in Europe* (Routledge, 2010) as well as co-editor *of Exterritorial Citizenship in Postcommunist* Europe (Rowman & Littlefield, 2015) and *European Identity Revisited* (Routledge, 2016).

Krajewska, Atina - is a Senior Lecturer at the School of Law, University of Sheffield, UK. She received her PhD from the University of Wroclaw, Poland. In her research she focuses on the developments of human rights law in the area of health and biomedicine. She is an author of numerous publications on issues of privacy, reproductive rights, and more recently global health law, in English, German, Polish, and Spanish. Her work bears diversely on distinct legal spheres of medical and public health law, public international law, and the sociology of law.

Kwasiborski, Piotr - is PhD candidate at the Chair of European Law, Institute of International Law, Faculty of Law and Administration University of Warsaw. His main field of scientific interests relates to issues concerning the challenges for EU integration process and the problem of social dumping on the EU internal market.

Maśnicki, Jędrzej - is PhD candidate at the Chair of European Law, Institute of International Law, Faculty of Law and Administration University of Warsaw. In 2013 he received a scientific grant from the Polish Ministry of Science and Higher Education to analyse implementation of EU secondary legislation in Poland. He was twice granted with The Ministry of Science and Higher Education Scholarship.

Mroczka, Kamil – PhD, Associate Professor of Political Science, The State School of Higher Education in Oświęcim and University of Warsaw, Poland. He received his PhD in political science from The University of Warsaw in 2014. He is the author of The impact of human resources policy in the Civil Service in Poland on the functioning of the state (Warsaw 2015) and co-author of Civil Service in Poland (Warsaw 2012). He held managerial positions in the government administration in The Ministry of Justice and Mazowieckie Province Office. Currently is employed as a general councillor in National Criminal Register Office in The Ministry of Justice.

Mucha, Jagna - is PhD candidate at the Chair of European Law, Institute of International Law, Faculty of Law and Administration University of Warsaw. Her academic interests revolve around alternative dispute resolution methods in the European Union with special focus on consumer disputes. She is a holder of the scholarship founded by the National Science Centre of Poland to finance the doctoral research conducted at the Centre for Socio-Legal Studies at the University of Oxford, UK.

Opiłowska, Elżbieta - is an Assistant Professor at the Willy Brandt Centre for German and European Studies and head of the Centre for Regional and Borderland Studies at the Institute of Sociology at the University of Wrocław; her main research interests and publications are on European border regions, German-Polish relations and regional policy of the EU.

Supernat, Jerzy - is Professor of Law at the University of Wrocław and Member of ReNEUAL (the Research Network on EU Administrative Law). His interests are in public administration and administrative law and he has published extensively in these areas. Among his books are *Administracja i prawo administracyjne. Słownik polsko-angielski* (2011) and *Administracja Unii Europejskiej. Zagadnienia wybrane* (2013).

Sus, Monika - is a Dahrendorf Postdoctoral Fellow at the Hertie School of Governance. Before coming to Berlin, she held an assistant professor position at the DAAD-founded Willy Brandt Centre for German and European Studies at the University of Wrocław in Poland. She has been granted scholarships by several European foundations and she has been a visiting fellow at the European University Institute in Florence, at the Centre Canadien d'études Allemandes et Européennes at the University of Montreal and the European Union Centre of Excellence at the University in Pittsburgh. She has published widely on European foreign policy, the Eastern Partnership, Europeanisation and policy advising.

Szpyrka, Michalina - is an Assistant of Judge (Supreme Court) and PhD candidate at the Chair of European Law, Institute of International Law, Faculty of Law and Administration, University of Warsaw. Her main field of scientific interests relates to issues concerning the protection of human rights, EU electronic communications law and EU competition law.

Tomczak, Małgorzata - is PhD candidate at the Chair of European Law, Institute of International Law, Faculty of Law and Administration University of Warsaw; a notarial apprentice in the Warsaw Chamber. Main interests: official documents and their turnover in the member states of the European Union.

Wiktorska-Święcka, Aldona - PhD, DS, MBA, Faculty of Social Science, University of Wrocław. She has been granted scholarships by the European Union, US Department of State, DAAD and Konrad-Adenauer Foundation. Profile: Public governance and public policy, territorial governance, sectoral governance, innovation in management and governance, normative assumptions of governance.